With ... Christmas '94 — John

Quotes and Anecdotes for Preachers and Teachers

compiled by

ANTHONY P. CASTLE

First published in Great Britain in 1979 by
KEVIN MAYHEW LTD
55 Leigh Road
Leigh-on-Sea, Essex

ISBN 0 905725 69 7

Printed and bound by E T Heron & Co. Ltd, Essex and London

Dedicated to
my parents—
source of
much homely
wisdom.

FOREWORD

Preachers and Teachers are forever searching for ideas to illustrate a point, spark the imagination and provoke reflection. If old truths are not dressed up in new clothes, they easily pass by unnoticed. And then a story is needed or a verbal picture to arouse interest and hold attention—not forgetting the touch of humour that is always so helpful. For the ones who face the same audience day by day or week by week, the task is that much harder.

This book is tailor-made to ease their burden. Anthony Castle has brought together an astonishing wealth of quotes and anecdotes conveniently arranged for those who are tied to the liturgical cycle. A good index shows the huge range of subjects that are touched on. What is not so apparent is the variety of sources. There are proverbs from many different cultures. Writers and poets, saints, popes and Fathers of the Church rub shoulders with Hitler, Gandhi and Mary O'Hara. It is refreshing to find something from Harpo and Groucho Marx as well as from Karl!

So there is much in these pages to cheer the priest preparing a Sunday homily or the teacher wondering about the next School Assembly. But I hope the book will be mainly blessed, albeit unknowingly, by the ones who have to sit at their feet and listen.

† Michael Bowen
Archbishop of Southwark

6th January, 1979

PREFACE

This book began life seventeen years ago, as a school exercise book jammed with useful stories and suitable sayings. Over the years it was, by turns, added to and neglected. The idea of arranging the material under theme headings and expanding the collection was prompted—as happens in life—by several experiences and the encouragement of one or two friends, notably Jim Freelove, the Deputy Headteacher of Sandown Court School, Tunbridge Wells. As the years passed, some of the 'pieces' came adrift from their sources. In preparing the book, I have made every effort to trace and provide the correct credit; should, however, the reader notice an incorrect source, the publishers will happily put the mistake right in any future edition.

'Quotes and Anecdotes' makes no claim to be anything but a pastoral aid for those who proclaim and promote the Christian message. Besides its obvious use in the preparation of sermons and school assemblies, the book may well prove useful in providing stimulation for prayer-groups, fillers for parish newsletters and spiritual reading for the private reader.

Finally it's 'thank-you' time; and first and foremost I would like to express my gratitude to Archbishop Michael Bowen for so kindly providing the Foreword. A big 'thank-you' too to Jacquie Galley and Margaret Fitzgerald, who spent many painstaking hours at their typewriters, and to Liz, my wife, who worked hard on the Indices.

Anthony P. Castle

THE VALUE OF TIME

'You know "the time" has come.' *Romans, 13:11*

Quotations

He who kills time commits suicide. *(Fred Beck)*

He who neglects the present moment throws away all he has. *(Schiller)*

Time deals gently with those who take it gently. *(Anatole France)*

One always has time enough if one will apply it. *(Goethe)*

Time is a circus, always packing up and moving away. *(Ben Hecht)*

Time must always ultimately teach. *(Hilaire Belloc)*

It is the wisest who grieve most at loss of time. *(Dante)*

Time hath a taming hand. *(Cardinal Newman)*

The enemy is glad to make you lose time when he cannot make you lose eternity. *(St. Francis de Sales)*

Time—that which man is always trying to kill, but which ends in killing him. *(Herbert Spencer)*

Dost thou love life? Then do not squander Time, for that's the stuff Life is made of. *(Benjamin Franklin)*

Come what, come may, time and the hour run through the roughest day. *(Shakespeare)*

The great rule of moral conduct is, next to God, to respect time. *(Lavater)*

You will find rest from vain fancies if you do every act in life as though it were your last. *(Marcus Aurelius)*

Proverb

All the treasures of earth cannot bring back one lost moment. *(French proverb)*

Humour

Teacher	Jimmy, name a great time saver.
Jimmy	Love at first sight!

Professor	Mr. Jones, will you tell me why you keep looking at your watch?
Jones	Yes, Sir, I was frightened that you might not have time to finish your interesting lecture!

Word-Pictures

When a man sits with a pretty girl for an hour, it seems like a minute. But let him sit on a hot stove for a minute—and it's longer than any hour. That's relativity. *(Albert Einstein)*

In a garden next to Gloucester Cathedral there is a sundial which bears this inscription:

'Give God thy heart, thy service and thy gold;
The day wears on and time is waxing old.'

Not long ago someone seemed bent upon defacing every public clock in Shrewsbury. One incident involved breaking the minute hand off of a clock 50 feet up a factory tower; on another occasion the culprit climbed 100 feet to wrench a minute hand from a public clock! But he could not stop time. As Thomas Carlyle said in 1840: 'The illimitable, silent, never-resting thing called time, rolling, rushing on, swift, silent, like an all-embracing ocean tide . . .'

'What of all things in the world, is the longest and the shortest, the swiftest and the slowest, the most divisible and the most extended, the most neglected and the most regretted, without which nothing can be done, which devours all that is little, and enlivens all that is great?' Question put to Zadig in Voltaire's 'Zadig—a Mystery of Fate.' Zadig replied: 'Time'.

When the ill-fated 'Titanic' steamed majestically through the darkness on her maiden voyage to New York, on 14th April 1912, there were more than two thousand people enjoying the liner's snug comforts. One of the tragic incidents of that night is recalled by the *Washington Post:*

'In the wheelroom, a nattily uniformed officer hummed at his task as he directed the destinies of an ocean greyhound that even then was setting a speed record. The phone rang. A minute passed! Another minute! The officer was busy! The third precious minute passed. The officer, his trivial task completed, stepped to the phone. From the "crow's nest" —"Iceberg dead ahead! Reverse engines!" But too late. As he rushed to the controls, the "pride of the seas" crashed into the iceberg amid a deafening roar.

Three precious minutes! Attention to trivial details and sixteen hundred people paid with their lives.'

See also: A19 Patience
B25 Quiet–time for prayer
C34 The Value of little things

INTEGRITY

'Integrity is the loincloth round his waist.' *Isaiah, 11:5*

Quotations

An honest man's the noblest work of God. *(Pope)*

Integrity without knowledge is weak and useless, and knowledge without integrity is dangerous and dreadful. *(Samuel Johnson)*

The less time it takes anyone to be led away from honesty, the more wicked he is. *(Erasmus)*

Some people are likeable in spite of their unswerving integrity! *(Don Marquis)*

It is a fine thing to be honest but it is also very important to be right. *(Winston Churchill)*

Honesty is the best policy; but he who is governed by that maxim is not an honest man. *(R. Whately)*

Everyone suspects himself of at least one of the cardinal virtues, and this is mine: I am one of the few honest people that I have ever known. *(F. Scott Fitzgerald)*

Proverbs

An honest man does not make himself a dog for the sake of a bone. *(Danish proverb)*

They are all honest men, but my cloak is not to be found. *(Spanish proverb)*

Humour

An honest fisherman is a pretty uninteresting person. *(Anon)*

'My boy,' said the business man to his son, 'there are two things that are essential if you are to succeed in business.'
'What are they, Dad?' asked the boy.
'Integrity and sagacity.'
'What is integrity?'
'Always, no matter what, always keep your word.'
'And sagacity?'
'Never give your word!'

Make yourself an honest man, and then you may be sure that there is one rascal less in the world. *(Carlyle)*

Word-Pictures

In Napoleon's expedition to Russia, a Russian peasant was captured, forced into Napoleon's service and branded on the arm with the letter 'N'. When he understood what it meant, he chopped off the arm that had been branded, rather than serve his country's enemy. *(Anon)*

I once knew a village joiner who was also undertaker when need arose. His language and manners were crude and as far as I know he only entered a church when his professional duties required him to do so. Yet there was an occasion after a funeral when he heard a group of bystanders saying how sorry they were for the widow who had been left with a young family. Roughly he pushed his way in. 'How much sorry are you?' he demanded, adding 'I'm sorry five pounds!' And he took the money from his pocket there and then to start a collection. *(Edmund Banyard)*

'While women weep as they do now, I'll fight; while little children go hungry as they do now, I'll fight; while men go to prison, in and out, in and out, I'll fight; while there is a poor lost girl upon the street, I'll fight; while there yet remains one dark soul without the light of God, I'll fight—I'll fight to the very end.' *(General William Booth)*

One good man—one man who does not put on his religion once a week with his Sunday coat, but wears it for his working dress, and lets the thought of God grow into him, and through and through him, till everything he says and does becomes religious—that man is worth a thousand sermons. He is a living Gospel—he is the image of God. And men see his good works, and admire them in spite of themselves, and see that they are Godlike, and that God's grace is no dream, but that the Holy Spirit is still among men, and that all nobleness and manliness is His gift, His stamp, His picture; and so they get a glimpse of God again in His saints and heroes, and glorify their Father who is in heaven. *(Charles Kingsley)*

Discovered on a monument dated 1629 in a Baltimore church:
Go placidly amid the noise and haste, and remember what peace there may be in silence. As far as possible, without surrender, be on good terms with all persons. Speak your truth quietly and clearly; and listen to others, even the dull and ignorant, they too have their story.

Avoid loud and aggressive persons, they are vexations to the spirit. If you compare yourself with others you may become vain and bitter, for always there will be greater and lesser persons than yourself. Enjoy your achievements as well as your plans. Keep interested in your own career, however humble; it is a real possession in the changing fortunes of time. Exercise caution in your business affairs, for the world is full of trickery. But let this not blind you to what virtue there is; many persons strive for high ideals and everywhere life is full of heroism.

Be yourself. Especially, do not feign affection. Neither be cynical about love for, in the face of aridity and disenchantment, it is perennial as the grass. Take kindly the counsel of the years, gracefully surrendering the things of youth. Nurture strength of spirit to shield you in sudden misfortune. But do not distress yourself with imaginings. Many fears are born of fatigue and loneliness. Beyond a wholesome discipline, be gentle with yourself.

You are a child of the Universe, no less than the trees and the stars you have a right to be here. And whether or not it is clear to you, no doubt the universe is unfolding as it should. Therefore, be at peace with God, whatever you conceive Him to be, and whatever your labours and aspirations in the noisy confusion of life, keep peace with your soul. With all its sham, drudgery and broken dreams, it is still a beautiful world. Be careful. Strive to be happy.

See also: B19 Conscience
B20 Growth to maturity
B26 The whole man
C23 Zeal for what is right

PERSEVERANCE

'Happy is the man who does not lose faith in me.' *Matthew, 11:6*

Quotations

Every noble work is at first impossible. *(Carlyle)*

The falling drops will at last wear the stone. *(Lucretius)*

'Tis known as perseverance in a good cause, and obstinancy in a bad one. *(Laurence Sterne)*

Though perseverance does not come from our power, yet it comes within our power. *(St. Francis de Sales)*

He greatly deceives himself who thinks that prayer perfects one without perseverance and obedience. *(St. Francis de Sales)*

We cannot command our final perseverance, but must ask it from God. *(St. Thomas Aquinas)*

He said not, 'Thou shalt not be tempested, thou shalt not be travailed, thou shalt not be afflicted,' but he said, 'Thou shalt not be overcome.' *(Julian of Norwich)*

A tree is shown by its fruits, and in the same way those who profess to belong to Christ will be seen by what they do. For what is needed is not mere present profession, but perseverance to the end in the power of faith. *(St. Ignatius of Antioch)*

Proverb

The man who removed the mountain began by carrying away small stones. *(Chinese proverb)*

Humour

Consider the postage stamp: its usefulness consists in the ability to stick to one thing till it gets there. *(Josh Billings)*

Even the woodpecker owes his success to the fact that he uses his head and keeps pecking away until he finishes the job he starts. *(Coleman Cox)*

Teacher 'Johnny, what is the difference between perseverance and obstinacy?'
Pupil 'One is a strong will and the other is a strong won't.'

'My boy,' said the wealthy man, 'when I was your age, I used to carry bricks for bricklayers.'
'I'm mighty proud of you, Dad. If it hadn't been for your perseverance I might have had to do something like that myself!'

Statements

If any one saith that he will for certain, of an absolute and infallible certainty, have that great gift of perseverance unto the end, unless he have learned this by special revelation; let him be anathema. *(Council of Trent, Session 6)*

If any man saith that the justified either is able to persevere without the special help of God in the justice received; or that with that help he is not able; let him be anathema. *(Council of Trent, Session 6)*

Word-Pictures

After Sir Walter Raleigh's introduction to the favour of Queen Elizabeth I, he wrote with a diamond on a window pane:
'Fain would I climb, but that I fear to fall.'
The Queen, seeing the words, wrote underneath with a diamond:
'If thy heart fail thee, do not climb at all.'

This is the romantic story of the father and mother of Thomas Becket, as told by Charles Dickens in his 'Child's History of England'.

Gilbert Becket, Thomas' father, made a pilgrimage to the Holy Land and was taken prisoner by a Saracen who had one fair daughter. She fell in love with Gilbert and told him she wanted to marry him, and was willing to become a christian if they could escape to a christian country. He returned her love until he found an opportunity to escape with his servant, Richard. When he returned to England, he forgot the Saracen girl.

But she had not forgotten Gilbert. She left her father's home in disguise and made her way to the coast. The merchant had taught her two English words, 'London' and 'Gilbert'. She went among the ships, saying again and again the same word, 'London'. Sailors showed her a ship bound for London, and she paid her passage with some of her jewels and arrived in London. As the merchant was sitting one day in his office, his servant came running in, saying, 'Master! The Saracen lady is here. As I live, she is going up and down the street calling out, "Gilbert, Gilbert".' The merchant hurried to find her. When she saw him, she fainted in his arms. Soon after they were married.

King Robert the Bruce of Scotland, pursued after defeat in battle, hid in a lonely cave. He tried to plan the future, but was tempted to despair. He had lost heart and had decided to give up when his eye was caught by a spider. The insect was carefully and painfully making its way up a slender thread to its web in the corner above. The king watched as it made several unsuccessful attempts, and thought, as it fell back to the bottom again and again, how it typified his own efforts. Then at last the spider made it! The king took courage and persevered and the example of the spider brought its reward.

Do you know the story of the two frogs that fell into a bucket of cream? They tried very hard to get out by climbing up the side of the bucket. But each time they slipped back again.

Finally one frog said: 'We'll never get out of here. I give up.' So down he went and drowned. The other frog decided to keep trying. Again and again he tried to climb with his front legs and kicked with his back legs. Suddenly he hit something hard. He turned to see what it was and discovered that all his kicking had churned up a lump of butter! He hopped on top of it and leaped out to safety.

On his voyage, which resulted in the discovery of America, Columbus refused to listen to the threats of his sailors. As day after day no land appeared, the sailors threatened to mutiny and demanded that they turn back. Columbus would not listen and each day entered two words in the ship's log, 'Sailed on'.

A suitor in Wales, who was rebuffed for forty-two years, eventually won his fair lady. After writing 2,184 love letters, the persistent but rather shy man, receiving neither written or spoken answer, summoned enough courage to present himself in person. He knocked on the lady's door and asked her hand. To his delight and surprise she accepted! The couple married at 74 years of age.

See also: A19 Patience
B49 Coping with doubt
C30 Increase our faith
C35 Hope

EMMANUEL—MARY'S CHILD

'The maiden is with child and will give birth to a son whom she will call Emmanuel.' *Isaiah, 7:14*

Quotations

It is the general rule, that all superior men inherit the elements of superiority from their mothers. *(Nichelet)*

God's presence is not discerned at the time when it is upon us, but afterwards, when we look back upon what is gone and over. *(Cardinal Newman)*

Who says I am not under the special protection of God? *(Adolf Hitler)*

There is only one way of being faithful to the Incarnation and that is to become an embodied testimony to the living God. Perhaps the core of the apologetic task in every age is to be created in lives rather than in arguments. *(Gabriel Marcel)*

The birth of Christ, for those who believe in Him, means that from this moment on, the indescribable mystery which we call God can only be found in someone entirely like you and me. What the Christian is really trying to say at Christmas is, 'I believe in Man'. *(H. J. Richards)*

Proverb

God often visits us, but most of the time we are not at home. *(French proverb)*

Humour

Imagine the Lord talking French! Aside from a few odd words in Hebrew, I took it completely for granted that God had never spoken anything but the most dignified English! *(Clarence Day)*

Word-Picture

One Christmas, Santa Claus brought me a toy engine. I took it with me to the convent, and played with it while mother and the nuns discussed old times. But it was a young nun who brought us in to see the crib. When I saw the Holy Child in the manger, I was distressed because little as I had, he had nothing at all. For me it was fresh proof of the incompetence of Santa Claus. I asked the young nun politely if the Holy Child didn't like toys, and she replied composedly enough, 'Oh, he does but his mother is too poor to afford them'. That settled it. My mother was poor too, but at Christmas she at least managed to buy me something even if it was only a box of crayons. I distinctly remember getting into the crib and putting the engine between his outstretched arms. I probably showed him how to wind it as well, because a small baby like that would not be clever enough to know. I remember too the tearful feeling of reckless generosity with which I left him there in the nightly darkness of the chapel, clutching my toy engine to his chest. *(Frank O'Connor—An Only Child)*

See also: A37 Christ the King
B4 Christ the Covenant of God
B8 The Cosmic Christ
B46 Christ the sacrament of God
C45 The divinity of Christ

MAN FOR OTHERS—UNSELFISHNESS

'You are my servant in whom I shall be glorified.' *Isaiah, 49:3*

Quotations

The love of liberty is the love of others; the love of power is the love of ourselves. *(William Hazlitt)*

We are more troublesome to ourselves than anyone else is to us. *(St. Francis de Sales)*

Self-sacrifice is good in its way, but we must take care that we don't sacrifice to the detriment of others. *(Kathleen Hinkson)*

Man's highest life does not consist in self-expression, but in self-sacrifice. *(R. H. Benson)*

Oysters are more beautiful than any religion . . . there's nothing in Christianity or Buddhism that quite matches the sympathetic unselfishness of an oyster. *(Siki)*

If a man is centred upon himself, the smallest risk is too great for him, because both success and failure can destroy him. If he is centred upon God, then no risk is too great, because success is already guaranteed—the successful union of Creator and creature, beside which everything else is meaningless. *(Morris West)*

They are slaves who fear to speak
For the fallen and the weak;
They are slaves who will not choose
Hatred, scoffing and abuse,
Rather than in silence shrink
From the truth they needs must think;
They are slaves who dare not be
In the right with two or three.
(James Russell Lowell)

Humour

If people knew how much ill-feeling Unselfishness occasions, it would not be so often recommended from the pulpit. *(C. S. Lewis)*

Teacher 'Unselfishness means going without something you need voluntarily. Can you give me an example, Jimmy?
Jimmy 'Yes, sometimes I go without a bath when I need one!'

Word-Pictures

Gandalf gives counsel . . . 'Other evils there are that may come; for Sauron is himself but a servant or emissary. Yet it is not our part to muster all the tides of the world, but to do what is in us for the succour of those years wherein we are set, uprooting the evil in the fields that we know, so that those who live after may have clean earth to till. What weather they shall have is not ours to rule.' *(J. R. R. Tolkien)*

In one of the terrible concentration camps of the Second World War there was a Polish priest, called Father Kolbe. He had been put there because he had published comments about the Nazi Regime. One of the prisoners escaped from the camp and the camp commandant, to punish the prisoners, ordered ten of them to be starved to death. Among the prisoners was a young man who had a wife and children. When the prisoners' numbers were called out, Father Kolbe stepped forward and insisted on taking the young man's place. In the death cell, Father Kolbe helped the others prepare for death. He was the last to die, and because he had taken too long, they injected poison into his arm. After his death, if you had gone into his cell, you would have seen a picture of Jesus on the cross scratched on the wall with his nails.

Rose was a young girl of 14 whose mother was dead and father often away, so she had to look after the younger children. She loved them all but especially her baby brother, Michael. The family was very poor. When her birthday came, the doctor, seeing her dressed in rags, sent her a present of a nice dress. When he saw her some days later she was still in her ragged dress. 'Where are your new clothes?' he asked. She replied, 'They're pawned. There was nothing in the house and Michael must have his milk.' She was making herself ill with work, so the doctor arranged for the children to be looked after and he sent her for a holiday with Michael in the country.

Then came a terrible blow. The family, where they were staying, wanted to adopt Michael. The father was willing but he left the decision to her. 'It's for his good. I wouldn't stand in his way,' she said. Some time later came the news that the baby was very ill. Immediately she decided to go to him and became his nurse. It was a very serious illness—the coughing of the baby was the worst part. She nursed Michael day and night until she was told the baby would recover. She got up, pressed her hands against her head and said, 'I have an awful headache.' She had caught the illness from Michael. She never recovered and died soon afterwards.

See also: A33 Love your neighbour
B41 Generosity
B47 Dying to self
C34 The value of little things

LIGHT OF THE WORLD

'The Lord is my light and my help.' *Psalm 27*

Quotations

God sometimes puts us in the dark to prove that He is light. *(Anon)*

No ray of light can shine
If severed from its source;
Without my inner light
I lose my course. *(Angelus Silesius)*

It is better to be saved by a lighthouse than by a lifeboat. *(Ernest Kunsch)*

A christian, like a candle, must keep cool and burn at the same time. *(M. Rosell)*

The Light of Lights
Looks always on the motive, not the deed,
The Shadow of Shadows on the deed alone. *(W. B. Yeats)*

Proverb

Don't curse the darkness—light a candle. *(Chinese proverb)*

Humour

The class had been told about the prodigious rate at which light travels. 'Isn't it wonderful,' the teacher said, 'to think of light coming to us from the sun at the speed of all those miles a second?'
'Not really,' said one boy, 'it's downhill all the way!'

Members of several religious Orders were together in a room one evening when suddenly the light went out, leaving them all in darkness. The Benedictine simply went on saying his Office, which he knew by heart anyway. The Franciscan knelt down and began to pray for light. The Dominican suggested to his companions that they should inquire into the nature of light, and consider the sequence of causes that might have led to its failure. But the Jesuit had left the room. He had gone to mend the fuse. *(Douglas Woodruff)*

Statement

The Second Vatican Council's document on 'The Church' opens with the words: 'Christ is the light of all nations. Hence this sacred Synod, which has been gathered in the Holy Spirit, eagerly desires to shed on all men that radiance of His which brightens the countenance of the Church. This it will do by proclaiming the gospel to every creature.'

Word-Pictures

'The Light of the World' is the title of a famous picture by Holman Hunt painted in 1854. It portrays Christ, thorn-crowned, and carrying a lantern, knocking at a closed door.

When the artist showed the completed picture to some friends, one pointed out what seemed to be an omission. 'You have put no handle on the door,' he said to Holman Hunt. The artist replied, 'We must open to the Light—the handle is on the inside.'

When the scientific oil lamp was invented in 1783 by a Swiss chemist, Ami Argand, many people felt man's genius had gone far enough. The new lamp produced a light equal to nine candles and burned whale oil. An encyclopedia of the time advised the use of a small screen between the eyes and the lamplight. At parties, ladies sometimes opened their parasols against the 'uncomplimentary' glare of the lamps.

Two legends enhance the lustre of the Koh-i-Noor diamond; that is that it must never be worn by a man, and its owner will rule the world.

The diamond's name means 'Mountain of Light'. It flashed among the possessions of the Mogul Emperor Mohammed when he fell to Nadir, the Shah of Persia who in turn died in a palace revolt of 1747. One hundred years later, it was the brightest jewel in the male-dominated Sikh empire that was conquered by the British Empire. Since then it has been worn by three English queens, but never by an English king.

There is a famous cave, some sixty miles from Auckland in New Zealand. It is known as the cave of the glow-worms. You reach it in a boat pulled by a wire for silence. As you glide down the stream, you suddenly come across a soft light gleaming in the distance; then you enter a magic world of fairyland. From the top of the cave, thousands of threads hang down from the glowing insects. So great is the light that it is possible to read a book there. But if there is the slightest noise, the bright light dies out, just as if a switch had been turned off.

See also: A37 Christ the King
B4 Christ the Covenant of God
B8 The Cosmic Christ
B46 Christ the Sacrament of God

POOR IN SPIRIT

'How happy are the poor in spirit; theirs is the kingdom of heaven.'
Matthew, 5:3

Quotations

We can alter ecclesiastical structures, recast our institutions, direct ourselves towards new goals, brush up our theology, scrap our liturgy and use a different one, but none of it is going to lead us to renewal, unless we acquire simplicity of heart. *(Hubert Van Zeller)*

He is rich enough who is poor with Christ. *(St. Jerome)*

No man should praise poverty but he who is poor. *(St. Bernard)*

Man is God's image; but a poor man is Christ's stamp to boot. *(G. Herbert)*

He is rich in spirit who has his riches in his spirit or his spirit in his riches; he is poor in spirit who has no riches in his spirit, nor his spirit in his riches. *(St. Francis de Sales)*

The poor man, rich in faith, who toils for the love of God and is generous of the little fruit of his labours, is much nearer to heaven than the rich man who spends a fortune in good works from no higher motive than his natural inclination to benevolence. *(Archbishop Ullathorme)*

The oligarchic character of the modern English commonwealth does not rest, like many oligarchies, on the cruelty of the rich to the poor. It does not even rest on the kindness of the rich to the poor. It rests on the perennial and unfailing kindness of the poor to the rich. *(G. K. Chesterton)*

Proverbs

Whoso stoppeth his ear at the poor shall cry himself and not be heard. *(Hebrew proverb)*

Not he who has little, but he who wishes for more, is poor. *(Latin proverb)*

Humour

I've worked myself up from nothing to a state of extreme poverty. *(Groucho Marx)*

A Franciscan and a Dominican came to a ford at a stream and the Dominican asked the Franciscan to carry him over, as the Franciscan was barefooted and his habit mattered less. The Franciscan lifted him up and carried him half-way, and then asked what money the Dominican had on him. 'Only two reales,' said the Dominican. But it was enough for the Franciscan, who promptly dropped his charge into the water, excusing himself by saying 'You know our rule: we are not allowed to carry money.' *(Douglas Woodruff)*

A Jesuit and a Franciscan were lunching together on a Friday. There were two pieces of fish on the dish, one large and the other very small. The Jesuit helped himself to the large piece and put the small one on the other's plate.

'Is that Jesuitry?' asked the Franciscan.

'What do you mean?' said the Jesuit.

'Only this,' the Franciscan replied. 'I've been trained in Holy Poverty. Had I served the fish, I should have put the large piece on your plate, and the small piece on mine.'

'That's exactly what you've got, isn't it'? said the Jesuit. 'What are you complaining about?' *(Douglas Woodruff)*

Statements

More that anything else is this vice of property to be cut off root and branch from the monastery. Let no one presume to give or receive anything without the leave of the abbot, or to retain anything as his own. He should have nothing at all; neither a book, nor tablets, nor a pen—nothing at all. For it is not allowed to the monks to have bodies or wills in their own power. *(Rule of St. Benedict)*

The brothers shall possess nothing, neither a house, nor a place, nor anything. But as pilgrims and strangers in this world, serving God in poverty and humility, they shall confidently seek alms, and not be ashamed, for the Lord made himself poor in this world for us. This is the highest degree of that sublime poverty, which has made you, my dearly beloved brethren, heirs and kings of the Kingdom of Heaven; which has made you poor in goods but exalted in virtues. *(Rule of St. Francis)*

Christians who take any active part in modern socio-economic development and defend justice and charity should be convinced that they can make a great contribution to the prosperity of mankind and the peace of the world. Whether they do so as individuals or in association, let their example be a shining one. After acquiring whatever skills and experience are absolutely necessary, they should in faithfulness to Christ and His Gospel observe the right order of values in their earthly activities. Thus their whole lives, both individual and social, will be permeated with the spirit of the beatitudes, notably with the spirit of poverty. *(Second Vatican Council—'The Church Today')*

Poverty voluntarily embraced in imitation of Christ provides a witness which is highly esteemed, especially today... By it, a man shares in the poverty of Christ, who became poor for our sake when before He had been rich, that we might be enriched by His poverty. *(Second Vatican Council—'The Religious Life')*

Word-Picture

Few missionaries have caught the popular imagination more than Gladys Aylward who, but for her own determination, would never have got to China.

'You've been with us now for three months, I see, Miss Aylward?' he said.

'Yes, sir'.

'Theology, now—?'

'I wasn't very good at Theology, was I?' she said quietly.

He had looked up under his eyebrows. 'No, you weren't. Not good at all... She knew she could never make him understand. She knew she lacked the persuasiveness to argue with him or the education to pass his examinations.

...'You see, Miss Aylward, all these scholastic shortcomings are important,' he said sympathetically, 'But most important of all is your age. If you stayed at the China Inland Mission Centre for another three years and then we sent you out, you would be about thirty by the time you arrived.' He had shaken his head doubtfully ... 'You will understand, I'm sure,' he continued, 'that there seems to be little point in your continuing your studies here'.

(Alan Burgess—'The Small Woman')

See also: A11 Divine Providence
C21 Rise above materialism
C29 Not through luxury
C25 Humility

THE LIGHT OF EXAMPLE

'Your light must shine in the sight of men.' *Matthew 5:16*

Quotations

A candle loses nothing by lighting another candle. *(Anon).*

There is just one way to bring up a child in the way he should go and that is to travel that way yourself. *(Abraham Lincoln)*

A holy life will produce the deepest impression. Lighthouses blow no horns; they only shine. *(D. L. Moody)*

As far as we can discern, the sole purpose of human existence is to kindle a light in the darkness of mere being. *(C. G. Jung)*

To reflect God in all that is, both here and now, my heart must be a mirror empty, bright and clear. *(Angelius Silesius)*

There are two ways of spreading light; to be a candle, or the mirror that reflects it. *(Edith Wharton)*

Example is always more efficacious than precept. *(Samuel Johnson)*

If you would convince a man that he does wrong, do right. Men will believe what they see. Let them see. *(Henry Thoreau)*

No man is so insignificant as to be sure his example can do no hurt. *(Lord Clarendon)*

Example is the school of mankind, and they will learn at no other. *(E. Burke)*

Jesus said, 'Within a man of light, there is light; and he lights the whole world.' *(Gospel according to Thomas)*

Proverbs

Example is the greatest of all seducers. *(French proverb)*

Precept begins, example accomplishes. *(French proverb)*

They do more harm by their evil example than by their actual sin. *(Latin proverb)*

Humour

In the nursery the children were shouting and making a din. Mother went in and asked what they were quarrelling about. 'We're not quarrelling,' said the eldest, 'we're just playing Mummy and Daddy'.

Word-Pictures

If all the matches produced in France were laid end to end they would stretch eight times the distance between the earth and the moon. So the state-controlled match industry reports.

What power to dispel darkness one little match has, if used properly. And what power for destruction when used carelessly—as witness many forest and city fires.

A blind man visited his friends. It was dark when he left and they gave him a lantern. 'Thank you, but I don't need it. Light or dark it's all the same to me.'

His friend replied, 'yes, but carry it anyway so people won't bump into you.'

Off he went, but soon someone collided into him and shouted, 'why don't you look where you are going?'

The blind man replied, 'why don't you see my lantern?'

'Sorry, brother,' the other said, 'your candle went out'. *(Anon)*

The following story is from Ernest Gordon's account of life and death in a Japanese P.O.W. camp on the river Kwai.

One incident concerned an Aussie private who had been caught outside the fence while trying to obtain medicine from the Thais for his sick friends. He was summarily tried and sentenced to death.

On the morning set for his execution he marched cheerfully between his guards to the parade ground. The Japanese were out in full force to observe the scene. The Aussie was permitted to have his Commanding Officer and a chaplain in attendance as witnesses. The party came to a halt. The C.O. and the chaplain were waved to one side and the Aussie was left standing alone. Calmly, he surveyed his executioners. He knelt down and drew a small copy of the New Testament from a pocket of his ragged shorts. Unhurriedly, his lips moving but no sound coming from them, he read a passage to himself. . . He finished reading, returned his New Testament to his pocket, looked up, and saw the distressed face of his chaplain. He smiled, waved to him, and called out, 'Cheer up, Padre, it isn't as bad as all that. I'll be all right.'

He nodded to his executioner as a sign that he was ready. He knelt down, and bent his head forward to expose his neck. The Samurai sword flashed in the sunlight. The examples set by such men shone like beacons. *(Ernest Gordon—'Miracle on the River Kwai')*

See also: A9 Relationships
A33 Love your neighbour
B24 Go tell everyone

RELATIONSHIPS

'All you need is "Yes" if you mean yes, "No" if you mean no.'
Matthew, 5:37

Quotations

Have a heart that never hardens, and a temper that never tires, and a touch that never hurts. *(Charles Dickens)*

Happiness is not perfected until it is shared. *(Jane Porter)*

We take care of our health, we lay up our money, we make our roof tight and our clothing sufficient, but who provides wisely that he shall not be wanting in the best property of all—friends? *(R. W. Emerson)*

I think people ought to fulfil sacredly their desires. And this means fulfilling the deepest desire, which is a desire to live unhampered by things that are extraneous, a desire for pure relationships and living truth. *(D. H. Lawrence)*

If a man does not make new acquaintances as he advances through life, he will soon find himself alone; one should keep his friendships in constant repair *(Samuel Johnson)*

We gain nothing by being with such as ourselves; we encourage each other in mediocrity. I am always longing to be with men more excellent than myself. *(Charles Lamb)*

Those are our best friends in whose presence we are able to be our best selves. *(C. W. Kohler)*

Lead the life that will make you kindly and friendly to everyone about you, and you will be surprised what a happy life you will live. *(C. M. Schwab)*

Life is mostly froth and bubble,
Two things stand like stone:
Kindness in another's trouble,
Courage in your own. *(Adam Lindsay Gordon)*

Christianity is not a religion, it is a relationship. *(Dr. Thieme)*

Every man is his own ancestor, and every man is his own heir. He

devises his own future; and he inherits his own past. *(H. F. Hedge)*
The first half of our lives is ruined by our parents and the second half by our children! *(C. S. Darrow)*

Proverbs

A faithful friend is an image of God. *(French proverb)*

Better a good enemy than a bad friend. *(Yiddish proverb)*

Word-Pictures

A blind man and a lame man happened to come at the same time to a piece of very bad road. The former begged the latter to guide him through his difficulties. 'How can I do that,' said the lame man, 'as I am scarcely able to drag myself along? But if you were to carry me I can warn you about anything in the way; my eyes will be your eyes and your feet will be mine.' 'With all my heart,' replied the blind man. 'Let us serve one another.' So taking his lame companion on his back, they travelled in this way with safety and pleasure. *(Aesop)*

The proud owner of the world's largest collection of termites, 230,000 of them, says that these insects have a 'secret formula' that helps them survive. The 'formula' is that they co-operate with one another. Zoologist Alfred Emerson says that 'one of the main ways that termites survive is through co-operation, not competition'.

In America in the 1860's, when covered wagons were heading west, the leaders always dreaded the fording of the River Platte. The current was so changeable in the broad, muddy stream that not even experienced scouts could tell where the pockets of quicksand and potholes lay. When an ox-team got stuck, the wagon was usually overturned, dumping family and possessions into the river. The difficulty was easily overcome. When a large number of wagons had arrived at the river, the oxen from all of them were hitched together in a long line to pull each of the families across in turn. Even though one team in the long line floundered, there were always enough on sure footing to keep the wagon on the move. *(Anon)*

See also: A33 Love your neighbour
B6 The Family
B30 Married love
B52 God is Love
C10 Love your enemies
C19 Friendships

SEEKING PERFECTION

'You must be perfect just as your heavenly Father is perfect.'
Matthew, 5:48

Quotations

Trifles make perfection, and perfection is no trifle. *(Michelangelo)*

Every man has in himself a continent of undiscovered character. Happy is he who acts the Columbus to his own soul. *(Sir J. Stevens)*

No one is suddenly made perfect. *(Bede the Venerable)*

Each and everything is said to be perfect in so far as it attains to its proper end; and this is its ultimate perfection. *(St. Thomas Aquinas)*

Not to go along the way to God is to go back. *(St. Thomas Aquinas)*

To obtain the gift of holiness is the work of a life. *(Cardinal Newman)*

Holiness consists not in doing uncommon things, but in doing all common things with an uncommon fervour. *(Cardinal Manning)*

It takes a long time to bring excellence to maturity. *(Publius Syrus)*

It is only imperfection that complains of what is imperfect. The more perfect we are, the more gentle and quiet we become towards the defects of others. *(Fenelon)*

The serene, silent beauty of a holy life is the most powerful influence in the world, next to the might of God. *(Pascal)*

No man can advance three paces on the road to perfection unless Jesus Christ walks beside him. *(R. H. Benson)*

That soul is perfect which is guided habitually by the instinct of the Holy Spirit. *(Isaac Hecker)*

Proverbs

The diamond cannot be polished without friction, nor the man perfected without trials. *(Chinese proverb)*

Fear less, hope more; Eat less, chew more;
Whine less, breathe more; Talk less, say more:
Hate less, love more; and all good things will be yours. *(Swedish proverb)*

Humour

'Charity, dear Miss Prism, charity! None of us are perfect. I myself am peculiarly susceptible to draughts.' *(Oscar Wilde)*

Wife (heatedly)	'Your're lazy, worthless, bad tempered; you're a liar.
Husband (reasonably)	'Well, dear, no man is perfect!'

Bachelors' wives and old maids' children are always perfect. *(Chamfort)*

Statements

All the faithful, whatever their condition or state, are called by the Lord each in his own way, to the perfect holiness whereby the Father Himself is perfect. *(Second Vatican Council—'The Church')*

The Church recalls to the mind of all that culture must be made to bear on the integral perfection of the human person, and on the good of the community and the whole of society. Therefore, the human spirit must be cultivated in such a way that there results a growth in its ability to wonder, to understand, to contemplate, to make personal judgements and to develop a religious, moral and social sense. *(Second Vatican Council—'The Church Today')*

Word-Pictures

Youth is not a time of life . . . it is a state of mind.
Nobody grows old by merely living a number of years;
people grow old only by deserting their ideals.
Years wrinkle the skin, but to give up enthusiasm wrinkles
the soul. Worry, doubt, self-distrust, fear and despair . . .
these are the long, long years that bow the head and turn
the growing spirit back to dust.
Whether seventy or sixteen, there is in every being's
heart the love of wonder, the sweet amazement at the stars
and the starlike things and thoughts, the undaunted
challenge of events, the unfailing childlike appetite for what next,
and the joy of the game of life.
You are as young as your faith, as old as your doubt;
as young as your self-confidence, as old as your fear;
as young as your hope, as old as your despair. *(Anon)*

Do all the good you can,
In all the ways you can,
In all the places you can,
At all the times you can,

To all the people you can,
As long as ever you can. *(John Wesley)*

You will never be sorry
For doing your level best,
For your faith in humanity,
For being kind to the poor,
For asking pardon when in error,
For being generous with an enemy,
For sympathising with the oppressed. *(Anon)*

Florence Nightingale who bandaged the world's battle wounds, said:

'I solemnly pledge myself before God and in the presence of this assembly:

To pass my life in purity and to practise my profession faithfully. I will abstain from whatever is deleterious and mischievous, and will not take or knowingly administer any harmful drug.

I will do all in my power to elevate the standard of my profession, and will hold in confidence all personal matters committed to my keeping and all family affairs coming to my knowledge in the practice of my profession.

With loyalty will I endeavour to aid the physician in his work, and devote myself to the welfare of those committed to my care.'

See also: A20 The Kingdom of God
A22 Seeking God
B26 The whole man
C47 The indwelling Spirit

GOD'S LOVING PROVIDENCE

'Surely life means more than food, and the body more than clothing! Look at the birds in the sky.' *Matthew 6:26*

Quotations

Men must pursue things which are just in present, and leave the future to the divine Providence. *(Francis Bacon)*

The beginning of anxiety is the end of faith, and the beginning of true faith is the end of anxiety. *(George Mueller)*

The crosses which we make for ourselves by a restless anxiety as to the future are not crosses which come from God. *(Anon)*

Let us hope . . . that a kind of Providence will put a speedy end to the acts of God under which we have been labouring. *(P. De Vries)*

I go the way that Providence dictates with the assurance of a sleep-walker. *(Adolf Hitler)*

All events that take place in this world, even those apparently fortuitous or casual, are comprehended in the order of divine Providence, on which fate depends. *(St. Thomas Aquinas)*

In all created things discern the providence and wisdom of God, and in all things give Him thanks. *(St. Teresa of Avila)*

The acts of our Maker ought always to be reverenced without examining, for they can never be unjust. *(Pope St. Gregory I)*

Not God alone in the still calm we find;
He mounts the storm, and walks upon the wind. *(Alexander Pope)*

Proverbs

Providence assists not the idle. *(Latin proverb)*

God builds the nest of the blind bird. *(Turkish proverb)*

He who gives us teeth will give us bread. *(Yiddish proverb)*

Humour

'We mustn't question the ways of Providence,' said the Rector. 'Providence,' said the old woman. 'Don't talk to me about Providence.

I've had enough of Providence. First he took my husband, and then he took my 'taters, but there's one above as'll teach him to mind his manners, if he doesn't look out!'

The Rector was much too distressed to challenge this remarkable piece of theology. *(Dorothy Sayers—'The Nine Tailors')*

Statement

The People of God believes that it is led by the Spirit of the Lord, who fills the earth. Motivated by this faith, it labours to decipher authentic signs of God's presence and purpose in the happenings, needs and desires in which this People has a part along with other men of our age. For faith throws a new light on everything, manifests God's design for man's total vocation and thus directs the mind to solutions which are fully human. *(Second Vatican Council—'The Church Today')*

Word-Pictures

Providence requires three things of us before it will help us—a stout heart, a strong arm and a stiff upper lip. *(Sam Slick)*

God's providence is not in baskets lowered from the sky, but through the hands and hearts of those who love him. The lad without food and without shoes made the proper answer to the cruel-minded woman who asked, 'But if God loved you, wouldn't he send you food and shoes?'
The boy replied, 'God told someone, but he forgot'. *(George Buttrick)*

The treasurer's voice droned on as he went through the accounts of the Papal States. Suddenly, Pope Pius V stood up, opened a window and stared out. After a few moments he relaxed, and turned back to his senior Vatican officials with eyes shining.

'Leave all this for now,' he said, waving towards the ledgers and financial statements, strewn about the table. 'We must go and give thanks to God. Victory has gone to the Christian fleet.'

The business-like treasurer made a note of the strange incident in the minutes. It happened, he wrote, just before 5 p.m. on October 7, 1571.

Exactly a fortnight later, on October 21, a messenger galloped into Rome from Venice with news of an historic naval victory.

A Christian fleet, under Don John of Austria, had trounced the Turkish fleet at Lepanto. According to the official report, it had become clear that victory was theirs just before 5 p.m. on October 7.

See also: A7 Poor in Spirit
A19 Patience
B21 Trust in God
C39 Doing God's will

HOLY SCRIPTURE

'Everyone who listens to these words of mine and acts on them will be like a sensible man who built his house on rocks.' *Matthew 7:24*

Quotations

The book of books, the storehouse and magazine of life and comfort, the holy scriptures. *(George Herbert)*

These writings bring back to you the living image of that most holy mind, the very Christ himself speaking, healing, dying, rising, in fact so entirely present, that you would see less of him if you beheld him with your eyes. *(Erasmus)*

Most people are bothered by those passages in Scripture which they cannot understand; but as for me, I always noticed that the passages in Scripture which trouble me most are those that I do understand. *(Mark Twain)*

In the twentieth century our highest praise is to call the Bible 'the World's Best-Seller'. And it has come to be more and more difficult to say whether we think it is a best-seller because it is great, or vice versa. *(D. Boorstin)*

The Scriptures of God, whether belonging to Christian or Jew, are much more ancient than any secular literature. *(Tertullian)*

To be ignorant of the Scripture is not to know Christ. *(St. Jerome)*

The Bible is a stream wherein the elephant may swim and the lamb may wade. *(Pope St. Gregory I)*

The whole series of the divine Scriptures is interpreted in a fourfold way. In all holy books one should ascertain what everlasting truths are therein intimated, what deeds are narrated, what future events are foretold, and what commands or counsels are there contained. *(Bede the Venerable)*

What you bring away from the Bible depends to some extent on what you carry to it. *(Oliver Wendell Holmes)*

If thou knewest the whole Bible by heart, and the sayings of all the philosophers, what would it profit thee without the love of God and without grace? *(Thomas à Kempis)*

In the Old Testament the New lies hidden, in the New Testament the Old is laid open. *(St. Augustine of Hippo)*

The Bible is a window in this prison-world, through which we may look into eternity. *(T. Dwight)*

England has two books, the Bible and Shakespeare. England made Shakespeare but the Bible made England. *(Victor Hugo)*

Humour

A lady was posting a gift of a Bible to a relative. The post office clerk examined the heavy parcel and inquired if it contained anything breakable. 'Nothing,' the lady told him, 'but the Ten Commandments.' *(Anon)*

In talking about the story of Jacob's dream, a Sunday School teacher asked the class, 'Why did the angels use the ladder when they had wings?'

One bright pupil quickly replied, 'Because they were moulting.'

After the teacher had told her class they could draw a picture of the Bible story she had told them, she went around to see what the children had done. She noticed that little Jenny hadn't drawn a Bible picture at all, so the teacher asked the child to tell the class about her picture.

'This is a car. The man in the front seat is God. The people in the back seat are Adam and Eve. God is driving them out of the Garden of Eden.'

There is a story of a Scottish minister who was reproved for only preaching from and thinking about the Old Testament, and was asked why he did not make more place in his ministry for the New. He replied, 'Aye, I know the New is there, and it is all very well in its way, but, as with other authors, the sequel is not quite up to the original work.' *(Douglas Woodruff)*

A German student, attempting to translate part of the New Testament into English, rendered a very famous text as 'The ghost is agreeable but the meat is soft.'

Statements

Let priests therefore . . . after they have themselves by diligent study perused the sacred pages and made them their own by prayer and meditation assiduously distribute the heavenly treasures of the divine word by sermons, homilies and exhortations; let them confirm the Christian doctrine by sentences from the Sacred Books . . .

let them set forth all this with such eloquence, lucidity and clearness that the faithful may not only be moved and inflamed to reform their lives, but may also conceive in their hearts the greatest veneration for the Sacred Scripture. *(Pius XII—'Divino Afflante Spiritu')*

Hence there exists a close connection and communication between sacred tradition and sacred Scripture. For both of them, flowing from the same divine wellspring, in a certain way merge into a unity and tend toward the same end. For sacred Scripture is the word of God inasmuch as it is consigned to writing under the inspiration of the divine Spirit. *(Second Vatican Council—'Revelation')*

Those who search out the intention of the sacred writer must, among other things, have regard for 'literary forms'. For truth is proposed and expressed in a variety of ways, depending on whether a text is history of one kind or another, or whether its form is that of prophecy, poetry, or some other type of speech. The interpreter must investigate what meaning the sacred writer intended to express and actually expressed in particular circumstances as he used contemporary literary forms in accordance with the situation of his own time and culture. *(Second Vatican Council—'Revelation')*

Word-Pictures

Item, that you shall provide on this side the feast of Easter next coming, one book of the whole Bible of the largest volume, in English, and the same set up in some convenient place within the said church that you have cure of, whereas your parishioners may most commodiously resort to the same, and read it . . . Item, that you shall discourage no man privily or apertly from the reading or hearing of the said Bible, but shall expressly provoke, stir, and exhort every person to read the same, as that which is the very lively word of God, that every Christian man is bound to embrace, believe, and follow, if he look to be saved. *(Drawn up by Cromwell, submitted to Cranmer 1538, and sent out by him)*

An atheist once said, in speaking of the Bible, that it was quite impossible these days to believe in any book whose author was unknown. A Christian friend asked him if the compiler of the multiplication table was known.
'No,' he answered.
'Then, of course, you do not believe in it?'
'Oh yes, I believe in it because it works well,' replied the sceptic.
'So does the Bible,' was the rejoinder, and the sceptic had no answer to make.

A young man heard with disgust that his wealthy old uncle had left him a Bible in his will. The will read thus: 'To my nephew I leave a copy of God's priceless Word which I trust he will use daily and find within its pages real treasure.'

The beneficiary threw the Bible into an old trunk in the attic, disgusted and disappointed with his share in his uncle's bequests. Years later, at a time of depression, he turned to the good Book for comfort. Between its pages he found many thousands of pounds.

The Seven Wonders of the Word

1. The wonder of its formation—the way in which it grew is one of the mysteries of time.
2. The wonder of its unification—a library of 66 books, yet one book.
3. The wonder of its age—most ancient of all books.
4. The wonder of its sale—best seller of any book.
5. The wonder of its interest—only book in the world read by all classes.
6. The wonder of its language—written largely by uneducated men, yet the best from a literary standpoint.
7. The wonder of its preservation—the most hated of all books, yet it continues to exist. 'The word of our God shall stand for ever.'

An American Soldier was taught a valuable lesson by a South Sea Islander during World War II.

The friendly host, trying to assure the visitor that they had many things in common, brought a copy of the Bible out of his hut and said: 'This is my most prized possession.'

With obvious disdain the soldier replied, 'We've outgrown that sort of thing, you know.'

The islander, who belonged to a tribe which had formerly practised cannibalism, was unimpressed by this lack of courtesy as well as faith. He calmly remarked, 'It's a good thing we haven't outgrown it here. If we had, you would have been a meal as soon as we saw you.'

A 15-year-old Bedouin boy named Muhammed adh-Dhib was searching for a stray goat in a desert region close to the Dead Sea, when he saw the opening of a small cave in a rocky cliff. He lazily threw a few stones through the hole and heard something break.

Thinking it might be hidden treasure, Muhammed ran back to camp and brought a friend, Ahmed Muhammed, to the cave. They squeezed through the opening into the cave and found among pieces of broken pottery, a number of clay cylinders, two feet high.

Hoping for gold or precious stones, the boys wrenched off the lids, but instead of the treasure they expected, they found only dark musty-swelling lumps of material. They were 11 scrolls made of thin strips of sheepskin sewn together, and coated in gummy, decomposed leather. The scrolls, between three feet and 24 feet long, were marked in an ancient form of Hebrew script. The boys were disappointed, but their families managed to sell the fragments to a dealer in Jerusalem for a few pounds. That was in 1947.

See also: B2 The Good News
B9 Revelation
B24 Go tell everyone
C6 The Old Testament Law

THE CHURCH IS FOR SINNERS

'Indeed I did not come to call the virtuous, but sinners.' *Matthew 9:13*

Quotations

The Church exists for the sake of those outside it. *(William Temple)*

There are many sheep without, many wolves within. *(St. Augustine of Hippo)*

The Church and the sacraments exist to rescue character and bring out the best in it. Christ did this during his lifetime and has been doing it ever since. *(Hubert Van Zeller)*

In the primitive Church the chalices were of wood, the prelates of gold. In these days, the Church hath chalices of gold and prelates of wood. *(Girolamo Savonarola)*

The Church, like the ark of Noah, is worth saving; not for the sake of the unclean beasts and vermin that almost filled it, and probably made most noise and clamour in it, but for the little corner of rationality, that was as much distressed by the stink within as by the tempest without. *(William Warburton—Bishop of Gloucester)*

The Church is not possession of the kingdom, it is the struggle for it. But it is a struggle consoled by the promise that the gates of hell will not prevail against it. *(A New Catechism)*

While I can not be regarded as a pillar, I must be regarded as a buttress of the Church, because I support from the outside. *(William Lamb)*

Don't stay away from Church because there are so many hypocrites. There's always room for one more. *(A. R. Adams)*

The Church is not made up of people who are better than the rest, but of people who want to become better than they are. *(Anon)*

Often times have I heard you speak of one who commits a wrong as though he were not one of you, but a stranger unto you and an intruder upon your world. But I say that even as the holy and the righteous cannot rise beyond the highest which is in each of you, so the wicked and the weak cannot fall lower than the lowest which is in you also. *(Kahlil Gibran)*

Humour

He was of the faith chiefly in the sense that the Church he currently did not attend was Catholic. *(Kingsley Amis—'One Fat Englishman')*

The retiring usher was instructing his youthful successor in the details of his office. 'And remember, my boy, that we have nothing but good, kind Christians in this Church—until you try to put someone else in their pew!'

There is one ingenious way of indulging in mild slander in the form of audible ejaculatory prayer, and I know a church in London where there is an Irish woman with a considerable gift for praying aloud in such a way as to make her personal opinions exceedingly clear.

One day, when the priest was a little late for Mass, she exclaimed as he came up the aisle, 'Oh, thanks be to the Mother of God, there's going to be the Holy Mass.' And at other times she has apostrophized before the statues of Our Lady and St. Joseph, making it very plain that the saints are not deceived about the real character of other parties praying in the church; and I have often wondered what the exact legal position would be, for, if any conversation is privileged, it is surely prayer. *(Douglas Woodruff)*

Statements

Although by the power of the Holy Spirit the Church has remained the faithful spouse of her Lord and has never ceased to be the sign of salvation on earth, still she is very well aware that among her members, both clerical and lay, some have been unfaithful to the Spirit of God during the course of many centuries. In the present age, too, it does not escape the Church how great a distance lies between the message she offers and the human failings of those to whom the gospel is entrusted. *(Second Vatican Council—'The Church Today')*

While Christ, 'holy, innocent, undefiled,' knew nothing of sin, but came to expiate only the sins of the people, the Church, embracing sinners in her bosom, is at the same time holy and always in need of being purified, and incessantly pursues the path of penance and renewal. *(Second Vatican Council—'The Church')*

Word-Pictures

Only one member has left the Church because of the behaviour of young people. It happened one hot summer evening. Bernice walked down the aisle and sat down with a bump in a pew. She kicked off her stiletto heels, hitched her skirt over her knees and placed her aching feet on the pew in front. She turned to the middle-aged man sitting next to her and said, 'Cor, ain't it bloody 'ot?' He left immediately and he has not been back since. In fact, it was bloody hot, and Bernice was just trying to be friendly in the only way she knew. Moreover, her greeting was in sharp distinction from the lack of welcome she received from him in the House of the Lord. Other adults have been driven close to despair at times by unexpected 'out of place' happenings, but it is to their credit that they still remain to tell the tale. *(Ernest Marvin:—'Odds Against')*

Dr. Philip Potter recalls the first world gathering he ever attended. It was in the Caribbean area.

A white South African explained apartheid in the Church by saying that the congregation was like any community in which people participated on the basis of sharing their life together. 'If we can't be friends, we can't feel at home with each other. Therefore it is better to be separated. Blacks don't feel at home with us, or we with them. Hence the separation.'

In the course of this explanation, the young Czech girl who was in the chair got redder and redder. She burst out, 'I do not understand what you are talking about. You speak of the Church as a community of friends. But that is not the Church of God. Friendship is what man makes. Fellowship is what God gives.'

This was posted on a Bronx, New York, Church notice board: 'Do come in—Trespassers will be forgiven.' *(Anon)*

Notice put up at the church door by an Italian congregation: 'Home for Abandoned Old Men.' *(Anon)*

Among the regulations for the tenants of a new block of flats near Marble Arch, occurs the injunction 'No religious services or immorality permitted in these flats.' *(Anon)*

See also: B17 The Church—Bride of Christ
C12 The Church for all men
C27 The Father who receives us back

THE SUCCESSORS OF THE APOSTLES

'He summoned his twelve disciples, and gave them authority over unclean spirits, with power to cast them out and to cure all kinds of diseases and sickness.' *Matthew 10:1*

Quotations

A bishop who is himself holy will most certainly have a following of holy priests, whose holiness will in turn redound to the religious perfection of the whole diocese.' *(Pope John XXIII)*

'*For* you, I am Bishop', said St. Augustine to his people, 'but *with* you, I am a Christian. The first is an office accepted, the second a grace received; one a danger, the other safety. If then, I am gladder by far to be redeemed *with you* than I am to be placed *over you,* I shall, as the Lord commanded, be more completely your servant.' *(St. Augustine of Hippo)*

It is very significant that in every recorded instance, the Apostles were busy at their daily work when the Master called them.
Peter and Andrew were fishing;
James and John were mending their nets;
Matthew was sitting at the receipt of custom.
God never visits an idle or unserviceable life. *(David Smith)*

Wherever the bishop appears, there let the people be; as wherever Jesus Christ is, there is the Catholic Church. *(St. Ignatius of Antioch)*

If the authority of Peter and his successors is plenary and supreme, it is not to be regarded as the sole authority. For He who made Peter the foundation of the Church also chose twelve, whom He called apostles (Luke 6, 13); and just as it is necessary that the authority of Peter should be perpetuated in the Roman pontiff, so by the fact that the bishops succeed the apostles, they inherit their ordinary power, and thus the episcopal order necessarily belongs to the essential constitution of the Church. *(Pope Leo XIII)*

To be a bishop (sacerdos) is much, to deserve to be one is more. *(St. Jerome)*

Be obedient to your bishop and welcome him as the parent of your soul. *(St. Jerome)*

Let him understand that he is no bishop, who loves to rule and not be useful to his flock. *(St. Augustine)*

Humour

The Bishop's Last Directions
Tell my Priests, when I am gone,
O'er me to shed no tears,
For I shall be no deader then
Than they have been for years. *(Anon)*

The Sunday School teacher asked a little girl if she knew who Matthew was. The answer was no. The teacher then asked if she knew who John was. Again the answer was no. Finally the teacher asked if she knew who Peter was.

She answered, 'I think he was a rabbit.'

A bishop in the South of London came out of his cathedral one day and saw a small boy playing in the gutter. He asked him what he was doing with the mud. 'I'm making a cathedral,' he said. 'Well,' said the bishop, 'If you have a cathedral, you must have a bishop.' 'Nah,' said the boy, 'I ain't got enough muck to make a bishop.'

Statements

As lawful successors of the apostles and as members of the episcopal college, bishops should always realize that they are linked one to the other, and should show concern for all the churches. *(Second Vatican Council—'Bishops')*

In discharging their apostolic office, which concerns the salvation of souls, bishops of themselves enjoy full and perfect freedom, and independence from civil authority. *(Second Vatican Council—'Bishops')*

In exercising his office of father and pastor, a bishop should stand in the midst of his people as one who serves. *(Second Vatican Council—'Bishops')*

The pastoral office or the habitual and daily care of their sheep, is entrusted to them completely. Nor are they to be regarded as vicars of the Roman Pontiff, for they exercise an authority which is proper to them, and are quite correctly called 'prelates', or heads of the people whom they govern. *(Second Vatican Council—'The Church')*

Word-Pictures

Edward Tucker and Robert Canton, salvage men working in Bermuda spotted an old wreck. Painstaking research identified the wreck as the Spanish Ship, San Pedro, which had sunk in 1595. In and around her, Tucker and Canton found 2000 silver coins, some assorted jewellery and gold bars, and a number of guns which threw

some light on the ship that had carried them.
But the most exciting find by far was a golden crucifix, three inches long by two inches wide, set with seven perfectly matched emeralds. The crucifix was identified as a pectoral cross, symbol of a bishop's authority. It is thought to be the most valuable single item ever recovered from the sea.
Estimates of its worth range from about £10,000 to £30,000—it is hard to put a price on it.

The Apostles' Symbols
The badges or symbols of the fourteen Apostles (i.e. the original twelve with Matthias and Paul) are as follows:
Andrew, an X-shaped cross because he was crucified on one.
Bartholomew, a knife, because he was flayed with a knife.
James the Great, a scallop shell, a pilgrim's staff or a gourd bottle, because he is the patron saint of pilgrims.
James the Less, a fuller's pole, because he is said to have been killed by a blow on the head with a pole, dealt him by Simeon the Fuller.
John, a cup with a winged serpent flying out of it, in allusion to the tradition about Aristodemos, priest of Diana, who challenged John to drink a cup of poison. John made the sign of a cross on the cup, Satan like a dragon flew from it, and John then drank the cup which was quite innocuous.
Judas Iscariot, a bag, because he acted as a treasurer for Jesus and the Apostles.
Jude, a club, because he was martyred with a club.
Matthew, a hatchet or halberd, because he was slain at Nadabar with a halberd.
Matthias, a battleaxe, because it is believed he was first stoned, and then beheaded with a battleaxe.
Paul, a sword, because his head was cut off with a sword.
Peter, a bunch of keys, because Christ gave him 'the keys of the kingdom of heaven.'
Philip, a long staff surmounted with a cross, because he suffered death by being suspended by the neck from a tall pillar.
Simon, a saw, because according to tradition, he was sawn to death.
Thomas, a lance, because he was pierced to death through the body, at Meliapore.

Who was the first priest ever to preach a sermon? The answer which seems to me very surprising, is that it was St. Augustine of Hippo, in the fourth century. Until his day, preaching was reserved to Bishops, but young Augustine was so particularly eloquent and gifted that he was allowed to preach while still only a priest, although the Bishop took care to be present. This was in the Western Church. In the more theologically-minded East, everybody seems to have been given to preaching. There is a curious complaint of St. Gregory of Nyssa about fourth-century Constantinople, where he says that 'if you ask a man for change he replies by giving you a philosophical treatise on the begotten and the unbegotten.' *(Douglas Woodruff)*

See also: A 24 The Papacy
A 45 The Priesthood
B 13 Authority

SIN

'Sin entered the world through one man, and through sin death.'
Romans 5:12

Quotations

There is only one calamity—sin. *(St. John Chrysostom)*

Sin is energy in the wrong channel. *(St. Augustine of Hippo)*

No man ever became extremely wicked all at once. *(Juvenal)*

Sin is essentially a departure from God. *(Martin Luther)*

To sin is nothing else than not to render to God his due. *(St. Anselm)*

For the religious man to do wrong is to defy his King; for the Christian, it is to wound his Friend. *(William Temple)*

Sin is not a monster to be mused on, but an impotence to be got rid of. *(Matthew Arnold)*

Keep yourself from opportunity and God will keep you from sins. *(Jacob Cats)*

The greatest fault is to be conscious of none. *(Thomas Carlyle)*

For evil to triumph, it is only necessary for good men to do nothing. *(Edmund Burke)*

Sins are like circles in the water when a stone is thrown into it; one produces another. When anger was in Cain's heart, murder was not far off. *(Philip Henry)*

I see no fault that I might not have committed myself. *(Goethe)*

Beware the pious fool, and the wise sinner. *(Ibn Gabirol)*

Proverbs

Sin can be well-guarded, but cannot be free from anxiety. *(Latin proverb)*

You can get to the ends of the earth by lying, but you'll never get back. *(Russian proverb)*

Who is not ashamed of his sins, sins double. *(German proverb)*

Humour

Mrs. Brown was shocked to learn that her son had told a lie. Taking the youngster aside for a heart-to-heart talk, she graphically explained the consequences of falsehood:

'A tall black man with red fiery eyes and two sharp horns grabs little boys who tell lies and carries them off at night. He takes them to Mars where they have to work in a dark canyon for 50 years! Now,' she concluded, satisfied, 'you won't tell a lie again, will you, dear?'

'No, Mum,' replied her son, gravely. 'You tell better ones.' *(F. G. Kernan)*

One minister told his congregation that there are 700 different sins. He has already received 46 requests for the list. *(Anon)*

'God knows how you Protestants can be expected to have any sense of direction,' she said. 'It's different with us. I haven't been to Mass for years, I've got every mortal sin on my conscience, but I know when I'm doing wrong. I'm still a Catholic.' *(Angus Wilson—'The Wrong Set')*

Statements

By himself and by his own power, no one is freed from sin or raised above himself, or completely rid of his sickness or his solitude or his servitude. On the contrary, all stand in need of Christ, their Model, their Mentor, their Liberator, their Saviour, their Source of Life. *(Second Vatican Council—'Missions')*

Man is obliged to regard his body as good and honourable since God has created it, and will raise it up on the last day. Nevertheless, wounded by sin, man experiences rebellious stirrings in his body. But the very dignity of man postulates that man glorify God in his body and forbid it to serve the evil inclinations of his heart. *(Second Vatican Council—'The Church Today')*

Word-pictures

When Leonardo da Vinci was painting his masterpiece 'The Last Supper', he looked for a model for his Christ. At last, he located a chorister in one of the churches of Rome who was lovely in life and features, a young man named Pietro Bandinelli.

Years passed, and the painting was still unfinished. All the disciples had been portrayed save one—Judas Iscariot. Now he started to look for a man whose face was hardened and distorted by sin—and at last he found a beggar on the streets of Rome with a face so villainous that he shuddered when he looked at him. He hired the man to sit for him as he painted the face of Judas on his canvas. When he was about to dismiss the man, he said, 'I have not yet found out your name.' 'I am Pietro Bandinelli,' he replied, 'I also sat for you as your model of Christ.'

The sinful life of years so disfigured the once fair face of the young man that it now looked as though it were the most villainous face in all Rome! *(Indian Christian)*

Persons called 'Sin-eaters' were hired at funerals in the Middle Ages to eat beside the corpse and so take upon themselves the sins of the deceased, that the soul might be delivered from Purgatory. In Carmarthenshire, the sin-eater used to rest a plate of salt on the breast of the deceased and place a piece of bread on the salt. After saying an incantation over the bread it was consumed by the sin-eater and it was thought that with it he ate the sins of the dead.

In the ruins of Pompeii there was found a petrified woman who, instead of trying to flee from the city, had spent her time in gathering up her jewels. In one of the houses was found the skeleton of a man who, for the sake of 60 coins, a small plate and a saucepan of silver, had remained in his house till the street was half-filled with volcanic matter, then was trying to escape from the window. *(Anon)*

It is pointless to complain that crime and sin receive more publicity than exemplary behaviour. It is, on the contrary, a matter of some satisfaction that evil is still regarded as news.

It will be a sad day if integrity and goodness become so rare as to be featured in the papers. *(Cardinal Heenan—'Through the Year with Cardinal Heenan')*

One summer afternoon on the River Mississippi, a steamer, crowded with passengers, many of them miners from California, suddenly struck a submerged wreck. In a moment her deck was a wild confusion. The boats were able to take off only one-quarter of the passengers. The rest, divesting themselves of their garments, succeeded in swimming to shore. Immediately after the last had quitted the vessel, a man appeared on deck. Seizing a spar, he leapt into the river but instantly sank like a stone. When his body was recovered, it was found that, while the other passengers were escaping, he had been rifling the miners' trunks, and round his waist he had fastened bags of gold. In a quarter of an hour he had amassed more than most men do in a lifetime, but he lost himself in an instant.
'Thou fool, this night thy soul shall be required of thee.' *(Anon)*

See also: A13 The Church is for sinners
A38 Original Sin
C37 Temptation

THE SAINTS

'Anyone who welcomes a holy man because he is a holy man will have a holy man's reward.' *Matthew 10:41*

Quotations

A vulgar man cannot be a saint. *(Rabbi Hillel)*

The saint is saint, not because he is 'good' but because he is transparent for something that is more than he himself is. *(Paul Tillich)*

Grace is indeed required to turn a man into a saint; and he who doubts this does not know what either a man or a saint is. *(Blaise Pascal)*

It is easier to make a saint out of a libertine than out of a prig. *(George Santayana)*

The great painter boasted that he mixed all his colours with brains, and the great saint may be said to mix all his thoughts with thanks. *(G. K. Chesterton)*

Nature requires the saint since he alone knows the miracle of transfiguration; growth and development, the very highest and most sustained incarnation, never weary him. *(Friedrick Wilhelm Nietzsche)*

The only difference between a saint and a sinner is that every saint has a past, and every sinner has a future. *(Oscar Wilde)*

The power of the soul for good is in proportion to the strength of its passions. Sanctity is not the negation of passion but its order. Hence great saints have often been great sinners. *(Coventry Patmore)*

What saint has ever won his crown without first contending for it? *(St. Jerome)*

No devotion to the saints is more acceptable and more proper than if you strive to express their virtues. *(Erasmus)*

The way of this world is to praise dead saints and persecute living ones. *(Anon)*

Proverb

Saint cannot, if God will not. *(French proverb)*

Humour

Every saint has a bee in his halo. *(E. V. Lucas)*

Saints are all right in heaven but they're hell on earth. *(Cardinal Cushing)*

Martyrdom, sir, is what these people like: it is the only way in which a man can become famous without ability. *(Bernard Shaw)*

There may have been disillusionments in the lives of the mediaeval saints, but they would scarcely have been better pleased if they could have foreseen that their names would be associated nowadays chiefly with racehorses and the cheaper clarets. *(Saki— H. H. Munro)*

There used to be an Italian who went about Liverpool selling plaster statues of the saints. One day he was barged into by a sailor who knocked St. Anthony out of his collection and broke off the arm with the Infant Jesus on it. The Italian was in the greatest distress. 'I can never sell him now,' he exclaimed. 'Sell him? Of course you can sell him,' said the sailor. 'Stick a patch on one of his eyes and sell him as Lord Nelson.' *(Douglas Woodruff)*

Statements

In the lives of those who shared in our humanity and yet were transformed into especially successful images of Christ, God vividly manifests to men His presence and His face. He speaks to us in them, and gives us a sign of His kingdom, to which we are powerfully drawn, surrounded as we are by so many witnesses and having such an argument for the truth of the gospel. *(Second Vatican Council —'The Church')*

Word-Pictures

The festival of Hallowe'en originated in a pagan celebration, even though its name derives from the Christian festival of All Hallows or All Saints.

It was introduced in the seventh century to commemorate all those saints and martyrs who had no special day to themselves, and was held on May 13. But in the eighth century, All Hallows day was moved to November 1, to counteract the pagan celebrations held on that date.

October 31, the eve of November 1, was the last night of the year in the ancient Celtic calendar, and was celebrated as the end of summer and its fruitfulness. It was a festival which the Celts of Northern Europe marked with bonfires to help the sun through the winter.

Only since the late eighteenth and early nineteenth centuries has Hallowe'en developed as a jolly time for children, with costumes, lanterns and games. Before then it was regarded as a night of fear, and wise men, respectful of hobgoblins and wandering demons, stayed indoors. *(Anon)*

The cult of Saints' relics began with the cult of the martyrs, as the faithful soaked small cloths—brandea—in their blood, or put them in contact with the coffin. The cult of relics spread rapidly when elevation and translation of the holy person's body began to be practised, and bones became easily available. Every altar of the growing Church was supposed to have a relic under it, and kings and princes collected them, housing them in reliquaries that became objects of art. The demand for relics exceeded supply, and some saints, particularly venerated in several places, have a head in each place. Gregory the Great refused a Byzantine empress' request for a piece of Saint Paul, but later on, there was no such hesitation about dismembering a body on the 'share-the-wealth' principle. Churchmen cut up the saints as farmers cut up seed potatoes, confident that the vital principle was in each fragment. Besides the relics of the saints, there were other relics with slips of ancient parchment attached to them saying that they were the bones of archangels. These brought a very high price and were thought to be particularly effective. The number of saints increased rapidly; there were over twenty-five thousand of them by the tenth century. Most of them were only local; getting a saint nationally recognised required the approval of a sovereign, international recognition that of the pope. The cults of really popular saints spread nearly as fast as the cults of motion-picture stars do today—the earliest representation we have of Saint Thomas Becket is in a Sicilian Cathedral. *(Ambrosini—'The Secret Archives of the Vatican')*

It is difficult to discover precisely how many relics of the saints are preserved and venerated throughout Italy. Some of the more than 2,000 saints in the Catholic calendar are nothing more than re-worked pagan deities. St Venerina, for example, who is patroness of a village in Calabria, is Venus in disguise. However, the great majority of saints did exist and an extraordinary number of these have left parts of their anatomy scattered profusely throughout the Catholic Churches of Italy. Some of their parts, reminiscent of the miracle of the loaves and fishes, have been multiplied. There are for instance nine breasts of St Eulalia throughout Italy, Sicily and Spain.

Multiplication of parts seems to be in direct ratio to the prestige of the saint. St John the Baptist, for example, would seem to have had four heads! One is to be found in Amiens, in France; a second in Damascus; a large part of a third is preserved in a gold chalice in St Mark's, Venice; and Rome, not to be outdone, has a piece of his cranium in the Church of San Silvestro.

St John's fingers and thumbs have also come in for much veneration, though his legs have totally disappeared! The church of St. Marcuola, Venice, possesses a complete hand, but twenty-eight fingers and thumbs can be discovered in other Italian churches, and this does not include the three fingers in the Cathedral Museum in Florence! His whole right arm and hand can be venerated in the Cathedral in Siena, and this particular relic was authenticated by Pope Pius II. It is a relief to know that, after all this dismembering, the Cathedral of Genoa claims the complete ashes of his whole body. *(Anon)*

Canonisation can have drawbacks. St. Swithin found it upset his wish to stay buried out of doors, where people would walk over his humble bones. It was the rain on the day of his translation on the 15th July, 983 which then continued for 40 days to prevent the monks from over-riding his wishes, which started the legend, still very much alive, that if it rains on the 15th July, it will rain for 40 days. It is of more academic interest that if it is fine on that day, it will continue fine for the same period. *(Douglas Woodruff)*

See also: A10 Seeking perfection
B26 The whole man
B51 One with Christ
C8 God's messengers

GENTLENESS

'Learn from me, for I am gentle and humble in heart.' *Matthew 11:30*

Quotations

The smile that you send out returns to you. *(Indian Wisdom)*

Nothing appeases an enraged elephant so much as the sight of a little lamb. *(St. Francis de Sales)*

It takes more oil than vinegar to make a good salad. *(Jean Pierre Camus)*

When you encounter difficulties and contradictions, do not try to break them, but bend them with gentleness and time. *(St. Francis de Sales)*

He who can preserve gentleness amid pains, and peace amid worry and multitude of affairs, is almost perfect. *(St. Francis de Sales)*

Nothing is so strong as gentleness, nothing so gentle as real strength. *(St. Francis de Sales)*

Hail the small sweet courtesies of life, for smooth do they make the road of it. *(Laurence Sterne)*

This is the final test of a gentleman: his respect for those who can be of no possible service to him. *(William Lyon Phelps)*

Good manners and soft words have brought many a difficult thing to pass. *(Aesop)*

Well bred thinking means kindly and sensitive thoughts. *(Francois de la Rochefoucauld)*

A gentleman is a man who can disagree without being disagreeable. *(Anon)*

Proverbs

The gentle ewe is sucked by every lamb. *(Italian proverb)*

Kind words don't wear out the tongue. *(Danish proverb)*

A gentle hand may lead the elephant with a hair. *(Persian proverb)*

Word-Pictures

Saint Anselm was riding one day with a group of young men, when one of them sighted a hare and the rest gave chase with their dogs. The hare took refuge under the feet of Anselm's horse. Anselm immediately reined in his steed, and forbade them to hunt the creature. When the men crowded round, noisy with the triumph of the capture, Anselm burst into tears.

'You laugh,' he said, 'but for this unhappy creature there is nothing to laugh at or be glad for, for its mortal foes are about it, and it flies to us for life, in its own way beseeching shelter.'

Then he rode on, and with a loud voice forbade that the dogs should touch the hare, while the creature, glad and at liberty, darted off to the fields and woods. *(Colin Goodman)*

'Go, give a penny to that blind beggar,' said the Rabbi of Witkowo to his son when they were walking together. The boy did so then rejoined his father. 'Why didst thou not raise thy hat?' asked the father. 'But he is blind,' replied the boy, 'he could not have seen me.' 'And how dost thou know,' retorted the Rabbi, 'that he is not an imposter? Go raise thy hat.' *(Moshe Hakotun)*

During the Crimean war, the allied forces tried to storm the Sebastopol defences on 18 June 1855, after heavy bombardment lasting some hours. The British share was an assault on the 'Redan', which was unsuccessful and cost 1,500 casualties. Following is an extract from a letter home from Capt. Henry Clifford, V.C.

'Did I tell you that when our troops went at the Redan, they got into some houses at the outskirts of Sebastopol. They rushed into one expecting to find Russian soldiers, but on bursting in the door, there sat three Sisters of Charity who went on working quietly and never once lifted up their heads. The point of the bayonet was raised and the rough soldiers withdrew respectfully and left the Sisters in peace. Shortly after, the position was found untenable, and our men retired, never injuring or molesting the house or its inmates. This was told me by one of the men who saw them. 'Bidads,' said the fellow, 'and I'd have blown the soul out of any of our chaps that had laid a finger on any of them!' *(Henry Clifford, V.C.—Letters and Sketches from the Crimea)*

The Wind and the Sun once had a quarrel. The Wind boasted that he was much stronger than the Sun. He said, 'I'll show you I'm stronger; see that old man over there with a big coat on? I bet I can make him take his coat off much quicker than you can.' 'All right,' said the Sun, 'we'll see.' So the Sun went behind a cloud, but left a little hole so that he could peep through and see what the Wind did. The Wind blew and blew as hard as he could, causing a terrible storm, but the harder he blew the tighter the old man wrapped his coat about him. In the end the poor old Wind had to become calm and give in. Then it was the Sun's turn. He came out from behind the cloud and smiled with sunshine at the old man. After a while, the old man began to mop his brow, then he pulled his coat off. So the Sun beat the Wind.

See also: A19 Patience
B41 Generosity
C18 Compassion
C46 Loving Kindness

BALANCE IN NATURE

'It was not for any fault on the part of creation that it was made unable to attain its purpose, it was made so by God' *Romans 8:20*

Quotations

Nature loves to hide. *(Heraclitus)*

An undevout astronomer is mad. *(Edward Young)*

Nature gives us life like a mother, but loves us like a step-mother. *(Giacomo Leopardi)*

Nature is not inanimate; its daily toil is intelligent; its works are duties. *(Cardinal Newman)*

Nature has some perfections, to show that she is the image of God; and some defects, to show that she is only His image. *(Pascal)*

Nature, the vicar of th' Almightie Lord. *(Geoffrey Chaucer)*

All things are artificial, for nature is the art of God. *(Thomas Browne)*

Looked at in the wrong way, nature can be a substitute for God. This is because relative beauty can be jealous of absolute beauty. *(Hubert Van Zeller)*

Every flower of the field, every fibre of a plant, every particle of an insect, carries with it the impress of its Maker, and can—if duly considered—read us lectures of ethics or divinity. *(Thomas Pope Blount)*

There is a sufficiency in the world for man's need but not for man's greed. *(Mahatma Gandhi)*

About nature, consult nature herself. *(Francis Bacon)*

Proverbs

Nature does not proceed by leaps. *(Latin proverb)*

Nature is the art of God. *(Latin proverb)*

What is natural is graceful. *(Greek proverb)*

Word-Pictures

St. Malo would not move his cloak because a wren had nested in it. The other day a professional in a golf championship let go his chance of winning because he would not play his ball out of a thrush's nest. *(Helen Waddell)*

Waste: man's single greatest product.
Each household discards about 3lb of glass a week—five bottles.
Each household discards about 12 cans a week.
Each household discards about 13lbs of paper a week.
Each household discards about 1½lbs of plastic a week.
Each household discards about 5½lbs of food a week.

In A.D. 1309, an Aztec Indian inhabitant of what is now Mexico City was found guilty of burning charcoal in the city and polluting the air. He was ordered to be hanged for the offence.

Today, Mexico City has a carbon-monoxide level greater than metropolitan New York, a sulphur-dioxide level greater than that of London, and ten times the industrial contaminants of the industrialised Rhine River valley. *(John McLaughlin)*

A great writer, called Sir Osbert Sitwell, tells the story of a man who once captured a very attractive little beaver. He decided to keep it as a pet and take it to his country home. To get there, he had to pass through New York and decided to spend the night at his flat. His wife received the unexpected visitor kindly and it was decided that the best place for the animal to spend the night was in the drawing room. They placed a wooden box lined with straw in the room so that the beaver could curl up in it. They then locked the door. When they entered the room next morning they found nothing there except the beaver and a dam! The animal had got out of its box and accidentally knocked over a small table on which was a vase of flowers. The spilt water on the floor had brought all the beaver's dam-building instincts into play. It had carefully sawn up the valuable chairs and tables and with the aid of cushions and books had made a wonderful dam. *(M. Nassan)*

See also: B32 The Wonders of God
B39 The Lord who works marvels
B42 Signs of the times
C34 The value of little things

PATIENCE

'Do you want us to go and weed it out?' But he said, 'No, because when you weed out the darnel, you might pull up the wheat with it. Let them both grow till the harvest'. *Matthew 13:28*

Quotations

Patience is the companion of wisdom. *(St. Augustine of Hippo)*

A lot of the road to heaven has to be taken at thirty miles an hour. *(Evelyn Underhill)*

Be long-suffering and prudent, and you will obtain the mastery over wickedness and accomplish all justice. *(Shepherd of Hermas)*

Patience is the root and guardian of all the virtues. *(Pope St. Gregory I)*

All men commend patience, although few be willing to practise it. *(Thomas à Kempis)*

One moment of patience may ward off great disaster, one moment of impatience may ruin a whole life. *(Chinese Wisdom)*

Patience is bitter, but its fruit is sweet. *(Jean Jacques Rousseau)*

On every level of life from housework to heights of prayer, in all judgement and all efforts to get things done, hurry and impatience are sure marks of the amateur. *(Evelyn Underhill)*

It takes patience to appreciate domestic bliss; volatile spirits prefer unhappiness. *(George Santayana)*

We must wait for God, long, meekly, in the wind and wet, in the thunder and lightning, in the cold and the dark. Wait, and he will come. He never comes to those who do not wait. *(Frederick W. Faber)*

'Take your needle, my child, and work at your pattern; it will come out a rose by and by.' Life is like that; one stitch at a time taken patiently, and the pattern will come out all right like embroidery. *(Oliver Wendell Holmes)*

Proverbs

Patience is power; with time and patience the mulberry leaf becomes silk. *(Chinese proverb)*

Patience is a bitter plant but it bears sweet fruit. *(German proverb)*

Humour

Angler 'You've been watching me for three hours. Why don't you try fishing yourself?'
Onlooker 'I ain't got the patience.'

That's the advantage of having lived 65 years. You don't feel the need to be impatient any longer. *(Thornton Wilder)*

Word-Pictures

An aged man, whom Abraham hospitably invited to his tent, refused to join him in prayer to the one spiritual God. Learning that he was a fire-worshipper, Abraham drove him from his door. That night God appeared to Abraham in a vision and said 'I have bourne with that ignorant man for 70 years; could you not have patiently suffered him one night?' *(The Talmud)*

Found scratched on a wall at the Tower of London by prisoners: 'It is not adversity that kills, but the impatience with which we bear with adversity.'

When Stanley went out in 1871 and found Livingstone, he spent months in his company, but Livingstone never spoke to Stanley about spiritual things. Throughout those months, Stanley watched the old man. Livingstone's habits were beyond his comprehension, and so was his patience. He could not understand Livingstone's sympathy for the Africans. For the sake of Christ and His Gospel, the missionary doctor was patient, untiring, eager, spending himself and being spent for his Master. Stanley wrote, 'When I saw that unwearied patience, that unflagging zeal, those enlightened sons of Africa, I became a Christian at his side, though he never spoke to me about it.' *(Anon)*

Some years ago, a fourteen-year strike came to an end in Dun Laoghaire, Ireland.

The strike at Downey's Public House had started in 1939 when publican Pat Downey fired a barman. As Downey refused to rehire the dismissed man, pickets began their marathon wait. Each year, Downey observed the anniversary of the strike by dressing his pub in flags and offering drinks to the pickets.

When Downey died in May of 1953, striker Val Murphy put aside his sandwich-board and walked into the pub to offer his sympathy to the widow.

A little Scottish schoolgirl was asked, 'What is patience?'
Her reply: 'Wait a wee while, and dinna weary.' *(Bob Edwards)*

Sir Isaac Newton was a famous scientist who owned a dog called Diamond. Diamond did him a very bad turn. Newton had taken eight whole years to write a very important book. One morning he came into his room and found that Diamond had knocked over a candle and the candle had set fire to the book on his desk. Think what that meant; eight whole years of work burnt up, but he could not be angry with a dog that did not know what it was doing. Newton said, 'Diamond, little do you know the labour and trouble to which you have put your master.' Then he did not look upon that great work as lost for ever as most people would have done. He sat down at his desk to start all over again. *(M. Nassan)*

See also: A11 Divine Providence
B21 Trust in God
C39 Doing God's Will

THE KINGDOM OF GOD

'A disciple of the kingdom of heaven is like a householder who brings out from his storeroom things both new and old." *Matthew 13:52*

Quotations

In the Gospel, Jesus is autobasileia, the kingdom himself. *(Origen of Alexandria)*

Power in complete subordination to love—that is something like a definition of the Kingdom of God. *(William Temple)*

To want all that God wants, always to want it, for all occasions and without reservations, this is the kingdom of God which is all within. *(Francois Fenelon)*

The kingdom of God is a kingdom of love; and love is never a stagnant pool. *(Henry W. Du Bose)*

Is the kingdom of God a big family? Yes, in a sense it is. But in another sense it is a prodigious biological operation—that of the Redeeming Incarnation. *(Pierre Teilhard De Chardin)*

If you want to work for the kingdom of God, and to bring it, and to enter into it, there is just one condition to be first accepted. You must enter it as children, or not at all. *(John Ruskin)*

The Kingdom of God will not come in a day; it will not be left with the morning milk. *(S. Parkes Cadman)*

Statements

In Christ's word, in His works, and in His presence this kingdom reveals itself to men. *(Second Vatican Council—'The Church')*

Before all things, however, the kingdom is clearly visible in the very person of Christ, Son of God and Son of Man, who came 'to serve and to give his life as a ransom for many' (*Mk.10:45*). *(Second Vatican Council—'The Church')*

For the Lord wishes to spread His kingdom by means of the laity also, a kingdom of truth and life, a kingdom of holiness and grace, a kingdom of justice, love and peace. In this kingdom, creation itself will be delivered out of its slavery to corruption and into the freedom of the glory of the sons of God. *(Second Vatican Council—'The Church')*

Word-Pictures

The kingdom is something within you which has the power of growth like a seed; something that you are searching for, and of whose values you become more confident and excited as the search proceeds and you discover truer, lovelier things which are constantly being surpassed; something for which you have to give everything you have, no less yet no more, including the earlier finds with which you were once so completely delighted. *(George Appleton)*

Though we achieve social justice, liberty, peace itself, though we give our bodies to be burned for these admirable causes, if we lack this—the transformation of the natural order by the Eternal Charity—we are nothing. For the kingdom is the Holy not the moral; the Beautiful not the correct; the perfect not the adequate; Charity not law. *(Evelyn Underhill)*

See, this kingdom of God is now found within us. The grace of the Holy Spirit shines forth and warms us, and, overflowing with many varied scents into the air around us, regales our senses with heavenly delight, as it fills our hearts with joy inexpressible. *(Seraphim of Sarov)*

See also: A31 Heaven
B17 The Church—Bride of Christ
B51 One with Christ
C38 Doing God's Will

FEEDING THE HUNGRY

'Give them something to eat yourselves' *Matthew 14:16*

Quotations

Ticker tape ain't spaghetti. *(F. La Guardia)*

To a man with an empty stomach, food is God. *(Mohandas Gandhi)*

When hunger comes through the door, love flees through the window. *(Jewish saying)*

It is not enough to free man from hunger imposed on him by an insufficiency of food. Man must be freed of all the forces that oppress him, of the natural, economic and political order. *(World Food Congress)*

If you give a man a fish, he will eat once.
If you teach a man to fish, he will eat for the rest of his life.
If you are thinking a year ahead, sow seed.
If you are thinking ten years ahead, plant a tree.
If you are thinking one hundred years ahead, educate the people.
By sowing seed, you will harvest once.
By planting a tree, you will harvest tenfold.
By educating the people, you will harvest one hundredfold. *(Kuantzu)*

I suggest that we are thieves in a way. If I take anything that I do not need for my own immediate use, and keep it, I thieve it from somebody else. . . In India, we have got three millions of people having to be satisfied with one meal a day, and that meal consisting of unleavened bread (chapati) containing no fat in it, and a pinch of salt. You and I have no right to anything that we really have until these three millions are clothed and fed better. You and I, who ought to know better, must adjust our wants, and even undergo voluntary starvation in order that they may be nursed, fed and clothed. *(Mohandas Gandhi)*

Proverbs

A man who wants bread is ready for anything. *(French proverb)*

When you're hungry, sing; when you're hurt, laugh. *(Jewish proverb)*

The full belly does not believe in hunger. *(Italian proverb)*

Humour

The absent-minded professor called his biology class to order shortly after the lunch hour.

'Our special work this afternoon,' he said, 'will be cutting up and inspecting the inner workings of a frog. I have a dead frog here in my pocket to be used as a specimen.'

He reached into his pocket and pulled out a paper bag, shook its contents on the table and out rolled a nice looking ham sandwich. The professor looked at it, perplexed, scratched his head and muttered, 'That's funny, I distinctly remember eating my lunch.' *(Anon)*

A Circus performer who boasted that he could digest anything, complained one day of a stomach ache. The pains became so acute that doctors ordered an examination. One look at the X-ray was enough to warrant an immediate operation.

The contents of the circus man's stomach astounded even the patient. Among the items extracted were 70 keys, 16 penknives, 36 nails and nuts, plus a quantity of iron and glass.

Statements

Conscience, a new conscience for our times, is calling each of us to self-review. Am I really doing all I can to help the poor and hungry? Am I prepared to pay more taxes in order that the government can do more for development? Am I prepared to pay more in the shops for goods imported from abroad so that the people who produce these goods are paid a decent wage? Am I prepared to leave my country to help the younger nations?. . . It is still true, today, to say that charity begins at home. But home, today, is all the world. *(Pope Paul VI 'Progressio Populorum')*

Since there are so many people in this world afflicted with hunger, this sacred Council urges all, both individuals and governments, to remember the saying of the Fathers: 'Feed the man dying of hunger, because if you have not fed him, you have killed him.' *(Second Vatican Council—'The Church Today')*

The distribution of goods should be directed toward providing employment and sufficient income for the people of today and of the future. *(Second Vatican Council—'The Church Today')*

Word-Pictures

When the British Government sought to reward General Gordon for his brilliant service in China, he declined all money and titles, but accepted a gold medal inscribed with the record of his thirty-three engagements. It was his most prized possession, but after his death the medal could not be found. Eventually it was learned that he had sent it to Manchester during a severe famine, directing that it should be melted down and used to buy bread for the poor. Under the date of its sending, these words were found written in his diary: 'The last earthly thing I had in this world that I valued I have given to the Lord Jesus Christ.' *(Indian Christian)*

It is the easiest thing in the world to buy a slave child. To prove the point, I bought one in Colombo last month. He is Raju, aged 8, from Nawalapittiya, near Kandy.

The sale was conducted among mounds of onions, chillies and coconuts in Colombo's crowded Wellawatta junction. Raju, wearing only a tattered sarong, was getting what food he could from a half-eaten coconut which he had found on the road. Raju's mother, looking incredibly worn out, was standing by, waiting to be paid. I asked her why she did it. The staccato answer had a familiar ring: 'Dry season. Very little work. No food for many days. Now we buy some. At least this one' (shot a glance at Raju) 'will not starve.' *(Anthony Mascarenhas)*

Christians alone straddle the whole spectrum of rich nations and therefore Christians can be a lobby of tremendous importance. When we come before our heavenly Father and he says, 'Did you feed them, did you give them to drink, did you clothe them, did you shelter them?' and we say, 'Sorry, Lord, but we did give them 0.3 per cent of our gross national product,' I don't think it will be enough. *(Barbara Ward)*

'Your poverty is greater than ours . . . the spiritual poverty of the West is much greater than the physical poverty of the East. In the West, there are millions of people who suffer loneliness and emptiness, who feel unloved and unwanted. They are not the hungry in the physical sense; what is missing is a relationship with God and each other.' *(Mother Teresa)*

See also: A33 Love your neighbour
B15 Jesus friend of outcasts
C21 Rise above materialism
C29 Not through luxury

SEEKING GOD

'After the fire there came the sound of a gentle breeze.' *1 Kings 19:12*

Quotations

The knowledge of God is naturally implanted in all. *(St. Thomas Aquinas)*

The difference between knowledge of God and love of Him! *(Pascal)*

It is in silence that God is known, and through mysteries that He declares Himself. *(R. H. Benson)*

It was the man in the street who understood our Lord, and the doctor of the law who was perplexed and offended. *(R. H. Benson)*

For the mind to attain to God in some degree is great beautitude. *(St. Augustine of Hippo)*

We know God better through grace than through unaided reason. *(St. Thomas Aquinas)*

We cannot form an adequate concept of man unless we include God. He is mysterious, transcendent and ineffable, the eternal principle of the universe. But he watches over us, knows and observes us, penetrates and preserves us unceasingly. He is our Father. *(Pope Paul VI)*

Each conception of spiritual beauty is a glimpse of God. *(Moses Mendelssohn)*

To have found God is not an end in itself but a beginning. *(Franz Rosenzweig)*

Proverb

Whosoever walks towards God one cubit, God runs towards him twain. *(Jewish proverb)*

Statements

From ancient times down to the present, there has existed among diverse peoples a certain perception of that hidden power which hovers over the course of things and over the events of human life; at times, indeed, recognition can be found of a Supreme Divinity and of a Supreme Father too. *(Second Vatican Council—'Non-Christians')*

Since it has been entrusted to the Church to reveal the mystery of God, who is the ultimate goal of man, she opens up to man at the same time the meaning of his own existence, that is, the innermost truth about himself. *(Second Vatican Council—'The Church Today')*

This sacred Synod affirms, 'God, the beginning and end of all things, can be known with certainty from created reality by the light of human reason.' *(Second Vatican Council—'Revelation'*

See also: A10 Seeking perfection
B28 The Father who draws us to Himself
C16 Come follow me
C38 Discerning God's Will

MERCY

'My salvation will come and my integrity be manifest.' *Isaiah 56:1*

Quotations

Dost thou wish to receive mercy? Show mercy to thy neighbour. *(St. John Chrysostom)*

Mercy is the fulfilment of justice, not the abolition. *(St. Thomas Aquinas)*

For mercy is a greater thing than right. *(Chaucer)*

Mercy, also, is a good thing, for it makes men perfect, in that it imitates the perfect Father. Nothing graces the Christian soul so much as mercy. *(St. Ambrose)*

Reason to rule, but mercy to forgive: The first is law, the last prerogative. *(Dryden)*

As freely as the firmament embraces the world, so mercy must encircle friend and foe. *(Schiller)*

Among the attributes of God, although they are all equal, mercy shines with even more brilliancy than justice. *(Cervantes)*

We hand folks over to God's mercy, and show none ourselves. *(George Eliot)*

Teach me to feel another's woe, to hide the fault I see;
that mercy I to others show, that mercy show to me. *(Alexander Pope)*

The mercy of God (may be found) between the bridge and the stream. *(St. Augustine of Hippo)*

Mercy imitates God and disappoints Satan. *(St. John Chrysostom)*

Proverbs

Mercy is better than vengeance. *(Greek proverb)*

Mercy often gives death instead of life. *(Latin proverb)*

Word-Pictures

A mother sought from Napoleon the pardon of her son. The

Emperor said it was the man's second offence, and justice demanded his death.

'I don't ask for justice,' said the mother, 'I plead for mercy.'

'But,' said the Emperor, 'he does not deserve mercy.'

'Sir,' cried the mother, 'it would not be mercy if he deserved it, and mercy is all I ask.'

'Well, then,' said the Emperor, 'I will have mercy.' And her son was saved. *(Anon)*

I say that we are wound with mercy round and round as if with air.
Gerald Manley Hopkins—'Mary Mother of Divine Grace'

Food was getting very low and water had almost run out, when, after nearly a year, Edward III forced Calais to surrender. The townspeople pleaded for their lives, but Edward was very displeased with their stubborn resistance to him. There had been bitter fighting and many Englishmen had died at the hands of the French. The King told the citizens that he would spare their lives if they would hand over to him six of their town council—six burghers—who would be made to suffer for the rest.

One of the six burghers threw himself at Edward's feet and pleaded for their lives, but the King would not listen; they were to die. One of the English knights pleaded with Edward; he took no notice. Queen Phillipa, who had been sitting at the King's side, got up and knelt before him. She begged him by his love for her and for Christ, his saviour, to forgive the six burghers. No one stirred and after a long silence, Edward said, 'Lady, your entreaties would melt the heart of a stone. Though it's not my will, I put their lives into your hands.' Taking the rope which was round the neck of the nearest prisoner, he handed it to the Queen. Phillipa thanked the King for his mercy and released the prisoners. *(Anon)*

See also: A17 Gentleness
C14 Forgiveness
C18 Compassion
C46 Loving Kindness

PAPACY

'You are Peter and on this rock I will build my Church.' *Matthew 16:18*

Quotations

When in the time of this Clement (Pope St. Clement I), no little dissension arose among the Christians at Corinth, the Church in Rome sent a most powerful letter to the Corinthians urging them to peace and renewing their faith and in the tradition which they had recently received from the apostles. *(Eusebius of Caesarea)*

Reckon up the priests from the days that Peter sat, and in their ancestral ranks, note who succeeded whom; for that is the rock over which the gates of hell shall never prevail. *(St. Augustine of Hippo)*

We think, too, that you should consult our holy brother, Bishop of the Church at Rome, for we presume that what you determine will in no way displease him. *(St. Ambrose)*

The rejection of the primacy of St. Peter has driven men on to a slippery course, where all the steps are downwards. *(Lord Acton)*

The action and the theory of the modern papacy are the outcome of an agelong growth, and we must seek in the pages of history less for a proof of the papal claims than for the evidence that they have shared in, and been central to, the general development of that society which is our only historical link with the origins of Christianity. *(Dom. Butler)*

Proverbs

We cannot all be Pope of Rome. *(German proverb)*

The corpse of the Pope takes up no more room than the sacristan's. *(Spanish proverb)*

Humour

He that has the Pope for his cousin need not fear hell fire. *(Spanish saying)*

The tale is told of a newly-appointed minister of the Kirk who was calling on his new parishioners. At one cottage where he had been warmly received, he apologised at the end, saying, 'You have been most courteous, but I should not have come, for I see you are not part of my congregation, but are Roman Catholics.' The old cottager protested with some warmth that this was not so; neither he nor his wife were Roman Catholics, nor ever would be. 'Then why,' said the minister, 'do you have that brightly coloured picture of Pope Leo XIII on your wall?' The old man looked at it, then he exclaimed, 'Wait till I catch that Izzy Cohen in Glasgow. He sold it to me, telling me it was Robert Burns in his Mason's regalia.' *(Douglas Woodruff)*

Statement

In order that the episcopate itself might be one and undivided, He placed Peter over the other apostles, and instituted in him a permanent and visible source and foundation of unity of faith and fellowship. And all this teaching about the institution, the perpetuity, the force and reason for the sacred primacy of the Roman Pontiff and of his infallible teaching authority, this sacred Synod again proposes to be firmly believed by all the faithful. *(Second Vatican Council—'The Church')*

Word-Pictures

Before a crowded concert in the Paris Conservatoire, the composer Gounod arrived in the audience, and found all seats occupied. A young priest rose and said, 'Please take my seat, you are older than I.' But Gounod replied: 'No, my friend, you are the Church. I recall a remark of Pope Gregory XVI. Some visitor said to him once 'Holy Father, I'm an older man than you.' The Pope said 'Older than me? I have lived over eighteen hundred years.'

'Your reverence is eighteen hundred years old: you must keep the seat.' *(Mgr. Luigi Vigna)*

The last non-Italian Pope, Adrian of Utrecht, had been the tutor of the young Emperor Charles V and enjoyed his confidence. He was ruling Spain for him when the messengers arrived at Vitoria with the disconcerting news that he had been elected Pope, and he set out on a very slow journey, not without dangers, to Rome, to his short and unhappy pontificate. *(Douglas Woodruff)*

When Hildebrand became Pope St. Gregory VII, with the new fashion, or fairly new one, of the Pope taking a new name, he chose to be Gregory VII because of his great respect for Gregory VI, a little known Pope, but a man with a most remarkable history.

Quite often, in bad patches of the extraordinary history of the See of Rome, ambitious cardinals or rulers have tried bribery. But Gregory bought the Papacy outright from his immediate predecessor, because that predecessor was a quite unfit young man, and Gregory, who was an elderly priest at Grottaferrata, bought the Papacy not from ambition, but to get it back into good hands.

He was apparently allowed to do so, and we can be sure that

Hildebrand, a leading figure in the great reform that began with St. Leo IX, would not have honoured Gregory VI as he did if the story had not been creditable to him. No-one has yet succeeded in purchasing the See of Westminster. *(Douglas Woodruff)*

In 1509, the Emperor Maximillian I wrote to his 'Very dear and beloved daughter, Margaret,' who ruled the Netherlands, to say that he could see no sensible reason why he should marry again; and went on to tell her his plans. 'Tomorrow we are sending the Bishop of Gurk to Rome to the Pope, for him to treat with him that he appoint Us his coadjutor, so that We may be assured of the Papacy after his death, later to become priest, and eventually saint, so that you will be obliged to pray to Me once I find myself in heavenly glory.' And he signed himself—'Your good father Maximilian, future Pope.'

See also: A14 Successors of the Apostles
B13 Authority
B17 The Church—Bride of Christ
C44 Feed my Sheep

COURAGE

'Jesus began to make it clear to his disciples that he was destined to suffer grievously at the hands of the elders.' *Matthew 16:21*

Quotations

Courage is a virtue only insofar as it is directed by prudence. *(Francois Fenelon)*

Courage is grace under pressure. *(Ernest Hemingway)*

Courage is doing what you're afraid to do. There can be no courage unless you're scared. *(Eddie Rickenbacker)*

Courage is almost a contradiction in terms. It means a strong desire to live taking the form of a readiness to die. *(G. K. Chesterton)*

The principal act of courage is to endure and withstand dangers doggedly rather than to attack them. *(St. Thomas Aquinas)*

Have courage for the great sorrows of life, and patience for the small ones. And when you have laboriously accomplished your daily task, go to sleep in peace. God is awake. *(Victor Hugo)*

To see what is right, and not to do it, is want of courage. *(Confucius)*

Most acts of assent require far more courage than most acts of protest, since courage is clearly a readiness to risk self-humiliation. *(Nigel Dennis)*

Courage is what it takes to stand up and speak; courage is also what it takes to sit down and listen. *(Anon)*

Mere physical courage—the absence of fear—simply is not worth calling bravery. It's the bravery of the tiger, not the moral bravery of the man. *(R. H. Benson)*

Every time we lose courage, we lose several days of our life. *(Maurice Maeterlinck)*

It is easy to be brave from a safe distance. *(Aesop)*

Proverbs

True courage grapples with misfortune. *(Latin proverb)*

You can't answer for your courage if you have never been in danger. *(French proverb)*

Word-Pictures

The Victoria Cross is the premier British award for conspicuous bravery in the presence of the enemy. Instituted by Queen Victoria in 1856, the ribbon is claret coloured, but was formerly blue for the Royal Navy and red for the Army. It consists of a bronze Maltese Cross with the royal crown surmounted by a lion under which is a scroll bearing the words *For Valour.* One of the first awards was to a boy-midshipman who when a bomb from a Russian battery fell on the deck of his warship, went and picked it up with its fuse burning, carried it to the side and dropped it into the sea.

After over a hundred years, the Victoria Cross had been awarded to 1,344 brave men altogether.*(Anon)*

One of the most famous stories of unselfishness and courage is the epic of Captain L. E. Oates, of the Inniskilling Dragoons, who marched with Scott to the South Pole. It was an illfated expedition. One disaster after another overtook the little party of men struggling over hundreds of miles of snow and ice in temperatures as low as minus 46, without machines or dogs to help them. Captain Oates was badly afflicted by frostbite; he could hardly hobble along, let alone pull his share of the weight of sledge and stores. March 17 (1912) was his birthday and, in the evening, he quietly left his tent and walked out into the blizzard knowing that without him to hamper them, his companions had a better chance of survival. His sacrifice was unavailing but is none the less memorable for that. Today in the Antarctic wastes, now crossed and recrossed by scientists with all their latest modern equipment, there is still a cairn and a cross and a plaque which begins, 'Hereabouts died a very gallant gentleman . . .' *(R. C. Macrobie)*

The word 'courage' takes on added meaning if you keep in mind that it is derived from the Latin term *cor* meaning 'heart'.

The dictionary defines it as a 'quality which enables one to pursue a course deemed right, through which one may incur contempt, disapproval, or opprobrium.'

Some 300 years ago, La Rochefoucauld went a step further when he said: 'Perfect courage is to do unwitnessed what we should be capable of doing before all men.' *(Anon)*

One Friday morning in February 1975, an underground train, with 300 people on it, crashed against a stone wall at Moorgate station killing 41 people. Among the passengers was a 19-year-old girl, named Margaret, who had just become a policewoman. When the train hit the wall, she found herself sitting on the floor with one of her legs under her body and a man on top of her. Neither could move without hurting the other. It was completely dark. The man on top said to her, 'you are being very brave.' 'I have to be,' she said, 'I am a policewoman.' For many hours, firemen tried to pull them out. Then they found that Margaret's left leg was trapped under a huge steel girder. The firemen marvelled that she could still laugh and joke. They could do nothing more to get her out. Then a surgeon came and told her that she was going to be put to sleep so that she could be got out. 'That's fine,' she said, 'who's going to take me?' Five minutes later, the surgeon took Margaret's left foot off above the ankle. Within two days she was sitting up in hospital, chatting cheerfully to visitors. She received more than 2,000 gifts and cards from all over the world. *(M. Nassan)*

See also: B35 The Grace of God
C13 Coping with grief
C41 Starting afresh

SACRAMENT OF PENANCE

'Whatever you bind on earth shall be considered bound in heaven; whatever you loose on earth shall be considered loosed in heaven.'
Matthew 18:18

Quotations

It is better for a man to confess his sins than to harden his heart. *(Pope St. Clement I)*

You shall confess your offences in church, and shall not come forward to your prayer with a bad conscience. *(Teaching of the Twelve Apostles)*

Even when one confesses his sins, he ought to do so with praise of God; nor is a confession of sins a pious one unless it be made without despair, and with a prayer for God's mercy. *(St. Augustine of Hippo)*

Within the Church, sins are forgiven in three ways; by baptism, by prayer and by the greater humility of penance. *(St. Augustine of Hippo)*

Through the office of priests, those should be reconciled to Holy Church by doing penance, who have departed from its society by sinning. *(St. Bede the Venerable)*

Be a lion in the pulpit, but a lamb in the confessional. *(St. Alphonsus of Liguori)*

So long as there is sin in the world, so long must there be penance. *(R. H. Benson)*

The Catholic religion does not compel indiscriminate confession of sins; it allows us to remain hidden from the sight of all other men, save one to whom she bids us reveal the depths of our heart, and show ourselves as we are. There is only this one man in the world, whom she bids us undeceive, and him she binds to inviolable secrecy, so that this knowledge remains with him as if it were not. Can anything be imagined more charitable, more tender? *(Pascal)*

Humour

A priest hearing children's confessions was puzzled to find child after child adding, after the recital of more familiar and intelligible sins, that of 'throwing peanuts in the river'. He wondered whether they were repenting of wasting food or of river pollution, and then decided to press for a little more explanation when the last and smallest child came in. But the smallest penitent failed to confess this. 'Yes,' said the priest, 'is that all—isn't there something you've forgotten? What about throwing peanuts in the river?' 'But, Father,' said a bewildered voice, 'I am Peanuts'. *(Douglas Woodruff)*

Fr. Vincent McNabb was once speaking in Hyde Park on the Sacrament of Penance. A heckler was positive that Catholics pay for absolution. 'You're really quite sure about that?' asked Fr. Vincent. The heckler said he was quite certain. 'Then I've been done!' said the priest. 'I've been hearing confessions for 50 years, and nobody ever paid me.'

My young brother had just made his first confession. When he returned to the pew, he tapped my mother on the shoulder, smiled, and said, 'I passed.' *(Pauline Ploughmas)*

Statement

In the spirit of Christ the Shepherd, priests should train them to submit their sins with a contrite heart to the Church in the sacrament of Penance. Thus mindful of the Lord's words: 'Repent, for the kingdom of God is at hand' (*Mt.4:17*), the people will be drawn ever closer to Him each day. *(Second Vatican Council—'Priests')*

Word-Picture

Few people are aware how long public penance went on in the Church of England. They may know that Oliver Cromwell, as the parish register of All Saints, Huntingdon, testifies, had to do it in 1626, after being publicly reprimanded five years before, and it may have had something to do with his antipathy to Bishops. The two great sins for which it was extracted were defamation of character and incest, and as late as 1835, a woman condemned to it only got off by producing a medical certificate. But all through the practical eighteenth century, the commutation of penance by money payments was growing.

In the seventeenth century, penance was more robust, and it generally consisted in having to ask pardon of the party wronged, followed by some public humiliation. And there is an entry from a Cornish church in 1672 kept at Exeter Cathedral: 'John Taprill, clerk, asked forgiveness of Rd. Grills Carpenter, within the parish church of Southill, upon a Sunday forenoon, after morning prayer, in the month of December last past, for reporting things not proven.

Whereupon the said Taprill, longing to be revenged, did sing some psalms as he thought fitting to lamentable tunes for sorrow of his disgrace'—making the congregation share his penance. *(Douglas Woodruff)*

See also: A27 As we forgive those
B16 Christ forgives our sin
C14 Forgiveness
C40 Reconciliation

AS WE FORGIVE THOSE

'Not seven, I tell you, but seventy-seven times.' *Matthew 18:22*

Quotations

To err is human, to forgive divine. *(Alexander Pope)*

We pardon to the extent that we love. *(Francois De La Rochefoucauld)*

'I can forgive, but I cannot forget' is only another way of saying 'I cannot forgive.' *(Henry Ward Beecher)*

Humanity is never so beautiful as when praying for forgiveness or else forgiving another. *(Jean Paul Richter)*

The more a man knows, the more he forgives. *(Catherine the Great)*

It is very easy to forgive others their mistakes; it takes more grit and gumption to forgive them for having witnessed your own. *(Jessamyn West)*

Every person should have a special cemetery plot in which to bury the faults of friends and loved ones. *(Anon)*

May God forgive him! I want him in heaven. *(Maria Goretti, 11, fatally stabbed while resisting the advances of a 19-year-old youth)*

Proverbs

He who forgives ends the quarrel. *(African proverb)*

To forgive is beautiful. *(Greek proverb)*

Forgiving the unrepentant is like drawing pictures on water. *(Japanese proverb)*

Word-Pictures

A minister tells the story of a clergyman who was given a flowery introduction before a speech. When he stood up to present his address, he said, 'May the Lord forgive this man for his excesses, and me for enjoying them so much.' *(Alice Murray)*

Brother Rufino was extremely gentle, and no one doubted his sincerity. Prayer came more naturally to him than preaching. Indeed, to speak in public terrified him. When he was asked to preach he became confused, then completely speechless. This handicap, however, could not be permitted when he had vowed to preach the Gospel of Christ.

Normally kind and tolerant, and ever prepared to counsel and befriend a brother, Francis could be harsh when a friar broke the Rule. He regarded it as an insult to Christ. Thus, hoping to overcome Rufino's weakness, he ordered him to go and preach in Assisi. Desperately Rufino pleaded to be excused and grew so obstinate that Francis fiercely rebuked him. As a penance, Francis again commanded Rufino to go, this time without his habit and wearing only his breeches.

It is easy to imagine Rufino's painful ordeal. People thought that this man, who had once walked Assisi as a prince, was now crazy as he entered the city half-naked. With urchins laughing and jeering at his heels, he passed through the streets, and when he started to preach on honesty, the words came so falteringly that the people laughed.

After Rufino had left the Porziuncola, Francis, regretting his treatment of him, turned his wrath upon himself. 'Please God,' he cried, 'thou shalt have experience of what thou hast made another endure.' With that, he threw off his habit and, dressed like Rufino, went to Assisi. Brother Leo, tactfully picking up both habits, followed some distance behind.

Rufino was still preaching when Francis reached the city. When the badly delivered sermon ended, Francis stood beside Rufino and spoke so marvellously on the poverty and nakedness of Christ that the congregation turned from laughter to tears. Leo then handed the habits to the friars, and the people crowded around them and kissed the hems of their robes. *(Douglas Liversidge)*

A small boy, repeating the Lord's Prayer one evening prayed: 'And forgive us our debts as we forgive those who are dead against us.' *(Anon)*

See also: A26 Sacrament of Penance
B16 Christ forgives our sins
C14 Forgiveness
C40 Reconciliation

WORK

'Call the workers and pay them their wages, starting with the last arrivals and ending with the first.' *Matthew 20:8*

Quotations

I like work, it fascinates me. I can sit and look at it for hours. *(Jerome K. Jerome)*

Work is the greatest thing in the world, so we should always save some of it for tomorrow. *(Don Herold)*

Light is the task where many share the toil. *(Homer)*

Some are bent with toil, and some get crooked trying to avoid it. *(Anon)*

God gives every bird its food, but he does not throw it into the nest. *(J. G. Holland)*

He who labours as he prays lifts his heart to God with his hands. *(St. Bernard)*

The great scandal of the nineteenth century is that the Church lost the working class. *(Pope Pius XI)*

Be thankful if you have a job a little harder than you like. A razor cannot be sharpened on a piece of velvet. *(Anon)*

The best worship, however, is stout working. *(Thomas Carlyle)*

Nothing is really work unless you would rather be doing something else. *(James M. Barrie)*

Proverbs

Work is worship. *(French proverb)*

Never was good work done without much trouble. *(Chinese proverb)*

Work is no disgrace: the disgrace is idleness. *(Greek proverb)*

Humour

A new employee had been caught coming in late for work three times and the fourth morning the foreman decided to read the riot act.

'Look here,' he snapped, 'don't you know what time we start work around here?'
'No, sir,' said the man, 'they're always working when I get here.'

'How many people work in the Vatican City, Holy Father?'
'About half.' *(Story told of Pope John XXIII)*

A man who needed a job saw an ad. in the local paper for a position open at the zoo. He accepted the job and was to dress up as a monkey and perform in one of the cages. All went well for several days and then, as he was going from limb to limb, he fell.
'Help, help,' he cried.
'Shut up,' said the lion in the next cage, 'or we'll both lose our jobs.'

Employer to new employee 'Young man, we have a record for doing the impossible in this place.'
Young man 'Yes, sir, I'll remember. I'll be as impossible as I can.'

'When I was a young man,' said Mr Jones, 'I thought nothing of working 12 or 14 hours a day.'
'Father,' replied the young man, 'I wish you wouldn't mention it. Those non-union sentiments are liable to make you unpopular.'

Statements

Everyone who works has the right to just and favourable remuneration insuring for himself and his family an existence worthy of human dignity . . . *(United Nations Universal Declaration of Human Rights, Article 23)*

According to natural reason and Christian philosophy, working for gain is creditable, not shameful, to a man, since it enables him to earn an honourable livelihood; but to misuse men as though they were things in the pursuit of gain, or to value them solely for their physical powers—that is truly shameful and inhuman. *(Pope Leo XIII: Rerum Novarum 1891)*

It is ordinarily by his labour that a man supports himself and his family, is joined to his fellow men and serves them, and is enabled to exercise genuine charity and be a partner in the work of bringing God's creation to perfection. Indeed, we hold that by offering his labour to God a man becomes associated with the redemptive work itself of Jesus Christ, who conferred an eminent dignity on labour when at Nazareth He worked with His own hands. *(Second Vatican Council—'The Church Today')*

Word-Pictures

A man who works with his hands is a labourer; a man who works with his hands and his brain is a craftsman; a man who works with his hands and his brain and his heart is an artist. *(Louis Nizer)*

Work is love made visible.
And if you cannot work with love, but only with distaste, it is better that you should leave your work and sit at the gate of the temple and take alms of those who work for joy.
For if you bake bread with indifference, you bake a bitter bread that feeds but half man's hunger.
And if you grudge the crushing of the grapes, your grudge distils a poison in the wine.
And if you sing though as angels, and love not the singing, you muffle man's ears to the voices of the day and the voices of the night. *(Kahlil Gibran)*

Work today has lost many traditional characteristics; so has play. Play has increasingly been transformed into organized sports, and sports, in turn, increasingly resemble work in the hard practice and preparation, in the intense involvement of coaches and athletes (in the spirit of work), and in actual economic productivity.

In a final paradox, only those sports which began as work—that is, hunting and fishing—are now dominated by the spirit of play. *(Charles Page)*

I think of a story my grandfather Stevenson, a devout Scotch-Presbyterian, told about the preacher who was driving along a back road in the south when he espied a parishioner wearily clearing up a poor, stony field. 'That is a fine job you and the Lord have done, cleaning up that rocky field,' he shouted. 'Thank you, parson,' the man replied. 'But I wish you could have seen it when the Lord had it all to himself.' *(Adlai Stevenson)*

John Wesley travelled 250,000 miles on horseback, averaging 20 miles a day for 40 years; preached 40,000 sermons; produced 400 hundred books; knew 10 languages. At 83, he was annoyed that he could not write more than 15 hours a day without hurting his eyes, and at 86, he was ashamed he could not preach more than twice a day. He complained in his diary that there was an increasing tendency to lie in bed until 5.30 in the morning! *(The Arkansas Baptist)*

Somebody said that it couldn't be done,
But he with a chuckle replied,
That maybe it couldn't, but he would be one
Who wouldn't say so till he'd tried.

So he buckled right in with a bit of a grin
On his face. If he worried, he hid it;
And he started to sing as he tackled the thing
That couldn't be done—and he did it! *(Anon)*

There are moments when things go well, and one feels encouraged. There are difficult moments, and one feels overwhelmed. But it is senseless to speak of optimism or pessimism. The only important thing is to know that if one works well in a potato field, the potatoes will grow. If one works well among men, they will grow. That's reality. The rest is smoke. *(Danilo Dolci)*

St. Benedict elevated work from a servile occupation to be avoided or limited as far as possible, often called the Curse of Adam, into something positively good.

It was my friend's thesis that St. Benedict's Rule never reached Russia where work continued to be looked down upon, just as further east, the Chinese delighted to grow their finger nails to enormous lengths as the visible proof they had no need to work. So while serfdom disappeared in Christian Europe, the opposite happened in Russia, and it became worse at the end of the Middle Ages. The western monks practised what they preached, especially the reformed Benedictines, Cistercians and Carthusians. The official marking for quality steel in France is still the Carthusian emblem, the ball and the cross. *(Douglas Woodruff)*

See also: A1 The value of time
A18 Balance in nature
A36 Using talents
A39 The glory of God

TRUE OBEDIENCE

'He became as men are; and being as all men are, he was humbler yet, even to accepting death, death on a cross.' *Philippians 2:7*

Quotations

Don't listen to friends when the Friend inside you says, 'Do this!' *(Mohandas Gandhi)*

Every revelation of God is a demand, and the way to knowledge of God is by obedience. *(William Temple)*

Obedience is the fruit of faith; patience the bloom on the fruit. *(Christina Rosetti)*

The devil does not fear austerity but holy obedience. *(St. Francis de Sales)*

The first degree of humility is obedience without delay. *(St. Benedict)*

No man securely commands but he who has learned to obey. *(Thomas à Kempis)*

Blessed are the obedient, for God will never suffer them to go astray. *(St.Francis de Sales)*

When God puts inspirations into a heart, the first he gives is obedience. *(St.Francis de Sales)*

Obedience responds to obedience. When someone obeys God, God obeys his request. *(Mios of Belos)*

How will you find good? It is not a thing of choices; it is a river that flows from the foot of the invisible throne, and flows by the path of obedience. *(George Eliot)*

Obedience is not servitude of man to man, but submission to the will of God, who governs through the medium of men. *(Pope Leo XIII)*

Proverbs

Obedience is the mother of success, the wife of safety. *(Greek proverb)*

No one can rule except one who can be ruled. *(Latin proverb)*

Humour

Teacher 'This is the fifth time this week that I have had to punish you. What have you to say, Charlie?'
Charlie 'I'm glad it's Friday!'

A teacher left her class one day and on returning found all the children sitting in profound silence with their arms folded. She was not only surprised at such silence, but bewildered and asked for an explanation. A little girl arose and said:

'Miss, you told us one day if you ever left the class room and came back and found all of us sitting perfectly silent, you would drop dead.'

Three year old Bobby insisted in standing up in his highchair although mother had admonished him to remain seated, then emphasized her admonishment twice reseating him. After the third time, little Bobby remained seated but looked at his mother searchingly and said, 'Mummy, I'm still standing up inside.'

Statements

With ready Christian obedience, laymen, as well as all disciples of Christ, should accept whatever their sacred pastors, as representatives of Christ, decree in their role as teachers and rulers in the Church. *(Second Vatican Council—'The Church Today')*

It also follows that political authority, whether in the community as such or in institutions representing the state, must always be exercised within the limits of morality and on behalf of the dynamically conceived common good, according to a juridical order enjoying legal status. When such is the case citizens are conscience-bound to obey. *(Second Vatican Council—'The Church Today')*

Word-Picture

Already in 1940, the order had gone out—incurables and the insane were no longer to be a burden on the Reich. Three high officials descended upon the Bethel institution (a huge hospital for epileptics and the mentally ill). 'Herr Pastor,' they said, 'the Fuehrer has decided that all these people must be gassed.' Von Bodelschwingh looked at them calmly. 'You can put me into a concentration camp, if you want; that is your affair. But as long as I am free, you do not touch one of my patients. I cannot change to fit the times or the wishes of the Fuehrer. I stand under orders from our Lord Jesus Christ.' *(John Foster)*

See also: A14 Successors of the Apostles
A32 Civic duty
B13 Authority
B31 The Commandments of Life
C25 Humility

THE JEWISH PEOPLE

'The vineyard of the Lord of hosts is the House of Israel and the men of Judah that chosen plant!' *Isaiah 5:7*

Quotations

The race of the Hebrews is not new but is honoured among all men for its antiquity and is itself well known to all. *(Eusebius of Caesarea)*

Jews are just like everyone else—only more so. *(Jewish saying)*

In Israel, in order to be a realist you must believe in miracles. *(David Ben-Gurion)*

The Jew's home has rarely been his 'castle'; throughout the ages it has been something far higher—his sanctuary. *(Joseph H. Hertz)*

If my theory of relativity is proven successful, Germany will claim me as a German and France will declare that I am a citizen of the world. Should my theory prove untrue, France will say that I am a German and Germany will declare that I am a Jew. *(Albert Einstein)*

The pursuit of knowledge for its own sake, an almost fanatical love of justice, and a desire for personal independence—these are features of the Jewish tradition which make me thank my stars that I belong to it. *(Albert Einstein)*

The Hebrews have done more to civilize men than any other nation. If I were an atheist, and believed in blind eternal fate, I should still believe that fate had ordained the Jews to be the most essential instrument for civilizing the nations. *(John Adams)*

Proverbs

No misfortune avoids a Jew. *(Yiddish proverb)*

No Jew is a fool, no hare is lazy. *(Spanish proverb)*

Even Moses couldn't get along with the Jews. *(Yiddish proverb)*

Statements

The Church cannot forget that she received the revelation of the Old Testament through the people with whom God in his inexpressible mercy deigned to establish the Ancient Covenant. Nor can she forget that she draws sustenance from the root of that good olive tree onto which have been grafted the wild olive branches of the Gentiles. *(Second Vatican Council—'Non-Christians')*

Since the spiritual patrimony common to Christians and Jews is thus so great, this sacred Synod wishes to foster and recommend that mutual understanding and respect which is the fruit above all of biblical and theological studies, and of brotherly dialogues. *(Second Vatican Council—'Non-Christians')*

Word-Pictures

Frederick the Great of Prussia asked his chaplain to prove the authenticity of the Bible in two words, and the chaplain immediately replied, 'The Jews, your Majesty!' *(Anon)*

The mud lay thick upon the stones and a black mist hung over the street; the rain fell sluggishly down, and everything felt cold and clammy to the touch. It seemed just the night when it befitted such a being as the Jew to be abroad. As he glided stealthily along, creeping behind the shelter of the walls and doorways, the hideous old man seemed like some loathsome reptile, engendered in the slime and darkness through which he moved: crawling forth, by night, in search of some rich offal for a meal. *(Charles Dickens)*

Hath not a Jew eyes? Hath not a Jew hands, organs, dimensions, senses, affections, passions, fed with the same food, hurt with the same weapons, subject to the same diseases, healed by the same means, warmed and cooled by the same winter and summer, as the Christian is? If you prick us, do we not bleed? If you tickle us, do we not laugh? If you poison us, do we not die? And if you wrong us, shall we not revenge? *(From the Merchant of Venice by William Shakespeare)*

There are three impudent creatures: among beasts, the dog; among birds, the cock; among people, Israel. But Rabbi Ammi added 'Do not consider this as blame; it is praise, for to be a Jew means to be ready to be martyred.' *(Midrash: Exodus Rabbah)*

Not long ago I was reading the Sermon on the Mount with a rabbi. At nearly every verse he showed me very similar passages in the Hebrew Bible and Talmud. When he reached the words 'Resist not evil', he did not say 'this too is in the Talmud', but asked, with a smile, 'Do the Christians obey this command?' I had nothing to say in reply, especially as at that particular time, Christians, far from turning the other cheek, were smiting the Jews on both cheeks. *(Leo Tolstoy)*

See also: A12 Holy Scripture
B36 The Family of God
C8 God's messengers

HEAVEN

'The Lord of hosts will remove the mourning veil covering all peoples, and the shroud enwrapping all nations, he will destroy Death for ever.'
Isaiah 25:7

Quotations

Heaven means to be one with God. *(Confucius)*

The main object of religion is not to get a man into heaven; but to get heaven into him. *(Thomas Hardy)*

Earth hath no sorrow that heaven cannot heal. *(Thomas Moore)*

When I reflect upon the number of disagreeable people who I know have gone to a better world, I am moved to lead a different life. *(Mark Twain)*

Heaven is not to be looked upon only as the reward, but as the natural effect, of a religious life. *(Joseph Addison)*

God may not give us an easy journey to the Promised Land, but He will give us a safe one. *(Bonar)*

One day, in my despair, I threw myself into a chair in the consulting room and groaned out, 'What a blockhead I was to come out here to doctor savages like these!' Whereupon Joseph quietly remarked, 'Yes, doctor, here on earth you are a great blockhead, but not in heaven.' *(Albert Schweitzer)*

If you insist on having your own way, you will get it. Hell is the enjoyment of your own way forever. If you really want God's way with you, you will get it in heaven, and the pains of purgatory will not deter you, they will be welcomed as means to that end. *(Dante Alighieri)*

Proverbs

Men go laughing to heaven. *(Dutch proverb)*

Heaven is mine if God says amen. *(Spanish proverb)*

Humour

The Irish have a story of an Irishman who appeared before St. Peter, expecting admission, and when his ledger showed pages and pages of heavy debit entries, said that the books had been badly kept, for he knew he had once given twopence to a beggar. St. Peter, after much flipping over of pages, found it was so indeed; but was twopence sufficient to outweigh all else? Then the Irishman said he had a friend called Patrick. If they would have the common politeness to call him, he would make it alright. St. Patrick was summoned, looked at the ledger, and he and St. Peter exchanged doubtful glances. 'What are we to do with this countryman of yours?' asked St. Peter. 'You see how it is.' 'Yes,' said St. Patrick, 'I see how it is. Give him back his twopence.' *(Douglas Woodruff)*

A teacher once said to a class of small boys, 'Hands up those who want to go to heaven.' All the boys put up their hands, except one. 'Don't you want to go to heaven, Georgie?' she asked, 'Nah, not if that lot's going.' The teacher did not ask Georgie where he would like to go.

An important man in advertising had a small daughter who came home from Sunday school one day carrying a bundle of pamphlets.
"And what do you have there?' asked the man.
'Oh, nothing much,' answered the little girl. 'Just some ads about heaven.'

'How is your wife?' the man asked a friend he hadn't seen for years.
'She's in heaven,' replied the friend.
'Oh, I'm sorry.' Then he realised that was not the thing to say, so he added, 'I mean, I'm glad.' And that was even worse. He finally came out with, 'Well, I'm surprised.' *(Christian Herald)*

Little Joan 'What do the angels do in Heaven, Mummy?'
Mother 'They sing and play harps.'
Little Joan 'Haven't they any radios?'

Statement

The Church, to which we are all called in Christ Jesus, and in which we acquire sanctity through the grace of God, will attain her full perfection only in the glory of heaven. Then will come the time of the restoration of all things. Then the human race as well as the entire world, which is intimately related to man and achieves its purpose through him, will be perfectly re-established in Christ. *(Second Vatican Council—'The Church')*

Word-pictures

A preacher, passing through an institution, was asked by a woman, 'Sir, what work of man will be in Heaven?' 'None, my dear lady,' he replied, thinking to escape quickly. 'O yes, there will; can you not tell me?' she persisted. 'No, I cannot, but will you not tell me?' said the preacher. 'Yes, sir,' she replied, 'it will be the print of the nails in the hands and feet of the Lord Jesus Christ. That is the only work of man that will be seen in heaven.' *(Anon)*

The Curé of Ars used to say in the pulpit, 'My dear parishioners, we must all do our very best to get to heaven. There we shall see God. How happy we shall be! We ought to go there all in a procession, with the parish priest in front. We must all of us get to heaven. If some of you get lost on the way, it will spoil everything!'

To over-fussy pilgrims who wanted to take too much time talking to him, he would say, 'We can talk in heaven.' *(Anon)*

Here lies a woman who was always tired,
She lived in a house where help was not hired.
Her last words on earth were: 'Dear friends, I am going
Where washing ain't done, nor sweeping, nor sewing;
But everything there is exact to my wishes;
For where they don't eat, there's no washing of dishes.
I'll be where loud anthems will always be ringing,
But having no voice, I'll be clear of the singing.
Don't mourn for me now, don't mourn for me never—
I'm going to do nothing for ever and ever.' *(Anon)*

See also: A20 The Kingdom of God
B3 Joy in Christ
B51 One with Christ
C48 One in us

CIVIC DUTY

'Give back to Caesar what belongs to Caesar—and to God what belongs to God.' *Matthew 22:21*

Quotations

Nothing is politically right which is morally wrong. *(Daniel O'Connell)*

Morality is the very soul of good citizenship. *(Archbishop Ireland)*

The office of government is not to confer happiness but to give men opportunity to work out happiness for themselves. *(William Ellery Channing)*

Liberty has never come from the government . . . The history of liberty is the history of the limitations of governmental power, not the increase of it. *(Woodrow Wilson)*

When a politican says, 'We're all in the same boat,' he usually means he wants to play captain while the rest of us do the rowing. *(Anon)*

No better citizen is there, whether in time of peace or war, than the Christian who is mindful of his duty; but such a one should be ready to suffer all things, even death itself, rather than abandon the cause of God or of the Church. *(Pope Leo XIII)*

A state without the means of some change is without the means of its conservation. *(Edmund Burke)*

A lesson that our country learned early and well, and which some countries unfortunately never learned or learned too late, is that each citizen had better take an active interest in running his country or he may suddenly find the country running him. *(Art Linkletter)*

Ghandi said that non-cooperation is 'with a method and a system, never with men' and that a hunger fast was 'never against an opponent but against a loved one, not to extract rights but to reform him'.

Humour

Hymn and Prayer for Civil Servants

O, Lord, grant that this day we come to no decisions, neither run we into any kind of responsibility, but that all our doings may be ordered to establish new departments, for ever and ever. Amen.

O Thou who seest all things below,
Grant that Thy servants may go slow,
That they may study to comply
With regulations till they die.

Teach us, O Lord, to reverence
Committees more than common sense;
To train our minds to make no plan
And pass the baby when we can.

So when the tempter seeks to give
Us feelings of initiative,
Or when alone we go too far,
Chastise us with a circular.

Mid war and tumult, fire and storms,
Give strength, O Lord, to deal out forms.
Thus may Thy servants ever be
A flock of perfect sheep for Thee.
(Published anonymously in the 'Daily Telegraph')

Statements

Citizens should develop a generous and loyal devotion to their country, but without any narrowing of mind. In other words, they must always look simultaneously to the welfare of the whole human family, which is tied together by the manifold bonds linking races, peoples, and nations. *(Second Vatican Council 'The Church Today')*

Let all Christians appreciate their special and personal vocation in the political community. This vocation requires that they give conspicuous example of devotion to the sense of duty and of service to the advancement of the common good. *(Second Vatican Council 'The Church Today')*

It is highly important, especially in pluralistic societies, that a proper view exist of the relation between the political community and the Church. Thus the faithful will be able to make a clear distinction between what a Christian conscience leads them to do in their own name as citizens, whether as individuals or in association, and what they do in the name of the Church and in union with her shepherds. *(Second Vatican Council 'The Church Today')*

Word-Pictures

The story is told of a king who placed a heavy stone in the road and then hid and watched to see who would remove it. Men of various classes came and worked their way round it, some loudly blaming the king for not keeping the highways clear, but all dodging the duty of getting it out of the way. At last a poor peasant on his way to town with his burden of vegetables for sale came, and, comptemplating the stone, laid down his load, and rolled the stone into the gutter. Then, turning round, he spied a purse that had lain right under the stone. He opened it and found it full of gold pieces with a note from the king saying it was for the one who should remove the stone. *(Indian Christian)*

Few people are aware that the word 'Govern' comes from the Latin term 'guberno' meaning 'to steer a ship.'

This thought was graphically illustrated by one man who said that a 'dictatorship is like a high-powered ocean liner. It can go straight ahead at a fast clip. The danger is that it may hit an iceberg.'

'Democracy,' he added, 'is like a log raft. You can't guide the thing very well; you wallow all over the place; your feet are always wet.'

'But you can never sink a log raft,' he concluded, 'and if you keep trying you eventually get there. That's what we've got to do, keep trying.'

The inefficiencies of self-government are often exasperating. But it is within the power of citizens, thank God, to right most wrongs.

Many years ago when a total eclipse of the sun became visible in Connecticut, USA, candles were lighted in many houses. Birds fell silent and disappeared, and domestic fowls retired to roost. The people were impressed by the idea that the day of judgement was at hand. This opinion was entertained by the Legislature, at that time sitting at Hartford. The House of Representatives adjourned; the Council proposed to follow the example. Colonel Davenport objected. 'The Day of Judgement,' he said, 'is either approaching, or it is not. If it is not, there is no cause for an adjournment; if it is, I choose to be found doing my duty. I move, therefore, that candles be brought.' *(Anon)*

See also: A29 True obedience
B14 Freedom to serve
B33 Faith and good works
B34 Human Rights

LOVE YOUR NEIGHBOUR

'The second commandment resembles it: You must love your neighbour as yourself.' *Matthew 22:39*

Quotations

No man can be a friend of Jesus Christ who is not a friend to his neighbour. *(R. H. Benson)*

To love our neighbour in charity is to love God in man. *(St. Francis de Sales)*

He alone loves the Creator perfectly who manifests a pure love for his neighbour. *(St. Bede the Venerable)*

Happy is the man who is able to love all men alike. *(St. Maximus the Confessor)*

Have a deaf ear for unkind remarks about others, and a blind eye to the trivial faults of your brethren. *(Walter Scott)*

We make our friends; we make our enemies; but God makes our next door neighbour. *(G. K. Chesterton)*

All is well with him who is beloved of his neighbours. *(George Herbert)*

Man becomes a holy thing, a neighbour, only if we realize that he is the property of God and that Jesus Christ died for him. *(Helmut Thielecke)*

The love of our neighbour is the only door out of the dungeon of self. *(George MacDonald)*

Though we do not have our Lord with us in bodily presence, we have our neighbour, who, for the ends of love and loving service, is as good as our Lord himself. *(St. Teresa of Avila)*

Next to the Blessed Sacrament itself, your neighbour is the holiest object presented to your senses. If he is your Christian neighbour, he is holy in almost the same way, for in him also Christ *vere latitat*—the glorifier and the glorified, Glory Himself, is truly hidden. *(C. S. Lewis)*

Proverbs

Love your neighbour, but don't pull down the hedge. *(Swiss proverb)*

No one is rich enough to do without a neighbour. *(Danish proverb)*

Love thy neighbour, even when he plays the trombone. *(Jewish proverb)*

He that will have none but a perfect brother must resign himself to remain brotherless. *(Italian proverb)*

Humour

Some Italian nuns of a nursing order printed this on the cover of their prospectus in English:

'We harbour all kinds of diseases, and have no respect for religion.'

A mother was telling her six-year-old about the Golden Rule. 'Always remember,' she said, 'that we are here to help others.'

The youngster mulled this over for a minute and then asked, 'Well, what are the others here for?' *(Christian Herald)*

Have you heard the story of the little girl who was sucking a lolly on the top of a bus and rubbing it now and again against the fur coat of the lady in front of her? Her mother said 'Don't do that, darling, you'll get hairs all over your lolly!' *(Anon)*

Statements

This Council lays stress on reverence for man; everyone must consider his every neighbour without exception as another self, taking into account first of all his life and the means necessary to living it with dignity. *(Second Vatican Council 'The Church Today')*

In our times a special obligation binds us to make ourselves the neighbour of absolutely every person, and of actively helping him when he comes across our path, whether he be an old person abandoned by all, a foreign labourer unjustly looked down upon, a refugee, a child born of an unlawful union and wrongly suffering for a sin he did not commit, or a hungry person who disturbs our conscience. *(Second Vatican Council 'The Church Today')*

Word-Pictures

Of the Tibetans it can be said that we respect them all the more for doing so little, to put it mildly, to attract a tourist trade. But this disengagement is perfectly compatible with a warmth of charity. The

French missionaries Huc and Gabet told a charming tale of a pious practice of Tibetan monks. When there was stormy weather, they would cut out paper horses and, taking them to the monastery roof, would release them into the wind with an appropriate prayer that they might be changed into real horses and carried to the travellers in distress. *(Douglas Woodruff)*

I chose Christianity because I felt that in it I had found the best way of serving my neighbour. I was elected by Christ to be a priest forever, motivated by the desire to devote myself full-time to loving my fellow man.

As a sociologist, I wished this love to become effective through science and technology. Upon analysing Colombian society, I realised the need for a revolution that would give food to the hungry, drink to the thirsty, clothing to the naked and bring about the well-being of the majorities in our country.

I feel that the revolutionary struggle is a Christian and priestly struggle. Only through this, given the concrete circumstances of our country, can we fulfil the love that men should have for their neighbours. *(Camilo Torres)*

A well-timed bite by a four-year-old girl with a good sense of smell saved her family from gas poisoning.

A peculiar odour awakened the child at three o'clock one morning and she hurried to her father's room to tell him.

When a vigorous shake failed to disturb his peaceful slumber, she bit him on the arm. That did the trick.

The police discovered that the strange smell was caused by monoxide fumes from the family car which had been left running in the adjoining garage.

The parents and all three children were in good condition after being administered a dose of oxygen.

The Rabbi Hillel was a renowned scribe in Jerusalem about the time of Christ's birth; he seems to have died about A.D.10, aged 80. He was called 'the Great' or 'the Elder', and his interpretations of the Law were less severe than others. He is said to have been the grandfather of Gamaliel *(Acts 22:3)* who taught St. Paul. Our Lord must have heard often of Hillel, and could possibly have spoken with him during the three days before the Finding in the Temple.

Here is one of the tales Our Lord might have heard. A certain gentile came to Shammai (Shammai was the leader of the more strict school of interpretation) and said that he would like to become a proselyte, but could not stay long in Jerusalem. 'Can you teach me the whole Torah while I am standing on one foot?' Shammai sent him away angrily. So the gentile went to Hillel with the same question. Hillel admitted him as a convert, and said, 'Whatever is hateful to thee, do not do to thy fellow-man. This is the whole Torah: all the rest is commentary. Now go and study.'

See also: A9 Relationships
B52 God is Love
C10 Love your enemies
C19 Friendship

HYPOCRISY AND AMBITION

'Do not be guided by what the Pharisees do; since they do not practise what they preach.' *Matthew 23:3*

Quotations

Thou shalt hate all hypocrisy, and everything that is not pleasing to the Lord. *(Teaching of the Twelve Apostles)*

I will have nought to do with a man who can blow hot and cold with the same breath. *(Aesop)*

Where there is no religion, hypocrisy becomes good taste. *(George Bernard Shaw)*

May the man be damned and never grow fat
Who wears two faces under one hat. *(H. G. Bohn)*

A Pharisee is a man who prays publicly and preys privately. *(Don Marquis)*

Ambition is like hunger; it obeys no law but its appetite. *(Josh Billings)*

Most people would suceed in small things if they were not troubled by great ambitions. *(Longfellow)*

Most of the trouble in the world is caused by people wanting to be important. *(T. S. Eliot)*

Hew not too high lest the chip fall in thine eye. *(John Heywood)*

Ambition is the mind's immodesty. *(Sir William Davenant)*

Well is it known that ambition can creep as well as soar. *(Edmund Burke)*

You cannot be anything if you want to be everything. *(Solomon Schechter)*

Proverbs

Many go out for wool and come back shorn. *(Spanish proverb)*

Every eel hopes to become a whale. *(German proverb)*

When the fox preaches, look to your geese. *(German proverb)*

Word-Pictures

Get place and wealth; if possible, with grace;
If not, by any means get wealth and place. *(Alexander Pope)*

Cineas when dissuading Pyrrhus from undertaking a war against the Romans, said, 'Sir, when you have conquered them, what will you do next?'

'Sicily is near at hand and easy to master,' replied Pyrrhus.

'And what when you have conquered Sicily?' 'Then we will pass on to Africa and take Carthage.'

'When these are conquered, what will be your next attempt?' asked Cineas.

'Then,' said Pyrrhus, 'we will fall upon Greece and Macedon and recover what we have lost there.'

'Well, when all are subdued, what fruit do you expect from all your victories?'

'Then,' said Pyrrhus, 'we will sit down and enjoy ourselves.'

'Sir!' said Cineas, 'may we not do it now? Have you not already a kingdom of your own? He that cannot enjoy himself with a kingdom cannot with a whole world.' *(Anon)*

Cardinal Wolsey, dying, charged Cromwell:
'I charge thee, Cromwell, fling away ambition. By that sin, fell the angels: how can man, then, the image of his Maker, hope to gain by't?' *(Shakespeare in Henry VIII)*

The original Jack Horner, the story goes, was steward to Richard Whiting, the last of the abbots of Glastonbury. In the 1530s, the time of the Dissolution of the Monasteries, it is said that the abbot, hoping to placate Henry VIII, sent His Majesty an enormous Christmas pie containing the deeds of 12 manors. Horner was entrusted to take the pie to the King. On the way he managed to open the pie and extract the deeds of the Manor of Mells in Somerset—presumably the 'plum' referred to in the rhyme.

An architect, who had worked for a large company for many years was called in one day by the board of directors and given plans for a fine house to be built in the best quarter of the town. The chairman instructed him to spare no expense, using the finest materials and best builders. As the house began to go up, the architect began to think, 'No expensive labour? Why use such costly materials?' So he began to use poor materials and to hire poor quality workmen, and he put the difference in the cost into his own pocket. When the house was finished, it looked very fine on the outside, but it certainly would not last long. Shortly after it was finished, the board of directors held another meeting to which the architect was called. The chairman made a speech, thanking the architect for his long service to the company, as a reward for which they were making him a present of the house! *(Anon)*

See also: A2 Integrity
A15 Sin
B26 The whole man
B44 The dignity of the individual

PREPARING FOR DEATH

'Stay awake, because you do not know either the day or the hour.'
Matthew 25:13

Quotations

Death ought to be our pleasure. *(Tertullian)*

What is death at most? It is a journey for a season: a sleep longer than usual. If thou fearest death, thou shouldest also fear sleep. *(St. John Chrysostom)*

Blessed be God for our sister, the death of the body. *(St. Francis)*

Of this at least I am certain, that no one has ever died who was not destined to die some time. *(St. Augustine of Hippo)*

For a perfect life is an imitation of death, which the righteous so lead with care that they escape the snares of sin. *(Pope St. Gregory I)*

Death has nothing terrible which life has not made so. A faithful Christian life in this world is the best preparation for the next. *(Tyron Edwards)*

Some people decide to be saved at the eleventh hour, and die at ten-thirty. *(Anon)*

Take heed, dear friend, in passing by,
As you are now, so once was I;
As I am now, you soon will be,
Prepare for death and follow me. *(On a tombstone)*

By God's body, master More, Indignatio principis mors est.
Is that all, my lord? quoth he. Then in good faith is there no more difference between your grace and me, but that I shall die today and you tomorrow. *(St. Thomas More at his trial)*

See me safe up: for my coming down, I can shift for myself. *(St. Thomas More, as he ascended the scaffold)*

There is a moment in every man's life when he has to make ready for a departure, and at last the moment comes for him to leave his earthly home, and to give an account of his labour. May every one of us then be able to say: I have looked those who did not share my ideals straight in the eyes and treated them with brotherly affection, in order not to impede the carrying out of God's great purpose, in his good time—a purpose which must bring about the fulfilment of the divine teaching and command of Jesus, 'that we may all be one.' *(Pope John XXIII)*

Proverbs

To die well is the chief part of virtue. *(Greek proverb)*

Six feet of earth make all men equal. *(Italian proverb)*

A good death does honour to a whole life. *(Italian proverb)*

Humour

Two small boys saw their grandmother walking up and down reading her prayer book. One boy said to the other, 'What's Grandma doing?' The other boy replied, 'She's swotting for her finals!'

Word Pictures

Francis of Assisi, hoeing his garden, was asked what he would do if he were suddenly to learn that he was to die at sunset that day. He said, ' I would finish hoeing my garden.' *(Anon)*

A 92-year-old man in Stanstead Abbots, England, is the proud possessor of a solid oak coffin, which he purchased 33 years ago, for £23. Every day since then, he has visited the shed in which he keeps the coffin to give it a polishing. If he feels drowsy after shining it, he crawls into it and takes a nap.

After doing this for 33 years, he is satisfied that his long rest will be comfortable for his body. He said: 'I even had my photograph taken in it! Wanted to see how I'd look when the undertaker lays me out, I came into the world a bit rough, as one of nine children. Now I'm making sure I go out respectable—with an oak coffin that has solid brass handles and everything.'

In years gone by, the Court Jester was an important member of the king's household. By means of quips, he kept the king in good humour, and entertained the members of the royal household.

Some writer tells us that what he believes to be the best retort any Court Jester gave. It was the retort given to his Sovereign, a dyspeptic dictator who had the ancient 'power of life or death' over all his subjects, and it was supposed to be legally impossible for the king to change any sentence he set on a subject. Becoming irritated by his Court Jester, in a sudden rage of wrath, the king sentenced his Court

Jester to death. Then realizing too late his rash decree, the king said to the Court Jester: 'In consideration of your faithful services, I will permit you to select the manner in which you prefer to die.' The Court Jester instantly answered: 'I select to die of old age.' *(Anon)*

A sick man asked Sengai to write something for the continued prosperity of his family, to be treasured from generation to generation. Sengai wrote: 'Father dies, son dies, grandson dies'. The sick, rich man was indignant. 'Is that what you write for the happiness of my family?'

Sengai replied, 'If your son would die before you, that would be very sad. If your grandson would die before you and your son, you would be broken-hearted. If your family dies in the order I have written down, isn't that prosperity and happiness?' *(Sengai)*

There is an old story of a jester who sometimes made very wise utterances. One day, the jester had said something so foolish that the king, handing him a staff, said to him, 'Take this, and keep it till you find a bigger fool than yourself.'

Some years later, the king was very ill, and lay on his deathbed. His courtiers were called; his family and his servants also stood round his bedside. The king, addressing them, said, 'I am about to leave you. I am going on a very long journey, and I shall not return again to this place: so I have called you all to say "Goodbye".' Then his jester stepped forward and, addressing the king, said, 'Your Majesty, may I ask a question? When you journeyed abroad visiting your people, staying with your nobles, or paying diplomatic visits to other courts, your heralds and servants always went before you, making preparations for you. May I ask what preparations your Majesty has made for this long journey that he is about to take?'

'Alas!' replied the king, 'I have made no preparations.'

'Then,' said the jester, 'take this staff with you, for now I have found a bigger fool than myself.' *(Anon)*

If I should never see the moon again
Rising red gold across the harvest field,
Or feel the stinging of soft April rain,
As the brown earth her hidden treasures yield.

If I should never taste the salt sea spray
As the ship beats her course against the breeze,
Or smell the dog-rose and the new mown hay,
Or moss and primrose beneath the tree.

If I should never hear the thrushes wake
Long before the sunrise in the glimmering dawn

Or watch the huge Atlantic rollers break
Against the rugged cliffs in baffling scorn.

If I have said goodbye to stream and wood,
To the wide ocean and the green clad hill,
I know that He who made this world so good
Has somewhere made a heaven better still.

This I bear witness with my latest breath
Knowing the love of God,
I fear not death.
(Lines found in the Bible of Major Malcolm Boyle, killed in action after the landing on 'D' Day, June 1944)

See also: A42 Life after death
B21 Trust in God
B22 Death
B23 The pastoral care of the sick
B41 Dying to self

USING TALENTS

'To one he gave five talents, to another two, to a third one; each in proportion to his ability.' *Matthew 25:15*

Quotations

No one respects a talent that is concealed. *(Erasmus)*

Talents are distributed unevenly, it is true: to one ten, and to another five; but each has one pound, all alike. *(R. H. Benson)*

Alas for those who never sing, but die with all their music in them. *(Oliver Wendell Holmes)*

The real tragedy of life is not in being limited to one talent, but in the failure to use the one talent. *(Edgar W. Work)*

There is a great deal of unmapped country within us. *(George Eliot)*

Doing easily what others find difficult is talent; doing what is impossible is genius. *(Amiel)*

If people knew how hard I have to work to gain my mastery, it would not seem wonderful at all. *(Michelangelo)*

Iron rusts from disuse; stagnant water loses its purity, and in cold weather becomes frozen; even so does inaction sap the vigours of the mind. *(Leonardo Da Vinci)*

Talent is the capacity of doing anything that depends on application and industry; it is voluntary power, while genius is involuntary. *(Hazlett)*

Nature has concealed at the bottom of our minds talents and abilities of which we are not aware. *(La Rochefoucauld)*

To do what others cannot do is talent. To do what talent cannot do is genius. *(Will Henry)*

Proverbs

Nobody don't never get nothing for nothing nowhere, no time, nohow. *(American proverb)*

Often the greatest talents lie unseen. *(Latin proverb)*

Humour

Author 'Well, sir, the upshot of it was that it took me ten years to discover that I had absolutely no talent for writing literature.'
Friend 'You gave up?'
Author 'Oh, no; by that time I was too famous.'

Teacher 'When George Washington was your age, he was head of his class.'
Pupil 'Yes, sir. And when he was your age, he was President of the United States!'

Statement

Since Christians have different gifts *(cf. Rom. 12:6)* each one must collaborate in the work of the gospel according to his own opportunity, ability, charismatic gifts, and call to service *(cf. 1 Cor. 3:10).*

Hence all alike, those who sow and those who reap *(cf. Jn. 4:37),* those who plant and those who irrigate, must be united *(cf. 1 Cor. 3:8).*

Thus, 'in a free and orderly fashion co-operating toward a common goal,' they can spend their forces harmoniously for the upbuilding of the Church. *(Second Vatican Council—'Missions')*

Word-Pictures

One day, Michelangelo saw a block of marble which the owner said was of no value. 'It's valuable to me,' said Michelangelo. 'There is an angel imprisoned in it and I must set it free.' *(Anon)*

An impoverished French farm lad was rated a genius by the recruiting officers who were inducting him into the army.

He amazed specialists in his aptitude test by scoring the highest of the 40,000 previously examined. One expert compared his mental capacity with that of Leonardo da Vinci and other great minds of the past.

The 20-year-old farmer never got more than rudimentary education because, as the ninth child of eleven children, he was needed to help at home.

Instead of inducting him immediately, the army sent him to a special school, where he completed six years of education in five months. *(Anon)*

You will ask where my ideas come from. I cannot say for certain. They come uncalled, sometimes independently, sometimes in association with other things. It seems to me that I could wrest them from Nature herself with my own hands, as I go walking in the woods. They come to me in the silence of the night or in the early morning, stirred into being by moods which the poet would translate into words, but which I put into sounds; and these go through my head ringing and singing and storming until at last I have them before me as notes. *(Ludwig van Beethoven)*

See also: A1 The value of time
A28 Work
A39 The Glory of God

CHRIST THE KING

'For he must be king until he has put all his enemies under his feet and the last of the enemies to be destroyed is death.' *1 Corinthians, 15:25*

Quotations

Eighty-six years I have served Him, and He has done me no wrong. How can I blaspheme my King who has saved me? *(St. Polycarp's answer when told to revile Christ)*

The true Christ, the divine and heavenly *Logos,* the only High Priest of the world, the only King of all creation, the only Archprophet of prophets of the Father. *(Eusebius of Caesarea)*

Christian Joy is the flag which is flown from the castle of the heart when the King is in residence there. *(P. Rainy)*

Wherever God rules over the human heart as King, there is the Kingdom of God established. *(Paul W. Harrison)*

Statement

Christ obeyed even at the cost of death, and was therefore raised up by the Father *(cf. Phil. 2:8–9).* Thus He entered into the glory of His kingdom. To Him all things are made subject until He subjects Himself and all created things to the Father that God may be all in all. *(cf. 1 Cor. 15:27–28).*

(Second Vatican Council—'The Church')

Word-Pictures

Some years ago, an American soldier on a bus in Sweden told the man sitting next to him, 'America is the most democratic country in the world. Ordinary citizens may go to the White House to see the President and discuss things with him.'

The man said, 'That's nothing. In Sweden, the King and the people travel on the same bus.'

When the man got off the bus, the American was told by other passengers that he had been sitting next to King Gustav Adolf VI. *(Anon)*

Dame Julian of Norwich tells us that Our Good Lord showed Himself to her in different ways, as on earth. One was His sweet Incarnation, when He was born of His Mother. Another was His blessed Passion, when He showed Himself dying on the Cross. Another time, she saw Him as if in a point, that is, His presence as Creator in everything, upholding it. Another time, He showed Himself as if leading a pilgrimage, with Himself going in front of us all, making the pilgrimage to heaven. At other times, He showed her Himself reigning as a king. But the way He showed Himself to her most often was as King reigning in man's soul. 'There He has fixed His resting place, and His royal city: and out of this worshipful throne He shall never rise, nor move His dwelling-place from it for ever.' *(Revelations of Divine Love)*

One of the famous stories of the early days of the Spanish civil war was that of Colonel José Moscardo, who, when it broke out, threw himself into the Alcazar fortress at Toledo with what troops he could collect, mostly cadets from a training school, to defend it to the end. Meanwhile, his wife and two youngest members of his family, still in the town, were arrested by the 'Reds' and held as hostages.

The siege had begun, but the telephone in the Alcazar was still working, and Colonel Moscardo was rung up by the commander of the besiegers, and told that if he did not surrender at once his son Luis, aged 17, would be shot.

'Neither the life of my son, nor of my whole family, will stop me doing my duty,' replied Moscardo.

'Your son shall speak to you on the 'phone himself. If you do not agree to surrender, he will be shot at once.'

The Colonel then heard the well-known voice of his son speaking from 200 yards away.

'What am I to do, father? They say they will shoot me if you do not surrender.'

'My dearest boy, these are the orders I give you, in the name of God. Call out "Arriba Espana" and "Viva Christo Rey", and die like a hero. Your father, for the honour of Spain, will never surrender.'

'Right, father.'

'Goodbye, my dearest boy.'

So Luis Moscardo was shot, and the siege went on for 72 long days. The Alcazar was bombed and shelled, mines were exploded, fires started, storming-parties driven back. The defenders lost 82 killed and 87 missing, while 580 were wounded. Two of the women died in the Alcazar of illness and two babies were born. When General Varela arrived and relieved the siege, Colonel Moscardo greeted him with the words 'Nothing to report, sir.' Moscardo died in 1958 aged 77.

During one of the Crusades, Philip Auguste, king of France, before he went into one of his battles, removed his royal crown from his head and, setting it on a table with the inscription *'Au plus digne'* (to the most worthy), he made his oration, as was the custom of leaders in those days. He asked his nobles, knights and men to forget that he was their king and commander, and to consider that the crown which he had laid aside for the battle would be the prize of the one who carried himself most worthily and bravely and contributed most to their victory. They entered the battle and returned victorious. All gathered round the table on which the crown had been placed. One of the nobles, stepping forward, took in his hands the royal crown and advancing toward the monarch, placed it on his head, saying 'Tu, O roi, es le plus digne' (Thou O king, art the most worthy).

See also: A4 Emmanuel—Mary's child
A44 Meeting Christ in the Sacraments
B4 Christ, the Covenant of God
B8 The Cosmic Christ

ORIGINAL SIN

'Sin entered the world through one man, and through sin death.'
Romans 5:12

Quotations

The whole clay of humanity is a condemned clay. *(St. Augustine of Hippo)*

Adam was but human—this explains it all. He did not want the apple for the apple's sake; he wanted it only because it was forbidden. The mistake was in not forbidding the serpent—then he would have eaten the serpent. *(Mark Twain)*

The kingdom of death dominated mankind to such an extent as to drive all, by due penalty, headlong into the second death, of which there is no end, except that the undue grace of God has delivered some. *(St. Augustine of Hippo)*

Carlyle said that men were mostly fools. Christianity, with its surer and more reverent realism, says that they are all fools. This doctrine is sometimes called the doctrine of original sin. It may also be described as the doctrine of the equality of men. *(G. K. Chesterton)*

Adam and Eve had many advantages, but the principal one was that they escaped teething. *(Mark Twain)*

The man without a navel still lives in me. *(Thomas Browne)*

Oh, he didn't believe in Adam or Eve,
He put no faith therein;
His doubts began with the fall of man,
And he laughed at original sin. *(H. Belloc: Song of the Pelagian Heresy)*

Sin; rub out the first and last letters, and you have I—or carnal self—the root of sin. *(Anon)*

Proverb

All the evil in the world was brought into it by an apple. *(Mala mali malo mala contulit omnia mundo.) (Medieval proverb)*

Statements

Affected by original sin, men have frequently fallen into multiple errors concerning the true God, the nature of man, and the principles of the moral law. The result has been the corruption of morals and human institutions and not rarely, contempt for the human person himself. *(Second Vatican Council—'Laity')*

If any one does confess that the first man Adam, when he had transgressed the command of God in Paradise, straightway lost that holiness and righteousness in which he had been established, and through the offence of this disobedience incurred the wrath and indignation of God, and therefore incurred death, which God had before threatened to him, and with death, captivity under the power of him who therefore had the power of death, namely the devil, and that the whole of Adam, through offence of that disobedience, was changed for the worse in respect of body and soul; let him be anathema. *(Council of Trent—Session 5)*

Word-Pictures

Sin has four characteristics; self sufficiency instead of faith, self-will instead of submission, self-seeking instead of benevolence, self-righteousness instead of humility. *(E. Paul Hovey)*

It is from the Talmud and not from Genesis that we get our traditional idea of Adam and Eve with a fig leave apiece, as though foliage had been rationed from the start: and from the Talmud, too, comes the story that Eve made all the animals eat some fruit too, so that they should all be involved in the same catastrophic consequences, and only the Phoenix had the sense to refuse and fly . . . *(Douglas Woodruff)*

There is an Indian fable of a swan, that, pitying a poor pig in its muddy environment, began to describe the beautiful country further up the river, with green banks and rising slopes, and invited the pig to join the happy company of white swans that lived there. The pig was willing enough to go, but asked the question, 'Is there any mire up in that fine country?' 'Oh no!' replied the swan, 'it is clean and free from mud and mire.' 'Then,' said the pig, 'I'm sorry I cannot accompany you. I must stay here in the mire.' *(Anon)*

Eden is on no map, and Adam's fall fits no historical calendar. Moses is not nearer the Fall than we are, because he lived 3,000 years before our time. The Fall refers not to some datable aboriginal calamity in the historic past but to a fact of human experience which is always present—namely, that we, who have been created for fellowship with God, repudiate it continually; and that the whole of mankind does this along with us. Every man is his own 'Adam,' and all men are solidarily 'Adam'. Thus Paradise before the Fall is. . . our 'memory' of a divinely intended quality of life, given to us along with our consciousness of guilt. *(J. S. Whale)*

Pointing to an unappetising cigar-butt in an ash-tray, a painter friend once said to me: 'That has, for me, all the beauty in the world.' She placated my raised eyebrows by explaining: 'Look at the subtle way the light plays on that mottled grey ash, upon the earthiness of the tobacco leaf, how it runs like spilt milk round the edge of the tray—it's a visual symphony.' My eyes began to discover nuances of colour and tone and form to which previously they had been blind. For a moment, sight regained its primal innocence, glimpsed a visual Garden of Eden in which everything was redeemed by the grace of light. *(John Alexander)*

It is said: It was because Adam ate the apple that he was lost and fell. I say: It was because of his arrogating something to himself, because of his I, Mine, Me and the like. Had he eaten seven apples, and yet never arrogated anything to himself, he would not have fallen: but as soon as he arrogated something to himself, he fell, and would have fallen if he had never bitten into the apple. *(Theologia Germanica)*

See also: A15 Sin
B10 Baptism
C26 The Human condition
C37 Temptation

THE GLORY OF GOD

'He was transfigured; his face shone like the sun and his clothes became as white as the light.' *Matthew 17:2*

Quotations

Though our lips can only stammer, we yet chant the high things of God. *(Pope St. Gregory I)*

Provided that God be glorified, we must not care by whom. *(St. Francis de Sales)*

God's majesty speaks to us by the works of his almighty Hands. *(R. H. Benson)*

If you say that God is good, great, blessed, wise or any such thing, the starting point is this: God is. *(St. Bernard)*

Short is the glory that is given and taken by men; and sorrow followeth ever the glory of this world. *(Thomas à Kempis)*

God is proved not only by the zeal of those who seek Him, but by the blindness of those who seek Him not. *(Pascal)*

To God alone be glory. *Soli Deo gloria. (Latin phrase (Mediaeval))*

But true glory and holy joy is to glory in Thee and not in one's self; to rejoice in Thy name, and not to be delighted in one's own virtue, nor in any creature, save only for Thy sake. *(Thomas à Kempis)*

Word-Pictures

On the margin of many of his masterpieces, Johann Sebastian Bach jotted down the words: 'To God Alone the Glory.'

And indeed, the prodigious quantity and sublime quality of his music, literally woven of religious contemplation and exaltation, reflect his lofty intention.

Although Bach was one of the greatest German organists of the 18th century, few besides his family and pupils knew of his genius in musical composition. At his death in 1750, after a lifetime of total dedication, poverty, and struggle, many of his priceless works were lost.

Music lovers today owe the 'rediscovery' of Bach to Felix Mendelssohn. As a young boy, he was enraptured by Bach's manuscript of the St. Matthew Passion. At the age of 20, he gave a private performance of it. As a result, Bach's genius was widely acclaimed. *(Anon)*

I AM is the unqualified fullness of being
is the supreme indication of presence
is the one statement that cannot be uttered without being completely true
is the one completely and immediately personal statement
is the presupposed in every intelligible utterance
is true equally of God and man
is true in every time and place
is the name of God. *(T. S. Gregory)*

It is not only prayer that gives God glory but work. Smiting on an anvil, sawing a beam, whitewashing a wall, driving horses, sweeping, scouring, everything gives God some glory if being in his grace you do it as your duty. To go to communion worthily gives God great glory, but to take food in thankfulness and temperance gives God glory too. To lift up the hands in prayer gives God glory, but a man with a dung fork in his hand, a woman with a slop pail, give him glory too. He is so great that all things give him glory if you mean they should. So then, my brethren, live. *(G. M. Hopkins)*

See also: A20 The Kingdom of God
B40 One God
C31 Thanksgiving
C39 Doing God's will

THE EQUALITY OF WOMEN

'His disciples returned, and were surprised to find him speaking to a woman.' *John 4:27*

Quotations

Men have sight; women insight. *(Victor Hugo)*

Women's styles may change, but their designs remain the same. *(Oscar Wilde)*

Mother is the name for God in the lips and hearts of little children. *(William Makepeace Thackeray)*

I think it must somewhere be written, that the virtues of the mothers shall be visited on their children as well as the sins of the fathers. *(Charles Dickens)*

Men shall always be what the women make them; if, therefore, you would have men great and virtuous, impress upon the minds of women what greatness and virtue are. *(J. J. Rousseau)*

Being a woman is a terribly difficult trade, since it consists principally of dealing with men. *(Joseph Conrad)*

Nature has given women so much power that the law has very wisely given them little. *(Samuel Johnson)*

There is no limit to the power of a good woman. *(R. H. Benson)*

A woman preacher is like a dog walking on his hind legs. It is not done well; but you are surprised to find it done at all. *(Dr. Johnson)*

Whatever women do, they must do twice as well as men to be thought half as good. Luckily, this is not difficult. *(Charlotte Whitton)*

When a king rules, his wife is the queen, but when a queen is a ruler, her husband is a prince. And then they talk about equality between the sexes. *(John Grigg)*

Proverbs

An ounce of mother is worth a pound of clergy. *(Spanish proverb)*

He who takes the child by the hand takes mother by the heart. *(Danish proverb)*

Humour

There was the sweet young thing who was being initiated into the mysteries of golf by her boyfriend. 'And now tell me,' she said coyly, 'which club do I use to make a hole-in-one?'

Actually, the original meaning of 'lady' was 'bread kneader' and if the dictionary adds 'See dough' it refers, we add sternly, to bread only. *(Cleveland Amory)*

My 13-year-old daughter and I were talking about women's liberation one day, and I said firmly, 'I don't want to be liberated.'

My daughter said, 'I don't want to be liberated either—at least not until I know how it feels to be captured.' *(Lynn Cannon)*

Statement

For in truth it must still be regretted that fundamental personal rights are not yet being universally honoured. Such is the case of a woman who is denied the right and freedom to choose a husband, to embrace a state of life, or to acquire an education or cultural benefits equal to those recognised for men. *(Second Vatican Council—'The Church Today')*

Word-Pictures

Henry VIII is no great favourite with Women's Lib, and I have unearthed another black mark against him. In his regulation about reading the Bible, chained in churches or elsewhere, he encourages it for all men except serving-men, but only for women of the upper class, of education and leisure, to instruct themselves so that they do not misunderstand what they read. *(Douglas Woodruff)*

Our daughter, who had entered a convent, ran up to us when we visited her one day and excitedly exclaimed, 'Mummy, guess what! I've just applied for the priesthood!' (It seemed the nuns wanted to be allowed to say Mass). Turning to her, I said, 'Look, when you came here you were my daughter. Now I call you sister, but if you think I'm going to call you father—well you can just forget the whole thing.' *(N.M.D.B.)*

In the beginning, said a Persian poet—Allah took a rose, a lily, a dove, a serpent, a little honey, a Dead Sea apple, and a handful of clay. When he looked at the amalgam—it was a woman. *(William Sharp)*

My sister and her fiancé were discussing their approaching marriage. 'I'm not having any of this woman's lib stuff,' he declared firmly. 'I'm going to be boss and you'll do as I say.'

Then he added: 'Is that all right with you?' *(C. Chamberlain)*

See also: B34 Human Rights
B44 The Diginity of the individual
C33 Equality

SPIRITUAL BLINDNESS

'I only know that I was blind and now I can see.' *(John 9:26)*

Quotations

The very limit of human blindness is to glory in being blind. *(St. Augustine of Hippo)*

The devil is ready to put out men's eyes that are content willing to wax blind. *(St. Thomas More)*

In the country of the blind, the one-eyed man is king. *(Erasmus)*

Blind men should judge no colours. *(John Heywood)*

A blind man will not thank you for a looking-glass. *(Anon)*

Proverbs

The eyes are blind when the mind is elsewhere. *(Latin proverb)*

When the blind man carries the banner, woe to those who follow. *(French proverb)*

Word-Pictures

A world of darkness and silence was the lot of Helen Keller who lived from 1880 to 1968. Blinded and made deaf by a fever when she was only 19 months old, she overcame her handicaps to become one of America's most famous authors and lecturers. When she was six-years-old, her teacher began to spell words into Helen's palm while the child felt the objects with the other hand. There was no progress. There came a breakthrough when the teacher spelled the word 'water' while holding Helen's other hand under a pump. Her sense of touch rapidly became her window to the world.

A three-year-old girl in Glasgow was the eyes of her blind mother and father.

Wearing a leather harness, the child was a familiar sight as she led her parents along streets, across intersections and in and out of shops.

'I trust her judgement completely,' said her totally blind father; 'She is a blessing to us,' agreed her nearly blind mother.

I noticed a man walking towards me down the village street. He was barefoot and dressed in a long robe. He came slowly along, feeling his way by tapping with his stick. He was blind. We sat down by the roadside to talk. He was the village postman, messenger and general errand man. He had heard that a stranger had arrived in the village, so he came along to greet me. He had two parcels with him. Out of one came a typewriter and there on the roadside he tapped out on a piece of rough paper a message, in the Braille language, of welcome to me and a greeting to friends in England.

Then he unwrapped his second parcel. Out came a large book about the size of a family Bible. Made of thick brown paper, the pages were studded with Braille characters. He ran his fingers along the lines until he found the passage from St. John 14: 'Let not your heart be troubled; believe in God, believe also in me.' We sat there by the side of the dusty road in silence. Then he packed away his treasures, shook hands, and away he padded down the road . . . I was moved by the man's inner serenity. He had turned blindness into sight and dark into light. *(Cecil Northcott: Christianity in Africa)*

In the African country of Ghana, a river was going to be used to make electricity and supply water for the people and their crops. But at the head of the river there was a place called 'the Valley of the Blind.' The people who lived there had trouble with their eyes. The trouble was caused by a fly which lived in the shrubs along the river. When this little fly bit someone it put into that person's blood a little creature called a parasite and this made the person blind. Before the huge work on the river could be properly started, it was necessary to find ways of getting rid of this little fly, *(M. Nassan)*

See also: A22 Seeking God
B49 Coping with doubt
C26 The human condition

LIFE AFTER DEATH

'I am the resurrection. If anyone believes in me, even though he dies he will live, and whoever lives and believes in me will never die!'
John 11:25

Quotations

To be immortal is to share in Divinity *(Clement of Alexandria)*

We maintain that after life has passed away, thou still remainest in existence, and look forward to a day of judgement, and according to thy deserts, art assigned to misery or bliss. *(Tertullian)*

After the royal throne comes death; after the dunghill comes the Kingdom of Heaven. *(St. John Chrysostom)*

After the resurrection of the body shall have taken place, being set free from the condition of time, we shall enjoy eternal life, with love ineffable and steadfastness without corruption. *(St. Augustine of Hippo)*

Nobody is excluded from the kingdom of heaven except through human fault. *(St. Thomas Aquinas)*

Primitive men did not philosophise; but for all that, they had their own way, an instinctive, non-conceptual way, of believing in the soul's immortality. It was a belief rooted in an obscure experience of the self, and in the natural aspirations of the spirit in us to overcome death. *(J. Maritain)*

For a small living, men run a great way; for eternal life, many will scarce move a single foot from the ground. *(Thomas à Kempis)*

He who provides for this life, but takes no care for eternity, is wise for a moment, but a fool forever. *(Tillotson)*

He who has no vision of eternity will never get a true hold of time. *(Carlyle)*

Proverbs

Those who live in the Lord never see each other for the last time. *(German proverb)*

When one is dead, it is for a long time. *(French proverb)*

Humour

There was a meeting of the board of directors going on in Hell. Satan was concerned over the fact that business was not increasing. He wanted to reach as many people as possible and draw them into Hell.

One demon jumped up and said: 'I'll go back to earth and convince the people that there is no Heaven.'

'That won't do,' said Satan. 'We've tried it before and it doesn't work.'

'I'll convince them that there is no Hell,' offered a second demon.

'No—that doesn't work either,' said Satan.

A wise old veteran in the back of the room rose and said, 'If you let me go back to earth, I can fill this place. I'll just convince them that there is no hurry.'

Four young bulls were standing in a field discussing what they wanted to be when they grew up. The first bull said he wanted to go to Rome and be a papal bull. The second said he wanted to go to London and be a bull in the City. The third said he wanted to go to Staffordshire and be a bull in a china shop. But the fourth bull said he just wanted to stay in the pasture for heifer and heifer and heifer. *(J.C.S.)*

Word-Pictures

Princess Tou Wan died about 104 B.C., but it was thought she would live forever, because she was buried in a jade suit. Her husband, who had died nine years earlier, was given a similar suit. The pair were laid to rest in vast tombs hollowed out of a rocky hillside. In China, in 1969, their tombs were discovered and they created a sensation because of the staggering wealth of the 2,800 funeral offerings. Most spectacular of all were the jade suits, each made up of more than 2,000 tiny plates of thin jade, sewn together with gold thread. Nobles of the period believed gold and jade would stand the ravages of time, and so confer immortality. *(A. P. Castle)*

Over the triple doorway of the Cathedral of Milan, there are three inscriptions spanning the spendid arches. Over one is carved a beautiful wreath of roses, and underneath is the legend 'All that pleases is but for a moment.'

Over the other is sculptured a cross, and these are the words beneath: 'All that troubles is but for a moment.' But underneath the great central entrance in the main aisle is the inscription 'That only is important which is eternal.'

Is there, I wonder, a kind of Gresham's law, by which, just as bad money drives out good, the more unpleasant ideas about purgatory have driven out the pleasanter ones? Towards the end of St. Bede's history of the first century of our national life as Christians and Catholics, he describes the vision of a fellow monk who at first thought he was seeing hell when he was only seeing purgatory. Hell was very much worse again. But then, a little later, he thought he was being shown heaven, so pleasant were the gardens, so enchanting the music, and so gracious the company. But this was not heaven: this too, was purgatory, and the kind of purgatory you went to varied according to the marks you had gained. But this notion of first-class waiting rooms so to speak, does not seem to have endured or taken root, and the popular view has always been that purgatory is not a place to stay in longer than can be helped; and it can be helped. *(Douglas Woodruff)*

See also: A31 Heaven
B22 Death
C35 Hope

BELIEVING COMMUNITY

'These remained faithful to the teaching of the apostles, to the brotherhood, to the breaking of bread and to the prayers.' *Acts 2:42*

Quotations

The union of men with God is the union of men with one another. *(St. Thomas Aquinas)*

Men are free when they are in a living homeland, not when they are straying and breaking away. Men are free when they belong to a living, organic, believing community, active in fulfilling some unfulfilled, perhaps some unrealised purpose. *(D. H. Lawrence)*

The individual man himself does not have the essence of man in himself as a moral or a thinking being. The essence of man is found only in the community, in the unity of man with man. *(Ludwig Feuerbach)*

A Church exists for the double purpose of gathering in and sending out. *(Anon)*

Proverb

There is little piety in big churches. *(Italian proverb)*

Humour

One Sunday morning, a man entered the church and sat down the front with his hat on. Noting the man, one of the ushers spoke to him, asking him if he knew he had forgotten to remove his hat.

'Yes,' the man replied, 'I realise I have my hat on. I've been coming to this church for two months and this is the only way I could get anyone to speak to me.'

Father told his little son that he couldn't go to church because he was suffering from a severe case of voluntary inertia.

'I bet you aren't,' the little boy answered, 'I bet you're just lazy.'

Statement

Thus the Church, at once a visible assembly and a spiritual community, goes forward together with humanity and experiences the same earthly lot which the world does. She serves as a leaven and as a kind of soul for human society as it is to be renewed in Christ and transformed into God's family. *(Second Vatican Council—'The Church Today')*

Word-Pictures

Humanity is one in Christ, men are branches of one vine, members of one body. The life of each man enlarges itself infinitely into the life of others, the communion of saints, and each man in the church lives the life of all men in the church; each man is humanity. He belongs not only to that part of humanity which, living on earth at the moment, stands before God in prayer and labour, for the present generation is only a page in the book of life. In God and in his church, there is no difference between living and dead, and all are one in the love of the Father. Even the generations yet to be born are part of this one divine humanity. *(Sergius Bulgakov)*

The traditional community was a mutual aid society. It was organised to satisfy the basic human needs of all its members and, therefore, individualism was discouraged. Most resources, such as land, might be communally owned and administered by chiefs and village headmen for the benefit of everyone. If, for example, a villager required a new hut, all the men would turn to forests and fetch poles to erect the frame and bring grass for thatching. The women might be responsible for making the mud-plaster for the walls and two or three of them would undoubtedly brew some beer so that all the workers would be refreshed after a hot but satisfying day's work. In the same spirit, the able-bodied would accept responsibility for tending and harvesting the gardens of the sick and infirm.

Human need was the supreme criterion of behaviour. The hungry stranger could, without penalty, enter the garden of a villager and take, say, some peanuts, a bunch of bananas, a mealie cob or a cassava plant root to satisfy his hunger. His action only became theft if he took more than was necessary to satisfy his needs. For then he was depriving others. *(Kenneth Kaunda: Humanism in Zambia—Reproduced from the World Council of Churches Newsletter July/August 1970)*

There was once a family who brought their youngest child, a girl, to be baptised. When it came time for the baptism, the family went forward, including a very happy three-year-old brother. When the baptism was over, the minister carried the baby into the middle of the congregation, expressing what a delight it was to welcome this child into the larger family, the Church. The three-year-old brother had followed the minister, and standing beside the minister, the little boy noticed a grandpa-aged man sitting and smiling with a very happy smile. In a voice that all could hear, the little boy said, 'Would you like to touch our baby?'

'I would,' said the elderly man.

So the minister gently held out the baby for the man to touch. The man seemed so pleased that the little boy said, 'Maybe someone else would like to touch her.'

The minister walked down the aisle, and hands reached out to touch the baby. 'Now,' said the minister, 'those of you who have touched this child should pass that loving touch to others around you, until all have been touched.' And so it happened. People were so thrilled with that service that they asked if the same thing might not be done at each baptism. *(John Ambrose)*

The church is never a place, but always a people; never a fold, but always a flock; never a sacred building, but always a believing assembly. The church is you who pray, not where you pray. A structure of brick or marble can no more be a church than your clothes of serge or satin can be you. There is in this world, nothing sacred but man, no sanctuary of God but the soul. *(Anon)*

See also: B17 The Church, Bride of Christ
B36 The Family of God
C12 The Church for all men

MEETING CHRIST IN THE SACRAMENTS

'He took the bread and said the blessing; then he broke it and handed it to them. And their eyes were opened and they recognised him.'
Luke 24:30–31

Quotations

A sacrament is a material object sanctified and consecrated by the Word of God. *(Peter Lombard)*

With these sacraments (i.e. baptism and the eucharist) Christ feeds His Church; by them, the soul's very being is strengthened. *(St. Ambrose)*

The liturgy is . . . not only a school of literary taste and a mine of marvellous subjects, but it is infinitely more; it is a great sacramental built around the six sacraments which surround the greatest sacrament who is Christ Himself dwelling among us even unto the consummation of the world. *(Thomas Merton)*

God had only one Son, and he was a missionary and a physician. *(David Livingstone)*

Statement

To accomplish so great a work, Christ is always present in His Church, especially in her liturgical celebrations. He is present in the sacrifice of the Mass, not only in the person of His minister, 'the same one now offering, through the ministry of priests, who formerly offered himself on the cross,' but especially under the Eucharist species. By His power, He is present in the sacraments, so that when a man baptises it is really Christ Himself who baptises. *(Second Vatican Council—'Liturgy')*

Word-Pictures

Walking down the street one day a lady noticed a little girl leaving the church by herself. When the child passed her, the lady inquired where she had been.

'In there,' replied the little girl, pointing to the church.

'And what were you doing in there?' the woman asked.

'Praying,' was the prompt reply.

Thinking the child was probably bothered with some problem, the lady inquired, 'What were you praying for, dear?'

'Nothing,' the child replied. 'I was just loving Jesus.'

At one of the settlements on a Red Indian reservation, where the priest was able to visit the Catholics only rarely, a Government agent came one day in his prairie-cart. He had things to give away, waistcoats and shirts and tobacco.

To one old man, who was a Catholic, the agent said jokingly, 'Your priest doesn't look after you, he doesn't seem to have brought you any presents, does he?'

The old man pointed to his bare chest, 'Can you see into my soul?'

'No, I can't,' said the agent.

'Well, if you could you would see the beautiful white garment that God gave me when the Blackrobe baptised me. And every time he comes he washes it clean for me in the blood of Jesus Christ. And when he gives me Communion, He puts Jesus Himself into my heart. Your tobacco soon goes off in smoke, and your shirts soon wear out, but the presents that the Blackrobe brings will stay with me and take me to heaven.

Se also: A37 Christ the King
B4 Christ the covenant of God
B46 Christ the Sacrament of God
B51 One with Christ
C45 The divinity of Christ

THE PRIESTHOOD

'The Lord is my Shepherd there is nothing I shall want.' *(Psalm 23)*

Quotations

The work of the ministry is an exalted work and leads to the kingdom of heaven. *(St. Basil)*

The priesthood requires a great soul; for the priest has many harassing troubles of his own, and has need of innumerable eyes on all sides. *(St. John Chrysostom)*

The priesthood is the spiritual power conferred on the ministers of the Church by Christ for the purpose of dispensing the sacraments to the faithful. *(John of Paris)*

The end of man is the glory of God. The end of a Christian is the greater glory of God. The end of a priest is the greatest glory of God. *(Cardinal Manning)*

A blot upon a layman's coat is little seen; a spot upon an alb cannot be hid. *(Cardinal Manning)*

A priest ought to be no place where his Master would not go, nor employ in anything which his Master would not do. *(Cardinal Manning)*

He cannot have the ordination of the Church who does not hold the unity of the church. *(St. Cyprian)*

I always like to associate with a lot of priests because it makes me understand anti-clerical things so well. *(Hilaire Belloc)*

Statement

The divinely established ecclesiastical ministry is exercised on different levels by those who from antiquity have been called bishops, priests and deacons. Although priests do not possess the highest degree of the priesthood, and although they are dependent on the bishops in the exercise of their power, they are nevertheles united with the bishops in sacerdotal dignity. By the power of the sacrament of orders, and in the image of Christ the eternal High Priest *(Heb. 5:1–10; 7:24; 9:11–28)*, they are consecrated to preach the gospel, shepherd the faithful and celebrate divine worship as true priests of the New Testament. *(Second Vatican Council—'The Church')*

Word-Pictures

During the Second World War, in the mountain village of Giazza, north of Verona, German paratroopers were going to execute some villagers, presumably for showing resistance. The parish priest, Fr. Domenico Mercante, offered himself as a hostage. The Germans accepted his offer, and decided to shoot him. When the time came, one of the firing-party refused to obey orders. 'I can't shoot a priest,' he said. He was placed at the priest's side, and both were shot together. The soldier's name is unknown. Fifteen years later, the Bishop of Verona unveiled a simple white monument commemorating the two heroes. The German Embassy in Rome was represented, and the Italian Minister of Justice gave an address. He said, 'The example of a priest and a soldier dying by the same rifle-fire, in order that not only the written law but the unwritten law too should be respected, provides an example of great moral value. It gives rise to the hope that the cause of peace amongst men may find its strongest protection in the conscience of humble but heroic spirits.' *(Anon)*

Almost every nation on earth has a proud record of priests who suffered and died in the name of the Christian religion. In previous centuries, in times of trouble, the priest was almost expected to play the hero. Elizabethan England, for example, saw the ruthless persecution of priests who took enormous risks to minister to their terrorised flocks—and all in the name of the Catholic faith.

The issues were quite clear—a political regime determined to crush the Catholic religion as something manifestly opposed to its aspirations and an obvious threat to its principles.

In more recent times, Nazi Germany also recognised the threat presented by the Catholic Church, as is attested by the presence of over 2,000 priests in Dachau alone. Behind the Iron Curtain, Hungary, Czechoslovakia, Lithuania and Russia have all had their generous share of priests suffering for their faith and usually the issues were as clearly defined as before. Priests represented a threat to a State determined to exterminate their ways and their attitudes.

More recently, however, the issues have been considerably more blurred. Where once it could be confidently asserted that those who persecuted the clergy would be quite obviously men determined to crush the Catholic Church, this is no longer the case. From various places, though especially from so-called Catholic countries—Chile, Brazil, Paraquay, Nicaragua, Bolivia, Argentina—come horrifying and distressing reports which change the traditional picture of the persecution of the clergy. Here, brutality and torture, harrassment and murder are perpetrated by people who claim to represent the very Catholic Church whose ministers they persecute. Here, priests and seminarians are attacked by forces who claim to be acting in the name of Christ and his Church.

Even Religious Sisters are not exempt from their hatred and blindness.

What terrible irony that those who serve the Church as its priests should now be martyred by cruel men and women whose faith in Christ they claim to share, and who are ostensibly as committed as the priests are to establishing his Kingdom on the Earth. *(Anon)*

Graham Greene's 'The Power and the Glory' was greatly influenced by the courageous underground work and death of Father Miguel Pro. During the Mexican religious persecution under President Calles, 35-year-old Miguel Pro, a Jesuit priest, secretly ministered to hundreds of Mexicans every day. A master of disguise, he escaped the police again and again. Finally he was arrested with his two brothers. No evidence was produced against them; there was not even a mock trial. When he faced the firing squad, Father Pro threw open his arms in the form of a cross and as the soldiers took aim cried, 'Long live Christ the King'. *(A. P. Castle)*

Our Lord's plan for each priest is personal partnership: 'We: Jesus and I'. This is how He would have each priest live and act—in the first person plural. Our Lord wants to share every moment of our life, especially every moment of our ministry. *(M. Eugene Boylan)*

See also: A14 Successors of the Apostles
A46 Priesthood of the laity
B13 Authority

PRIESTHOOD OF THE LAITY

'You are a chosen race, a royal priesthood, a consecrated nation, a people set apart, to sing the praises of God.' *1 Peter 2:9*

Quotations

What is the people itself but priestly? To whom it was said, 'You are a chosen race, a royal priesthood, a consecrated nation' *(1 Peter 2,9)*, as the apostle Peter says. Everyone is anointed to the priesthood, is anointed to the kingdom also; but it is a spiritual kingdom and a spiritual priesthood. *(St. Ambrose)*

By the waters of baptism, as by common right, Christians are made members of the mystical Body of Christ the Priest, and by the 'character' which is imprinted on their souls, they are appointed to give worship to God; thus they participate, according to their condition, in the priesthood of Christ. *(Pope Pius XII)*

Confirmation is the sacrament of the common priesthood of the laity. *(Gerald Vann)*

Statements

The earth's goods must be divided fairly and this right of every man to a just share comes first. Even the right to private property, and the right to free enterprise, must yield to justice.

Those who have money, cannot just spend as they please, or speculate, regardless of the way that others are affected.

The laity must act, using their initiative, not waiting for instructions. The laity must take the Christian spirit into the minds and hearts of men, into morality and laws, into the structures of society. The laity must breathe the spirit of the Gospel into the changes and reforms that have to come. *(Pope Paul VI: This is Progress)*

The Lord Jesus, 'whom the Father has made holy and sent into the world' *(Jn.10:36)*, has made His whole Mystical Body share in the anointing by the Spirit with which He Himself has been anointed. For in Him all the faithful are made a holy and royal priesthood. They offer spiritual sacrifices to God through Jesus Christ, and they proclaim the perfections of Him who has called them out of darkness into His marvellous light. Hence, there is no member who does not have a part in the mission of the whole Body. Rather, each one ought to hallow Jesus in his heart and bear witness to Jesus in the spirit of prophecy. *(Second Vatican Council—'Priests')*

It is through the sacraments and the exercise of the virtues that the sacred nature and organic structure of the priestly community is brought into operation. Incorporated into the Church through baptism, the faithful are consecrated by the baptismal character to the exercise of the cult of the Christian religion. *(Second Vatican Council—'The Church')*

Are not we laymen priests also? It is written: 'He hath also made us a kingdom and priests to God and his Father.' The difference between the Order and the people is due to the authority of the church and the consecration of their rank by the reservation of a special bench for the order. *(Tertullian, writing as a Montanist)*

See also: B10 Baptism
B44 The dignity of the individual
C49 Confirmation

THE SPIRIT OF TRUTH

'The Father will give you another Advocate to be with you for ever, that Spirit of truth whom the world can never receive.' *John 14: 16–17*

Quotations

All truth, wherever it is found, belongs to us as Christians. *(St. Justin Martyr)*

Nothing conquers except truth: the victory of truth is charity. *(St. Augustine of Hippo)*

Every truth without exception—and whoever may utter it—is from the Holy Ghost. *(St. Thomas Aquinas)*

We arrive at the truth, not by the reason only, but also by the heart. *(Pascal)*

No truth can really exist external to Christianity. *(Cardinal Newman)*

Let us rejoice in the Truth, wherever we find its lamp burning. *(Albert Schweitzer)*

I thirst for truth, but shall not reach it till I reach the source. *(Robert Browning)*

The truth is cruel, but it can be loved, and it makes free those who have loved it. *(George Santayana)*

Truth is the foundation of all knowledge and the cement of all societies. *(John Dryden)*

Proverbs

Individuals may perish; but truth is eternal. *(French proverb)*

Time discovers truth. *(Latin proverb)*

Tell the truth and run. *(Jugoslav proverb)*

The name of God is Truth. *(Hindu proverb)*

Statement

Truth, however, is to be sought after in a manner proper to the dignity of the human person and his social nature. The inquiry is to be free, carried on with the aid of teaching or instruction, communication and dialogue. In the course of these, men explain to one another the truth they have discovered, or think they have discovered, in order thus to assist one another in the quest for truth. Moreover, as the truth is discovered, it is by a personal assent that men are to adhere to it. *(Second Vatican Council—'Religious Freedom')*

Word-Pictures

Daniel O'Connell became an extremely skilled and quite untiring cross-examiner, with a great knowledge of the subterfuges by which Irish witnesses endeavoured to avoid perjuring themselves and to maintain a verbal truthfulness.

There is one story of a witness, in a case where a will had been forged after death, and the witness kept protesting that the testator 'had life in him' when he signed. After a time, O'Connell noticed that this witness took care never to vary the words 'he had life in him,' and following up the hint, he soon extracted the admission that the life in question was a live fly in the dead testator's mouth. Small wonder that with such an apprenticeship, O'Connell, on whom there were never any flies, was a full match for the English. *(Douglas Woodruff)*

But there are seven sisters ever serving Truth,
Porters of the Posterns, one called Abstinence,
Humility, Charity, Chastity be the chief maidens there;
Patience and Peace help many a one;
Lady Almsgiving lets in full many. *(William Longland, 'Piers Plowman')*

What a shaking thing
The truth can be,
Especially when found
On the family tree. *(Anon)*

Truth does not consist in minute accuracy of detail, but in conveying a right impression; and there are vague ways of speaking that are truer than strict facts would be. When the Psalmist said, 'Rivers of water run down mine eyes, because men keep not thy law, he did not state the fact, but he stated a truth deeper than fact, and truer. *(Henry Alford)*

See also: B53 Consecrated in Truth
C47 The indwelling Spirit
C48 Confirmation—Receive the Holy Spirit

WORSHIP

'All these joined in continuous prayer, together with several women, including Mary the mother of Jesus, and with his brothers.' *Acts 1:14*

Quotations

God respects me when I work, but he loves me when I sing. *(Tagore)*

For men invariably worship what they like best. *(St. Jerome)*

Great liturgies cannot be manufactured; they grow. *(Arnold Lunn)*

Human society as such is bound to offer to God public and social worship. It is bound to acknowledge in Him its supreme Lord and first beginning, and to strive toward Him as to its last end, to give Him thanks and offer Him propitiation. *(Pope Pius XI)*

Let the law of prayer determine the law of belief. *(Legem credendi lex statuat supplicandi) (St. Prosper of Aquitaine)*

The most pressing duty of Christians is to live the liturgical life, and increase and cherish its supernatural spirit. *(Pope Pius XII)*

It is a law of man's nature, written into his very essence, and just as much a part of him as the desire to build houses and cultivate the land and marry and have children and read books and sing songs, that he should want to stand together with other men in order to acknowledge their common dependence on God, their Father and Creator. *(Thomas Merton)*

Proverbs

Prayers travel faster when said in unison. *(Latin proverb)*

They that worship God merely from fear, would worship the devil too, if he appear. *(Anon)*

Humour

The shopkeeper had just handed me a demonstration pair of binoculars. I was getting the distant wall nicely into focus when a passer-by, seeing my Roman collar, quietly advised, 'Just tell them to move to the front of the church, Father.' *(John Stewart)*

There is an old traditional Jewish story that 'the three pillars' of Judaism, Torah (learning), Avodah (worship) and Gemilus hasadim (kind deeds) at the dispersion of the Jews came before God and cried that they would now be forgotten. 'No,' said God, 'I am going to tell the Jews to build synagogues wherever they go. The rabbi will teach the Torah, and the cantor will lead the Avodah.' 'What about me,' asked Kind Deeds. 'Ah,' said the Lord,' 'during the service each Jew will turn to his neighbour and offer him a pinch from his snuffbox.'

Word-Pictures

God is the supreme artist. He loves to have things beautiful. Look at the sunset and flowers and the snow-capped mountains and the stars. They are beautiful because they come from God. God loves to have things beautiful in Church, too. And the same goes for church courtesies. To show our reverence for the Cross on which he died for us, and for the Sacrament in which he comes to our hearts, is just to be polite to God. This is not required, but it is the part of Christian good breeding. It has the importance that courtesy has the world over. *(John S. Baldwin)*

The centuries which followed the fall of the Empire in the West, in spite of the impoverishment of their material culture, were from the liturgical point of view a great creative age, and it is remarkable that this is no less true of the semi-barbarian West than of the stable and comparatively prosperous Byzantine world. All these ages possessed of poetry, music and art found expression in the liturgy—an expression no later age has been able to surpass. *(C. Dawson)*

I have a treasured missal of the Sarum or old English rite, printed at Ingoldstadt in 1555. When it was planned, Edward VI was still on the throne, and when I peruse it I regret more than ever that there was no Englishman in Rome in 1570 when St. Pius V, while tidying up the immemorial Roman rite, exempted from the discipline of that rite any other which could show 200 years of continuity. The Sarum rite shows how confusing a misnomer it is to call the Roman rite 'tridentine' when it is incomparably older than Trent. The canon of the Mass in the Sarum rite is identical all the way from *Te igitur* until the communion. One of the small differences was that in the *Te igutur* prayer, after mentioning the Pope and the local bishop, the King was also prayed for, as he was not prayed for at Rome where the Pope was also the King. Let us repair the omission of 1570 and apply now for Sarum to be licensed. *(Douglas Woodruff)*

The champions of the sweeping liturgical changes of the last few years are fond of claiming that they have sought simplicity to remove duplications and reiterations, that the essentials may stand out more clearly. It is a dangerous principle for ceremonies that need to be invested with a proper solemnity. They might make their patron that

Indiana magistrate who acquired some notoriety in the last century for the way in which he stripped the marriage ceremony of all accessories and came straight to fundamentals, so that the ceremony lasted under a minute. He just asked the bridegroom, 'Have her?' and when the bridegroom had said yes, turned to the bride and said 'Have him?' and after her yes, announced 'Married. Five dollars.' *(Douglas Woodruff)*

The word 'Worship' is an Anglo-Saxon word and means 'worthship' or 'worthiness'. The word commonly translated 'worship' in the New Testament—though there are several other Greek words—is *'Proskuneo'*, to kiss the hand toward. This is thought to be derived from the slave's manner of salutation and homage when he entered the presence of his master, the act being a mark of reverence and respect, and also implying affection. Hence, in ascriptions of worship, we have the expression 'Thou art worthy'. *(Anon)*

When it comes to reading at Mass for the benefit of others, Eamonn Andrews believes it deserves the same effort as if he were preparing for one of his television shows.

This point comes across in an article on involving parishioners in the Dublin Diocesan Bulletin.

A priest in the Dublin northside resort of Portmarnock, where Eamonn lives, asked him if he would read at Sunday Mass. Eamonn gladly agreed, and was told he would be given the date and time later.

One Saturday an altar boy called to his home and told him he was 'on' at the 11 o'clock Mass next morning. Later the same day Eamonn explained to the priest why he would have to refuse this time.

'The word of God,' he said, 'as far as I am concerned, is something which is absolutely precious. It means an awful lot to me. I have made a lot of sacrifices during my life because of the convictions I have about the Gospel, and therefore I will not take the Gospel for granted.

'You have asked me to come along tomorrow to go out and read something I never saw before. If I were doing a television programme I would spend a whole week planning and preparing it. I will not go out there just to read in front of the people without putting a lot of preparation into it; without having it explained to me. I want to know what it is about. I want to know what the people are to get out of it. I want to pray about it.' *(The Universe)*

See also: B25 Quiet time for prayer
B29 The Mass
C32 Prayer

WAITING ON THE LORD

'Stay awake, because you do not know when the master of the house is coming.' *Mark 13:35*

Quotations

When you do not know what to do—wait. *(Anon)*

True waiting means waiting without anxiety. *(St. Francis de Sales)*

They also serve who only stand and wait. *(John Milton)*

There are three distinct comings of the Lord of which I know, His coming to men, His coming into men, and His coming against men. *(St. Bernard)*

Proverbs

Everything comes to those who wait. *(French proverb)*

The future belongs to him who knows how to wait. *(Russian proverb)*

It's good to hope, it's the waiting that spoils it. *(Yiddish proverb)*

Word-Pictures

Three hundred years ago, a man condemned to the Tower of London carved these words on the stone wall of the prison:

> 'It is not adversity that kills,
> but the impatience with which we bear adversity.'

The Emperor Hadrian once said to Rabbi Joshua, 'I want to see your God.' The Rabbi replied, 'That is impossible.' The Emperor said, 'You must show Him to me.' The Rabbi made the Emperor go outside with him. It was summer. He said to the Emperor, 'Look at the sun,' 'I cannot,' answered the Emperor. Then the rabbi replied, 'If you cannot even look at the sun, which is but one of the servants of the Holy One, blessed be He, how shall you look at the Holy One Himself?' *(The Talmud)*

One morning in the early 1890's, four workers were busy in a cornfield. One man with a scythe was cutting the corn and leaving it in long swathes. He was followed by a lad who was making bands of twisted cornstalks and laying them on the ground at intervals, side by side. The third worker had a small wooden rake with three six-inch teeth on it, and with this he was gathering bundles of the cut corn, and placing each bundle on one of the bands left by the lad. The fourth worker, following the others, was making each bundle into a sheaf by twisting the band tightly round it and tucking in the end.

At half-past-10, they stopped for a lunch break. They sat down and opened their lunch packets which contained sandwiches of home-fed cold bacon. The lad looked at his food as it lay open upon a cloth. He had been converted the night before at a chapel meeting, so he clasped his hands and closed his eyes to say grace. When he opened his eyes, his sandwiches had gone. The dog had taken them!

The farmer had seen it all. Much amused, he said to the lad, 'It is a good thing to pray—but you must also watch!' *(Peter Hargreaves)*

See also: A1 Value of time
A22 Seeking God
A35 Preparing for Death
B21 Trust in God
C1 Liberation from fear
C36 The Day of the Lord

THE GOOD NEWS

'Go up on a high mountain, joyful messenger to Zion. Shout with a loud voice, joyful messenger to Jerusalem.' *Isaiah 40:9*

Quotations

The unpardonable sin is to deny the Word of God within. *(John Whittier)*

The Gospel was not good advice but good news. *(William Ralph Inge)*

How petty are the books of the philosophers with all their pomp, compared with the gospels! *(Jean Jacques Rousseau)*

Our reading of the Gospel story can be and should be an act of personal communion with the living Lord. *(William Temple)*

God writes the gospel not in the Bible alone, but on trees, and flowers, and clouds, and stars. *(Martin Luther)*

Thanks be to the Gospel, by means of which we also, who did not see Christ when He came into this world, seem to be with Him when we read His deeds. *(St. Ambrose)*

Humour

The sexton had been laying the new carpet on the pulpit platform and had left a number of tacks scattered on the floor. 'See here, James,' said the parson, 'what do you suppose would happen if I stepped on one of those tacks right in the middle of my sermon?'

'Well, sir,' replied the sexton, 'I reckon there'd be one point you wouldn't linger on!' *(Anon)*

Statements

In His gracious goodness, God has seen to it that what He had revealed for the salvation of all nations would abide perpetually in its full integrity and be handed on to all generations. Therefore, Christ the Lord, in whom the full revelation of the supreme God is brought to completion *(cf. 2 Cor. 1:20; 3:16; 4:6.)*, commissioned the apostles to preach to all men that gospel which is the source of all saving truth and moral teaching, and thus to impart to them divine gifts. This gospel had been promised in former times through the prophets and Christ Himself fulfilled it and promulgated it with His own lips. *(Second Vatican Council—'Revelation')*

Holy Mother Church has firmly and with absolute constancy held, and continues to hold, that the four Gospels just named, whose historical character the Church unhesitatingly asserts, faithfully hand on what Jesus Christ, while living among men, really did and taught for their eternal salvation until the day He was taken up into heaven (*see Acts 1:1*–2). *(Second Vatican Council—'Revelation')*

Word-Pictures

That the Gospel is to be opposed is inevitable—
That the Gospel is to be disbelieved is to be expected—
But that it should be made dull is intolerable! *(Gerald Kennedy)*

GOOD North
East
West
South FOR ALL. *(Anon)*

You are writing a Gospel,
A chapter each day,
By the deeds that you do,
And the words that you say.

Men read what you write,
If it's false or it's true.
Now what is the Gospel
According to you? *(Anon)*

The curate stepped into the pulpit to preach with all the apprehension of a young man recently ordained. He hesitated for a moment. Then his face broke into a wide grin as he shared with us the message someone had left near his notes. 'Give 'em Heaven!' *(M. L. Rogness)*

Ruskin says that many people read the Scriptures as the hedgehog gets grapes. The old monks said that this animal rolled over among the grapes and carried what happened to stick to its spines or quills. So the 'hedgehoggy' readers roll themselves over on a portion of the Scriptures and get only what happens to stick. But you can get only the skins of Bible verses that way. If we want the juice, we must press them in clusters. *(Anon)*

Author Lloyd Douglas used to tell how he loved to visit an old violin teacher who had a homely wisdom that refreshed him. One morning, Douglas walked in and said 'Well, what's the good news today?' Putting down his violin, the teacher stepped over to a tuning fork suspended from a cord and struck it.

'*There* is the good news for today,' he said. 'That, my friend, is the musical note A. It was A all day yesterday, will be A next week and for a thousand years.' *(Purnell Bailey)*

See also: B9 Revelation
B12 On a mission
B24 Go tell everyone
C2 Joy of Salvation

JOY IN CHRIST

'Be happy at all times.' *1 Thessalonians 5:16*

Quotations

God is infinite fun. *(Mary O'Hara)*

Happiness is the practice of the virtues. *(St. Clement of Alexandria)*

We are all strings in the concert of his joy. *(Jakob Boehme)*

Happiness is the art of making a bouquet of those flowers within reach. *(Bob Goddard)*

The life without festival is a long road without an inn. *(Democritus of Abdera)*

The thought of God, and nothing short of it, is the happiness of man. *(Cardinal Newman)*

If there is joy in the world, surely the man of pure heart possesses it. *(Thomas à Kempis)*

Happiness is not a matter of events; it depends upon the tides of the mind. *(Alice Meynell)*

Happiness is a mystery like religion, and should never be rationalised. *(G. K. Chesterton)*

Happiness consists in the attainment of our desires, and in our having only right desires. *(St. Augustine of Hippo)*

The supreme happiness of life is the conviction of being loved for yourself, or more correctly, of being loved of yourself. *(Victor Hugo)*

When I think upon my God, my heart is so full of joy that the notes dance and leap from my pen; and since God has given me a cheerful heart, it will be pardoned me that I serve Him with a cheerful spirit. *(Franz Josef Haydn)*

Proverbs

Those who wish to sing always find a song. *(Swedish proverb)*

Great joys weep, great sorrows laugh. *(French proverb)*

Humour

Happiness, according to many philosophers, is a state of being that nobody recognises while they are happy but can recollect all too clearly when they are unhappy—like the bachelor who ran after women and caught one. *(Carl Riblet)*

Word-Pictures

An Athenian one day found Aesop amusing himself by talking to a group of boys and began to laugh and jeer at him for it. Aesop took a bow unstrung and laid it upon the ground. Then, calling the Athenian, 'Now, philosopher,' said he, 'expound the riddle if you can, and tell me what the unstrung bow implies.' The man, after racking his brain a considerable time to no purpose, at last gave it up. 'Why,' said Aesop, smiling, if you keep a bow always bent, it will presently lose its elasticity; but if you let it go slack, it will be fitter for use when you want it. *(Aesop)*

Can we not say to the young apprentice who has just learnt the use of a high precision lathe, and is thrilled at his new ability to use so apparently heavy and bulky a machine to prepare a piece of metal to a given shape with an accuracy of one ten-thousandth of an inch, that God is equally thrilled, and that this sheer joy in the situation is not wholly different from that of the angels who behold God's glory and rejoice? *(C. A. Coulson)*

There was a mediaeval king who regularly used the advice of a wise man. This sage was summoned to the king's presence. The monarch asked him how to get rid of his anxiety and depression of spirits, how he might be really happy, for he was sick in body and mind. The sage replied, 'There is but one cure for the king. Your Majesty must sleep one night in the shirt of a happy man.'

Messengers were dispatched throughout the realm to search for a man who was truly happy. But everyone who was approached had some cause for misery, something that robbed them of true and complete happiness. At last they found a man—a poor beggar—who sat smiling by the roadside and, when they asked him if he was really happy and had no sorrows, he confessed that he was a truly happy man. Then they told him what they wanted. The king must sleep one night in the shirt of a happy man, and had given them a large sum of money to procure such a shirt. Would he sell them his shirt that the king might wear it? The beggar burst into uncontrollable laughter, and replied, 'I am sorry I cannot oblige the king. I haven't a shirt on my back.' *(Anon)*

See also: B51 One with Christ
C2 Joy of Salvation
C47 The indwelling Spirit

CHRIST, THE COVENANT OF GOD

'I proclaim Jesus Christ, the revelation of a mystery kept secret for endless ages.' *Romans 16; 25*

Quotations

Jesus alone is able to offer himself as the sufficient illustration of his own doctrine. *(Hensley Henson)*

In his life Christ is an example,
showing us how to live;
In his death he is a sacrifice,
satisfying for our sins;
In his resurrection, a conqueror;
In his ascension, a king;
In his intercession, a high priest. *(Martin Luther)*

I believe that he belongs not only to Christianity but to the entire world, to all races and people; it matters little under what flag, name, or doctrine they may work, profess a faith, or worship a God inherited from the ancestors. *(Mahatma Gandhi)*

There is one physician, fleshy and spiritual, begotten and unbegotten, God in man, true life in death, both of Mary and of God, first passible then impassible, Jesus Christ our Lord. *(St. Ignatius)*

Therefore, four Catholic covenants were given to mankind. The first, Noah's, was that of the rainbow after the flood; the second, Abraham's, being that of the circumcision. The third was the giving of the law in the time of Moses; and the fourth is that of the gospel given through our Lord Jesus Christ. *(St. Irenaeus)*

Statement

He therefore chose the race of Israel as a people unto Himself. With it, he set up a covenant. Step by step He taught this people by manifesting in its history both Himself and the decree of His will, and by making it holy unto Himself. All these things, however, were done by way of preparation and as a figure of that new and perfect covenant which was to be ratified in Christ, and of that more luminous revelation which was to be given through God's very Word made flesh. *(Second Vatican Council—'Revelation')*

Word-Pictures

The Incarnation broke the wall between time and eternity, temple and market, church and shop, sacred and secular. The Incarnation allows no division of the Gospel into personal and social, permits no surrender of the group to the devil in order to rescue one member of it from him, lets no public injustice escape the Gospel's judgment while the Gospel tends some private man's grief. The God who assumed flesh sought the redemption of the whole man in all his circumstances and conditions. Forgetting this, the Church ceases to be the Church of the Incarnated Christ. *(K. Haselden)*

During a cruel and bloody war, a commander took an oath in the presence of his troops that he would slaughter the entire population of a certain town, and in due course the bloodhounds of war were let loose on the defenceless people.

Now it so happens that a fugitive, seeking for shelter, saw a sight which was indirectly the means of saving both his own life and the lives of others. He spied a number of soldiers as they broke into a house, the inmates of which they put to the sword. On leaving it, they fastened up the place again, and one of them, dipping a cloth in a pool of blood, splashed it on the door, as a token to any who might follow of what had taken place inside.

Quick as his feet could carry him, the poor fugitive sped away to a large house in the centre of the town where a number of his friends were concealed, and breathlessly told them what he had seen. At once it flashed upon them how to act. A goat was in the yard. It was immediately killed, and its blood splashed on the door. Scarcely could they close the door again when a band of soldiers rushed into the street and began to slay right and left. But when they came to the blood-marked door, they made no attempt to enter.

The sword—so they thought—had already entered and performed its work in that house. Thus, while the many around were put to death, all inside the blood-sprinkled door were saved. *(Anon)*

See also: A37 Christ the King
A44 Meeting Christ in the Sacraments
B10 The Cosmic Christ
B46 Christ the Sacrament of God

A SAVIOUR IS BORN FOR US

'Today in the town of David a Saviour has been born to you; he is Christ the Lord.' *Luke 2;11*

Quotations

For he was made Man that we might be made God. *(St. Athanasius)*

By His divine nature, Christ is simple,
By His human nature, He is complex. *(St. Thomas Aquinas)*

The incarnation is not an event; but an institution. What Jesus once took up He never laid down. *(Vincent McNabb)*

The greatness of God was not cast off, but the slightness of human nature was put on. *(St. Thomas Aquinas)*

He is what God means by man.
He is what man means by God. *(J. S. Whale)*

Since we are not yet ready for the banquet of our Father, let us grow familiar with the manger of our Lord Jesus Christ. *(St. Augustine of Hippo)*

I think that the purpose and cause of the Incarnation was that God might illuminate the world by his wisdom and excite it to the love of Himself. *(Peter Abelard)*

The manger is heaven, yea, greater than heaven. Heaven is the handiwork of this child. *(The Greek Anthology)*

Let us not flutter too high, but remain by the manger and the swaddling clothes of Christ, 'in whom dwelleth all the fullness of the God-head bodily.' There a man cannot fail of God, but finds him most certainly. *(Martin Luther)*

The Word of God, Jesus Christ, on account of His great love for mankind, became what we are in order to make us what He is Himself. *(St. Irenaeus)*

Every thought, word, action, silence, and self-repression in the incarnate life of the Word of God is full of spiritual significance and effectiveness. *(R. H. Benson)*

I once talked to a continental pastor who had seen Hitler, and had, by all human standards, good cause to hate him. 'What did he look like?' I asked. 'Like all men,' he replied. 'That is, like Christ.' *(C. S. Lewis)*

Humour

Wife to husband on Christmas morning
'You angel! Just what I need to exchange for just what I wanted. *(Anon)*

An older sister was trying to motivate her younger brother to good behaviour. 'If you are not better, Santa Claus will not stop and see you next week,' she told the four-year-old. 'He'll pass right over this house.'

'What?' said the tot. 'Won't he even stop for you?' *(Anon)*

Little Jennie was being taught that it was the proper thing to do to write a 'thank-you' letter to those persons who sent her gifts at Christmas. She seemed to do pretty well until it came to Aunt Martha's gift. Finally she finished her note which read: 'Thank you for your Christmas present. I always wanted a pin-cushion, although not very much.' *(Anon)*

I once asked a Christmas Eve group of children if they believed in Santa Claus. The very smallest ones answered without hesitation, 'Why, of course!' The older ones shook their heads. The little girls smiled sadly but said nothing. One future scientist asserted boldly, 'I know who it is,' while one little boy, with his eye on gain, said: 'I believe in it all; I can believe anything.' That boy, I realised, would one day be a bishop. *(Stephen Leacock)*

Statement

Since human nature as He assumed it was not annulled, by that very fact it has been raised up to a divine dignity in our respect too. For by His incarnation the Son of God has united Himself in some fashion with every man. He worked with human hands, He thought with a human mind, acted by human choice, and loved with a human heart. Born of the Virgin Mary, He has truly been made one of us, like us in all things except sin. *(Second Vatican Council—'The Church Today')*

Word-Pictures

All men living today belong to a single species, *Homo sapiens,* and are derived from a common stock. Pure races—in the sense of genetically homogeneous populations—do not exist in the human species. *(UNESCO Report 1964)*

The first Christmas card was believed to have been sent by W. C. T. Dobson, R.A., in 1844. Sir Henry Cole and J. C. Horsley produced the first commercial Christmas card in 1846, although it was condemned by temperance enthusiasts because members of the family group in the centrepiece were cheerfully drinking wine. After Tucks, the art printers, took to printing them in the 1870s, they really came into vogue. *(Anon)*

The first Christmas that little Linda learned to read, she was allowed to distribute the family gifts on Christmas Eve.

According to the family custom, the one who distributed the gifts could open the first package. After all the gifts were distributed with loving care, Linda kept looking and looking around the tree and among the branches. Finally father asked, 'What are you looking for, dear?' To which Linda replied, 'I thought Christmas was Jesus' birthday and I was just wondering where his present is. I guess everyone forgot him.' *(Anon)*

A wealthy family in England, many years ago, took their children for a holiday in the country. Their host toured over his estate for a weekend. The children went swimming in a pool. One of the boys began to drown, and the other boys screamed for help. The son of the gardener jumped in and rescued the helpless one. Later, the grateful parents asked the gardener what they could do for the youthful hero. The gardener said his son wanted to go to college. 'He wants to be a doctor,' he said. The visitors shook hands on that. 'We'll be glad to pay his way through,' they told him.

When Winston Churchill was stricken with pneumonia after the Teheran conference, the King of England instructed that the best doctor be found to save the Prime Minister. The doctor turned out to be Dr. Fleming, the developer of penicillin. 'Rarely,' said Churchill to Fleming, 'has one man owed his life twice to the same rescuer.' It was Fleming who saved Churchill in that pool. *(Anon)*

See also: A4 Mary's Child—Emmanuel
B3 Joy in Christ
C2 Joy of Salvation
C7 The humanity of Christ

THE FAMILY

'The Lord honours the father in his children, and upholds the rights of a mother over her sons.' *Ecclesiasticus 3:2*

Quotations

Home is where the heart is. *(Pliny the Elder)*

Wife and children are a kind of discipline of humanity. *(Francis Bacon)*

What a father says to his children is not heard by the world, but it will be heard by posterity. *(Jean Paul Eixhter)*

The union of the family lies in love; and love is the only reconciliation of authority and liberty. *(R. H. Benson)*

Where does the family start? It starts with a young man falling in love with a girl—no superior alternative has yet been found. *(Sir Winston Churchill)*

The family, grounded on marriage freely contracted, monogamous and indissoluble, is and must be considered the first and essential cell of human society. *(Pope John XXIII)*

The family is more sacred than the state, and men are begotten not for the earth and for time, but for heaven and eternity. *(Pope Pius XI)*

The family may be regarded as the cradle of civil society, and it is in great measure within the circle of family life that the destiny of states is fostered. *(Pope Leo XIII)*

Proverbs

None but a mule denies his family. *(Moroccan proverb)*

Pity the home where everyone is the head. *(Jewish proverb)*

There are no praises and no blessings for those who are ashamed of their families. *(Jewish proverb)*

Nobody's family can hang out the sign 'Nothing the matter here.' *(Chinese proverb)*

Humour

The one thing children wear out faster than shoes is parents. *(John Plomp)*

As I understand it, heredity is what a man believes in until his son begins to act like a delinquent. *(Presbyterian Life)*

Children are very adept at comprehending modern statistics. When they say, 'Everyone else is allowed to,' it is usually based on a survey of one. *(Paul Sweeney)*

Two boys were walking home from Sunday School. They had had a lesson that morning on the devil.

'What do you think of this devil business?' one boy asked the other.

'Well,' the other boy replied, 'you know how Santa Claus turned out—it is either your mother or your dad.' *(Anon)*

Little Alice was allowed to sit on her mother's place at the dinner table one evening when her mother was absent. Her slightly older brother, resenting the arrangement, sneered, 'So you're the mother tonight. All right, how much is two times seven?'

Without a moment's hesitation, Alice replied nonchalantly, 'I'm busy. Ask your father.' *(Anon)*

Statements

The family has received from God its mission to be the first and vital cell of society. It will fulfil this mission if it shows itself to be the domestic sanctuary of the Church through the mutual affection of its members and the common prayer they offer to God, if the whole family is caught up in the liturgical worship of the Church and if it provides active hospitality and promotes justice and other good works for the service of all the brethren in need. *(Second Vatican Council—'The Laity')*

Thus the Christian family, which springs from marriage as a reflection of the loving covenant uniting Christ with the Church, and as a participation in that covenant, will manifest to all men the Saviour's living presence in the world and the genuine nature of the Church. *(Second Vatican Council—'The Church Today')*

Word-Pictures

Most people have forgotten nowadays what a home can mean, though some of us have come to realise it as never before. It is a kingdom of its own in the midst of the world, a haven of refuge amid the turmoil of our age, nay more, a sanctuary. It is not founded on the shifting sands of private and public life, but has its peace in God. For it is God who gave it its special meaning and dignity, its nature and privilege, its destiny and worth. It is an ordinance God has established in the world, the place where peace, quietness, joy, love, purity, continence, respect, obedience, tradition, and, to crown them all, happiness may dwell, whatever else may pass away in the world. *(Dietrich Bonhoeffer)*

'Stinkers of the Season'
An article by Marj Proops in The Daily Mirror
There's the mother who nominates her husband as a Christmas stinker. She says: 'Our daughter got a part in the school play, and was very excited when she brought home an invitation for us to go and see it. Her father, though, has turned it down. He says his darts match is more important!'

Every Christmas brings its stinkers and I know in advance who'll head the list . . .

Dad, the stinker, who goes to the pub Christmas morning and comes home plastered at 3 p.m. to the dried up dinner, the angry wife and the hungry, fractious kids.

Dad, again, who got so tight at the Christmas office party that he left the turkey on the train.

There will be the mother-in-law who blighted the family party by criticising her daughter-in-law's cooking, making the children sick by giving them too many sweets, stirring up a fight or two, snoring through the Queen's speech and putting the boot in for the teenagers by insisting on staying around for the party.

There will be the daughter who wouldn't help mum and sat around all afternoon with her boyfriend on the sofa. There will be the son who spent all his money on his motor-bike and his girlfriend and borrowed 50p from his father to buy two handkerchiefs for his mother.

There will be the martyred wife nominated by her husband a stinker because she worked her fingers to the bone and never stopped pointing out how hard she worked and refused every offer of help.

See also: A9 Relationships
B30 Married Love
C5 Marriage

MARY, MOTHER OF GOD

'The shepherds found Mary and Joseph, and the baby lying in the manger.' *Luke 2:16*

Quotations

The dignity of virginity began with the Mother of the Lord. *(St. Augustine of Hippo)*

Though she was the Mother of the Lord, yet she desired to learn the precepts of the Lord, and she who brought forth God, yet desired to know God. *(St. Ambrose)*

They all were looking for a king
To slay their foes and lift them high;
Thou cam'st, a little baby thing
That made a woman cry. *(George MacDonald)*

Upon these two titles, Mary Mother of God, and Mary the Mother of mankind, the whole practice of the Catholic's devotion to the Blessed Virgin Mary is built. *(Archbishop Goodier)*

I fully grant that devotion towards the blessed Virgin has increased among Catholics with the progress of centuries; I do not allow that the doctrine concerning her has undergone a growth, for I believe that it has been in substance one and the same from the beginning. *(Cardinal Newman)*

If anyone believes that holy Mary is not the mother of God *(theotokos),* he has no share in the divine inheritance. If anyone says that Christ passed through the virgin as through a tube but was not formed in her in both a divine and human manner, divine without the assistance of man, human in accordance with the law of pregnancies, he likewise is ungodly. *(St. Gregory of Nazianzen)*

The Church cannot insist too much on the true position of Mary, for it is a strong hedge round the doctrine of the Incarnation. Every grace of Mary's, every prerogative, every dignity she has, is hers simply because she is the Mother of Christ; and it is wholly for His sake that we honour her, nor do we give her any honour which does not in consequence redound to Him of necessity. *(Abbot Chapman)*

In Marian piety, the role of the Trinity and of Christ should clearly be seen as essential and intrinsic. And this because Christian worship is essentially worship of the Father, the Son and the Holy Spirit, or as the liturgy says, worship of the Father through the Son in the Holy Spirit. In the case of Mary, everything is related to Christ and everything depends on him. It was because of the part she was to play in the life of Christ that the Father chose her from all eternity as the mother full of grace and adorned her with gifts of the Spirit granted to no other. *(Pope Paul VI)*

Proverb

God could not be everywhere, so He made mothers. *(Jewish proverb)*

Statements

If anyone does not confess that Emmanuel is true God, and that therefore the holy Virgin is Mother of God *(Dei genetricem-Theotokon)*, since she bore, after the flesh, the incarnate Word of God, let him be anathema. *(Council of Alexandria)*

At the message of the angel, the Virgin Mary received the Word of God in her heart and in her body, and gave Life to the world. Hence she is acknowledged and honoured as being truly the Mother of God and Mother of the Redeemer. Redeemed in an especially sublime manner by reason of the merits of Her Son, and united to Him by a close and indissoluble tie, she is endowed with the supreme office and dignity of being the Mother of the Son of God. *(Second Vatican Council—'The Church')*

Word-pictures

In Michelangelo's masterpiece of sculpture, the Pietà, the Mother seems far too young to be the Mother of the dead Son. Someone said this to Michelangelo, and he replied, 'You don't know anything. Chaste women retain their fresh looks longer than those who are not chaste. The Madonna was without sin, without even the least unchaste desire, and so she was always young.'

The great importunity of Sir Walter Raleigh, court favourite during part of the reign of good Queen Bess, wearied Queen Elizabeth. One day, when he came to ask a fresh favour from her, she turned and said, 'Raleigh, when will you cease to be a beggar?' Immediately came Raleigh's reply, 'When your Majesty ceases to be a benefactress and to grant me favours.' *(Anon)*

Behold, how completely Mary traces all to God, lays claim to no works, no honour, no fame. She seeks not any glory, but goes about her wonted household duties, milking the cows, cooking the meals, washing pots and kettles, sweeping out the rooms, and performing the work of maidservant or housemother in lowly and despised tasks, as though she cared naught for such exceeding great gifts and graces. She was esteemed among other women and her neighbours no more highly than before, nor desired to be, but remained a poor townswoman, one of the great multitude. When men accord us praise and honour . . . we ought neither to reject this praise and honour as though they were wrong, nor to despise them as though they were not; but . . . ascribe them to Him in heaven to whom they belong. *(Martin Luther)*

See also: A4 Mary's Child-Emmanuel
A40 Equality of Women
C7 The Humanity of Christ
C45 The Divinity of Christ

THE COSMIC CHRIST

'In the beginning was the Word, the Word was with God, and the Word was God. He was with God in the beginning.' *John 1:1*

Quotations

Jesus Christ is the centre of all, and the goal to which all tends. *(Blaise Pascal)*

The beauty of the world is Christ's tender smile for us coming through matter. *(Simone Weil)*

God is not a cosmic bell-boy for whom we can press a button to get things. *(Harry Emerson Fosdick)*

Only religion, only revelation, can explain things. Only God, Who made the cosmos, can say what He made it for, what end it is to serve. *(Abbot Chapman)*

The story of the universe is another Person's, and we are part of the story, it's characterisation, not its author. *(M. C. D'Arcy)*

With all the multiplicity of knowledge, there is one thing happily that no man knows: whether the world is old or young. *(G. K. Chesterton)*

As the print of the seal on the wax is the express image of the seal itself, so Christ is the express image—the perfect representation—of God. *(St. Ambrose)*

When Christ appears in the clouds, he will simply be manifesting a metamorphosis that has been slowly accomplished under his influence in the heart of the mass of mankind. *(Pierre Teilhard De Chardin)*

For it has been clearly demonstrated that the Word which exists from the beginning with God, by whom all things were made, who was also present with the race of men at all times, this Word has in these last times, according to the time appointed by the Father, been united to his own workmanship and has been made passible man. *(St. Irenaeus)*

Statement

For God's Word, by whom all things were made, was Himself made flesh so that as perfect man He might save all men and sum up all things in Himself. The Lord is the goal of human history, the focal point of the longings of history and of civilisation, the centre of the human race, the joy of every heart, and the answer to all its yearnings. *(Second Vatican Council—'The Church Today)*

See also: A4 Mary's Child—Emmanuel
A37 Christ the King
B4 Christ the Covenant of God
C45 The Divinity of Christ

REVELATION

'It was by a revelation that I was given the knowledge of the mystery.'
Ephesians 3:3

Quotations

How wonderful it is that nobody need wait a single moment before beginning to improve the world. *(Anne Frank, just before being taken off to her death in 1944)*

As prayer is the voice of man to God, so revelation is the voice of God to man. *(Cardinal Newman)*

Human salvation demands the divine disclosure of truths surpassing reason. *(St. Thomas Aquinas)*

Truths above reason can be believed on authority alone; where that is lacking, we have to take hints from the workings of nature. *(St. Thomas Aquinas)*

Every revelation of truth felt with interior savour and spiritual joy is a secret whispering of God in the ear of a pure soul *(Walter Hilton)*

He who shall introduce into public affairs the principles of primitive Christianity will revolutionise the world. *(Benjamin Franklin)*

The Lord Jesus Christ loves to reveal Himself to those who dare to take the bleak side of the hill with Him. *(Anon)*

A revelation is religious doctrine viewed on its illuminated side; a mystery is the self-same doctrine viewed on the side unilluminated. *(Cardinal Newman)*

A Christian cannot live by philosophy. Only the light of Christian revelation gives the end as well as the means of life. It is the same for you as for me and the man in the street. If one has more learning, another has more grace, it is all one. *(Abbot Chapman)*

We do not believe that God has added, or ever will add, anything to His revelation in His Son. But we can now see many things in that revelation which could not be seen by those who first received it. Each generation of Christians, and each people to which the Christian Gospel is preached, makes its own contribution to the understanding of the riches of Jesus Christ. *(C. B. Moss)*

Statement

Then, after speaking in many places and varied ways through the prophets, God 'last of all in these days has spoken to us by His son' *(Heb. 1:1–2).* For He sent His Son, the eternal Word, who enlightens all men, so that He might dwell among men and tell them the innermost realities about God *(cf. Jn. 1:1–12).* Jesus Christ, therefore, the Word made flesh, sent as 'a man to men' speaks the words of God *(Jn. 3:34),* and completes the work of salvation which His Father gave Him to do *(cf Jn. 5:36, 17:4).* To see Jesus is to see His Father *(Jn. 14:9).* For this reason, Jesus perfected revelation by fulfilling it through His whole work of making Himself present and manifesting Himself: through His words and deeds, His signs and wonders, but especially through His death and glorious resurrection from the dead and final sending of the Spirit of Truth. *(Second Vatican Council—'Revelation')*

Word-Pictures

Jesus said: 'You test the face of the sky and of the earth: but Him who is before your face you have not known, and you do not know how to test this moment.' *(The Gospel according to Thomas)*

By the prices of the 70's, the financial cost, it was revealed, of the gifts of the 12 days of Christmas ('a partridge in a pear tree . . .') would be something like £28,400. *(Heard on BBC Radio 4)*

We must be saved together or we will not be saved at all. That would seem to be the deepest truth about the atonement, a profoundly mysterious truth, not wholly congenial to our mutual self-centredness, but lying as it were somewhere near the base of the whole structure of divine revelation. The Bible is a book about Man and not about individual men, except insofar as they show us Man in his infinite need and Man as the object of God's infinite grace. *(Max Warren)*

See also: A12 Holy Scripture
B2 The Good News
B24 Go tell everyone
C8 God's messengers
C38 Discerning God's Will

BAPTISM

'He will baptise you with the Holy Spirit.' *(Mark 1:8)*

Quotations

In baptism, Christ's passion works a regeneration; a person dies entirely to the old life and takes on the new. Therefore baptism washes away the whole guilt of punishment belonging to the past. *(St. Thomas Aquinas)*

Our adoptive sonship is in its supernatural reality a reflection of the sonship of the Word. God has not communicated to us the whole of his nature but a participation of it. *(R. Garrigou-Lagrange)*

Baptise as follows: After first explaining all these points, baptise in the name of the Father and of the Son and of the Holy Spirit, in running water. But if you have no running water, baptise in other water; and if you cannot in cold, then in warm. But if you have neither, pour water on the head three times in the name of the Father and of the Son and of the Holy Spirit. *(Teaching of the Twelve Apostles)*

Christians are made, not born. *(St. Jerome)*

Happy is our sacrament of water, in that by washing away the sins of our early blindness, we are set free and admitted into eternal life. . . But we, little fishes, after the example of our ICHTHYS (*Jesous Christos Theou Uios Soter:* Jesus Christ Son of God Saviour) are born in water, nor have we safety in any other way than by permanently abiding in water. *(Tertullian) (The Greek word for fish is* ichthys*)*

You have been baptised, but think not that you are straightway a Christian. . . The flesh is touched with salt: what then if the mind remains unsalted? The body is anointed, yet the mind remains unanointed. But if you are buried with Christ within, and already practise walking with Him in newness of life, I acknowledge you as a Christian. *(Erasmus)*

Humour

When a negro was asked whether he believed in baptism, he replied, 'Sure I believe in it, boss, I've seen it done.' *(Anon)*

A Presbyterian and a Baptist minister were discussing baptism. After a beautiful dissertation on the subject by the Baptist minister, the

Presbyterian minister asked if the Baptist considered a person baptised if he were immersed in water up to his chin. 'No,' said the Baptist.

'Is he considered baptised if he is immersed up to his nose?' asked the Presbyterian.

Again the Baptist's answer was, 'No.'

'Well, if you immerse him up to his eyebrows, do you consider him baptised?' queried the Presbyterian.

'You don't seem to understand,' said the Baptist. 'He must be immersed completely in water—until his head is covered.'

'That's what I've been trying to tell you all along,' said the Presbyterian, 'it's only a little water on the top of the head that counts.' *(Anon)*

Statement

By the sacrament of baptism, whenever it is properly conferred in the way the Lord determined, and received with the appropriate dispositions of soul, a man becomes truly incorporated into the crucified and glorified Christ and is reborn to a sharing of the divine life, as the apostle says: 'For you were buried together with Him in Baptism, and in Him also rose again through faith in the working of God who raised Him from the dead.' *(Col. 2:12; cf. Rom. 6:4)*

Baptism, therefore, constitutes a sacramental bond of unity linking all who have been reborn by means of it. But baptism, of itself, is only a beginning, a point of departure, for it is wholly directed toward the acquiring of fullness of life in Christ. Baptism is thus oriented toward a complete profession of faith, a complete incorporation into the system of salvation such as Christ Himself willed it to be, and finally, toward a complete participation in Eucharistic communion. *(Second Vatican Council—'Ecumenism')*

Word Pictures

Earth retains all the water ever created—an estimated 326 million cubic miles of it. Water responds to a variety of powerful forces—the heat of the sun, the pull of earth's gravity and the tidal forces of the sun and moon. The result is a natural cycle in which water has been used, purified and re-used for 3,000 million years. *(Anon)*

On the Moscow radio, March 1963, Christian baptism was castigated as a 'health menace' and 'a senseless and dangerous rite.' In the weekly pro-atheist broadcast, the communist commentator said that 'thousands' of babies died of pneumonia following christening ceremonies and that 'weak hearts' and 'weak lungs' in adults had been traced to baptism in their early years.

In an all-out attack upon religious practices, the broadcast had as its theme 'religion's threat to health.' Life expectancy in the time of the Czars, it said, was only 32 years because religion was widespread and baptism was administered to almost all Russians.

It added that during the communist regime, life expectancy has risen to 69 years, largely because of government health services and the fact that fewer baptisms take place. *(Anon)*

When the Roman youth reached manhood, he put on the Toga Virilis, the robe of manhood. The day was one of special ceremonial, a great day for him.

When the Hindu youths of certain castes reached manhood, they put on the Yagnopavitam or sacred cord. The day is one of special ceremonial, a great day for the youth who is invested with the sacred cord.

So the believer at his baptism acknowledges that he has 'put on Christ'—a new robe of righteousness to display to the world, a new cord of holiness that links him with the holiness of his God, a 'Holy Father'. *(Anon)*

St. Louis of France used to sign his documents not, 'Louis IX, King' but 'Louis of Poissy.' Someone asked him why, and he answered: 'Poissy is the place where I was baptised. I think more of the place where I was baptised than of Rheims Cathedral where I was crowned. It is a greater thing to be a child of God than to be the ruler of a Kingdom: this last I shall lose at death, but the other will be my passport to an everlasting glory.' *(Anon)*

St. Ambrose, in a disquisition on baptism, makes a big point that the newly baptised is about to be received in the very best society. With baptism, one becomes a member of the communion of saints, one of the richest Catholic doctrines, but one which I feel is being increasingly neglected today. This is not at all the mind of the Church, and word 'holidays' serve as a constant reminder how important the Church always thought it to keep in remembrance, for encouragement and edification, the lives of heroic sanctity, and impressive as the company was of which St. Ambrose was thinking in the 4th century, it is vastly more numerous now, with striking additions every generation. *(Douglas Woodruff)*

See also: A38 Original Sin
B36 The Family of God
C26 The Human Condition
C49 Confirmation
C47 The Indwelling Spirit

VOCATION

'Speak, Lord, your servant is listening.' *1 Samuel 3:10*

Quotations

The vocation of every man and woman is to serve other people. *(Leo Tolstoy)*

The test of a vocation is the love of the drudgery it involves. *(Logan Pearsall Smith)*

Blessed is he who has found his work; let him ask no other blessedness. *(Thomas Carlyle)*

We must not forget that our vocation is so to practise virtue that men are won to it; it is possible to be morally upright repulsively. *(William Temple)*

Do not despise your situation. In it you must act, suffer and conquer. From every point on earth, we are equally near to heaven and the infinite. *(Henri F. Amiel)*

A good vocation is simply a firm and constant will in which the called person has to serve God in the way and in the places to which Almighty God has called him. *(St. Francis de Sales)*

If a person shows a firm and persevering determination to serve God in the manner and place to which His divine majesty calls her, she gives the best proof she can that she has a true vocation. *(St. Francis de Sales)*

It seems to me that it is the right thing for a director to discourage people who think they have a vocation. If it is real, it will vanquish all obstacles, and will stand out, not as a mere invitation, but as a categorical imperative. *(Abbot Chapman)*

Humour

This story comes from Rome, but I expect the rest of the world has its variants. Two American Catholic young men encountered a little nun seated alone just outside a bar. Conversation began, and ended thus:

'Well Sister, we're just going along to the bar for a drink. Can we bring you out anything? A coca-cola or something?'

'Well, that's very kind of you. What are you going to drink? I don't care much for coca-cola.'

'We're having a dry Martini.'

'Well, so will I. But bring it to me in a cup and saucer, not a glass.'

Boys to waiter 'Three large dry Martinis. Put one in a tea-cup please.'

Waiter 'Gee, is that little nun STILL sittin' there?' *(Douglas Woodruff)*

This is the season when American nuns peregrinate and arrive at the London Hotels. Of two of them I am told this tale, that, sitting in the restaurant-car opposite two young men, the youths thought they would try to shock them. Said one, 'I am going home for my parents' wedding, they think it's about time.' Said the other, 'Mine thought of getting married but they've turned it down for the expense.' Said one of the nuns, 'Would one of you two bastards mind passing the mustard?' *(Douglas Woodruff)*

Statement

Yet a man must so respond to God's call that, without consulting flesh and blood (*cf. Gal. 1:16)*, he can devote himself wholly to the work of the Gospel. This response, however, can be made only when the Holy Spirit gives His inspiration and strength. For he who is sent enters upon the life and mission of Him who 'emptied himself, taking the nature of a slave' *(Phil. 2:7)*. Therefore, he must be ready to stand by his vocation for a lifetime, and to renounce himself and all those whom he thus far considered as his own, and instead to become 'all things to all men' *(1 Cor. 9:22)*. *(Second Vatican Council—'Missions')*

Word-pictures

When Christ calls a man, He bids him come and die. It may be a death like that of the first disciples who had to leave home and work to follow Him, or it may be a death like Luther's, who had to leave the monastery and go out into the world. But it is the same death every time—death in Jesus Christ, the death of the old man at His call. That is why the rich young man was so loath to follow Jesus, for the cost of following was the death of his will. In fact every command of Jesus is a call to die, with all our affections and lusts. But we do not want to die, and therefore Jesus Christ and His call are necessarily our death and our life. *(Dietrich Bonhoeffer, The Cost of Discipleship)*

Seven young nuns of the Franciscan Missionaries of Mary, none older than 36, martyred in China in 1900, were beatified by Pius XII in 1946.

This order first sent its Sisters to China in 1886, and in 1899,

Mother M. Hermine, aged 33, was sent with a party to start a new orphanage at Taiyuanfu in Shansi province. They quickly won the love of the children and the respect of the townsfolk. But the 'Boxer' society against foreigners was already working havoc in the neighbouring province, and by June 1900, the population of Shansi also were being stirred up to 'destroy the devils from the West and slay all Christians'. The storm came near to Taiyuanfu. Bishop Grassi advised the nuns to flee while there was time, but Mother Hermine said she and her Sisters must remain with the orphans. She begged the Bishop 'not to deprive them of the palm of martyrdom which God in his mercy was reaching down to them from heaven'.

On 28th June, they started out with their orphans to reach a safer place, but at the gates of the town they were turned back. There was nothing to do but wait for the arrival of the Boxer troops. Two Bishops and three other Franciscans waited also. The Sisters remained quiet and calm. Soldiers came and took away the orphans by force. Then on 9th July, the Boxers, led by the Governor Yu-Hsien, broke into the building. Bishop Grassi at once pronounced the final absolution. Yu-Hsien gave orders for the Catholics to be bound, and bundled them roughly out into the yard, where, without even the pretence of a trial, the butchery began. First of all, the nuns had to witnesss the brutal murder of the Bishops and friars, then came their own turn. With the words of the *Te Deum* on their lips, the sisters knelt and raised their veils, baring their necks to receive the blow from the sword which cut off their heads. One after another, these holy women gladly laid down their lives for Christ. *(M. R. Walsh)*

I asked God for strength that I might achieve;
I was made weak that I might learn humbly to obey.

I asked for help that I might do greater things;
I was given infirmity that I might do better things.

I asked for riches that I might be happy;
I was given poverty that I might be wise.

I asked for all things that I might enjoy life;
I was given life that I might enjoy all things.

I was given nothing that I asked for;
But everything that I had hoped for.

Despite myself, my prayers were answered;
I am among all men most richly blessed. *(Anon)*

See also: A10 Seeking Perfection
A22 Seeking God
C16 Come follow me
C38 Discerning God's Will

ON A MISSION

'The time has come,' Jesus said, 'and the kingdom of God is close at hand. Repent, and believe the Good News.' *Mark 1:15*

Quotations

The Church exists by mission, as fire exists by burning. *(Emil Brunner)*

The world has many religions; it has but one Gospel. *(George Owen)*

The fact of the missions reveals the Church's faith in herself as the Catholic unity of mankind. *(J. C. Murray)*

The reason some folks don't believe in mission is the brand of religion they have isn't worth propagating. *(Anon)*

If God calls you to be missionary, don't stoop to be a king. *(Jordan Grooms)*

Your love has a broken wing if it cannot fly across the sea. *(Maltbie D. Babcock)*

If people ask 'Why did he not appear by means of other parts of creation, and use some nobler instrument, as the sun or moon or stars or fire or air, instead of man merely?', let them know that the Lord came not to to make a display, but to teach and heal those who were suffering. *(Athanasius of Alexandria)*

To practical people like Americans there is no oral or written evidence of the true religion so valid as the spectacle of its power to change bad men into good ones. Such a people will not accept arguments from history and from Scripture, but those of a moral kind they demand; they must see the theories at work. A mission is a microcosm of the Church as a moral force. *W. Elliott)*

Humour

Missionaries, my dear! Don't you realise that missionaries are the divinely provided food for destitute and underfed cannibals? Whenever they are on the brink of starvation, Heaven in its infinite mercy sends them a nice plump missionary. *(Oscar Wilde)*

Statements

The members of the Church are impelled to carry on such missionary activity by reason of the love with which they love God and by which they desire to share with all men in the spiritual goods of both this life and the life to come. *(Second Vatican Council—'Missions')*

Missionary activity is nothing else and nothing less than a manifestation or epiphany of God's will and the fulfilment of that will in the world and in world history. *(Second Vatican Council—'Missions')*

Word-Pictures

One cannot be Christian in name alone. It is not enough to say that one possesses the faith in one's own individual conscience. The faith is both a communal and outgoing thing. Consequently, it carries with it the obligation of involving oneself with it and of spreading it. You yourselves must be apostles of the faith, and grow in love for the Church. You must foster within yourselves a deep missionary spirit, showing interest and zeal not only for the missionary countries but also for all those people you meet in the contacts of daily life. *(Pope Paul VI)*

Fr. Nussbaum was martyred in Tibet in 1941. He was a tough little blue-eyed Alsatian, 50-years-old, with a blond beard; always gentle and good humoured, he lived in Tibetan-fashion at a post in Chinese Tibet. After years of efforts, he got some Swiss priests from the St. Bernard Pass to start a mountain hospice at the Latsa Pass (1935). Leaving his mission to the Swiss, Fr. Nassbaum moved on into Tibet proper (a forbidden land) to start a mission again at Yerkalo. (Over the years many priests had tried to set up a mission there but all had died martyrs deaths.)

Fr. Nussbaum duly established himself in the village of Yerkalo, with one of the Swiss priests, and in three years, they had baptised 350 Tibetans. They then earned the enmity of the chief Lama of the nearby monastery of Karmda. He sent messages to the Dalai Lama demanding expulsion of all Western priests, but got no reply. Meanwhile the Second World War broke out, and the Lama of Karmda took counsel with a local bandit-leader.

In September 1941, Fr. Nussbaum went to Mission headquarters at Tse-chung for a retreat. Returning to Yerkalo, with his bearer and three Tibetan girl-catechists whom he had recruited, he was warned of an ambush and camped in the village of Napu, where no house would give them shelter.

During the night, bandits attacked, but were bought off with some money and blankets and all the caravan's tea. Next day, they moved on to the mission-house at Pamé. There another night attack took place and the priest and his party were all bound while they watched the looting of the mission. Then they were dragged along a rocky path (Fr. Nussbaum with bare and bleeding feet) and at the edge of a ravine the priest was shot in the back. The other prisoners were then allowed to go. A group of Christians from Pamé came and recovered the body. *(Henri Daniel-Rops)*

Azariah was tall and very dark, quick in movement and speech, with the knack of stirring up enthusiasm by his swift passionate words. A phrase that was constantly on his lips was 'Every Christian a witness'. It was absolutely necessary, he said, that every convert should at once bear witness. He drove this home at Madras in his own vivid way. 'It was,' he said, 'by the witness of the common man that the Gospel spread in the early church, from slave to slave, from soldier to soldier, from artisan to artisan: and as I have gone around among the churches, I have had the baptised members place their hands on their heads and repeat after me, "I am a baptised Christian. Woe is me if I preach not the Gospel".' *(A. M. Chirgwin—'These I have Known')*

See also: B2 The Good News
B24 Go tell everyone
C12 The Church for all men
C16 Come follow me

AUTHORITY

'Here is a teaching that is new,' they said, 'and with authority behind it.'
(Mark 1:27)

Quotations

People who are masters in their own house are never tyrants. *(Napoleon)*

The man who cannot control himself becomes absurd when he wants to rule over others. *(Isaac Arama)*

It is right to submit to higher authority whenever a command of God would not be violated. *(St. Basil)*

The highest duty is to respect authority, and obediently to submit to just law. *(Pope Leo XIII)*

To despise legitimate authority, no matter in whom it is invested, is unlawful; it is a rebellion against God's will. *(Pope Leo XIII)*

There are three theories of power and therefore of authority, to wit: the robber theory that all power is for mastery; the hireling theory that all power is for wealth; the good shepherd theory that all power is for service. *(Vincent McNabb)*

No authority has power to impose error, and if it resists the truth, the truth must be upheld until it is admitted. *(Lord Acton)*

Authority is not a short way to the truth; it is the only way to many truths; and for men on earth, it is the only way to divine truths. *(Vincent McNabb)*

Next to power without honour, the most dangerous thing in the world is power without humour. *(Eric Sevareid)*

Statements

Now, if the political community is not to be torn to pieces as each man follows his own viewpoint, authority is needed. This authority must dispose the energies of the whole citizenry toward the common good, not mechanically or despotically, but primarily as a moral force which depends on freedom and the conscientious discharge of the burdens of any office which has been undertaken. *(Second Vatican Council—'The Church Today')*

Therefore, this Vatican Synod urges everyone, especially those who are charged with the task of educating others, to do their utmost to form men who will respect the moral order and be obedient to lawful authority. Let them form men who will be lovers of true freedom—men, in other words, who will come to decisions on their own judgement and in the light of truth, govern their activities with a sense of responsibility, and strive after what is true and right, willing always to join with others in co-operative effort.*(Second Vatican Council—'Religous Freedom')*

Word-Pictures

One of the most solemn facts in all history—one of the most significant for anybody who cares to ponder over it—is the fact that Jesus Christ was not merely murdered by hooligans in a country road; he was condemned by everything that was most respectable in that day, everything that pretended to be most righteous—the religious leaders of the time, the authority of the Roman Government, and even the democracy itself which shouted to save Barabbas rather than Christ. *(Herbert Butterfield 'History and Human Relations')*

A Government surveyor one day brought his theodolite along to a farm, called on the farmer and asked permission to set it up in a field nearby to take readings. Seeing the farmer's unwillingness to let him enter the field, he produced his papers and explained that he had Government authority for entering the field and could, on the same authority, go anywhere in the country to take necessary readings. Reluctantly the farmer opened the barred gate and allowed him to enter and set up his survey table, but went to the other end of the field and let in the fiercest of his bulls. The surveyor was greatly alarmed at seeing the bull approach, and the farmer from the other side of the gate shouted to him, 'Show him you credentials: show him your authority.' The surveyor had the authority to enter but had not the power to resist the bull. *(Anon)*

See also: A14 Successors of the Apostles
A24 Papacy
A29 True Obedience
A32 Civic Duty
B14 Freedom to serve

FREEDOM TO SERVE

'I made myself all things to all men in order to save some at any cost'
1 Corinthians 9:22

Quotations

Freedom is participation in power. *(Marcus Tullius Cicero)*

For what is liberty but the umhampered translation of will into act? *(Dante)*

Freedom is that faculty which enlarges the usefulness of all other faculties. *(Immanuel Kant)*

Freedom is not worth having if it does not include the freedom to make mistakes. *(Gandhi)*

There are two freedoms—the false, where a man is free to do what he likes; the true, where a man is free to do what he ought. *(Charles Kingsley)*

Liberty of spirit is a detachment of the Christian heart from all things to follow the known will of God. *(St. Francis de Sales)*

No freedom is so great as that of the children of God who are fast bound by the perfect law of love and liberty. *(R. H. Benson)*

A Christian man is the most free lord of all, and subject to none; a Christian man is the most dutiful servant of all, and subject to everyone. *(Martin Luther)*

He who does not enjoy solitude will not love freedom. *(Arthur Schopenhauer)*

True liberty is liberty to do what we ought to do. It is not liberty to do as we like. *(Field-Marshal Lord Montgomery)*

God forces no one, for love cannot compel, and God's service, therefore, is a thing of perfect freedom. *(Hans Denk)*

Proverbs

Better to be a free bird than a captive king. *(Danish proverb)*

No bad man is free. *(Greek proverb)*

No man is free who is not master of himself. *(Greek proverb)*

Humour

It is by the goodness on God that in our country we have those three unspeakably precious things: freedom of speech, freedom of conscience and the prudence never to practise either of them. *(Mark Twain)*

We are not free; it was not intended we should be. A book of rules is placed in our cradle and we never get rid of it until we reach our graves. Then we are free and only then. *(E. W. Howe)*

Statement

For its part, authentic freedom is an exceptional sign of the divine image within man. For God has willed that man be left 'in the hand of his own counsel' so that he can seek his Creator spontaneously, and come freely to utter and blissful perfection through loyalty to Him. Hence man's dignity demands that he act according to a knowing and free choice. Such a choice is personally motivated and prompted from within. It does not result from blind internal impulse nor from mere external pressure. *(Second Vatican Council—'The Church Today')*

Word-Pictures

When Jean Jacques Rousseau was hunted and hounded from one place to another on account of his opinions, Voltaire heard of it and although Voltaire did not share Rousseau's views, he invited him to come and live in his home. And when Rousseau finally arrived, Voltaire embraced him and said, 'I do not agree with a word you say, but I will fight to the death for your right to say it.' *(Anon)*

Incredible as it is, 2,370 years after Socrates drank hemlock, 1,970 years after the crucifixion of Christ, 435 years after Thomas More was beheaded and 370 years after Giordano Bruno was burnt at the stake, thousands of men and women waste away their days in prison for their opinions. But opinions should be free, and if he is behind bars it is not he but those who keep him there that are dishonoured. *(Salvador de Madariaga)*

In a daring maneouvre, ships of three nations combined to save a refugee family from Communist pursuers in busy shipping lanes in the Baltic Sea.

An East German police boat was bearing down with its machine guns on the little kayak whose tiny outboard motor had failed. Ignoring the danger of collision, a Danish ferry captain swung his vessel sharply, putting it between pursuers and pursued.

The police boat began to swing around the Danish boat but then a Swedish ferry speedily moved in to block it again as passengers on both ships cheered. Finally a West German freighter reached the terrified refugees, lowered a ladder and hauled them aboard.

The yearning for freedom, whether it is political, social, intellectual, economic, racial or religious, is imbedded so deeply in every man that he will often risk life itself to achieve it. *(Anon)*

See also: B34 Human Rights
B45 Free Will
C1 Liberation from fear

JESUS, FRIEND OF OUTCASTS

A leper came to Jesus and pleaded on his knees; 'If you want to' he said, 'you can cure me.' *Mark 1:40*

Quotations

God says to man 'With thy very wounds I will heal thee' *(The Talmud)*

If Jesus had been indicted in a modern court, he would have been examined by two doctors, found to be obsessed by a delusion, declared to be incapable of pleading, and sent to an asylum. . . *(George Bernard Shaw)*

Proverbs

A poor man is hungry after eating. *(Portuguese proverb)*

Not he who has little, but he who wishes for more, is poor. *(Latin proverb)*

Many can bear adversity, but few contempt. *(English proverb)*

Statement

The greatest commandment in the law is to love God with one's whole heart and one's neighbour as oneself *(cf. Mt.22:37–40)*. Christ made this commandment of love of neighbour His own and enriched it with a new meaning. For He wanted to identify Himself with His brethren as the object of this love when He said, 'As long as you did it for one of these, the least of my brethren, you did it for me' *(Mt. 25:40)*. *(Second Vatican Council—'The Laity')*

Word-Pictures

Chad Varah was an Anglican priest. In 1953, he buried a girl of 18 who had killed herself. The coroner, at her inquest, suggested that she might not have done this desperate act if someone had been around who would have listened to her troubles. Chad Varah decided to use his London church and a telephone to listen to people who were in despair. He put a small advertisement in the local paper, and during the first week he had 27 calls.

Soon he was listening and advising people 12 hours each day. There were so many people waiting in his outer office to see him that he asked some of his congregation to come and provide cups of tea for them. Then he found that often people who had come into the outer office in great distress had become different people by the time they reached him, and some did not even wait to see him because one of the helpers had befriended them. So he decided to train a group of his congregation so that they could be more helpful in the way they befriended the clients.

That is how the Samaritans were formed. *(Patricia Curley)*

Two or three years ago, I was fortunate enough to take part, on Christmas Eve, in a 'soup-run' to the down-and-outs of Central London. This was a very simple but a very worthwhile operation. It consisted in taking rather stale bread, cut up into thick wedges, and a couple of tureens of soup, to four points in Central London where down-and-outs would gather. There were six of us engaged in this work on this particular night; some were full-time while two, including myself, were having our first experience.

I was staggered to find that when we arrived at the Waterloo arches, under the station, at about 1 a.m. there were already about 50 down-and-outs waiting patiently for our soup. I was equally surprised when we drew up along the embankment beside Charing Cross, 45 minutes later, to find a similar number. We called later at two other places, both near Covent Garden, where the numbers were smaller but the sight equally depressing. There were women as well as men, young as well as old. Some wanted to talk, some shuffled off in silence. Over all hung a great air of sadness. We finished our work on Christmas morning about 5.15 a.m. I had been surprised by many small happenings during the course of that night, but above all else remarkably impressed by the kindness, consideration and love shown by the young people who had given up their night to do this work. *(A. P. Castle)*

They borrowed a bed to lay His head
  When Christ the Lord came down;
They borrowed an ass in the mountain pass
  For Him to ride to town;
But the crown He wore and the cross He bore
  Were His own -
  The cross was His own *(Anon)*

See also: A21 Feeding the hungry
A33 Love your neighbour
B38 The suffering servant
C3 Sharing possessions

CHRIST FORGIVES OUR SINS

Jesus said to the paralytic, 'my child, your sins are forgiven.' *Mark 2:5*

Quotations

Nothing in this lost world bears the impress of the Son of God so surely as forgiveness. *(Alice Cary)*

From a parish newsletter inviting parishioners to a communal celebration of penance: 'If you don't have any sins, bring a friend who does.' *(Anon)*

Statement

God, who 'wishes all men to be saved and come to the knowledge of the truth' *(1 Tim.2:4)*, 'in many and various ways. . . spoke of old to our fathers by the prophets' *(Heb. 1:1)*. When the fullness of time had come He sent His Son, the Word made flesh, anointed by the Holy Spirit, to preach the gospel to the poor, to heal the contrite of heart *(cf. Is.61:1; Lk4:18)*, to be a 'bodily and spiritual medicine', the Mediator between God and man *(cf. 1 Tim. 2:5)*. *(Second Vatican Council—'Liturgy')*

Word-Pictures

The story is told by a missionary who works in Arab countries of a woman catechist who visited the tents of the nomadic tribesmen who camped near the town where she lived. On one of her visits, she came to a tent where a woman stood, engulfed in deep sorrow and anxiety. Entering, she saw lying on a mat on the floor, an Arab lad, sick, emaciated and evidently dying of tuberculosis. She asked the mother, 'May I tell him a story?' Receiving a nodded assent, she knelt down beside the lad and began to tell the story of Our Lord and His sufferings and death for sinners. She described how he was beaten, crowned with thorns, led out of the city of Jerusalem, nailed to a cross and left to die. The lad lay with closed eyes, but toward the end of her narration, he opened them and appeared to take some interest in the story. She left, to return the next day, when she told the same story, emphasising the fact that the blood of Jesus Christ was shed on the cross for the forgiveness of the lad's sins if he would only come to Jesus. This time the sick boy showed a greater interest and his face seemed to lighten up toward the end of her narration. Next day, thinking it might be well to introduce something new into her message, she began to tell of the birth of Christ and was describing the place where He was born when the sick lad raised his hand and said, 'Not that! Not that! Tell me about the cross and the blood and the forgiveness of my sins.' And again the same moving story was told.

When the lady missionary returned again some days later, she found the woman still sad and weeping bitterly: but there was no lad on the mat inside the tent. She asked the mother how he had died. The mother, when she saw he was dying, had called the Mohammedan priest who came with the Koran and began to read aloud to the dying lad. Then she described how he had feebly raised his thin hand and said 'Not that! Tell me about the cross and the blood and the forgiveness of sins.' *(Anon)*

A Christian doctor in Scotland was very lenient with his poor patients, and when he found that it was difficult for them to pay his fees he wrote in red ink across the record of their indebtedness the one word—'Forgiven'. This was of such frequent occurrence that his case book had few pages where the red letters did not appear. After his death, his executors thought the doctor's estate would be greatly benefited if some of the "Forgiven" debts could be collected. After unsuccessful applications to the poor patients, the executors took legal proceedings to recover the amounts. But when the judge examined the case book and saw the word 'Forgiven' cancelling the entry, he said, 'There is no tribunal in the land that could enforce payment of these accounts marked "Forgiven",' and he dismissed the case. *(Indian Christian)*

During October 1806, John Newton entered his pulpit to preach for the last time. The occasion was a special service to raise money for the sufferers from the battle of Trafalgar. A friend of the First Lord of the Admiralty, and an old sailor himself, he was exerting his last strength on behalf of the victims of war. But as he addressed the crowded congregation, his mind wandered away. Perhaps it was to the day when he had been taken by the Press Gang, or to the time he had himself seen action as a midshipman, or to the disgrace and agony of the flogging for desertion, or even to his voyages as a slave captain. Wherever his mind went, he clean forgot what he was doing and somebody had to go into the pulpit to remind him. He lived for another year, and a few weeks before the end, said to a friend, 'My memory is nearly gone; but I remember two things, that I am a great sinner and that Christ is a great Saviour'. He died on 21st December 1807, and his epitaph written by his own hand is 'John Newton (Clerk), Once an infidel and libertine, A servant of slaves in Africa: Was by the rich mercy of our Lord and Saviour Jesus Christ,

Preserved, restored, pardoned, And appointed to preach the faith he had long laboured to destroy.' *(Anon)*

See also: A15 Sin
A26 Sacrament of Penance
A27 As we forgive those
C22 Forgiveness
C27 The Father who receives us back
C40 Reconciliation

THE CHURCH—BRIDE OF CHRIST

'I will betroth you to myself for ever, betroth you with integrity and justice, with tenderness and love.' *Hosea 2:21*

Quotations

The Church is in Christ as Eve was in Adam. *(Richard Hooker)*

What matters in the Church is not religion but the form of Christ, and its taking form amidst a band of men. *(Dietrich Bonhoeffer)*

The Church of Christ is not an institution; it is a new life with Christ and in Christ, guided by the Holy Spirit. *(Sergius Belgakov)*

This Church, imitating His (i.e. Christ's) Mother, daily gives birth to His members, and likewise remains a virgin.
St. Augustine of Hippo)

I have laboured with all my might that holy Church, the bride of God, our mistress and our mother, should recover her honour and remain chaste, and free and Catholic. *(Pope St. Gregory VII)*

The Church, like blessed Mary ever Virgin, both espoused and immaculate, conceives us as a virgin by the Spirit, bears us as a virgin without pain, and both espoused as it were to one, but made fruitful by another, through the single parts which compose the one Catholic Church is joined visibly to the pontiff set over it, but is increased through the visible power of the Holy Spirit. *(St. Bede the Venerable)*

Statement

Having become the model of a man loving his wife as his own body, Christ loves the Church as His Bride *(cf. Eph.5:25*–28). For her part, the Church is subject to her Head *(cf. Eph.5:22*–23). 'For in him dwells all the fullness of the Godhead bodily' *(Col.2:9)*. He fills the Church, which is His Body and His fullness, with His divine gifts *(cf. Eph1:22*–23) so that she may grow and reach the fullness of God *(cf. Eph.3:19)*. *(Second Vatican Council —'The Church')*

Word-Pictures

'I cannot get used to being called a Person of God,' said the layman, 'when I was brought up to think of myself as a sheep; and I quite understand why I was a sheep for my pastors to count, because counting sheep is the best way to enable our pastors to go to sleep.' *(Douglas Woodruff)*

When I found myself singing—a courtesy term in my case—with my fellow parishioners the rousing hymn that assures us that 'The Church's one foundation is Jesus Christ Our Lord', the memory came back to me of the very different circumstances in which I had first learnt it among the Evangelicals of the Church of England. I recalled how lustily my Protestant uncles and aunts sang it, as one in the eye for the Pope, for it was written against the Roman claim 'Thou art Peter and upon this Rock I will build my Church'. The one foundation, says the hymn, is elsewhere. Still, this is not said in so many words, and there is nothing in the words which Catholics cannot sing with full conviction.

Anglicans, for their part, have never hesitated about 'Lead, Kindly Light' either, though they do not like the scene to which the 'Kindly Light' eventually led the author of the Hymn which was, when he wrote it, the very much distant scene he did not ask to see, and would have shuddered at, had he glimpsed it. *(Douglas Woodruff)*

See also: A13 The Church is for sinners
B36 The family of God
C12 The Church for all men

SUNDAY

'The Sabbath was made for man, not man for the Sabbath; so the Son of Man is master even of the Sabbath.' *Mark 2:27*

Quotations

Everything has its weekday side and its Sunday side.
(G. C. Lichtenberg)

The Sabbath is the golden clasp that binds together the volume of the week. *(Macauley)*

Going to church doesn't make you a Christian any more than going to a garage makes you an automobile. *(Billy Sunday)*

Better a man ne'er be born.
Than he trims his nails on a Sunday morn.
(Warwickshire: Traditional)

God ended all the world's array,
And rested on the seventh day:
His holy voice proclaimed it blest,
And named it for the sabbath rest. *(St. Bede the Venerable)*

The Lord's Day is so called, because on that day, the joy of our Lord's resurrection is celebrated. This day the Jews did not observe, but it was declared by the Christians in honour of the Lord's resurrection, and the celebration began from that time. *(St. Isidore)*

Sunday, indeed, is the day on which we hold our common assembly because it is the first day on which God, transforming the darkness and matter, created the world; and our Saviour, Jesus Christ, arose from the dead on the same day. For they crucified Him on the day before, that of Saturn, and on the day after, Sunday, He appeared to His apostles and disciples, and taught them the things which we have passed on to you also for consideration.
(St. Justin Martyr)

Humour

A small boy, on his way to church for the first time, was being briefed by his elder sister. 'They won't allow you to talk,' she warned him. 'Who won't?' asked the boy. 'The Hushers.' *(Sign, London)*

A child—one of the many who get taken to church these days much too young, partly with the idea of accustoming them to church as a normal part of life, but often because there is nobody to leave them with—was bored and restless, kept looking at the sanctuary lamp, and finally whispered: 'When the red light changes to green, can we go?' *(Douglas Woodruff)*

Statement

By an apostolic tradition which took its origin from the very day of Christ's resurrection, the Church celebrates the paschal mystery every eighth day; with good reason, this, then, bears the name of the Lord's day or the day of the Lord. For on this day Christ's faithful should come together into one place so that, by hearing the word of God and taking part in the Eucharist, they may call to mind the passion, the resurrection and the glorification of the Lord Jesus, and may thank God who 'has begotten us again, through the resurrection of Jesus Christ from the dead, unto a living hope' (*1 Pet. 1:3*). Hence the Lord's day is the original feast day, and it should be proposed to the piety of the faithful and taught to them in such a way that it may become in fact a day of joy and of freedom from work. Other celebrations, unless they be truly of overriding importance, must not have precedence over this day, which is the foundation and nucleus of the whole liturgical year. *(Second Vatican Council—'The Liturgy')*

Word-pictures

Even in the slave-camps of Russia under Stalin, Sunday was not always forgotten.

Slavomir Rawicz, in *The Long Walk,* describes his experiences in forced-labour Camp 303, in northern Siberia, from which he escaped with a few others, reaching India after many months of terrible endurance across the Gobi desert and the Himalayas.

At Camp 303, soup and bread were the regular diet, but 'There was an occasional treat on Sunday when we were given dried fish . . . We worked hard for six days and had an easy day on the seventh.'

'Sunday was the day when the Commandant addressed the prisoners.' *(Anon)*

One Sunday, our young minister announced that he would dispense with the formality of standing at the door to shake hands with the faithful at the end of the service.

Instead, he now goes out and shakes hands with the parents waiting to pick up their children from Sunday-school. *(C.W.F.)*

It is a theory cherished by those who love to find the continuity in history, that the Puritans were really the down-trodden Saxons and poor Danes taking a very belated revenge on the haughty Norma-

French nobility. One line of argument is the attitude to Sunday, which was treated very seriously in Saxon England, with colossal penalties for working or making servants work—penalties that might include being reduced to bondage.

Then came the Normans, bringing what later came to be called 'the Continental Sunday', choosing it as the most auspicious day of the week for every kind of public event, the lucky day, and the day for jollification. This, it is thought, was always secretly disapproved of, though there was for a long time no gainsaying the feudal lords, who did as they pleased.

Sunday was so gay that there were some French missionaries who came to England in 1200 to preach against the excessively Continental English Sunday. But they got a bad reception in southern England, and their leader, Eustatius, went back to France for more ammunition. He returned in the following year with a letter from the Almighty, which had come via Jerusalem, having been found on St. Simeon's altar in the church of the Holy Sepulchre. When the letter arrived, those in the church had prostrated themselves and nobody liked to touch it, till the Patriarch had the boldness to do so, and read out a terrible denunciation from the Lord for those who did not keep the Lord's Day holy, as ordered in the Ten Commandments. There followed a threat that from the Heavens there would rain down on them stones and wood and scalding water, to be followed by a new set of ravenous and loathsome beasts, with the heads of lions and the tails of camels.

Eustatius, on his second visit to England, left the south alone, and had a better reception in York, where it was agreed to stop Sunday marketing. Stories soon circulated round Yorkshire of the misfortunes that had promptly overtaken millers and others who had worked on the Sabbath. These injunctions applied any time after three o'clock on Saturday afternoon, when the observance of the Sabbath should begin.

But this was only a foretaste of Wycliffe's time, when the Lollards started in earnest to enforce the English Sunday, and there was plenty of legislation to stop tradesmen and shopkeepers. Well before the 17th century, Sunday had been tightened up, by Henry VIII among others. Queen Mary tried to go back to an earlier and laxer tradition, in a way that no doubt had its contrary effect on the growing Puritans of Elizabeth's reign. Although the Commonwealth Puritans lost their cause, they left their mark on the 18th-century Sabbath, and after the French Revolution it tightened up again. *(Douglas Woodruff)*

See also: A48 Prayer and Worship
B29 The Eucharist

CONSCIENCE

'Let anyone blaspheme against the Holy Spirit and he will never have forgiveness.' *Mark 3:29*

Quotations

Conscience is God's presence in man. *(Emmanuel Swedenborg)*

A good conscience is a continual Christmas. *(Benjamin Franklin)*

No more conscience than a fox in a poultry farm. *(George Bernard Shaw)*

Conscience warns us as a friend before it punishes us as a judge. *(King Stanislas I)*

Conscience is the royalty and prerogative of every private man. *(Dryden)*

Conscience is nearer to me than any other means of knowledge. *(Cardinal Newman)*

Conscience and reputation are two things. Conscience is due to yourself, reputation to your neighbour. *(St. Augustine of Hippo)*

Conscience is the voice of the soul, as the passions are the voice of the body. No wonder they often contradict each other. *(Jean Jacques Rousseau)*

The best preacher is the heart; the best teacher is time; the best book is the world; the best friend is God. *(The Talmud)*

Though the dungeon, the scourge, and the executioner be absent, the guilty mind can apply the goad and scorch with blows. *(Lucretius)*

A good conscience is a mine of wealth. And in truth, what greater riches can there be, what thing more sweet than a good conscience? *(St. Bernard)*

Proverbs

All too often a clear conscience is merely the result of a bad memory. *(Ancient proverb)*

There is no pillow so soft as a clear conscience. *(French proverb)*

A bad conscience is a snake in one's heart. *(Yiddish proverb)*

Humour

Hewitt 'You don't seem to think much of him.'
Jewell 'If he had his conscience taken out, it would be a minor operation.' *(Anon)*

Small boy's definition of conscience: 'Something that makes you tell your mother before your sister does.' *(Anon)*

The teacher had given her English class a test. As she began to read off the correct answers, one of the boys changed an answer further down on the page. This troubled him as he thought the teacher might think he had changed the answer she had just given. He raised his hand and asked what he should do about changing answers after the teacher started reading the correct ones.

'Let you conscience be your guide,' the teacher told him.

The boy scratched his head and seemed so puzzled that the teacher asked him what was the matter.

'My conscience can't make up its mind,' the boy replied. *(Anon)*

Statements

Conscience is the most secret core and sanctuary of a man. There he is alone with God, whose voice echoes in his depths. In a wonderful manner conscience reveals that law which is fulfilled by love of God and neighbour. *(Second Vatican Council—'The Church Today')*

On his part, man perceives and acknowledges the imperatives of the divine law through the mediation of conscience. In all his activity, a man is bound to follow his conscience faithfully, in order that he may come to God, for whom he was created. It follows that he is not to be forced to act in a manner contrary to his conscience. Nor on the other hand, is he to be restrained from acting in accordance with his conscience, especially in matters religious. *(Second Vatican Council—'Religious Freedom')*

Word-Pictures

King David and King Solomon led merry, merry lives,
With many, many lady friends and many, many wives,
But when old age crept over them, with many, many qualms,
King Solomon wrote Proverbs and King David wrote the Psalms.
(Dr. James Ball Naylor)

And I will place within them as a guide
My umpire Conscience, whom if they will hear,
Light after light well used they shall attain,
And to the end persisting, safe arrive. *(John Milton)*

Cowardice asks, Is it safe?
Expediency asks, Is it politic?
Vanity asks, Is it popular?
But Conscience asks, Is it right? *(W. Morley Punshon)*

'Oh, yes,' said the Indian, 'I know what my conscience is. It is a little three-cornered thing in here,' he laid his hand on his heart, 'that stands still when I am good; but when I am bad, it turns round, and the corners hurt very much. But if I keep on doing wrong, by-and-by the corners wear off and it doesn't hurt any more.' *(J. Ellis)*

A CAT'S CONSCIENCE

A dog will often steal a bone,
But conscience lets him not alone,
And by his tail his guilt is known.

But cats consider theft a game,
And, howsoever you may blame,
Refuse the slightest sign of shame.

When food mysteriously goes,
The chances are that Pussy knows
More than she leads you to suppose.

And hence there is no need for you,
If Puss declines a meal or two,
To feel her pulse and make ado. *(Anon)*

Two men once visited a holy man to ask his advice. 'We have done wrong actions,' they said 'and our consciences are troubled. Can you tell us what we must do so that we may be forgiven and feel clear of our guilt?'

'Tell me of your wrong doings, my sons,' said the old man.

The first man said, 'I have committed a great and grievous sin.'

'What about you?' the holy man asked the second.

'Oh,' said he, 'I have done quite a number of wrong things, but they are all quite small, and not at all important.'

The holy man considered for a while. 'This is what you must do,' he said at last. 'Each of you must go and bring me a stone for each of his misdeeds.'

Off went the men: and presently the first came back staggering with an enormous boulder, so heavy that he could hardly lift it, and with a groan he let it fall at the feet of the holy man. Then along came the second, cheerfully carrying a bag of small pebbles. This he also laid at the feet of the saint.

'Now,' said the holy man, 'take all those stones and put them back where you found them.'

The first man shouldered his rock again, and staggered back to the place from which he had brought it. But the second man could only remember where a few of his pebbles had lain. After some time, he came back, and said that the task was too difficult.

'You must know, my son,' said the old man, 'that sins are like these stones. If a man has committed a great sin, it lies like a heavy stone on his conscience; but if he is truly sorry, he is forgiven and the load is taken away. But if a man is constantly doing small things that are wrong, he does not feel any very great load of guilt, and so he is not sorry, and remains a sinner. So, you see, my son, it is as important to avoid little sins as big ones.' *(Anon)*

See also: A2 Integrity
A10 Seeking Perfection
A34 Hypocrisy, Ambition
B45 Free Will
C47 The Indwelling Spirit

GROWTH TO MATURITY

'Of its own accord the land produces first the shoot, then the ear, then the full grain in the ear.' *Mark 4:28*

Quotations

Difficulties are things that show what men are. *(Epictetus)*

God gets His best soldiers out of the highlands of affliction. *(Anon)*

If God sends us on stony paths, He will provide us with strong shoes. *(Alexander Maclaren)*

Men come to their meridian at various periods of their lives. *(Cardinal Newman)*

Sometimes great difficulties are permitted only in order to strengthen character. *(R. H. Benson)*

A woman deserves no credit for her beauty at 16 but beauty at 60 is her own soul's doing. *(Anon)*

God develops spiritual power in our lives through pressure of hard places. *(Anon)*

Experience is not what happens to a man; it is what a man does with what happens to him. *(A. Huxley)*

Your theology, fancy or plain, is what you are when the talking stops and the action starts. *(Colin Morris)*

For it is the part of a truly great man not merely to be equal to great things, but also to make little things great by his own power. *(St. Basil)*

The greater the difficulty, the more glory in surmounting it. Skilful pilots gain their reputation from storms and tempests. *(Epicurus)*

'Whenever I find myself in the cellar of affliction, I always look about for the wine.' *(Samuel Rutherford)*

Statements

The law of Christian maturity demands that we lose ourselves in concern for others. One must not wait until all problems at home are solved before beginning to address oneself to those of the neighbour. In fact, an awareness of the immensity of the tasks and problems of progress which face humanity as a whole can stir individuals to work more seriously for progress in their own society. *(Pope Paul VI)*

Indeed, everyone should painstakingly ready himself personally for the apostolate, especially as an adult. For the advance of age brings with it better self-knowledge, thus enabling each person to evaluate more accurately the talents with which God has enriched his soul and to exercise more effectively those charismatic gifts which the Holy Spirit has bestowed on him for the good of his brothers.
(Second Vatican Council—'The Laity')

Word-Pictures

A MATURITY CHECK-UP

1. A mature person does not take himself too seriously—his job, yes!
2. A mature person keeps himself alert in mind.
3. A mature person does not always 'view with alarm' every adverse situation that arises.
4. A mature person is too big to be little.
5. A mature person has faith in himself which becomes stronger as it is fortified by his faith in God.
6. A mature person never feels too great to do the little things and never too proud to do the humble things.
7. A mature person never accepts either success or failure in themselves as permanent.
8. A mature person never accepts any one of his moods as permanent.
9. A mature person is one who is able to control his impulses.
10. A mature person is not afraid to make mistakes. *(Leonard Wedel)*

Benjamin Franklin's practical suggestions on how to get along with others are as timely today as they were when he wrote them nearly 200 years ago.
'The best thing to give your enemy is forgiveness;
— to an opponent, tolerance;
— to a friend, your ear;
— to your child, good example;
— to a father, reverence;
— to your mother, conduct that will make her proud of you;
— to yourself, respect;
— to all men, charity.'

'What is REAL?' asked the rabbit one day, when they were lying side by side near the nursery fender, before Nana came to tidy the room. 'Doesn't it mean having things that buzz inside you and a stick-out handle?'

'Real isn't how you are made,' said the skin horse. 'It's a thing that happens to you. When a child loves you for a long, long time, not just to play with, but REALLY loves you, then you become REAL.'

'Does it happen all at once, like being wound up,' he asked, 'or bit by bit?' 'It doesn't happen all at once,' said the skin horse. 'You become. It takes a long time. That's why it doesn't often happen to people who break easily, or have sharp edges, or who have to be carefully kept. Generally, by the time you are REAL, most of your hair has been loved off, and your eyes drop out and you get loose in the joints and very shabby.' *(Margery Williams—'The Velveteen Rabbit')*

When Sir Thomas More resigned the Lord Chancellorship, his daughter wrote:

He looks younger every day; and yet not with the same kind of youth before his back was bowed under the Chancellorship. 'Tis a more composed, chastised sort of rejuvenescence; rather the soft warmth of autumn, which sometimes seems like May, than May itself: the enkindling, within this mortal tabernacle, of a Heavenly light that never grows dim, because it is immortal, and burns the same yesterday, today and forever; a youthfulness of soul and mind characterised by growth; something with which this world and its fleeting fancies has nothing to do: something that a King can neither impart nor take away. *(Elizabeth More)*

See also: A2 Integrity
A7 Poor in Spirit
A10 Seeking perfection
B28 The whole man

TRUST IN GOD

'Why are you so frightened? How is it that you have no faith?'
Mark 4:40

Quotations

Never trouble trouble, till trouble troubles you. *(Anon)*

Trouble is only opportunity in work clothes. *(Anon)*

Today is the tomorrow you worried about yesterday—and all is well. *(Anon)*

Put your trust in God, but keep your powder dry. *(Oliver Cromwell)*

God hides things by putting them near us. *(Anon)*

Nothing is so bad as not trusting God. *(R. H. Benson)*

All things work together for good, if one will but trust God. *(R. H. Benson)*

What is more elevating and transporting, than the generosity of heart which risks everything on God's word? *(Cardinal Newman)*

Consider seriously how quickly people change, and how little trust is to be had in them; and cleave fast unto God, Who changeth not. *(St. Teresa of Avila)*

When you see the lilies spinning in distress,
Taking thought to manufacture loveliness,
When you see the little birds build barns for store,
That's the time for you to worry not before. *(Anon)*

Cast off indecision and doubt not in the least, when asking anything from God . . . Those who are divided in purpose are they who waver before the Lord and altogether fail to obtain any of their requests. But those who are wholly perfect in the faith ask everything with reliance on the Lord and they receive. *(Shepherd of Hermas)*

Proverbs

One of them, a grave and sensible man . . . repeated a Spanish proverb, which though I cannot repeat in just the same words that he spoke it in, yet I remember I made it into an English proverb of my own thus:

'In trouble to be troubled
Is to have your trouble doubled.' *(Daniel Defoe)*

Trust in God, but mind your business. *(Russian proverb)*

From those I trust, God guard me;
from those I mistrust, I will guard myself. *(Italian proverb)*

Word-Pictures

My God and I will walk the plank together.
My God and I will jump into the sea.
My God and I will meet all kinds of weather.
My God and I will walk triumphantly. *(Anon)*

Bishop Taylor Smith used to write the following in autograph books:

The worried cow would have lived till now
If she had saved her breath;
But she feared her hay wouldn't last all day,
And she mooed herself to death.

In all your affairs, rely wholly on God's Providence . . . Imitate little children, who with one hand hold fast to their father, and with the other hand gather strawberries or blackberries along the hedges. So too, as you gather and handle the goods of this world with one hand, you must with the other always hold fast the hand of your heavenly Father, turning yourself towards him from time to time to see if your actions or occupations be pleasing to him. Above all things, take heed that you never leave his hand or think to gather more or to gain some advantage. For should he forsake you, you will not be able to go a step further without falling to the ground.
(St Francis de Sales)

'Worry' we are told, is from an Anglo-Saxon word which means 'harm' and is another form of the word 'wolf'. It is something harmful and bites and tears as a wolf which mangles a sheep. There are times, no doubt, when we must feel anxious because of harm suffered or anticipated by ourselves or others, and this may be beneficial because it rouses to necessary activity; but often worry has the opposite effect, it paralyses us and unfits us for duty, and also distracts our thoughts and obscures our vision.

An old story tells of an angel who met a man carrying a heavy sack and enquired what was in it. 'My worries,' said the man. 'Let me see them,' asked the angel. When the sack was opened, it was empty. The man was astonished and said he had two great worries. One was of yesterday which he now saw was past; the other of tomorrow which had not yet arrived. The angel told him he needed no sack, and the man gladly threw it away. *(Anon)*

See also: A11 Divine Providence
A19 Patience
B52 God is love
C39 Doing God's Will

DEATH

'Death was not God's doing, he takes no pleasure in the extinction of the living.' *Wisdom 1:13*

Quotations

Death is the side of life which is turned away from us. *(Rainer Maria Rilke)*

I depart from life as from an inn, and not as from my home. *(Marcus Tullius Cicero)*

It is a poor thing for anyone to fear that which is inevitable. *(Tertullian)*

Who knows but life be that which men call death, and death what men call life? *(Euripides)*

It was a truly human tombstone which bore the inscription, 'I expected this, but not yet.' *(Anon)*

We understand death for the first time when he puts his hand upon one whom we love. *(Mme. de Stael)*

Death is but a sharp corner near the beginning of life's procession down eternity. *(John Ayscough)*

When a man dies he clutches in his hands only that which he has given away in his lifetime. *(Jean Jacques Rousseau)*

The foolish fear death as the greatest of evils, the wise desire it as a rest after labours and the end of ills. *(St Ambrose)*

Men fear death as children fear to go in the dark; and as that natural fear in children is increased with tales, so is the other. *(Francis Bacon)*

Why is it that we rejoice at a birth and grieve at a funeral? It is because we are not the person involved. *(Mark Twain)*

Proverbs

Death is a debt we must all pay. *(Greek proverb)*

Death does not take the old but the ripe. *(Russian proverb)*

The angel of Death has many eyes. *(Yiddish proverb)*

Humour

I am ready to meet my Maker. Whether my Maker is prepared for the ordeal of meeting me is another matter. *(Sir Winston Churchill)*

Here I lie at the chancel door,
Here I lie, because I'm poor;
The farther in, the more you pay,
Here I lie, as warm as they. *(William Andres)*

EPITAPHS

For a Mr Box

Here lies one Box within another.
The one of wood was very good,
We cannot say so much for t'other.

For the Earl of Kildare

Who killed Kildare? Who dared Kildare to kill?
Death killed Kildare—who dare kill whom he will.

For Dr Chard

Here lies the corpse of Chard,
Who filled the half of this church yard.

For Arabella

Here rests in silent clay
Miss Arabella Young,
Who on the 21st May,
Began to hold her tongue.

At the last moment, a minister was asked to preach a funeral sermon for another minister who had suddenly become ill.

Realising he had forgotten to ask if the deceased had been a man or woman, he frantically tried to catch a mourner's eye. Finally succeeding, he pointed to the casket and whispered, 'Brother or sister?'

'Cousin' came the faint reply. *(Together)*

Vicar 'I was grieved to hear your husband has gone at last'.
Mrs Black 'Yas, 'e 'as, sir, and I only hope e's gone where I know 'e ain't.' *(Anon)*

The fence around a cemetery is foolish, for those inside can't come out and those outside don't want to get in. *(Arthur Brisbane)*

He (the author's father) said he was dying of fast women, slow horses, crooked cards and straight whisky. *(Kenneth Rexroth)*

It's not that I'm afraid to die. I just don't want to be there when it happens. *(Woody Allen)*

Statements

It is in the face of death that the riddle of human existence becomes more acute. Not only is man tormented by pain and by the advancing deterioration of his body, but even more so by a dread of perpetual extinction. He rightly follows the intuition of his heart when he abhors and repudiates the absolute ruin and total disappearance of his own person. *(Second Vatican Council—'The Church Today')*

Such is the mystery of man, and it is a great one, as seen by believers in the light of Christian revelation. Through Christ and in Christ, the riddles of sorrow and death grow meaningful. Apart from His gospel, they overwhelm us. Christ has risen, destroying death by His death. He has lavished life upon us so that, as sons in the Son, we can cry out in the Spirit: Abba, Father! *(Second Vatican Council—'The Church Today')*

Word-Pictures

I have seen death too often to believe in death.
It is not ending—but a withdrawal.
As one who finished a long journey,
  Stills the motor,
  Turns off the lights,
  Steps from his car,
And walks up the path
To the home that awaits him. *(Blanding)*

In different countries and societies, death is associated with different colours. In the west, mourners traditionally wear black. In China, white has always been acceptable because it represents happiness and prosperity in the next world. Gypsies used to wear red at funerals to symbolise physical life and energy. Red was also the colour representing death in the Celtic world and foretelling disaster. Moslems believe that the souls of the just assume the form of white birds. This idea spread to Europe in the Middle Ages, and mourners in England wore white for centuries before black became the fashion. *(Anon)*

Church bells were once believed to have supernatural powers. When England was ravaged by the Black Death in the 14th century, ringing the church bells was widely believed to help to disperse the plague. Almost three centuries later, Dr Francis Hering wrote, 'Let the bells of cities be rung often, thereby the air is purified.' *(Anon)*

The ringing of bells at a funeral was once supposed to drive away the dead person's ghost. When the ancient Romans held their feast in honour of the family dead in the month of May, it was customary to ring bronze bells and intone 'Ghosts of my fathers, go forth.' *(Anon)*

Yona was a pastor in Rwanda when inter-tribal fighting broke out in 1963. He knew he was a marked man but he refused to leave his post for a more remote village. One evening he was taken from his home by soldiers and shot at a bridge where the invaders had fought with the national army. Two others taken with him by the soldiers were set free, his bearing in face of death having apparently shamed their captors. 'They were all amazed; they had never seen anyone go singing to his death, or walking, as he did, like a man just taking a stroll.' On being taken out of the army jeep at the bridge, he had asked permission to write in his diary. He wrote: 'We are going to heaven': and then added, as completely as he could in the time, an account of the church's funds left in his house. *(T.A. Beetham—'Christians and the New Africa')*

See also: A35 Preparing for death
A42 Life after death
B47 Dying to self
C36 Day of the Lord

PASTORAL CARE OF THE SICK

'My grace is enough for you; my power is at its best in weakness.'
2 Corinthians, 12:9

Quotations

The best prayers have often more groans than words. *(John Bunyan)*

We are so fond of one another, because our ailments are the same. *(Jonathan Swift)*

I enjoy convalescence. It is the part that makes the illness worthwhile. *(George Bernard Shaw)*

Disease makes men more physical; it leaves them nothing but body. *(Thomas Mann)*

The sick on the other hand are to be admonished to realise that they are sons of God by the very fact that the scourge of discipline chastises them. For unless it were His plan to give them an inheritance after their chastisements, He would not trouble to school them in affliction. *(Pope St Gregory I)*

Now the custom of the Church is that the sick should be anointed by the priests with consecrated oil and through the accompanying prayer restored to health. If, therefore, the sick be in sins and shall have confessed these to the priests of the Church and shall have sincerely undertaken to relinquish and amend them, they shall be remitted to them. For sins cannot be remitted without the confession of amendment. *(Venerable Bede)*

Before all things and above all things, care must be taken of the sick, so that they may be served in very deed as Christ himself. . . But let the sick on their part consider that they are being served for the honour of God, and not provoke their brethren who are serving them by their unreasonable demands. Yet they should be patiently borne with, because from such as these is gained a more abundant reward. *(St Benedict)*

Proverbs

In time of sickness the soul collects itself anew. *(Latin proverb)*

Sickness shows us what we are. *(Latin proverb)*

Sickness is every man's master. *(Danish proverb)*

Every invalid is a physician. *(Irish proverb)*

Humour

It is a cold, which God Almighty in justice did give me while I sat lewdly sporting with Mrs Lane the other day with the broken window in my neck. *(Samuel Pepys)*

Word-Pictures

Hilary Pole was a young woman who was totally physically handicapped, while being extremely active, mentally and intellectually. She was only able to move her left big toe one-sixteenth of an inch.

To make it possible for Hilary to communicate with her family and the world around her, Reg Maling, a medical scientist, who had invented the Possum, developed in 1967, a special mechanism to make use of Hilary's minute movement.

The Possum is a machine which makes it possible to dial a telephone number, open a front door, switch on a light or fire without lifting a finger, by using special electronic equipment. A sequence of lights on a display board is operated by blowing on a stem pipe, or in Hilary's case, tapping lightly with her big toe. The release of pressure activates the gadget. A code of sucks and blows enables disabled people to operate an electric typewriter at up to 40 words a minute.

Hilary made good use of her Possum, winning the MBE in 1973 for her work for the handicapped! She died on 18th June 1975, aged 37. *(A. P. Castle)*

On a parcel sent from Norway to England was affixed a label with the words—'Glass with anxiety'—in large letters, to indicate the fragile nature of the contents and obtain for the parcel cautious handling. The sender, with a limited knowledge of English, evidently thought that 'anxiety' was a synonym for 'care'. Perhaps we should speak of pastoral anxiety for the sick! *(Anon)*

See also: A35 Preparing for death
B38 The Suffering Servant

GO TELL EVERYONE

'Jesus summoned the Twelve and began to send them out in pairs . . to preach repentance.' *Mark 6:7,13*

Quotations

Preaching is truth through personality. *(Phillips Brooks)*

The half-baked sermon causes spiritual indigestion. *(Austin O'Malley)*

When you preach the Gospel, beware of preaching it as the religion which explains everything. *(Albert Schweitzer)*

To love to preach is one thing—to love those to whom we preach, quite another. *(Richard Cecil)*

The authority of those who preach is often an obstacle to those who wish to learn. *(Cicero)*

Many good speakers have a head of steam and a fine train of thought but no terminal facilities. *(Anon)*

The test of a preacher is that his congregation goes away saying, not 'What a lovely sermon!' but 'I will do something.' *(St Francis de Sales)*

When I preach I regard neither doctors nor magistrates, of whom I have above 40 in my congregation; I have all my eyes on the servant maids and on the children. And if the learned men are not well pleased with what they hear, well, the door is open. *(Martin Luther)*

Proverbs

Who teaches, often learns himself. *(Italian proverb)*

Those having torches will pass them on to others. *(Greek proverb)*

The teacher is like the candle, which lights others in consuming itself. *(Italian proverb)*

Humour

A famous preacher once told his congregation, 'Every blade of grass is a sermon.'

A few days later, a parishioner saw him mowing his lawn. 'That's right, Father,' the man said, 'cut your sermons short.' *(Anon)*

A preacher was disturbed by the snoring of grandfather in the front bench. He stopped and asked a little boy to wake him.

He promptly answered, 'You wake him up, you put him to sleep.' *(Anon)*

Pastor Jones in our church had been paying five-year-old Tommy Brown 10 cents a week to keep his grandfather awake during the sermon. Last week Tommy didn't deliver, and that night Pastor Jones jumped him. 'I know, sir,' explained the lad, 'but Grandfather pays me 15 cents to let him sleep.' *(Presbyterian Life)*

A preacher whose sermon had gone down very badly asked a friend afterwards, 'How would you have delivered that sermon?'
'Under an assumed name,' he replied. *(Anon)*

Word-Pictures

Paganini, the great violinist, came out before his audience one day and made the discovery just as they ended their applause that there was something wrong with his violin. He looked at it a second and then saw that it was not his famous and valuable one. He felt paralysed for a moment, then turned to his audience and told them there had been some mistake and he did not have his own violin. He stepped back behind the curtain thinking that it was still where he had left it, but discovered that someone had stolen his and left that old second-hand one in its place. He remained back of the curtain a moment, then came out before his audience and said,

'Ladies and gentlemen: I will show you that the music is not in the instrument but in the soul.' And he played as he had never played before; and out of that second-hand instrument, the music poured forth until the audience was enraptured with enthusiasm and the applause almost lifted the roof off the building, because the man had revealed to them that the music was not in the machine but in his own soul.

It is your mission . . . to walk out on the stage of this world and reveal to all earth and Heaven that the music is not in conditions, not in things, not in externals, but the music of life is in your own soul. *(Anon)*

The news of the result of the Battle of Waterloo was eagerly awaited by the people of Great Britain, for so much depended on it. Somehow or other the message came with one word short, and only two words got across—'Wellington defeated'. The country was plunged into mourning, and great was the lamentation until the mistake was discovered, and the omitted third word arrived—'Napoleon'—so that it read 'Wellington defeated Napoleon'. Their sorrow was turned to joy. *(Anon)*

Somewhere, I read about an Eskimo hunter who asked the local missionary priest, 'If I did not know about God and sin, would I go to hell?' 'No,' said the priest, 'not if you did not know.' 'Then why,' asked the Eskimo earnestly, 'did you tell me?' *(Annie Dillard)*

The late Duke of Windsor tells about his first attempts at public speaking after he became the Prince of Wales.

'The more appearances I had to make, the more I came to respect the really first-class speech as one of the highest human accomplishments. No one I knew seemed to possess that rare and envied gift of speaking well in so high a degree as Mr Winston Churchill, who was a sympathetic witness of some of my earliest attempts. "If you have an important point to make," he advised, "don't try to be subtle and clever about it. Use the pile driver. Hit the point once, and then come back and hit it again, and then hit it the third time, a tremendous whack!" ' *(Anon)*

The decline of the Ministry of the Word in Protestant England can perhaps be traced in hour glasses. In the seventeenth century they lived up to their name, and it was really at the end of an hour that the preacher, if in good form, would turn them over and say 'another glass'. If he stopped before the sand, he was thought an idle, shirking dog.

But early in the last century, habits changed, and Queen Victoria restoring the Chapel Royal in 1867 had an hour-glass fitted which gave the preachers 18 minutes. Her son, Edward, improved on this royal hint, and made it known that to go beyond 10 minutes was to displease him.

Of Isaac Barrow, in Charles II's reign, it is related that 'he was three-and-a-half hours delivering a sermon on charity before the Lord Mayor and aldermen; and on one occasion when preaching in Westminster Abbey the servants of the Church caused the organ to be struck up against him and he was fairly blown out of the pulpit'. *(Douglas Woodruff)*

See also: B2 The Good News
B12 On a Mission
C8 God's messengers

QUIET—TIME FOR PRAYER

'You must come away to some lonely place all by yourselves and rest for a while.' *Mark 6:31*

Quotations

It is difficult to be quiet if you have nothing to do. *(Arthur Schopenhauer)*

Recollection is the only paradise from which we cannot be turned out. *(Jean Paul Richter)*

All the troubles of life come upon us because we refuse to sit quietly for a while each day in our rooms. *(Blaise Pascal)*

If we have not quiet in our minds, outward comfort will do no more for us than a golden slipper on a gouty foot. *(John Bunyan)*

To go up alone into the mountain and come back as an ambassador to the world, has ever been the method of humanity's best friends. *(Evelyn Underhill)*

Solitude, though it be silent as light, is like light, the mightiest of agencies; for solitude is essential to man. All men come into this world alone; all leave it alone. *(Thomas De Quincey)*

How can you expect God to speak in that gentle and inward voice which melts the soul, when you are making so much noise with your rapid reflections? Be silent, and God will speak again. *(Francois Fenelon)*

It is easy in the world to live after the world's opinion; it is easy in solitude to live after your own; but the great man is he who in the midst of the crowd keeps with perfect sweetness the independence of solitude.
(Ralph Waldo Emerson)

There is no true solitude except interior solitude. *(Thomas Merton)*

Mere silence is not wisdom, for wisdom consists in knowing when and how to speak and when and where to keep silent. *(J. P. Camus)*

I need wide spaces in my heart
Where Faith and I can go apart

And grow serene.
Life gets so choked by busy living,
Kindness so lost in fussy giving
That Love slips by unseen. *(Anon)*

Proverb

Quiet sow, quiet mow. *(English proverb)*

Word-Pictures

Luigi Tarisio was found dead one morning with scarce a comfort in his home, but with 246 fiddles, which he had been collecting all his life, crammed into an attic, the best in the bottom drawer of an old rickety bureau. In very devotion to the violin, he had robbed the world of all that music all the time he treasured them; others before him had done the same, so that when the greatest Stradivarius was first played, it had had 147 speechless years. *(W. Y. Fullerton)*

Come now, little man! Flee for a while from your tasks, hide yourself for a little space from the turmoil of your thoughts. Come, cast aside your burdensome cares, and put aside your laborious pursuits. For a little while, give your time to God, and rest in him for a little while. Enter into the chamber of your mind, shut out all things save God and whatever may aid you in seeking God; and having barred the door of your chamber, seek him. *(St. Anselm of Canterbury)*

It has always been worthy of note that, while the French have led mankind in appreciation of the pleasures of the table, they have produced the severest religious Orders, the Carthusians and the Trappists, men with a love of silence remarkable in the world's most fluent conversationalists. One of the Avignon Popes, Urban V, when he thought of the Charterhouse, no great distance away, thought he must use his high authority over all religious Orders to make the monks eat meat sometimes.

Very much perturbed, the monks sent a deputation of their oldest and halest members to thank the Pope for his kindly interest. They said they had thought of sending a deputation of monks between 70 and 80, but had judged it would be more efficacious still if their seniors came, and so the youngest monk in the deputation was 87 and the oldest, who did the talking, was 99. The cause, the vegetarian rule, was saved. *(Douglas Woodruff)*

See also: A1 Value of time
A10 Seeking Perfection
C32 Prayer
C47 The Indwelling Spirit

THE WHOLE MAN

'Bear with one another charitably, in complete selflessness, gentleness and patience.' *Ephesians 4:2*

Quotations

The body is the socket of the soul. *(Anon)*

The soul, like the body, lives by what it feeds on. *(J. Gilbert Holland)*

You can easily judge the character of a man by how he treats those who can do nothing for him. *(James Miles)*

I wished for all things that I might enjoy life, and was granted life that I might enjoy all things. *(An anonymous soldier)*

Despise the flesh, for it passes away; be solicitous for your soul which will never die. *(St. Basil)*

It is the glory of man to continue and remain in the service of God. *(St. Irenaeus)*

The soul is the user, the body for use; hence the one is master, the other servant. *(St. Ambrose)*

What a man is in the sight of God, so much he is and no more. *(St. Francis of Assisi)*

The eyes of the soul should not be hindered by the eyes of the body. *(R. H. Benson)*

Never has there been so little discussion about the nature of men as now, when, for the first time, anyone can discuss.
(G. K. Chesterton)

Man is an exception, whatever else he is. If he is not the image of God, then he is a disease of the dust. If it is not true that a divine being fell, then we can only say that one of the animals went entirely off his head. *(G. K. Chesterton)*

Proverbs

What soap is for the body, tears are for the soul. *(Jewish proverb)*

The diamond cannot be polished without friction, nor the man perfected without trials. *(Chinese proverb)*

Statements

According to the almost unanimous opinion of believers and unbelievers alike, all things on earth should be related to man as their centre and crown. *(Second Vatican Council—'The Church Today')*

Thus the ideal of 'the universal man' is disappearing more and more. Nevertheless, it remains each man's duty to preserve a view of the whole human person, a view in which the values of intellect, will, conscience, and fraternity are pre-eminent. These values are all rooted in God the Creator and have been wonderfully restored and elevated in Christ. *(Second Vatican Council—'The Church Today')*

Word-Pictures

Mankind has taken up just a fraction of earth's time. It is almost impossible to imagine the vast expanse of time since the earth was born out of gas and cosmic dust 5,000 million years ago.

Imagine the planet's history condensed into a single century. On the time scale produced by this leap of imagination, the oldest-known rocks began to form at the dawn of year 15, and life in its most primitive form of bacteria and algae appeared in the year 26. Until the year 80 life evolved slowly as the continents drifted about, and it was not until eight years ago that the first amphibians struggled ashore.

Dinosaurs were dominant three years ago, but by the following year they had become extinct.

Three weeks ago, the first man emerged in Africa, using tools and walking upright. The last Ice Age ended two hours ago, the Industrial Revolution started two minutes ago . . . and four seconds ago man set foot on the moon. *(Anon)*

A crippled woman left her crutches and ran up a flight of stairs to rescue her three-year-old daughter when fire threatened to trap the child in an upstairs bedroom.

The mother, injured in a car crash two years previously, had been unable to walk without crutches ever since the accident.

She was in the kitchen when she suddenly discovered that the house was on fire.

Realising that the life of her little daughter was at stake, she momentarily forgot her own physical handicap. She rushed to the upper floor, grabbed the sleeping child and carried her to safety. *(Anon)*

There are three qualities you must have if you are going to succeed finally, however technically proficient you may be.

First, you must have integrity, which I would say in your own profession (of commerce) is particularly important.

Second, you must have courage, not necessarily physical courage, because not everyone has that, but moral courage, standing firm by what one believes to be right.

Third, you must have enthusiasm, the ability to get something out of life by putting something into it in an enthusiastic way. *(Lord Montgomery)*

See also: A2 Integrity
A10 Seeking perfection
B20 Growth to maturity

BREAD FROM HEAVEN

'It is my Father who gives you the bread from heaven, the true bread; for the bread of God is that which comes down from heaven and gives life to the world.' *John 6:32–33*

Quotations

The history of man from the beginning has been the history of the struggle for daily bread. *(Jesue de Castro)*

Bread for myself is a material matter: bread for other people is a spiritual matter. *(Nikolai Berdyaev)*

Christ is food for me; Christ is drink for me; the Flesh of God is food for me, the Blood of God is drink for me. Christ is ministered to me daily. *(St. Ambrose)*

As to the truth of the Flesh and Blood there is no room left for doubt. For both from the declaration of the Lord Himself and from our own faith, it is truly Flesh and truly Blood. And when These are eaten and drunk, it is brought to pass that we are both in Christ and Christ is in us. Is this not so? *(St. Hilary of Poitiers)*

Therefore you hear that as often as sacrifice is offered, the Lord's death, the Lord's resurrection, the Lord's ascension and the remission of sins is signified, and will you not take the Bread of life daily? He who has a wound needs medicine. The wound is that we are under sin; the medicine is the heavenly and venerable Sacrament. *(St. Ambrose)*

Proverbs

When God gives us bread, men will supply the butter. *(Yiddish proverb)*

A mother's bread costs dear. *(Spanish proverb)*

Whose bread I eat, his song I sing. *(German proverb)*

Statement

The Lord left behind a pledge of this hope and strength for life's journey in that sacrament of faith where natural elements refined by man are changed into His glorified Body and Blood, providing a meal of brotherly solidarity and a foretaste of the heavenly banquet. *(Second Vatican Council—'The Church Today')*

Word-Pictures

In 1956, news came through about one of Stalin's forced-labour camps in Siberia, by way of a Dr. Joseph Scholmer who had been a prisoner there. He said that four bishops, 700 priests and 700 monks and nuns had been deported from Lithuania, as well as many lay Catholics. They worked in mines 600 feet below ground, and Mass was said often down there by some priest dressed in his usual overalls. The altar-wafers came by post from Lithuania, allowed through as 'Lithuanian bread', and the wine was from the Crimea. The miners had made a tiny silver chalice only one-and-a-quarter inches high. At Easter (said Dr. Scholmer) over 400 of the Lithuanian miners received their Easter communion hidden in tins of cigarettes which were being distributed. Each host, wrapped in a small piece of linen, was hidden under a top layer of cigarettes, and broken up for four communicants. *(Anon)*

The story is told of a certain minister who was disturbed to see a shabby old man go into his church at noon every day and come out again after a few minutes. What could he be doing? He informed the caretaker and bade him question the old man. After all, the place contained valuable furnishings.

'I go to pray,' the old man said in reply to the caretaker's questioning.

'Come, come now,' said the other, 'you are never long enough in the church to pray.'

'Well, you see,' the shabby old man went on, 'I cannot pray a long prayer, but every day at 12 o'clock, I just comes and says, "Jesus, it's Jim" and waits a minute and then comes away. It's just a little prayer, but I guess He hears me.'

When Jim was injured some time later and taken to hospital, he had a wonderful influence in the ward. Grumbling patients became cheerful and often the ward would ring with laughter.

'Well, Jim,' said the sister to him one day, 'the men say you are responsible for this change in the ward. They say you are always happy.'

'Aye, sister, that I am. I can't help being happy. You see, it's my visitor. Every day he makes me happy.'

'Your visitor?' The sister was puzzled. She always noticed that Jim's chair was empty on visiting days, for he was a lonely old man, with no relations. 'Your visitor? But when does he come?'

'Every day,' Jim replied, the light in his eyes growing brighter. 'Yes, every day at 12 o'clock he comes and stands at the foot of my bed. I see him and he smiles and says, "Jim, it's Jesus" '. *(William Aitken)*

Napoleon won his victories largely by concentrating his forces with unexpected speed. But this meant forced marches for his soldiers, living in the country, where supplies soon ran out. Lack of food meant much illness and many casualties. 'An army marches on its stomach' he said, and offered a prize of 20,000 francs to anybody who would invent some way of preserving food. A Parisian chef won the prize with a plan for a process of bottling food previously heated. Later in London this was improved on, by substituting tins for glass bottles (the beginning of the canning industry). The manufacturers kept the French name boeuf bouilli, so the English soldiers called it bully beef.

The Eucharist supplies Christ's army on the march to heaven with the food it needs. *(Anon)*

See also: A21 Feeding the Hungry
A52 Meeting Christ in the Sacraments
B29 The Eucharist

THE FATHER WHO DRAWS US TO HIMSELF

'No one can come to me unless he is drawn by the Father who sent me.'
John 6:44

Quotations

The Father is the principle of the whole Deity. *(St. Augustine of Hippo)*

Our Heavenly Father never takes anything from His children unless He means to give them something better. *(George Mueller)*

The Mohammedans have 99 names for God, but among them all they have not 'Our Father'. *(Anon)*

Whosoever walks toward God one cubit, God runs toward him twain. *(Anon)*

God does not ask about our ability or our inability, but our availability. *(The Arkansas Baptist)*

An old mystic says somewhere, 'God is an unutterable sigh in the innermost depths of the soul.' With still greater justice, we may reverse the proposition and say the soul is a never ending sigh after God. *(Theodor Christlieb)*

Proverbs

He who has no friend has God. *(Egyptian proverb)*

God never shuts one door but He opens another. *(Irish proverb)*

With God, go over the sea—without Him, not over the threshold. *(Russian proverb)*

Word-Pictures

I can say this of Naseby, that when I saw the enemy draw up and march in gallant order towards us, and we a company of poor ignorant men, to seek how to order our battle—I could not (riding alone about my business) but smile out to God in praises, in assurance of victory, because God would, by the things that are not, bring to naught things that are. Of which I had great assurance; and God did it. *(Oliver Cromwell)*

It was the widespread rebellion against the central government in 1964 which was to bring persecution and death to many Congo Christians. The actions of the Simbas, or Lions, were usually unpredictable...'Why did you shelter a white woman?' asked the Simba military court of one pastor. 'Because she is my sister in Christ, the child of my own Heavenly Father,' was the reply. Although he was condemned by the court to be shot, the effect of his bearing on the Simba major was such that he set him free. *(T. A. Beetham 'Christianity and the New Africa')*

The daughter of Karl Marx once confessed to a friend that she had never been brought up in any religion and had never been religious. 'But,' she said, 'the other day I came across a beautiful little prayer which I very much wish could be true'. 'And what was the prayer?' She was asked. Slowly the daughter of Karl Marx began repeating in German, 'Our Father, which art in heaven. . .' *(Robert Latham—'God for all Men')*

Have you ever realised that the words 'I', 'my' and 'me' do not occur once in the Lord's Prayer?

Yet while saying 'Our Father', it is easy to mean only 'my Father'; to utter the words 'give us this day our daily bread' and still think only in terms of 'give me my daily bread'.

These lines of Charles Thompson may help you avoid the tendency to be self-centred while praying:

You can not pray the Lord's Prayer,
And even once say 'I'.
You can not pray the Lord's Prayer,
And even once say 'My'.
Nor can you pray the Lord's Prayer,
And not pray for another;
For when you ask for daily bread,
You must include your brother.
For others are included
In each and every plea:
From the beginning to the end of it,
It does not once say 'Me'.

See also: B40 One God
C20 Our Father in Heaven
C27 The Father who receives us back

THE EUCHARIST

'For my flesh is real food and my blood is real drink. He who eats my flesh and drinks my blood lives in me and I live in him.'
John 6:55–56

Quotations

If you have received worthily, you are what you have received. *(St. Augustine of Hippo)*

The Christian metaphysics is—that he eats God. *(Theodor Hoecker)*

At the Sacrament of the Body and Blood of Christ, nothing shall be offered but bread and wine mixed with water. *(Council of Hippo)*

The worthiest thing, most of goodness, in all this world, it is the mass. *(Lay Folk's Mass Book. 13th Cent.)*

The effect of our communion in the Body and Blood of Christ is that we are transformed into what we consume, and that he in whom we have died and in whom we have risen from the dead lives and is manifested in every movement of our body and of our spirit. *(Pope Leo I)*

The sacrament (mystery) of sacraments. *(Pseudo-Dionysius)*

Here, Lord Jesus, art Thou both Shepherd and Green Pasture. *(St. Thomas Aquinas)*

The noblest sacrament, consequently, is that wherein His Body is really present. The Eucharist crowns all the other sacraments. *(St. Thomas Aquinas)*

I am God's wheat; I am ground by the teeth of the wild beasts that I may end as the pure bread of Christ. *(St. Ignatius of Antioch)*

Great is this mystery, and great the dignity of priests, to whom that is given which is not granted to angels. For priests alone, rightly ordained in the Church, have power to celebrate and to consecrate the body of Christ. *(Thomas à Kempis)*

For all the other things which are said in the earlier parts of the service are said by the priest . . . when it comes to the consecration of the venerable sacrament, the priest no longer uses his own language, but he uses the language of Christ. Therefore, the word of Christ consecrates this sacrament. *(St. Ambrose)*

Be zealous, then, in the observance of one Eucharist. For there is one Flesh of our Lord, Jesus Christ, and one Chalice that brings union in His Blood. There is one altar, as there is one bishop with the priests and deacons, who are my fellow workers. And so, whatever you do, let it be done in the name of the Lord. *(St. Ignatius of Antioch)*

Humour

Up in the north-west of England, they told me the tale of two Irish labourers over here for work who, having inadvertently and carelessly strayed into a very advanced Anglo-Catholic church, were resolved to be particularly careful about Mass the following Sunday. They watched everything closely and suspiciously until the second collection came round, and then, with great relief, one whispered to the other, 'It's alright, Mick, we're all right this time.' *(Douglas Woodruff)*

This is an appropriate moment to tell the tale of the half-crown and the penny. As they came down adjoining chutes at the Royal Mint they agreed to try to keep in touch, and to recount their adventures when they met. After a good while, meet they did. The half-crown had had quite a good time, being gratefully fondled as a tip of a generous order, and had crossed many counters for useful purposes, and the penny could not match the history. His story was largely of slot machines, bus rides, and buying newspapers in the street; but, he said triumphantly, he had one big thing to boast about, that he had never once missed Mass. *(Douglas Woodruff)*

Statement

As often as the sacrifice of the cross in which 'Christ, our passover has been sacrificed' *(1 Cor. 5:7)* is celebrated on an altar, the work of our redemption is carried on. At the same time, in the sacrament of the Eucharistic bread, the unity of all believers who form one body in Christ *(cf. 1 Cor. 10:17)* is both expressed and brought about. All men are called to this union with Christ, who is the light of the world, from whom we go forth, through whom we live, and toward whom our journey leads us. *(Second Vatican Council—The Church')*

Word-Pictures

Stories continue to come out of China, from time to time, of the heroic efforts of the few remaining bishops and priests to keep the Faith alive and nourish the underground Church. One such story tells of a priest who lives and works as a coolie. By means of prearranged sign language, he gets messages around of where he is to be found—usually in the corner of a local market ostensibly selling soap. Customers who, like the early Christians, give a secret sign, are given a piece of soap, between the wrappings of which is hidden a small wafer of consecrated bread. The Chinese Christian takes his purchase home and usually, after a short family service, receives Communion. *(Anon)*

As Christ willed it and spake it
And thankfully blessed it and brake it,
And as the sacred words do make it
So I believe and take it.

My life to give therefor,
In earth to live no more.
(Lines appearing in various Catholic sources, quoted by Princess Elizabeth when pressed to declare her opinion of the holy eucharist. She characteristically omitted the last two. 16th Cent.)

See also: A44 Meeting Christ in the Sacraments
B18 Sunday
B27 Bread from Heaven

MARRIED LOVE

'A man must leave his father and mother and be joined to his wife, and the two will become one body.' *Genesis 2:24*

Quotations

Let there be spaces in your togetherness. *(Kahlil Gibran)*

A successful marriage is an edifice that must be rebuilt every day. *(André Maurois)*

Don't over-analyse your marriage; it's like yanking up a fragile indoor plant every 20 minutes to see how its roots are growing. *(Anon)*

Success in marriage is more than finding the right person: it is a matter of being the right person. *(Rabbi B. R. Brickner)*

The sum which two married people owe to one another defies calculation. It is an infinite debt, which can only be discharged through all eternity. *(Goethe)*

The state of marriage is one that requires more virtue and constancy than any other; it is a perpetual exercise of mortification. *(St. Francis de Sales)*

The best way to compliment your wife is frequently. *(Anon)*

It is necessary to be almost a genius to make a good husband. *(Balzac)*

Many a man in love with a dimple makes the mistake of marrying the whole girl. *(Anon)*

A good marriage is that in which each appoints the other guardian of his solitude. *(Rainer Maria Rilke)*

To be happy with a man you must understand him a lot and love him a little. To be happy with a woman you must love her a lot and not try to understand her at all. *(Helen Rowland)*

Proverbs

A man too good for the world is no good for his wife. *(Yiddish proverb)*

For a good dinner and a gentle wife you can afford to wait. *(Danish proverb)*

Everyone can keep house better than her mother until she trieth. *(English proverb)*

A good husband should be deaf and a good wife blind. *(French proverb)*

Humour

Every woman should marry, and no man. *(Disraeli)*

Marriage halves our griefs, doubles our joys and quadruples our expenses. *(Anon)*

'Doctors say that married men live longer than bachelors,' the young miss said to the bachelor.
'Well, I've heard that too,' he replied, 'but my married friends claim that it only seems longer.' *(Anon)*

Bride 'How can I keep my wedding ring clean?'
Mother 'Soak gently in dishwater three times a day!' *(Anon)*

Before marriage a man yearns for a woman. After marriage the 'Y' is silent. *(Anon)*

Problems in marriage often arise because a man too often shows his worst side to his better half. *(Anon)*

Boy 'Do you know, Dad, that in some parts of Africa a man doesn't know his wife until he marries her?'
Dad 'Why single out Africa?' *(Anon)*

Husband to wife 'Did you see that pretty girl smile at me?'
Wife 'That's nothing, the first time I saw you, I laughed out loud.' *(Anon)*

'How come you never married?'
'It was like this. I kept looking for an ideal woman.'
'And you never found her?'
'Oh, sure, but just my luck—she was looking for the ideal man.' *(Anon)*

Young Father 'In your sermon this morning you spoke about a baby being a new wave on the ocean of life.'
Priest 'That's right.'

Young Father 'Don't you think a fresh squall would have been nearer the truth?' *(Anon)*

When the late Mr. and Mrs. Henry Ford celebrated their golden wedding anniversary, a reporter asked them, 'To what do you attribute your 50 years of successful life?'

'The formula,' said Ford, 'is the same formula I have always used in making cars—just stick to one model.' *(Anon)*

Questioning the children before Confirmation, the Bishop asked one nervous little girl, 'What is matrimony?' She answered, 'a place where souls suffer for a time on account of their sins.'

'No, no,' said the parish priest, 'that's purgatory.'

'Let her alone,' said the Bishop. 'She may be right. What do you and I know about it?' *(Anon)*

Statements

Authentic married love is caught up into divine love and is governed and enriched by Christ's redeeming power and the saving activity of the Church. Thus this love can lead the spouses to God with powerful effect and can aid and strengthen them in the sublime office of being a father or a mother. *(Second Vatican Council—'The Church Today')*

Such love, merging the human with the divine, leads the spouses to a free and mutual gift of themselves, a gift proving itself by gentle affection and by deed. Such love pervades the whole of their lives. Indeed, by its generous activity it grows better and grows greater. Therefore, it far excels mere erotic inclination, which, selfishly pursued, soon enough fades wretchedly away.

This love is uniquely expressed and perfected through the marital act. The actions within marriage by which the couple are united intimately and chastely are noble and worthy ones. Expressed in a manner which is truly human, these actions signify and promote that mutual self-giving by which spouses enrich each other with a joyful and a thankful will.

Sealed by mutual faithfulness and hallowed above all by Christ's sacrament, this love remains steadfastly true in body and in mind, in bright days or dark. It will never be profaned by adultery or divorce. Firmly established by the Lord, the unity of marriage will radiate from the equal personal dignity of wife and husband, a dignity acknowledged by mutual and total love. *(Second Vatican Council—'The Church Today')*

Word-Pictures

Marriage is like a three-speed gearbox: affection, friendship, love. It is not advisable to crash your gears and go right through to love straight away. You need to ease your way through. The basis of love is respect, and that needs to be learnt from affection and friendship. *(Peter Ustinov)*

Before President Ford married Elizabeth Bloomer, in 1948, they drew up a private marriage contract together.

'We sat down before the wedding and, in a very businesslike way, defined our objectives,' says Mrs Ford.

'We decided the number of children we would have, and ardently agreed to the mutual promise that one would never try to "change" the other.'

'We decided, too, that a successful marriage is never really a 50–50 proposition and settled for a 75–25 arrangement. Sometimes the 75 would emanate from my side. Sometimes it would have to be Jerry's gesture. We have carefully worked out the art of generous compromise.' *(Marian Christy)*

In Imperial China, where wise justice was legendary, the law maintained a careful balance between the sexes. The first time a wife was unfaithful, it was her seducer who was punished, for he was presumed to have taken advantage of her innocence. At the second breach, it was the fickle spouse herself who was whipped. On the third occasion, her husband was imprisoned for having brought the venerable institution of marriage into disrepute. *(James de Coquet)*

Paolina and Ake Viking were married in Sicily in the autumn of 1958, thanks to a far-travelled bottle. Two years earlier, Ake, a bored young Swedish sailor on a ship far out at sea, had dropped a bottle overboard with a message asking any pretty girl who found it to write.

Paolina's father, a Sicilian fisherman, picked it up and passed it to his daughter for a joke. Continuing the joke, Paolina sent off a note to the young sailor. The correspondence quickly grew warmer. Ake visited Sicily and the marriage soon followed their first meeting. *(Anon)*

See also: B8 The Family
C13 Marriage
A46 Priesthood of the Laity

THE COMMANDMENTS OF LIFE

'Accept and submit to the word which has been planted in you and can save your souls.' *James 1:21*

Quotations

Live by the commandments; do not die by them. *(Talmud)*

Wherever law ends, tyranny begins. *(John Locke)*

Man is an able creature, but he has made 32,647,389 laws and hasn't yet improved on the Ten Commandments. *(Anon)*

What else are the laws of God written in our hearts but the very presence of the Holy Ghost? *(St Augustine of Hippo)*

The precepts of the law are these: to live honorably, to injure no other man, to render to every man his due. *(Institutes of Justinian)*

God's precepts are light to the loving, heavy to the fearful. *(St Thomas Aquinas)*

To say 'It is only a man-made law' is to miss the point. Only when civil laws are at variance with the laws of God are they strictly man-made. *(Hubert Van Zeller)*

Love of God is the root, love of our neighbour the fruit, of the Tree of Life. Neither can exist without the other; but the one is cause and the other effect, and the order of the Two Great Commandments must not be inverted. *(William Temple)*

All laws are promulgated for this end: that every man may know his duty; and therefore the plainest and most obvious sense of the words is that which must be put on them. *(St Thomas More)*

Humour

Overheard 'If God believed in today's permissiveness, He would have given us the Ten Suggestions!' *(Anon)*

'The boys are in such a mood that if someone introduced the Ten Commandments, they'd cut them down to eight'. *(Senator Norris Cotton (Reference to economy-minded Senate))*

Word-Pictures

Life must be based on positive and permanent values. The value of love will always be stronger than the value of hate; since any nation which employs hatred is eventually torn to pieces by hatred within itself. The value of truth and sincerity is always stronger than the value of lies and cynicism. No process has been invented which can permanently separate men from their own hearts and consciences or prevent them from seeing the results of their own false ideas. You cannot make men believe that a way of life is good when it spreads poverty, misery, disease and death. Men cannot be everlastingly loyal unless they are free. *(Franklin D. Roosevelt)*

In Oscoda, Michigan, Rev John Silen gives the Ten Commandments the Chippewa Indians had long ago.
They are:

1. Never steal, except from an enemy.
2. Respect the aged and harken to them.
3. Be kind to the sick and deformed.
4. Obey your parents.
5. Be modest.
6. Be charitable.
7. Be of good courage, suffer in silence.
8. Avenge personal and family wrongs.
9. Be hospitable.
10. Pray to the Great Spirit.

Many people criticise some of these Chippewa commandments and at the same time look upon God's Ten Commandments as ghostly whispers of a dead age.

Six hundred and thirteen commandments were given to Moses: 365 negative, corresponding to the days of the year, and 248 positive, corresponding to the number of joints in the human body. *(Talmud)*

See also: A28 True Obedience
C6 The Old Testament Law
C39 Doing God's Will.

THE WONDERS OF GOD

'He has done all things well,' they said 'he makes the deaf hear and the dumb speak.' *Mark 7:37*

Quotations

It is impossible on reasonable grounds to disbelieve miracles. *(Pascal)*

God raises the level of the impossible. *(Corrie Ten Boom)*

Miracles are not contrary to nature, but only contrary to what we know about nature. *(St Augustine of Hippo)*

A miracle is no argument to one who is deliberately, and on principle, an atheist. *(Cardinal Newman)*

It would have approached nearer to the idea of miracle if Jonah had swallowed the whale. *(Thomas Paine)*

I should not be a Christian but for the miracles.
(St Augustine of Hippo)

All miracles are simply feeble lights like beacons on our way to the port where shines the light, the total light of the resurrection. *(Jacques Ellul)*

For those who believe in God, no explanation is needed; for those who do not believe in God, no explanation is possible. *(John LaFarge)*

The miracles of Jesus were the ordinary works of his Father, wrought small and swift that we might take them in. *(George MacDonald)*

I cannot understand people having historical difficulties about miracles. For, once you grant that miracles *can* happen, all the historical evidence at our disposal bids us believe that sometimes they do. *(R. A. Knox)*

Miracles are important, and are only important because they provide evidence of the fact that the universe is not a closed system, and that effects in the natural world can be produced by the reactions of non-human will. *(Arnold Lunn)*

The Incarnation is the most stupendous event which ever can take place on earth; and after it and henceforth, I do not see how we can scruple at any miracle on the mere ground of it being unlikely to happen. *(Cardinal Newman)*

Proverbs

Miracles are the swaddling-clothes of infant churches. *(English proverb)*

Little saints also perform miracles. *(Danish proverb)*

Statement

If any one shall say that miracles are impossible, and therefore that all the accounts regarding them, even those contained in Holy Scripture, are to be dismissed as fabulous or mythical; or that miracles can never be known with certainty, and that the divine origin of Christianity is not rightly proved by them; let him be anathema. *(First Vatican Council—Session 3)*

Word-Pictures

When Moses threw the wand into the Red Sea, the sea quite contrary to the expected miracle, did not divide itself to leave a dry passage for the Jews. Not until the first man had jumped into the sea did the promised miracle happen and the waves recede. *(Jewish legend)*

If you say, but no one has seen miracles performed, then I answer that once upon a time everybody worshipped false gods and persecuted Christians, and then afterwards all were converted including the wise, noble, powerful, by a few poor and unlettered preachers. Either this was miraculous or not. If so, then the point is granted; if not, then I ask, what greater miracle could there have been than to convert so many without miracles? *(St Thomas Aquinas)*

A miracle may be considered as an event inconsistent with the constitution of nature, that is, with the established course of things in which it is found. Or, again, an event in a given system which cannot be referred to any law, or accounted for by the operation of any principle, in that system. It does not necessarily imply a violation of nature, as some have supposed—merely the interposition of an external cause, which, we shall hereafter show, can be no other than the agency of the Deity. And the effect produced is that of an unusual or increased action in the parts of the system. *(Cardinal Newman)*

Jack Traynor, of Liverpool, was hit in the head with a piece of shrapnel at the start of the First World War, but he recovered and was posted to Egypt, where as a result of the wound he began to have epileptic fits. In May 1915, at Gallipoli, he was cut down by three Turkish machine-gun bullets. Two passed through his chest and the third went through his right arm and lodged under his collar bone, severing the main nerves in his armpit and paralysing the limb. After four unsuccessful attempts to reunite the severed nerves, he was awarded a one hundred per cent pension in 1917.

A statement signed by three doctors who accompanied him to Lourdes in 1923 attested that he was then epileptic and incontinent, and without any voluntary movement in his legs. His arm was still paralysed and there was a resultant atrophy of chest and shoulder muscles.

It was after Traynor's ninth and last visit to the baths that he suddenly felt he could walk, and the following day, during the Procession of the Blessed Sacrament, his right arm began to twitch. On the third day, the same three doctors confirmed that Traynor could walk, had recovered the use of his arm and that a hole in his skull, through which it had been possible to see his brain pulsating, had completely closed.

Traynor returned to Liverpool to take charge of the family coal business and, being an honest man, informed the Ministry of Pensions of his recovery. Since they had no administrative machinery to cope with miracles, he continued to receive his pension until he died, aged 64. *(Anon)*

Some of the Christians referred to in the documents we present are in prison for the crime of 'miraculous healings'. According to the Communist authorities, such things are impossible!

However, I myself was sick in prison with lung, spinal and intestinal tuberculosis and recurring jaundice. The 'medicines' I received were beatings, neglect and lack of food. Doctors in Oslo who later examined me and took X-rays could not believe at first that I had survived the Rumanian prison conditions, with four vertebrae infected with tuberculosis, lungs like sieves, and without food and drugs. The healing virtue of Christ had proved to be the same as in the times of the Gospel. Today He delivers many of the fighters of the Underground Church from their infirmities through the prayers of the faithful.

We read in the *Journal* of George Fox, the founder of the Quakers, that when he was released from the prison in Newcastle he could heal. So can many who have passed through Communist jails.

The Communists may mock such healings as fakes—again they put the dunce's caps on our heads! But I know that I was mortally sick and I know that I am now very much alive! Thousands can tell the same story. *(Richard Wurmbrand)*

See also: A18 Balance in Nature
B39 The Lord Who works marvels

FAITH AND GOOD WORKS

'Faith is like that, if good works do not go with it, it is quite dead.'
James 2:17

Quotations

As the flower is before the fruit, so is faith before good works. *(Richard Whately)*

You can do very little with faith, but you can do nothing without it. *(Nicholas Murray Butler)*

Faith is the root of works. A root that produces nothing is dead. *(Thomas Wilson)*

The greatest pleasure I know is to do a good action by stealth and have it found out by accident. *(Charles Lamb)*

All work that is worth anything is done in faith. *(Albert Schweitzer)*

We do the works, but God works in us the doing of the works. *(St Augustine of Hippo)*

For faith without works cannot please, nor can good works without faith. *(St Bede the Venerable)*

A work is then truly excellent, when the intention of the workman is struck out from the love of God, and returns again and again to rest in charity. *(St Augustine of Hippo)*

He who would obey the gospel must first be purged of all defilement of the flesh and the spirit that so he may be acceptable to God in the good works of holiness. *(St Basil)*

Think not that pleasing God lies so much in performing good works as in performing them with good will, and without attachment and respect to persons. *(St John of the Cross)*

To be active in works and unfaithful in heart is like raising a beautiful and lofty building on an unsound foundation. The higher the building, the greater the fall. Without the support of faith, good works cannot stand. *(St Ambrose)*

God chose that man should seek salvation by faith rather than by works, lest anyone should glory in his deeds and thereby incur sin. *(St Ambrose)*

Proverb

Faith sees by the ears. *(English proverb)*

Humour

Two priests were driving in a cab to the station, and were in some anxiety lest they should miss their train. One of them pulled out his watch and discovered it had stopped

'How annoying!' he exclaimed. 'And I always put such faith in that watch!'

'In a case like this,' answered the other, 'good works would evidently have answered the purpose better.'

Word-Pictures

St Frances Cabrini, the first US citizen to be canonised, had her own ways of supporting the many charitable institutions she founded. When bills for upkeep came, for example, she was known to stamp them PAID and send them back—explaining gently that she knew the senders really wished to contribute to God's work, so she was saving them a lot of time and trouble. No one ever complained. *(Adela Rogers St Johns)*

Faith is not merely praying
Upon our knees at night;
Faith is not merely straying
Through darkness into light;
Faith is not merely waiting
For glory that may be.
Faith is the brave endeavour,
The splendid enterprise,
The strength to serve, whatever
conditions may arise. *(Anon)*

See also: C22 The Light of Faith
C30 Increase our Faith

HUMAN RIGHTS

'Wherever you find jealousy and ambition, you find disharmony and wicked things of every kind being done.' *James 3:16*

Quotations

'All human beings are born free and equal in dignity and rights.' *(Adopted by U.N.O. 10th December 1948)*

Every man bears the whole stamp of the human condition. *(Michael de Montaigne)*

Rights that do not flow from duty well performed are not worth having. *(Mohandas Gandhi)*

I am the inferior of any man whose rights I trample under foot. *(Robert Ingersoll)*

They have rights who dare maintain them. *(James Russell Lowell)*

Wherever there is a human being, I see God-given rights inherent in that being, whatever may be the sex or complexion. *(William Lloyd Garrison)*

A right is worth fighting for only when it can be put into operation. *(Woodrow Wilson)*

But the world *can* be different. Human society is not more than the people of that society. And nothing makes its progress more inevitable than people who decide that it is. *(Thomas Cullinan)*

No one can be perfectly free till all are free; no one can be perfectly moral till all are moral; no one can be perfectly happy till all are happy. *(Herbert Spencer)*

To shelter or give medical aid to a man on the run, from a police force which will torture and perhaps kill him, is an act of Christian love demanded by Christ in the Gospel and is no more a political act than giving first aid and a cup of tea to a Member of Parliament who has a car smash outside your door. *(Sheila Cassidy)*

Justice requires that all men acknowledge and defend the sacrosanct rights of human freedom and human dignity, and that the infinite wealth and resources with which God has endowed the whole of the earth, shall be distributed, in conformity with right reason for the use of all His children. *(Pope Pius XII)*

Humour

Man's inhumanity to man is hard,
In fact, 'tis scarce in line with aught that's human;
And yet—'tis quite angelic, as compared
With woman's inhumanity to woman. *(Anon)*

Statement

At the same time, however, there is a growing awareness of the exalted dignity proper to the human person, since he stands above all things, and his rights and duties are universal and inviolable. Therefore, there must be made available to all men everything necessary for leading a life truly human, such as food, clothing and shelter; the right to education, to employment, to a good reputation, to respect, to appropriate information, to activity in accord with the upright norm of one's own conscience, to protection of privacy and to rightful freedom in matters religious too. *(Second Vatican Council—'The Church Today')*

Word-Pictures

To those who find it difficult to believe stories of torture and ask (not unreasonably) for medical evidence, it is important to explain that a good deal of care is taken by torturers to see that no lashing marks are made on the subject.

Electric shock, the most commonly used torture in many countries, leaves no mark at all, as anyone who likes to touch a live wire can verify.

Likewise, immersion of the head in a bucket of water contaminated by excrement, unless it causes death by drowning, cannot be proved. I could go on, but the point is simple: modern torture is designed to leave no scars.

To those people who believe that people who become 'involved in politics' deserve what they get, it is worth pointing out that Article 5 of the Universal Declaration on Human Rights states clearly, 'No one shall be submitted to torture or cruel, inhuman or degrading treatment or punishment.' *(Sheila Cassidy)*

A big landowner invited me to celebrate Mass at his establishment. All his workers were there, hundreds of them. If I preach and say, for example, that one must obey one's employer, that one must work with patience and goodwill and do one's duty, for this landowner I am 'a tremendous bishop', 'a holy bishop'. I can expect to be invited again to preach. But if, while speaking of the worker's duty and the landowner's rights, I have the audacity, yes the audacity, to mention the worker's rights and the landowner's duty, then it is quite a different matter. 'This is a revolutionary, a progressive, he is pro-communist . . .' *(Dom Helder Camara)*

I have the audacity to believe that peoples everywhere can have three meals a day for their bodies, education and culture for their minds, and dignity, equality and freedom for their spirits. I believe that what self-centred men have torn down, other-centred can build up. I still believe that one day mankind will bow before the altars of God and be crowned triumphant over war and bloodshed, and nonviolent redemptive good will proclaim the rule of the land. 'And the lion and the lamb shall lie down together and every man shall sit under his own vine and fig tree and none shall be afraid.' I still believe that we shall overcome. *(Martin Luther King)*

A father, who had been working hard all day, came home wanting rest and quiet. But his young daughter kept pestering him. To keep her quiet, he cut out a map of the world from a newspaper and cut it up into pieces of different sizes. He then told her that he would give her a bar of chocolate when she had 'put the world together'. He hoped that this would give him an hour of peace. Five minutes later she came back telling him that the map was finished and was laid out on the floor. The father was surprised and asked, 'How did you get it together so quickly?' 'That was easy,' she said, 'I just turned the pieces over, and on the other side, I saw the picture of a man. When the man was put together right, the world was right.' *(Anon)*

THE RIGHT–
To affection, love and understanding.
To adequate nutrition and medical care.
To free education.
To full opportunity for play and recreation.
To a name and nationality.
To special care, if handicapped.
To be among the first to receive relief in times of disaster.
To learn to be a useful member of society and to develop individual abilities.
To be brought up in a spirit of peace and universal brotherhood.
To enjoy these rights, regardless of race, colour, sex, religion, national, or social origin. *(UN Declaration of the Rights of The Child)*

See also: A21 Feeding the Hungry
A40 Equality of Women
B44 The dignity of the individual
C1 Liberation from fear
C33 Equality

THE GRACE OF GOD

'The Lord spoke with Moses, but took some of the Spirit that was on him and put it on the 70 elders. When the Spirit came on them, they prophesied.' *Numbers 11:25*

Quotations

Grace does not destroy nature, it perfects it. *(St. Thomas Aquinas)*

They travel lightly whom God's grace carries. *(Thomas à Kempis)*

Grace is God himself, his loving energy at work within his church and within our souls. *(Evelyn Underhill)*

A state of mind that sees God in everything is evidence of growth in grace and a thankful heart. *(Charles G. Finney)*

There is no such way to attain to a greater measure of grace as for a man to live up to the little grace he has. *(Phillips Brooks)*

The law detects, grace alone conquers sin. *(St. Augustine of Hippo)*

Every holy thought is the gift of God, the inspiration of God, the grace of God. *(St. Ambrose)*

Let grace be the beginning, grace the consummation, grace the crown. *(St. Bede the Venerable)*

The burden of life is from ourselves, its lightness from the grace of Christ and the love of God. *(Archbishop Ullathorne)*

The private and personal blessings we enjoy, the blessings of immunity, safeguard, liberty and integrity, deserve the thanksgiving of a whole life. *(Jeremy Taylor)*

It would seem that grace has a certain power, accumulating through the centuries, of saturating even physical objects with its force, however men may rebel. *(R. H. Benson)*

Proverbs

In space comes grace. *(English proverb)*

God does not refuse grace to one who does what he can. *(Latin proverb)*

Word-Pictures

When I want to move my hand, it moves. I don't have to stop and think, 'How shall I move it?' It happens. But if I find myself to be a selfish kind of person and want to be unselfish, it doesn't happen. Therefore, something has got to take hold of us from outside. *(William Temple)*

If grace perfects nature, it must expand all our natures into the full richness of the diversity which God intended when he made them, and heaven will display far more variety than hell. 'One fold' doesn't mean 'one pool'. Cultivated roses and daffodils are no more alike than wild roses and daffodils. *(C. S. Lewis)*

At Tara today in this fateful hour
I place all Heaven with its power,
and the sun with its brightness,
and the snow with its whiteness,
and the fire with all the strength it hath,
and lightning with its rapid wrath,
and the winds with their swiftness along their path,
and the sea with its deepness,
and the rocks with their steepness,
and the earth with its starkness:
all these I place,
by God's almighty help and grace,
between myself and the powers of darkness.

'Rune of St. Patrick'
(Anon)

As the earth can produce nothing unless it is fertilised by the sun, so we can do nothing without the grace of God. *(St. John Vianney)*

See also: B51 One with Christ
B52 God is Love
C55 The Indwelling Spirit

THE FAMILY OF GOD

'The one who sanctifies, and the ones who are sanctified, are of the same stock; that is why he openly calls them brothers.' *Hebrews 2:11*

Quotations

Christ and the Church are two in one flesh. *(St. Augustine of Hippo)*

Men become what they are, sons of God, by becoming what they are, brothers of their brothers. *(Martin Buber)*

In all my travels, the thing that has impressed me most is the universal brotherhood of man—what there is of it. *(Mark Twain)*

Let us be like the lines that lead to the centre of a circle—uniting there, and not like parallel lines, which never join. *(Hasidic saying)*

Perfect virtue is when you behave to everyone as if you were receiving a great guest. Not to do to others as you would not have them do to you. Within the four seas all are brothers. *(Confucius)*

The supreme reality of our time is our indivisibility as children of God and the common vulnerability of this planet. *(John F. Kennedy)*

Our true nationality is mankind. *(H. G. Wells)*

While there is a lower class, I am in it,
While there is a criminal element, I am of it,
While there is a soul in prison, I am not free. *(Eugene V. Debs)*

Word-Pictures

Mankind is a single nation. One of God's signs is the creation of the heavens and the earth and the diversity of your tongues and your colours. Surely there are signs in this for the learned. O mankind, surely we have created you from a male and a female and made you nations and families that you may know each other. Surely the noblest of you with God is the most dutiful of you. Surely God is knowing awareness. *(The Qu'ran)*

Recognise all mankind, whether Hindu or Muslim, as one:
The same Lord is the Creator and Nourisher of all;
Recognise no distinctions among them.
The monastery and the mosque are the same;
So the Hindu worship and the Muslim prayer;
Men are all one. *(Guru Gobind Singh)*

So the world is not one, its peoples are more divided now, and also more conscious of their divisions, than they have ever been before. They are divided between those who are satisfied and those who are hungry; they are divided between those with power and those without power; they are divided between those who dominate and those who are dominated, between those who exploit and those who are exploited. And it is the minority which is well fed and the minority which has secured control of the world's wealth and over their fellow men. Further, in general, that minority is distinguished by the colour of their skin, and by their race. And the nations in which most of the minority of the world's people live have a further distinguishing characteristic—their adoption of the Christian religion. *(Julius K. Nyerere)*

Perhaps few among you have so many dealings with men of different races, different religions, different beliefs and different cultures as I—unworthily—have. In all these dealings, I have always found a great love, a wide-open heart, always opens the heart of others. This great love must be not mere diplomacy but the result of a sincere conviction that, as I have already said, we are all the children of God, who has created mankind, who has created each one of us, and whose children we all are. *(Cardinal Bea)*

The Grand Rabbi of Lyons was a Jewish chaplain to the French forces in the 1914–18 war. One day, a wounded man staggered into a trench and told the Rabbi that a Roman Catholic was on the point of death in no-man's-land, and was begging that his padre should come to him with a crucifix. The padre could not quickly be found. The Jew rapidly improvised a cross, ran out with it into no-man's-land and was seen to hold it before the dying man's eyes. He was almost immediately shot by a sniper; the bodies of the Catholic and the Jew were found together. *(Victor Gollancz)*

No man is an island, entire of itself: every man is a piece of the continent, a part of the main; if a clod be washed away by the sea, Europe is the less, as well as if a promontory were, as well as if a manor of thy friends or of thine were. Any man's death diminishes me, because I am involved in mankind. And therefore never send to know for whom the bell tolls; it tolls for thee. *(John Donne)*

During a battle between Muslims and Sikhs, a Sikh water carrier called Ghanaya was seen giving water to wounded Muslim soldiers as they lay suffering from thirst under the hot sun. He was brought to Guru Gobind Singh and accused of being a traitor. The Guru heard the charges and asked Ghanaya to answer them. 'When I walked through the battlefields I saw no Muslims and no Sikhs, only your face in every man,' said Ghanaya. 'You are a true Sikh,' replied the Guru. 'Continue the work; and here is some ointment to put on the wounds. You shall be known as Bhai Ghanaya from now on.' Bhai means brother; it is a term of honour among Sikhs, reserved for the best of men. *(W. Owen Cole)*

See also: B34 Human Rights
C12 The Church for all men
C17 International Peace
C24 Lord of all nations

TRUE WISDOM

'I prayed, and understanding was given me; I entreated, and the Spirit of Wisdom came to me.' *Wisdom 7:7*

Quotations

Knowledge comes, but wisdom lingers. *(Alfred, Lord Tennyson)*

The art of being wise is the art of knowing what to overlook. *(William James)*

Wisdom is oftentimes nearer when we stoop than when we soar. *(William Wordsworth)*

He is truly wise who gains wisdom from another's mishap. *(Publius Syrus)*

Fruitless is the wisdom of him who has no knowledge of himself. *(Erasmus)*

It is great folly to wish to be wise with an impossible wisdom. *(St. Francis de Sales)*

A knife of the keenest steel requires the whetstone, and the wisest man needs advice. *(Zoroaster)*

Wisdom is the foundation, and justice the work without which a foundation cannot stand. *(St. Ambrose)*

The first key to wisdom is assiduous and frequent questioning. For by doubting we come to inquiry and by inquiry we arrive at truth. *(Peter Abelard)*

Common sense, in an uncommon degree, is what the world calls wisdom. *(Coleridge)*

Wisdom is the ability to use knowledge so as to meet successfully the emergencies of life. Men may acquire knowledge, but wisdom is a gift direct from God. *(Dr. Bob Jones)*

To have a low opinion of our own merits, and to think highly of others, is an evidence of wisdom. All men are frail, but thou shouldst reckon none as frail as thyself. *(Thomas à Kempis)*

Proverbs

Wisdom comes by suffering. *(Greek proverb)*

There is often wisdom under a shabby cloak. *(Latin proverb)*

The great wisdom in man consists in knowing his follies *(French proverb)*

Humour

Fools make feasts and wise men eat them;
Wise men make jests and fools repeat them. *(Traditional)*

Some men are wise,
And some are otherwise.
(Traditional)

Wisdom is a hen, whose cackling we must value and consider because it is attended with an egg; but, then, lastly, it is a nut, which, unless you choose with judgment, may cost you a tooth, and pay you with nothing but a worm. *(Jonathan Swift)*

Word-Pictures

Who knows not, and knows not that he knows not, is foolish; shun him.
Who knows not, and knows that he knows not, is humble; teach him.
Who knows, but knows not that he knows, is asleep; wake him.
Who knows, and knows that he knows, is wise; follow him.
(Anon)

I remember the story of the old Scot on his deathbed. He was being taken through his baptismal vows, to renew them, and was asked, did he renounce the Devil and all his works? To which he answered, 'At the present very delicate juncture in my affairs, I can have no wish to give unnecessary offence in any quarter.' *(Douglas Woodruff)*

Perfect wisdom hath four parts, viz., wisdom, the principle of doing things aright; justice, the principle of doing things equally in public and private; fortitude, the principle of not flying danger but meeting it; and temperance, the principle of subduing desires and living moderately. *(Plato)*

When a youth was giving himself airs in the theatre and saying, 'I am wise for I have talked with many wise men.' Epictetus replied, 'I too have conversed with many rich men, yet I am not rich.' *(Anon)*

A famous astronomer was amused by the remark of a 15-year-old girl who sat next to him at dinner.

With youthful candour, she spontaneously asked, 'What do you do for a living?'

'I study astronomy,' the scientist replied.

'Really?' gasped the wide-eyed teenager. 'I finished astronomy last year!' *(Anon)*

A wise old owl sat on an oak
The more he saw the less he spoke;
The less he spoke the more he heard;
Why aren't we like that wise old bird? *(Edward Hersey Richards)*

An executive from the aircraft industry watched a small plane, full of passengers, being prepared for take-off. He went to the pilot and said, 'Surely you are not going to take off in this dreadful weather are you?' 'Of course I am,' said the pilot. 'But you won't make it,' said the man. 'I'm the one who flies it and I know I can,' said the pilot. 'I come from the firm that built the plane,' said the man, 'and I say you can't.' Not long after the plane had taken off, it crashed and killed everybody on board! *(Anon)*

Professor Albert Einstein, the mathematical genius, was travelling by train in the United States. The dinner-gong sounded, so he left his seat in the carriage and walked down the corridor to the dining-car, taking with him a book he was reading.

When he had sat down at a table, he found that he had left his reading glasses in his compartment, but as he could manage to read the book without them he decided not to go back. As he read on, he came to a footnote which was printed in very small type which he could not decipher.

He called to Sam, one of the dining-car attendants, and pointed to the footnote.

'Would you be good enough to read that for me?' he asked.

'Ah sho' am sorry, sir,' said Sam, 'but Ah ain't educated either.' *(Peter Hargreaves)*

See also: A2 Integrity
B19 Conscience
B20 Growth to maturity
B26 The whole man

THE SUFFERING SERVANT

'By his sufferings shall my servant justify many, taking their faults on himself.' *Isaiah 53:11*

Quotations

Unearned suffering is redemptive. *(Martin Luther King)*

Take the cross *he* sends, as it is, and not as *you* imagine it to be. *(Mother Cornelia Connelly)*

One ounce of patient suffering is worth far more than a pound of action. *(Jean P. Camus)*

Desire earnestly always to suffer for God in everything and on every occasion. *(St. Teresa of Avila)*

It is a glorious thing to be indifferent to suffering, but only to one's own suffering. *(Robert Lynd)*

The chief pang of most trials is not so much the actual suffering itself as our own spirit of resistance to it. *(Jean Nicholas Grou)*

The hardest heart and grossest ignorance must disappear before the fire of suffering without anger and malice. *(Mohandas Gandhi)*

There is nothing that we suffer for the honour of God, however little it may be, that is not more serviceable to us than if we possessed the dominion of the world. *(Archbishop Ullathorne)*

Torture us, rack us, condemn us, crush us; your cruelty only proves our innocence. That is why God suffers us to suffer all this. *(Tertullian)*

He who knoweth how to suffer will enjoy much peace. Such a one is a conqueror of himself and lord of the world, a friend of Christ, and an heir of heaven. *(Thomas à Kempis)*

We all suffer for each other, and gain by each other's sufferings; for man never stands alone here, though he will stand by himself one day hereafter; but here he is a social being, and goes forward to his long home as one of a large company. *(Cardinal Newman)*

Proverbs

He who suffers much will know much. *(Greek proverb)*

Of suffering comes ease. *(English proverb)*

Statement

By suffering for us He not only provided us with an example for our imitation. He blazed a trail and if we follow it, life and death are made holy and take on a new meaning. *(Second Vatican Council—'The Church Today')*

Word-Pictures

From the Will of Count Schwerin von Schwanenfeld who was executed September 8, 1944, for his part in the plot against Hitler . . . Further it is my desire that in that part of the gravel bed in my forest of Sartowitz where the victims of the massacres of the late autumn of 1939 are laid to rest, a very high oaken cross he erected as soon as the conditions of the time permit, with the following inscription:

> Here lie from 1,400 to 1,500 Christians and Jews.
> May God have mercy on their souls and on their murderers.

(Kathe Kuhn 'Dying We Live')

During the First World War, a village behind the lines in the Somme valley had been shelled, and there were many civilian casualties. The church too had been damaged, but it was the largest building available for a dressing-station in the sudden emergency. The altar was turned into an improvised operating table. One of the casualties brought in was a young soldier who belonged to the village and was at home on a few days leave. He was badly wounded and his leg would have to come off at once. 'You'll have to be brave,' said the doctor, 'This is going to be rather painful. We've got no anaesthetic—it was all destroyed when the hospital was hit.'

The young man looked at the altar, and pointed with his head towards the crucifix over it. 'I shall be all right,' he said, 'Put me there. So long as I can look at Him, I'll manage.' *(Anon)*

Let nothing disturb thee,
Nothing affright thee;
All things are passing;
God never changeth;
Patient endurance
Attaineth to all things;
Who God possesseth
In nothing is wanting;
Alone God sufficeth. *(St. Teresa of Avila)*

The following story is from Ernest Gordon's account of life and death in a Japanese P.O.W. camp on the River Kwai:

One story that went the rounds soon after, concerned another soldier of the Argyll regiment, who was in a work detail on the railway.

The day's work had ended; the tools were being counted, as usual. As the party was about to be dismissed, the Japanese guard shouted that a shovel was missing. He insisted that someone had stolen it to sell to the Thais. Striding up and down before the men, he ranted and denounced them for their wickedness and their ingratitude to the Emperor. As he raved, he worked himself up into a paranoid fury. Screaming in broken English, he demanded that the guilty one step forward to take his punishment. No one moved; the guard's rage reached new heights of violence. 'All die! All die!' he shrieked.

To show that he meant what he said, he cocked his rifle, put it on his shoulder and looked down the sights, ready to fire at the first man at the end of them. At that moment the Argyll stepped forward, stood stiffly to attention, and said calmly, 'I did it.'

The guard unleashed all his whipped-up hate; he kicked the helpless prisoner and beat him with his fists. Still the Argyll stood rigidly to attention, with the blood streaming down his face. His silence goaded the guard to an excess of rage. Seizing his rifle by the barrel, he lifted it high over his head and, with a final howl, brought it down on the skull of the Argyll, who sank limply to the ground and did not move. Although it was perfectly clear that he was dead, the guard continued to beat him and stopped only when he was exhausted.

The men of the work detail picked up their comrade's body, shouldered their tools and marched back to camp. When the tools were counted again at the guard-house, no shovel was missing.

(Ernest Gordon 'Miracle on the River Kwai')

See also: B15 Jesus, friend of outcasts
C13 Coping with grief
B49 Coping with doubt

THE LORD WHO WORKS MARVELS

'What marvels the Lord worked for us. Indeed we were glad.'
Psalm 126:3

Quotations

Wonder is the basis of worship. *(Thomas Carlyle)*

To be surprised, to wonder, is to begin to understand. *(José Ortega y Gasset)*

Quality is never an accident. It is always the result of intelligent effort. There must be the will to produce a superior thing. *(John Ruskin)*

You will find something far greater in the woods than you will in books. Stones and trees will teach you what you can never learn from masters. *(St. Bernard)*

A monk asks: 'Is there anything more miraculous than the wonders of nature?' The Master answers: 'Yes, your awareness of the wonders of nature.' *(Anon)*

Day after day, O Lord of my life, shall I stand before thee face to face. With folded hands, O Lord of all worlds, shall I stand before thee face to face... And when my work shall be done in this world, King of kings, alone and speechless shall I stand before thee face to face. *(Rabindranath Tagore)*

I feel that a man may be happy in this world and I know that this world is a world of imagination and vision. I see everything I paint in this world, but everybody does not see alike. To the eye of a miser, a guinea is far more beautiful than the sun, and a bag worn with the use of money has more beautiful proportions than a vine filled with grapes. The tree which moves some to tears of joy is, in the eyes of others, only a green thing which stands in the way. As a man is, so he sees. *(William Blake)*

Proverbs

A wonder lasts but nine days. *(English proverb)*

God made us and we wonder at it. *(Spanish proverb)*

Humour

'Can you tell me, Johnny, who made you?'

'God made part of me.'
'What do you mean?'
'I mean he made me little. I grow'd the rest myself.' *(Anon)*

A Sunday school teacher was examining her pupils after a series of lessons on God's omnipotence. She asked, 'Is there anything God can't do?'

There was silence. Finally, one lad held up his hand. The teacher, disappointed that the lesson's point had been missed, asked resignedly, 'Well, just what is it that God can't do?'

'Well,' replied the boy, 'He can't please everybody.' *(Anon)*

Word-Pictures

In a little church in the far South of Ireland, every window but one is of stained glass, representing Christ and his saints. Through the one window which is plain glass may be seen a breath-taking view: a lake of deepest blue, studded with green islets, and backed by range after range of purple hills. Under the window is the inscription: 'The heavens declare the glory of God, and the firmament showeth His handiwork.' *(Robert Gibbings)*

A little girl who lived in a remote part of the country was receiving her first Bible instruction at the hands of her elderly grandmother, and the old lady was reading the child the story of the creation. After the story had been finished the little girl seemed lost in thought.

'Well, dear,' said the grandmother, 'what do you think of it?'

'Oh, I love it. It's so exciting,' exclaimed the youngster. 'You never know what God is going to do next!' *(Anon)*

The Seven Wonders of the ancient world were:

1. The Great Pyramid.
2. The Colossus of Rhodes.
3. The Hanging Gardens of Babylon.
4. The Temple of Diana in Ephesus.
5. The Statue of Jupiter in Athens.
6. The Halicarnassus (Mausoleum).
7. The Pharos Lighthouse at Alexandria.

God's wonders of creation far exceed any and all of these. *(Anon)*

There is a West Indian folk tale about a contest for youth. The young men of the village were sent off to search for the most beautiful thing in the world, and to return with it to show it to the elders. One young enthusiast named Amarli Bakoff raced for the distant hills which had always fascinated him. He climbed higher and higher, up through the forest and across the scrubland until he came to snowfields for the first time in his life. 'Surely,' he thought, as he reached the dazzling whiteness, 'this must be the most beautiful thing in the world!' He plunged his hand into the stinging coldness and clutched a handful of snow in its marvellous purity.

With his hand held tightly closed, he raced back to the village, eager to be back for the appointed day of the judging of the contest. The villagers were assembled, and the elders were inspecting the priceless treasures which the other youths had discovered; jewels, silks, marvels of art and craft, and wonders of nature. Suddenly Amarli Bakoff broke into their midst.

'What have you brought us?' they asked excitedly.

'See!' he cried triumphantly—and he opened his hand.

There was nothing there. They saw nothing. Only Amarli Bakoff knew the meaning of what had happened.

'The most beautiful thing in the world,' he said, 'is what eye cannot see and what hand cannot hold.' *(Peter Hargreaves)*

One of the popular poems that came to us after World War I was "Trees" by Joyce Kilmer, sergeant in the 165th infantry (69th New York) A.E.F. who was killed in action near Ourcy, July 30th, 1918.

I think that I shall never see
A poem lovely as a tree.

A tree whose hungry mouth is prest
Against the earth's sweet flowing breast;

A tree that looks at God all day,
And lifts her leafy arms to pray;

A tree that may in Summer wear
A nest of robins in her hair;

Upon whose bosom snow has lain;
Who intimately lives with rain.

Poems are made by fools like me,
But only God can make a tree.

In his book *Confessions,* St. Augustine describes his search:

'What is this God?' I asked the earth, and it answered, 'I am not He,' and all things that are in the earth made the same confession. I asked the sea and the deeps and the creeping things, and they answered, 'We are not your God; seek higher . . .'

I asked the heavens, the sun, the moon, the stars, and they answered, 'Neither are we the God whom you seek.' And I said to all the things that throng about the gateways of the senses, 'Tell me something of Him.' And they cried out in a great voice, 'He made us.' My question was my gazing upon them, and their answer was their beauty . . . I asked the whole frame of the universe about my God and it answered me, 'I am not He, but He made me.'

H. G. Wells went to visit his fellow writer, Henry James, and noticed an unusually large stuffed bird in the drawing room. He was perplexed and intrigued.

'My dear James,' he asked, 'what is that?'

'That,' James informed him, 'is a stork.'

'Humph,' Wells snorted, 'it's not my idea of a stork.'

'Apparently, however,' James remarked, 'it was God's idea of one.'
(Anon)

See also: A18 Balance in Nature
B32 The Wonders of God

ONE GOD

'Listen, Israel: The Lord our God is the one Lord.' *Deuteronomy 6:4*

Quotations

Beware of the man whose god is in the skies. *(Bernard Shaw)*

If God did not exist, it would be necessary to invent him. *(Voltaire)*

God and other artists are always a little obscure. *(Oscar Wilde)*

Do not seek God in outer space—your heart is the only place in which to meet Him face to face. *(Angelus Silesius)*

Mysterious Being, infinitely far from me, who yet in every beating of this heart must be. *(Angelus Silesius)*

Change and decay in all around I see;
O thou, who changest not, abide with me. *(Henry Francis Lyte)*

Anything that makes religion a second object makes it no object.
He who offers to God a second place offers him no place. *(Ruskin)*

Two men please God—who serves Him with all his heart because he knows Him; who seeks Him with all his heart because he knows Him not. *(Panin)*

The God to whom little boys say their prayers has a face very like their mothers. *(James M. Barrie)*

Now nobody denies what nobody is ignorant of—for nature herself is teacher of it—that God is the Maker of the universe, and that it is good, and that it is man's by free gift of its Maker. *(Tertullian)*

The world is so empty if one thinks only of mountains, rivers and cities, but to know someone here and there who thinks and feels with us and who, though distant, is close to us in spirit, this makes the earth for us an inhabitated garden. *(Goethe)*

It has been the universal opinion of mankind from ancient times, from the earliest tradition of the protoplast, that there is one God, the Maker of heaven and earth . . .

For nature reveals its Author, the work suggests the Artist, and the world manifests its Designer. But the whole Church throughout the world has received this tradition from the apostles. *(St. Irenaeus)*

Proverbs

God is one; what He does, sees none. *(Yiddish proverb)*

God often visits us, but most of the time we are not at home. *(French proverb)*

Humour

Johnny, aged five, was told by his mother that he must finish his breakfast porridge. He said he didn't want to.

His mother replied, 'You must finish it. If you don't, God will be very angry.'

She went into the kitchen to wash up, leaving Johnny looking with a sullen determination at the porridge. Outside it was raining, and suddenly there was a heavy roll of thunder.

Johnny's mother came back into the room and found him eating his porridge as quickly as he could, and meanwhile muttering to himself, 'All that fuss for a small plate of porridge!' *(Redemptorist Record)*

Word-Pictures

Augustus Toplady was one day overtaken by a severe thunderstorm in Burrington Combe, a rocky glen running into the heart of the Mendip Hills. There was no habitation anywhere near, and no place to which he could turn for shelter from the storm.

Looking about him, he saw two massive pillars of rock, a deep fissure in the centre of a precipitous crag of limestone, and took refuge there. Standing there in safety, he escaped the storm. Finding a piece of paper lying near, he picked it up and with his pencil wrote the famous familiar hymn, first published in 1775, 'Rock of Ages, cleft for me, Let me hide myself in Thee.' *(Anon)*

Four Hebrew letters, YHVH (which appear 6,823 times in the Old Testament) form the Hebrew name for God. 'Adonai' is a substitute for these sacred letters. The title 'Adonai' is never pronounced by pious Jews except during solemn prayer and with the head covered. *(Anon)*

You see many stars at night in the sky but find them not when the sun rises, can you say there are no stars in the heaven by day? So, O man! Because you behold not God in the days of your ignorance, say not that there is no God. As one and the same material, water, is called by different names by different peoples, one calling it water, another calling it eau, a third aqua, and another pani, so the one Sat-chit-ananda, the everlasting intelligent-bliss, is invoked by some as

God, by some as Allah, by some as Jehovah, by some as Hari, and by others as Brahman. As one can ascend to the top of a house by means of a ladder or a bamboo or a staircase or a rope, so divers are the ways and means to approach God, and every religion in the world shows one of these ways. Different creeds are but different paths to reach the Almighty. *(Sri Ramakrishna)*

See also: B30 The Father who draws us to himself
B54 The Trinity
C27 The Father who receives us back

GENEROSITY

'I tell you solemnly, this poor widow has put more in than all who have contributed to the treasury.' *Mark 12:43*

Quotations

One of the most difficult things to give away is kindness—it is usually returned. *(C. Flint)*

Too many people have decided to do without generosity in order to practise charity. *(Albert Camus)*

He who gives when he is asked has waited too long. *(Anon)*

You do not have to be rich to be generous. If he has the spirit of true generosity, a pauper can give like a prince. *(Corinne V. Wells)*

The truly generous is the truly wise. *(Anon)*

It is possible to give without loving, but it is impossible to love without giving. *(Richard Braunstein)*

Humour cannot be learnt. Besides wit and keenness of mind, it presupposes a large measure of goodness of heart, of patience, of tolerance and of human kindness. *(Curt Goetz)*

Proverbs

The hand that gives, gathers. *(English proverb)*

The man who gives little with a smile gives more than the man who gives much with a frown. *(Jewish proverb)*

Give with a warm hand, not a cold one. *(Jewish proverb)*

Humour

A German monk, dining recently in an English Benedictine monastery, looked doubtful when, at the end of the meal, a whole cheese was brought in and, since he was the principal guest, placed first before him. 'No, no,' he said after consideration, 'It is too much—give me half.' *(Douglas Woodruff)*

A northern Canon, noted for his hospitality, greeted a 'supply' priest with an offer of refreshment. 'A drop of whiskey, Father?' 'No thanks,' answered the visitor. 'A cup of tea, then, or perhaps you prefer coffee?' 'No thanks,' repeated the priest. 'Then you'll have a cigar or a cigarette?' 'I don't smoke.' A pause and the perplexed Canon asked, 'Well Father, will you have a holy picture? *(Douglas Woodruff)*

A pig was lamenting his lack of popularity. He complained to the cow that people were always talking about the cow's gentleness and kind eyes, whereas his name was used as an insult. The pig admitted that the cow gave milk and cream, but maintained that pigs gave more. 'Why,' the animal complained, 'we pigs give bacon and ham and bristles and people even pickle our feet. I don't see why you cows are esteemed so much more.'

The cow thought awhile and said gently, 'Maybe it's because we give while we're still living.' *(Anon)*

A small boy observed his mother put a penny in the offering plate at the morning service. On the way home from church, she freely criticised the poor sermon they had heard. 'But, mother,' said the boy, 'what could you expect for a penny?' *(Anon)*

I enjoyed the tale of the elderly money-lender and the Salvation Army lass. She accosted him in Bond Street in Self-Denial Week, and said, 'Will you give a shilling to the Lord?'

'How old are you?' said he, and she answered, 'Nineteen.'

'Well,' said the money-lender, 'I am seventy-five, so I shall be seeing Him before you do, so I'll give it to him.' *(Anon)*

Word-Pictures

Alexander the Great had a famous but poor philosopher in his court. Being pressed for money, the philosopher made application to his patron for relief. Alexander had commissioned him to draw whatever cash he needed from the Treasury, so the philosopher presented a request for a very large sum. The Treasurer refused to honour the draft until he consulted his royal master, adding that he thought the amount exhorbitant. Alexander replied, 'Pay the money at once. The philosopher has done me a singular honour. By the largeness of his request he shows the idea he has conceived both of my wealth and my generosity.' *(Anon)*

The best thing to give . . .

to your enemy is forgiveness;
to an opponent, tolerance;
to a friend, your heart;
to your child, a good example;
to a father, deference;

to your mother, conduct that will make her proud of you;
to yourself, respect;
to all men, charity. *(Lord Balfour)*

A report from an elementary school near Chicago tells about a Christmas pageant held in the school. A third grader was the innkeeper. He had only one line to say: 'Sorry. There is no room in the inn.' But the little boy entered into the spirit of the play and said his part with real feeling. And then, as Mary and Joseph turned away to leave, the little fellow called out, 'Come back, Joseph. I will give you my room!' (Didn't the Lord say something about becoming like little children?) *(Anon)*

There is a fable well known in India of a poor beggar who lived in a State ruled by a Maharaja. The beggar had no home but put up every night in a free lodging-house, sleeping on a mat on the floor, and covering himself in the cooler nights with old rags. His clothing was tattered and old and, having no means of earning a livelihood other than begging, he used to go out in the morning after a meal of cold rice left over from the previous day and sit by the wayside with his beggar's bowl. For 'punyam' (merit), passers-by used to throw some grains of rice or copper coins his way, so he usually had enough rice for two meals a day, and enough money to buy sticks for a fire and a few vegetables, fish or dhall for curry, which he ate at the choultry.

One day he heard that on the morrow, the Maharaja himself was coming that way in his chariot. That raised his hopes, as he said to himself, 'The Maharaja will not give me a handful of rice or a copper coin, or even a few annas, but nothing less than a golden Varaha.' The next day he took up his usual position by the side of the road, and patiently awaited the Maharaja's coming. The sun stood overhead and still he waited in the noonday heat, but no sign of the ruler. Patiently he waited, still full of hope, until almost sunset, and then he heard the welcome sound of the horses' hoofs and the chariot wheels. Stepping into the road, he brought the chariot to a standstill, approached the Maharaja and begged for alms. Instead of giving him anything, the Maharaja extended his hands and asked the beggar to give him something. Extremely disappointed and disgusted at a wealthy ruler begging from a poor beggar, he counted out five grains of rice from his bowl and placed them angrily in the hands of the Maharaja. 'Namasthe,' said the Maharaja, and continued his journey.

With a sore heart and very disappointed, the beggar went that evening to his choultry, took out his winnowing fan and began to clean his rice for his meal. As he did so, a small glittering object attracted his attention. Picking it up, he saw that it was a grain of gold. Laying it carefully on one side, he went on winnowing till he found another glittering golden grain, then another. Now the search began in real earnest, and a fourth was found among the rice. After another search he saw a fifth and put it with the others. But no matter how long he searched after that, he found not another grain of gold.

Then the truth dawned on him. Five grains of rice given to the Maharaja had brought him in return five grains of gold. 'What a fool I was!' he exclaimed regretfully. 'If I'd known, I'd have given him it all.' *(Anon)*

The following story is from Ernest Gordon's account of life and death in a Japanese P.O.W. camp on the River Kwai:

Farther on, we were shunted on to a siding for a lengthy stay. We found ourselves on the same track with several carloads of Japanese wounded. They were on their own and without medical care. No longer fit for action, they had been packed into railway trucks which were being returned to Bangkok. Whenever one of them died en route, he was thrown off into the jungle. The ones who survived to reach Bangkok would presumably receive some form of medical treatment there. But they were given none on the way. They were in a shocking state; I have never seen men filthier. Their uniforms were encrusted with mud, blood and excrement. Their wounds, sorely inflamed and full of pus, crawled with maggots . . . Without a word, most of the officers in my section unbuckled their packs, took out part of their ration and a rag or two, and with water canteens in their hands went over to the Japanese train to help them. Our guards tried to prevent us, bawling, 'No goodka! No goodka!' But we ignored them and knelt by the side of the enemy to give them food and water, to clean and bind their wounds, to smile and say a kind word. Grateful cries of 'Aragatto!' (thank you) followed us when we left. An allied officer from another section of the train had been taking it all in. 'What bloody fools you all are!' he said to me. 'Don't you realise that those are the enemy?'

(*Ernest Gordon 'Miracle on the River Kwai'*)

See also: A5 Unselfishness
C18 Compassion
C46 Loving Kindness

SIGNS OF THE TIMES

'Take the fig tree as a parable: as soon as its twigs grow supple and its leaves come out, you know that summer is near.' *Mark 13:28*

Quotations

I am in difficulty both summer and winter about my salary. *(Egyptian letter 256 BC)*

Politicians have strained their ingenuity to discover new sources of public revenue. *(Socrates, 50 BC)*

Philosophy has struggled to find some substitute for the divine commandments and the surveillance of God. *(Socrates)*

Who has not seen with his own eyes the present spirit. . . which forces up the price of commodities to such a degree that human language cannot find words to express the transaction? *(Diocletian, AD 301)*

Even though a god, I have learned to obey the times. *(Palladas, AD 400)*

The golden age was the age in which gold did not reign. The golden calf is still made of mud. *(Graffiti written during French Student Revolt, May 1968)*

Every age has its pleasures, its style of wit, and its own ways. *(Nicolas Boileau 1674)*

Future ages will wonder at us, as the present age wonders at us now. . . our love of what is beautiful does not lead to extravagance. . . mighty indeed are the marks and monuments we have left. *(Pericles of Athens, Fifth century BC)*

Proverb

The golden age was never the present age. *(English proverb)*

Word-Pictures

Two tablets dating back to 2800 B.C. were unearthed in Babylon not long ago. They both commented on the trends of the day.
One reads: 'Times are not what they used to be.'
The other tablet reflected a major concern of many people living 28

centuries ago. Their complaint: 'The world must be coming to an end. Children no longer obey their parents and every man wants to write a book.' *(Anon)*

Aristotle, the great Greek philosopher who lived more than two thousand years ago, wrote this about the young people of his time: 'Their faults are nearly all errors of exaggeration. They overdo in cases of love and in all other things. They imagine that they know everything, and stubbornly stand on their point. They like to crack jokes for joking is the bad manneredness of the well mannered.'

General William Booth once said, 'I consider the greatest dangers of the twentieth century to be:
i, Religion without the Holy Ghost;
ii, Christianity without Christ;
iii, Forgiveness without regeneration;
iv, Morality without God;
v, Heaven without Hell.'

Buttes, in 'Dyets Dry Dinner' (1599) gives the following:
Heresie and beere came hopping into
England both in a yeere.

The world is passing through troublous times. The young people of today think of nothing but themselves. They have no reverence for parents or old age. They are impatient of all restraint. They talk as if they knew everything, and what passes for wisdom with us is foolishness to them. As for the girls, they are immodest and unwomanly in speech, behaviour and dress. *(Peter the Monk in AD 1274)*

The Anglo-Saxon Chronicle for the year 1137 says:
'Every powerful man built his castles and when the castles were built, they filled them with devils and wicked men. But by night and day, they took those people that they thought had any goods—men and women—and put them in prison and tortured them with indescribable torture to extort gold and silver. Many thousands they killed by starvation. They levied taxes on the villages every so often and called it protection money. When the wretched people had no more to give, they robbed and burned all the villages, so that you could easily go a whole day's journey and never find anyone occupying a village, nor land tilled. Then corn was dear, and meat and butter, and cheese, because there was none in the country. Wretched people died of starvation; some lived by begging for alms who had once been rich men; some fled the country. There had never been till

then greater misery in the country, nor had heathens done worse than they did. Men said openly that Christ and the saints were asleep.

See also: A18 Balance in nature
B34 Human Rights
C17 International Peace

FORTY DAYS OF LENT

'The Spirit drove Jesus out into the wilderness and he remained there for forty days.' *Mark 1:12*

Quotations

Fasting is better than prayer. *(St. Clement)*

Fasting is more effective than charity, for the latter is done with money, but the former can be done only by one's own person. *(Talmud)*

As to the repugnance felt by our (modern) Catholics for fasting, it is not without some interest to note that it is occurring in the very time when disciples of Gandhi have demonstrated the virtues of fasting on the level of natural mystique and non-violent resistance. *(Jacques Maritain)*

In these days, therefore, let us add something beyond the wonted measure of our service, such as private prayers and abstinence in food and drink. Let each one, over and above the measure prescribed for him, offer God something of his own freewill in the joy of the Holy Spirit. *(St. Benedict)*

If any bishop, or presbyter, or deacon, or reader, or singer, does not fast the fast of forty days, or the fourth day of the week, and the day of the Preparation (Friday), let him be deprived, except he be hindered by weakness of body. But if he be one of the laity, let him be suspended. *(Ecclesiastical Canons of the Holy Apostles)*

Proverbs

A fast is better than a bad meal. *(Irish proverb)*

Who fasts, but does no other good, saves his bread but goes to Hell. *(Italian proverb)*

Statement

The Lenten season has a twofold character: 1, it recalls baptism or prepares for it; 2, it stresses a penitential spirit. By these means especially, Lent readies the faithful for celebrating the paschal mystery, after a period of closer attention to the Word of God, and more ardent prayer. In the liturgy itself, and in liturgy-centered instructions, these baptismal and penitential themes should be more pronounced. *(Second Vatican Council—'Liturgy')*

Word-Pictures

As Ash Wednesday approaches each year, Catholics are brought into touch with what is, perhaps, the oldest kind of soap. Some scholars connect the cleansing symbolism of ashes with fire, saying that the Parsees and the Brahmins have used ashes for purification on this basis. More practical men say it comes from countries where water is scarce, and sand and ashes are used instead. Tertullian talks about sackcloth and ashes, and they seem to be one of the Jewish symbols which the Church continued. But they were kept originally for public penitents, people whom we do not see in our churches nowadays, which seems, perhaps, odd, unless it be thought that we all, on Ash Wednesday, achieve that status.

In the Middle Ages, public penitents used to be expelled from a church, being cast out by the Bishop, as Adam, the first man, had been cast out of Paradise, and Urban II, the Pope of the Crusades, decreed ashes for everybody. The English, at any rate, were already by then firmly fixed in the Ash Wednesday ritual. *(Douglas Woodruff)*

The Saxons called March 'lencten monath' because in this month, the days noticeably lengthen. As the chief part of the great fast, from Ash Wednesday to Easter, falls in March, it received the name Lencten-faesten or Lent.

The fast of 36 days was introduced in the 4th century, but it did not become fixed at 40 days until the early seventh century, thus corresponding with Our Lord's fast in the wilderness.

See also: B47 Dying to self
C37 Temptation
C40 Reconciliation
C41 Starting afresh

THE DIGNITY OF THE INDIVIDUAL

'He not only died for us—he rose from the dead, and there at God's right hand he stands and pleads for us.' *Romans 8:34*

Quotations

What is dignity without honesty?. *(Cicero)*

Men are born equal but they are also born different. *(Erich Fromm)*

Perhaps the only true dignity of man is his capacity to despise himself. *(George Santayana)*

You can't expect a person to see eye to eye with you when you're looking down on him. *(Anon)*

Even one ear of corn is not exactly like another. *(Talmud)*

Man is more interesting than men. God made him and not them in his image. Each one is more precious than all. *(André Gide)*

A whole bushel of wheat is made up of single grains. *(Thomas Fuller)*

Let not a man guard his dignity, but let his dignity guard him. *(Emerson)*

Proverbs

The easiest way to dignity is humility. *(English proverb)*

Not all horses enjoy the same thing. *(Jewish proverb)*

Humour

The two things that a healthy person hates most between heaven and hell are a woman who is not dignified and a man who is. *(G. K. Chesterton)*

The butler entered the room, a solemn procession of one. *(P. G. Wodehouse)*

It is only people of small moral stature who have to stand on their dignity. *(Arnold Bennett)*

Statement

Coming down to practical and particularly urgent consequence, this Council lays stress on reverence for man; everyone must consider his every neighbour without exception as another self, taking into account first of all his life and the means necessary to living it with dignity, so as not to imitate the rich man who had no concern for the poor man Lazarus. *(Second Vatican Council—'The Church Today')*

Word-Pictures

A quarter of a century ago, amidst the great hopes of all mankind, the United Nations Organisation was born. Alas, in an immoral world, it too grew up immoral. It is not a United Nations Organisation but a United Governments Organisation, which equates those governments which were freely elected, those which were imposed by force and those which seized power by force of arms. Thanks to the venal prejudice of the majority of its members, the United Nations jealously guards the liberty of certain nations and neglects the liberty of others. It obsequiously voted against investigating private grievances—the groans, cries and entreaties of simple, humble individuals, insects too tiny for such a large organisation to concern itself with. The best document it put out in all its twenty-five years was the Declaration of Human Rights, yet the United Nations did not endeavour to make endorsement of it an obligatory condition of membership, and thus it left ordinary people at the mercy of governments not of their choosing. *(Alexander Solzhenitsyn)*

I cannot bear the universal categorisation of human beings: 'bourgeois,' 'bolshevist,' 'capitalist,' 'nigger,' 'hippie,' 'pig,' 'imperialist.' The one so labelled may be reviled, imprisoned, tortured, killed or exiled because he is no longer a human being, but a symbol. He does not bleed when pricked; his heart does not cry in the night. By this conjuring trick, conscience is made to disappear. It is, perhaps, the profoundest corruption of our time. *(Eric Sevareid)*

I could tell you the story of Jonas—of Jonas who was home from school for his summer holidays and who was arrested one morning and charged with being a vagrant. I heard about it late in the afternoon and by the time I reached the police station, he was waiting in the yard to be locked up for the night.

'Where was your school pass?' I asked him.

'They tore it up,' he replied.

Luckily the waste paper basket was still there; luckily I found the pass, in four pieces. And when I refused to give it up to the sergeant in charge, I was arrested myself. . .

You see, a native must carry a pass. A pass is his title to existence in the white man's city, his only excuse to authority for being where he is and doing what he does. And this, because he is black; he is a thing rather than a person. *(Trevor Huddleston)*

Maurice Baring used to tell the following story.

One doctor said to another doctor:

'About the termination of a pregnancy, I want your opinion. The father was a syphilitic. The mother was tuberculous. Of the four children born, the first was blind, the second died, the third was deaf and dumb, the fourth also tuberculous. What would you have done?'

'I would have ended the pregnancy.'

'Then you would have murdered Beethoven.'

'Dear Daddy'—in her best handwriting, eleven-year-old Jane wrote a letter to her make-believe father every week. She addressed the envelope to herself, and every week without fail, she wrote back—'Dear Jane'. For this shy youngster living in a local authority home, two postage stamps and a dream father were the only cure she had available for an affliction that is so pathetically easy to diagnose—loneliness. At this moment, there are four million desperately lonely people in this country. Before someone like young Jane grows into a lonely Mrs X I know who rings up the telephone speaking clock for company, why don't we act? *(Daily Express)*

See also: B26 The Whole man
B34 Human Rights
B45 Free Will
C47 The Indwelling Spirit

FREE WILL

'Jesus never needed evidence about any man; he could tell what a man had in him.' *John 2:25*

Quotations

Skill is nil without will. *(Ibn Tibbon)*

No one can rob us of our free will. *(Epictetus)*

God presses us but does not oppress our liberty. *(St. Francis de Sales)*

He who has a firm will moulds the world to himself. *(Goethe)*

People do not lack strength; they lack will. *(Hugo)*

To deny the freedom of the will is to make morality impossible. *(Froude)*

At twenty years of age the will reigns; at thirty, the wit; and at forty, the judgement. *(Gratian)*

We have freedom to do good or evil; yet to make choice of evil, is not to use, but to abuse our freedom. *(St. Francis de Sales)*

The power of choosing good and evil is within the reach of all. *(Origen)*

We are not constrained by servile necessity, but act with free will, whether we are disposed to virtue or incline to vice. *(St. Ambrose)*

Not only in works, but also in faith, God has given man freedom of the will. *(St. Irenaeus)*

The freedom of the will is then true freedom, when it does not serve vices and sins. *(St. Augustine of Hippo)*

If man does not have the free faculty to shun evil and to choose good, then, whatever his actions may be, he is not responsible for them. *(St. Justin Martyr)*

There are no galley slaves in the royal vessel of divine love—every man works his oar voluntarily. *(Jean Pierre Camus)*

Proverbs

When the will is ready, the feet are light. *(French proverb)*

Where there's a will, there's a way. *(English proverb)*

There is nothing good or evil save in the will. *(Greek proverb)*

Our eyes and ears are not subject to our will—but our tongues are. *(Jewish proverb)*

Statement

It is in accordance with their dignity as persons—that is, beings endowed with reason and free will and therefore privileged to bear personal responsibility—that all men should be at once impelled by nature and also bound by a moral obligation to seek the truth, especially religious truth. *(Second Vatican Council—'Religious Freedom')*

Word-Picture

A tourist standing by Niagara Falls saw an eagle swoop upon a frozen lamb encased in a piece of floating ice. The eagle stood upon it as it drifted towards the rapids. Every now and then, the eagle would proudly lift its head into the air to look around him, as much as to say, 'I am drifting on towards danger. I know what I am doing. I shall fly away and make good my escape before it is too late.'

When he reached the edge, he stooped, spread his powerful wings, and leaped for flight; but alas, while he was feeding on the carcase, his feet had frozen to its fleece. He leaped and shrieked, and beat upon the air with his wings until he went over into the chasm and darkness below. *(Anon)*

See also: A2 Integrity
B26 The Whole Man
B44 The Dignity of the Individual

CHRIST THE SACRAMENT OF GOD

'The Son of Man must be lifted up as Moses lifted up the serpent in the desert, so that everyone who believes may have eternal life in him.'
John 3:14–15

Quotations

He changed sunset into sunshine. *(Clement of Alexandria)*

Jesus alone is able to offer himself as the sufficient illustration of his own doctrine. *(Hensley Henson)*

Something fiery and star-like gleamed from his eyes and the majesty of Godhead shone from his countenance. *(St. Jerome)*

Our faith is sound if we believe that no man, old or young, is delivered from the contagion of death and the bonds of sin, except by one Mediator of God and men, Jesus Christ. *(St. Augustine of Hippo)*

Whenever Christianity has struck out a new path on her journey, it has been because the personality of Jesus has again become living, and a ray from His Being has once more illuminated the world. *(Anon)*

Word-Pictures

A group of women teachers from a Christian school had fled to an outlying village in another part of Burma, when their town was invaded. It was during the disastrous days of our retreat. Stragglers from our forces came staggering in, British lads, with blistered feet and torn clothing. Famished, parched and sleepless, they were done. These women, both Burmese and Karen, took them in . . . There were some in the neighbourhood ready to inform against the women. Armed men surrounded the house. 'You have been helping the enemy,' they said. 'You shall die.' They asked for mercy, tried to buy it, offering all they had. Then they said, 'If we must die, give us a moment to get ready.' The company of them knelt in prayer, and were cut to pieces. One of them was a girl of 17. When the Japanese were gone, the Bishop held his first confirmation. In the front row of those to be confirmed, he recognised a Burmese who had been a prominent anti-Christian leader.

'My friend,' said the Bishop, 'how did you come to be baptised?' 'It was the way those girls in that village died two years ago,' he said. 'I knew they had something which I had not.' *(John Foster)*

Christ is all-sufficient. For the

ARTIST, He is the altogether lovely—*(Song of Solomon 5:16)*

ARCHITECT, He is the chief cornerstone—*(1 Peter 2:6)*

ASTRONOMER, He is the sun of righteousness—*(Malachi 4:2)*

BAKER, He is the living bread—*(John 6:51)*

BANKER, He is the unsearchable riches—*(Ephesians 3:8)*

BUILDER, He is the sure foundation—*(Isaiah 28:16) (1 Corinthians 3:11)*

CARPENTER, He is the door—*(John 10:9)*

EDITOR, He is good tidings of great joy—*(Luke 2:10)*

ELECTRICIAN, He is the light of the world—*(John 8:12)*

FARMER, He is sower and the Lord of the harvest—*(Matthew 13:37) (Luke 10:2)*

FLORIST, He is the rose of Sharon and the lily of the valley—*(Song of Solomon 2:1)*

JEWELLER, He is the living precious stone—*(1 Peter 2:4)*

LAWYER, He is the counselor, lawgiver and advocate—*(Isaiah 9:6) (1 John 2:1)*

LABOURER, He is the giver of rest—*(Matthew 11:28)* *(Anon)*

See also: A44 Meeting Christ in the Sacraments
B4 Christ, the covenant of God
B16 Christ forgives our sins
B51 One with Christ

DYING TO SELF

'I tell you, most solemnly, unless a wheat grain falls on the ground and dies, it remains only a single grain, but if it dies it yields a rich harvest.'
John 12:24

Quotations

Self-centredness completely vitiates communication—with either God or man. *(Hubert Van Zeller)*

Love is like death—it kills the self-willed me, it breaks its stranglehold and sets the Spirit free. *(Angelus Silesius)*

Let our praise be with God, and not from ourselves, for God hates those who praise themselves. *(Pope St. Clement I)*

Self-love is cunning, it pushes and insinuates itself into everything, while making us believe it is not there at all. *(St. Francis de Sales)*

No death has greatness but that from which new life can spring. No life more vital than that which from the death of self takes wing. *(Angelus Silesius)*

Man's highest life does not consist in self-expression, but in self-sacrifice. *(R. H. Benson)*

He who lives to benefit himself confers on the world a benefit when he dies. *(Tertullian)*

Make it thy business to know thyself, which is the most difficult lesson in the world. *(Cervantes)*

When a man is wrapped up in himself, he makes a pretty small package. *(John Ruskin)*

You give but little when you give of your possessions. It is when you give of yourself that you truly give. *(Kahlil Gibran)*

Your life is without a foundation, if in any matter, you choose on your own behalf. *(Dag Hammarskjold)*

Proverbs

He is unworthy to live who lives only for himself. *(English proverb)*

He who wants to know himself should offend two or three of his neighbours. *(Chinese proverb)*

Word-Pictures

A. J. Cronin tells of his days as medical officer to a Welsh mining company in his book 'Adventures in Two Worlds'.

I have told you of Olwen Davies, the middle-aged district nurse who for more than twenty years, with fortitude and patience, calmness and cheerfulness, served the people of Tregenny. This unconscious selflessness, which above all seemed the keynote of her character, was so poorly rewarded, it worried me. Although she was much beloved by the people, her salary was most inadequate. And late one night after a particularly strenuous case, I ventured to protest to her as we drank a cup of tea together. 'Nurse,' I said, 'Why don't you make them pay you more? It's ridiculous that you should work for so little.' She raised her eyebrows slightly. But she smiled. 'I have enough to get along.' 'No, really,' I persisted, 'you ought to have an extra pound a week at least. God knows you're worth it.' There was a pause. Her smile remained, but her gaze held a gravity, an intensity which startled me. 'Doctor,' she said, 'if God knows I'm worth it, that's all that matters to me.' *(A. J. Cronin)*

Ira Dutton (as his name was) was born on a farm in Vermont, and was made to go to school though he hated it. He was 17 when the Civil War broke out. He enlisted in the Northern army and soon became an officer. When the war ended, he was 22, and says he allowed the demon of drink to get him into its clutches. For years he led a kind of double life, sober in daytime, but at night associating with disreputable acquaintances. However, somehow he came to a better mind, and was received into the Church when he was 40. He changed his first name to Joseph. Two years later he read about Damien, and determined to go and help him with the lepers, partly to begin a new life and partly to make reparation for his sins. He sailed (in the roughest and most uncomfortable way) to the South Seas and met Damien on the beach of Molokai (1886). He told him he asked for no special treatment or consideration: 'I just want to consider myself a servant to my fellow men.' Damien already had leprosy, and in another year or two was dead. Brother Joseph lived for another 40 years on Molokai, devoting himself to the lepers. *(Anon)*

Are you willing to be sponged out, erased, cancelled,
made nothing?
Are you willing to be made nothing,
dipped into oblivion?

If not, you will never really change.

The phoenix renews her youth
only when she is burnt, burnt alive, burnt down
to hot and flocculent ash.
Then the small stirring of a new small bub in the nest
with strands of down like floating ash
Shows that she is renewing her youth like an eagle,
Immortal bird. *(D. H. Lawrence)*

See also: A5 Unselfishness
A7 Poor in spirit
A10 Seeking Perfection
B26 The Whole Man

CHRISTIAN UNITY

'The whole group of believers was united, heart and soul.' *Acts 4:32*

Quotations

From many to make one. *(Ex pluribus unum facere.) (St. Augustine of Hippo)*

There are three unions in this world: Christ and the Church, husband and wife, spirit and flesh. *(St. Augustine of Hippo)*

Putting all the ecclesiastical corpses into one graveyard will not bring about a resurrection. *(David M. Lloyd-Jones)*

Some of us worked long enough in a shipbuilding district to know that welding is impossible except the materials to be joined are at white heat temperature; and none of our denominational convictions is at white heat. When you try to weld them, they only fall apart. *(George F. MacLeod)*

Form all together one choir, so that, with the symphony of your feelings and having all taken the tone of God, you may sing with one voice to the Father through Jesus Christ, that He may listen to you and know you from your chant as the canticle of His only Son.
(St. Ignatius of Antioch)

Proverbs

Union gives strength to the humble. *(Latin proverb)*

Strength united is greater. *(Latin proverb)*

Humour

The tale is told of two Irish labourers, new to traffic lights. Having watched the transient amber and the more enduring green, one said to the other, 'they don't allow the Protestants much time to get across.' *(Anon)*

One Sunday in an Irish village, three Protestant women visited a Roman Catholic church. Recognising them and wishing to show respect, the priest whispered to his server, 'Three chairs for the Protestant ladies.'

The server jumped to his feet and shouted, 'Three cheers for the Protestant ladies.' The congregation rose, responded heartily, and the service continued. *(The Sign)*

Statement

There can be no ecumenism worthy of the name without a change of heart. For it is from newness of attitudes *(cf. Eph. 4:23)* from self-denial and unstinted love, that yearnings for unity take their rise and grow toward maturity. We should therefore pray to the divine Spirit for the grace to be genuinely self-denying, humble, gentle in the service of others, and to have an attitude of brotherly generosity toward them. *(Second Vatican Council—'Ecumenism')*

Word-Pictures

I read of an industrious German, the father of a large family, who, with the help of willing child labour, compiled a dictionary of Protestant sects. His name is Gruendler, and he has often kept his children in on a Sunday to help him arrange the cards, listing 2,639 different Christian denominations, the glorious fruit of the Protestant Reformation. *(Douglas Woodruff)*

Speaking from the moon, the astronaut Frank Borman said, 'We are one hunk of ground, water, air, clouds, floating around in space. From here it really is one world.' *(Frank Borman)*

See also: A20 The Kingdom of God
B17 The Church, Bride of Christ
B36 The Family of God
B51 One with Christ

COPING WITH DOUBT

'Why are you so agitated, and why are these doubts rising in your hearts?' *Luke 24:38*

Quotations

Time trieth truth in every doubt. *(John Heywood)*

Cleave ever to the sunnier side of doubts. *(Anon)*

Feed your faith, and your doubts will starve to death. *(Anon)*

Doubt charms me no less than knowledge. *(Dante)*

He is a dull man who is always sure, and a sure man who is always dull. *(H. L. Mencken)*

Ten thousand difficulties do not make one doubt, as I understand the subject; difficulty and doubt are incommensurate. *(Cardinal Newman)*

Faith keeps many doubts in her pay. If I could not doubt, I should not believe. *(Henry David Thoreau)*

Our doubts are traitors
And make us lose the good we oft might win
By fearing to attempt. *(Shakespeare)*

Who can determine when it is, that the scales in the balance of opinion begin to turn, and what was a greater probability in behalf of a belief becomes a positive doubt against it? *(Cardinal Newman)*

There lives more faith in honest doubt, believe me, than in half the creeds. *(Alfred Lord Tennyson)*

Proverbs

To believe with certainty we must begin with doubting. *(Polish proverb)*

The wise are prone to doubt. *(Greek proverb)*

Who knows nothing doubts nothing. *(French proverb)*

Word-Pictures

Seeing the immense design of the world, one image of wonder mirrored by another image of wonder—the pattern of fern and of feather echoed by the frost of the window-pane, the six rays of the snowflake mirrored by the rock crystal's six-rayed eternity—I ask myself, 'Were those shapes moulded by blindness? Who, then, shall teach me doubt?' *(Dame Edith Sitwell)*

A man went to stay with a friend in Cornwall, in a part where there was a large number of deep holes in the ground. These were disused mine-shafts, some of which had no rails round them. He went for a walk one day and got lost. Darkness came and he realised that he was near these holes and it was dangerous to walk in the dark. But it was too cold to sit down and wait till morning, so he walked on with great care. In spite of this, his feet slipped and he started to slide down a mine-shaft. He managed to grasp a rock that was sticking out of the side of the shaft. There he hung, terrified, with his feet dangling. He managed to hang on for about twenty minutes, but the agony in his arms got so great that he knew he would soon have to let go and plunge to his death. He was about to let go when he saw, to his immense relief, a little light in the distance which began to grow greater and he knew that help was coming. He shouted loud with all the energy he had left. When the rescuers arrived and shone their light down on him the first thing they saw was that his feet were dangling within a foot of solid earth. This mine-shaft had been filled in! All his agony and fears had been for nothing. *(M. Nassan)*

See also: C13 Coping with grief
C22 The Light of Faith
C30 Increase our faith
C41 Starting Afresh

THE GOOD SHEPHERD

'I am the good shepherd: the good shepherd is one who lays down his life for his sheep.' *John 10:11*

Quotations

The Saviour of our souls and helmsman of our bodies, the Shepherd of the Catholic Church throughout the world. *(Martyrdom of St. Polycarp)*

He is the Good Shepherd, Who gives His life for the sheep—His life for them, His flesh to them, the one for their redemption, the other for their food. O mighty marvel! He is Himself the Shepherd of the sheep, their Pasturage and their redemption's Price. *(St. Bernard)*

Proverbs

The death of the wolf is the health of the sheep. *(Italian proverb)*

It is a foolish sheep that makes the wolf his confessor. *(English proverb)*

Good pastures make fat sheep. *(English proverb)*

Statement

Thus the Church is a sheepfold whose one and necessary door is Christ *(Jn. 10:1–10)*. She is a flock which God Himself foretold that He would be the Shepherd *(cf. Is. 40:11; Ez. 34:11 ff.)*. Although guided by human shepherds, her sheep are nevertheless ceaselessly led and nourished by Christ Himself, the Good Shepherd and the Prince of Shepherds *(cf. Jn. 10:11; 1 Pet. 5:4)* who gave His life for the sheep *(cf. Jn. 10:11–15)*. *(Second Vatican Council—'The Church')*

Word-Pictures

One night, a tall American doctor told me a story of Commissioner Lord, of the Salvation Army, also a prisoner of the Chinese in Korea.

'We were dead beat. Another terrible day's march lay ahead. The men were lying cold and half-starved in the lousy shacks waiting for the command to get going. A lot of those guys thought they couldn't make it—they felt they'd had it. Suddenly old Commissioner Lord appeared in the doorway of our shack. He seemed very confidential about something. "Boys," he said, "boys, I've got news for you—great news—listen." We all took notice. We all thought, "What's with this guy?" That old Commissioner, why he just stood among us and said, "The Lord is my shepherd; I shall not want," and he went right through that psalm, like it was God's personal message to us. Chaplain, I'm telling you, you could hear the silence. I never felt so moved in all my life. Then the guards came—it was get going or die. Those men rose like they had new strength. Can't tell you where they got it from. They marched and they stuck it out.' *(S. J. Davies)*

The world's longest fence, 3,500 miles from end to end, has been built in Queensland, Australia.

The six-foot-high barrier was begun to keep dingoes (wild dogs) out of the 135 million acres of high quality grazing land.

Since 20 million sheep and 600,000 head of cattle are at stake, landlords willingly pay charges for the fence and maintain six full-time inspectors.

Before the barrier's erection, dingoes ravaged the sheep and cattle, causing widespread destruction. *(Anon)*

There was once a man who owned several hundred sheep. His servants used to take these sheep out for feeding, and each evening, as they brought them back, they found two or three missing. He asked his servants to go and look for them, but for fear of wild beasts, they did not trouble themselves about them. The owner had a love for them and wanted to save them. 'If I go myself, searching for these sheep, they will not recognise me, as they have not seen me before. They would recognise my servants, but the servants will not go. So I must become like a sheep. He went out and found that some had gone astray and some had been wounded. They readily followed him, thinking he was a sheep like one of themselves. He brought them in and sat with them and fed them. When he had saved all the sheep and brought them home, then he took off his sheep skin. He was not sheep, but man. He became a sheep in order to save those lost sheep. So God is not man, He became man in order to save men. *(Sadhu Sundar Singh)*

See also: B15 Jesus friend of outcasts
B38 The suffering servant
C44 Feed my sheep

ONE WITH CHRIST

'As a branch cannot bear fruit all by itself, but must remain part of the vine, neither can you unless you remain in me.' *John 15:4*

Quotations

The greatness of contemplation can be given to none but them that love. *(Pope St. Gregory I)*

We become contemplatives when God discovers Himself in us. *(Thomas Merton)*

The perfect soul desires to be rapt by contemplation in the chaste embraces of her Spouse. *(St. Bernard)*

How many there must be who have smothered the first sparks of contemplation by piling wood on the fire before it was well lit. *(Thomas Merton)*

The acts of contemplation are four: to seek after God, to find Him, to feel His sacred touch in the soul, and to be united with Him and to enjoy Him. *(Archbishop Ullathorne)*

Seek in reading and thou shalt find in meditation; knock in prayer and it shall be opened to thee in contemplation. *(St. John of the Cross)*

To live according to the spirit is to think, speak and act according to the virtues that are in the spirit, and not according to the sense and sentiments which are in the flesh. *(St. Francis de Sales)*

Holiness consists not in doing uncommon things, but in doing all common things with an uncommon fervour. *(Cardinal Manning)*

Though Christ a thousand times
In Bethlehem be born.
If he's not born in thee,
Thy soul is still forlorn.

The cross on Golgotha
Will never save thy soul,
The cross in thine own heart
Alone can make thee whole. *(Angelus Silesius)*

Too late I loved you, O beauty so ancient yet ever new! Too late I loved you! And, behold, you were within me, and I out of myself and there I searched for you. *(St. Augustine of Hippo)*

Contemplative prayer is a deep and simplified spiritual activity in which the mind and will are fused into one. They rest in a unified and simple concentration upon God, turned to Him and intent upon Him and absorbed in His own light, with a simple gaze which is perfect adoration because it silently tells God that we have left everything else and desire even to leave our own selves for His sake, and that He alone is important to us, He alone is our desire and consumed with love and enveloped in spiritual light, worthy to be called and to be the spouse of Christ. *(Walter Hilton)*

Statement

Since Christ in His mission from the Father is the fountain and source of the whole apostolate of the Church, the success of the lay apostolate depends upon the laity's living union with Christ. For the Lord has said, 'He who abides in me, and I in him, he bears much fruit: for without me you can do nothing.' *(Jn. 15:5) (Second Vatican Council—'Laity')*

Word-Pictures

Jesus said: 'Cleave the wood and thou shalt find me; lift the stone and I am there. Let him-who-seeks not cease seeking until he finds; and when he finds he will be troubled and when he has been troubled, he will marvel and he will reign over the All.' *(The Gospel according to St. Thomas)*

As Brother Lawrence had found such comfort and blessing in walking in the Presence of God, it was natural for him to recommend it earnestly to others; but his example was a stronger inducement than any arguments he could use. His very countenance was a lesson in itself; such a sweet and calm devotion appearing in it, as could not but affect all beholders. And it was noticed that in the greatest hurry of business in the kitchen, he still preserved his recollection and his heavenly mindedness. He was never hasty nor loitering, but did each thing at its right time, with a steady, uninterrupted composure and tranquility of spirit.

'The time of business,' said he, 'does not with me differ from the time of prayer, and in the noise and clatter of my kitchen, while several persons are at the same time calling for different things, I possess God in as great tranquility as if I were upon my knees at the Blessed Sacrament.'

Brother Lawrence said that the most excellent method which he had found of going to God was that of doing our ordinary work without any idea of pleasing men, and (as far as we are capable) purely for the love of God. *(Peter Hargreaves)*

Who sees his lord
Within every creature
Deathlessly dwelling
Amidst the mortal:
That man sees truly...
Who sees the separate
Lives of all creatures
United in Brahman,
Brought forth from Brahman,
Himself finds Brahman. *(The Bhagavad-Gita)*

See also: B25 Quiet—time for prayer
C47 The Indwelling Spirit
C48 One in us

GOD IS LOVE

'Anyone who fails to love can never have known God, because God is love.' *1 John 4:8*

Quotations

Love can deny nothing to love. *(Andreas Capellanus)*

There is no living in love without suffering. *(Thomas à Kempis)*

To love is to wish the other's highest good. *(R. H. Benson)*

It is only the souls that do not love that go empty in this world. *(R. H. Benson)*

Love is the movement, effusion and advancement of the heart toward the good. *(St. Francis de Sales)*

It is always springtime in the heart that loves God. *(St. John Vianney)*

Give me such love for God and men, as will blot out all hatred and bitterness. *(Dietrich Bonhoffer)*

Love seeketh not itself to please,
nor for itself have any care,
but for another gives its ease,
and builds a heaven in hell's despair. *(William Blake)*

You had pierced our hearts with the arrow of Your love, and our minds were pierced with the arrows of Your words. *(St. Augustine of Hippo)*

Love has a hem to its garment
That touches the very dust;
It can reach the stains of the streets and lanes,
And because it can, it must. *(Anon)*

The longest way to God, the indirect,
lies through the intellect.
The shortest way lies through the heart.
Here is my journey's end and here its start. *(Angelus Silesius)*

The reason why God's servants love creatures so much is that they see how much Christ loves them, and it is one of the properties of love to love what is loved by the person we love. *(St. Catherine of Siena)*

Proverbs

Who God loves, he punishes *(Yiddish proverb)*

Love is a glass which shatters if you hold it too tightly or too loosely. *(Russian proverb)*

Humour

God wants spiritual fruit, not religious nuts. *(Ethel Wilcox)*

Statement

What does the most to reveal God's presence, however, is the brotherly charity of the faithful who are united in spirit as they work together for the faith of the gospel and who prove themselves a sign of unity. *(Second Vatican Council—'The Church Today')*

Word-Pictures

Some people want to see God with their eyes as they see a cow, and to love him as they love their cow for the milk and cheese and profit it brings them. This is how it is with people who love God for the sake of outward wealth or inward comfort. They do not rightly love God, when they love him for their own advantage. Indeed, I tell you the truth, any object you have in your mind, however good, will be a barrier between you and the inmost Truth. *(Meister Eckhart)*

An eminent baby specialist had a standard treatment for frail newborn infants who failed to gain weight.

When he came to the baby's chart during his rounds in the hospital, he invariably scrawled the following direction to the nurse in attendance:

'This baby to be loved every three hours.' *(Anon)*

Some 800 years after her death, the solicitude of an Englishwoman for the poor continues to have its effects.

To this day, as a result of her remarkable bequest, a supply of six pounds of flour is given to each adult and three pounds to each child in two small Hampshire villages.

Her husband, the story goes, who had little compassion for the poor, was impatient when she asked, shortly before her death in the 12th century, that he give something to the poor every year in her memory.

Setting fire to a branch, he told her he would donate the produce from as much land as she could crawl around while the branch still burned.

Despite her weakened condition, she is said to have crawled around twenty-three acres before the flame died out. Touched by her love for others, her husband kept his word. *(Anon)*

A father complained to the Besht that his son had forsaken God.

'What, Rabbi, shall I do?'

'Love him more than ever,' was the Besht's reply. *(Jewish saying)*

A great American story-teller wrote about two young people who were very much in love. Christmas Eve was coming and they wanted to give presents to one another. But they were very poor and had no money for presents. So each one, without telling the other, decided to sell his or her most precious possession. The girl's most precious possession was her long golden hair and she went to a hairdresser and had it cut off. She sold it then to buy a lovely watch chain for her lover's watch. He, meanwhile, had gone to a jeweller and sold his watch to buy two beautiful combs for his beloved's hair. Then they made their gifts. There were tears at first and then laughter. There was no hair for the combs and no watch for the watch chain. But there was something more precious and that was their self-sacrificing love for one another. *(Anon)*

See also: A9 Relationships
A33 Love your neighbour
B30 Married Love
C10 Love your enemies

CONSECRATED IN TRUTH

'I have sent them into the world, and for their sake I consecrate myself so that they too may be consecrated in truth.' *John 17:19*

Quotations

If God were able to backslide from truth, I would fain cling to truth and let God go. *(Meister Eckhart)*

Truth which is merely told is quick to be forgotten: truth which is discovered lasts a lifetime. *(William Barclay)*

If the world goes against truth, then Athanasius goes against the world. *(Athanasius)*

Any human being can penetrate to the kingdom of truth, if only he longs for truth and perpetually concentrates all his attention upon its attainment. *(Simone Weil)*

Error is none the better for being common, nor truth the worse for having lain neglected. *(John Locke)*

Let us rejoice in the Truth, wherever we find its lamp burning. *(Albert Schweitzer)*

A truth that's told with bad intent
Beats all the lies you can invent. *(William Blake)*

Facts that are not frankly faced have a habit of stabbing us in the back. *(Sir Harold Bowden)*

Seven years of silent inquiry are needful for a man to learn the truth, but fourteen in order to learn how to make it known to his fellow men. *(Plato)*

Sit down before the facts as a little child; be prepared to give up every preconceived notion, follow humbly and to whatever abysses nature leads, or you shall learn nothing. *(Thomas Huxley)*

Truth is the perfect correlation of mind and reality; and this is actualised in the Lord's person. If the gospel is true and God is, as the Bible declares, a living God, the ultimate truth is not a system of propositions grasped by a perfect intelligence, but is a personal being apprehended in the only way in which persons are ever fully apprehended, that is, by love. *(William Temple)*

Proverbs

A half truth is a whole lie. *(Yiddish proverb)*

Truth is heavy; few therefore can bear it. *(Hebrew proverb)*

Truth is God's daughter. *(Spanish proverb)*

Humour

Father 'I want an explanation and I want the truth.'
Son 'Make up your mind, Dad, you can't have both. *(Anon)*

It is always the best policy to speak the truth, unless of course you are an exceptionally good liar. *(Jerome K. Jerome)*

The English are always degrading truth into facts. When a truth becomes a fact, it loses all its intellectual value. *(Oscar Wilde)*

Word-Pictures

One can tell lies without literal mis-statement. During a lull in the cold war, a Russian diplomat was explaining to an English one the difference between Russian and British newspapers.

'Suppose you and I had a race, and you came in first. Your newspapers would report: "The Soviet and British ambassadors yesterday had a race. The British Ambassador won." In "Pravda', the report would be: "A race took place yesterday between diplomats. The Soviet Ambassador came in second. The British Ambassador finished only just in front of the last man".' *(Anon)*

In a village in India, five blind men lived together. One day, they happened to come near an animal which someone told them was an elephant. 'What is an elephant like?' they asked. They were invited to feel its body. 'Why, an elephant is like a pillar,' said the first. He had felt only its leg. 'No, no, it is like a barrel,' said another, who had felt only the belly. A third said, 'It is like a rope,' for he had felt the tail; and a fourth, 'Like a hose,'—he had felt the trunk. 'It is like a winnowing-fan,' said the last man, who had felt only the ear. So they began to argue among themselves. Each said that his description of the elephant was the true one.

It is the same with Truth, says the Hindu, who loves telling this story. His ancient books, the Vedas, say, 'The Truth is One; people call it by various names.' All of us, like the blind men, find a part of the truth and think we have grasped it all. But truth itself must always be One and the same. *(Swami Yogeshananda)*

'The Jesuits were originally a savage Indian tribe, who emigrated very early in history to Spain via Arabia, and settled down in Northern Spain where they were made Catholics. For their savage and unscrupulous fierceness, the Popes took them into their service as the Church's vanguard. How disastrous they proved for Germany is clearly shown by the historical fact that it was the Jesuits who urged Charlemagne to the merciless massacre of the Saxons at Verden.' (Extract of a lesson on history in a labour camp in Nazi Germany.) *(Douglas Woodruff)*

A six-year-old daughter gave her mother a real shock when she came home from school and announced that her class was going to see 'the handsome gorilla.'

The startled parent decided to check with the school officials without delay. She gave a sigh of relief when she learned that what the first graders were due to see was the play 'Hansel and Gretel.'

When little children confuse fantasy with reality, they do so harmlessly and therefore due allowance is usually made.

But when those who know better distort the truth that God has entrusted to them, whether deliberately or through negligence, far-reaching damage can result.

Make sure that under all circumstances you are a transmitter of 'the truth and nothing but the truth.' Be a stickler for accuracy. Check and double check information that you pass on, especially if it is detrimental to others. *(Anon)*

See also: A47 The spirit of truth
C11 Conversation
C23 Zeal is for the right

THE TRINITY

'Baptise them in the name of the Father and of the Son and of the Holy Spirit, and teach them to observe all the commands I gave you.'
Matthew 28:19-20

Quotations

Among all things called one, the Unity of the Divine Trinity holds the first place. *(St. Bernard)*

How can plurality consist with unity, or unity with plurality? To examine the fact closely is rashness, to believe it is piety, to know it is life, and life eternal. *(St. Bernard)*

Tell me how it is that in this room there are three candles and but one light, and I will explain to you the mode of the divine existence. *(John Wesley)*

The Father is my trust, the Son is my refuge, the Holy Ghost is my protection. O Holy Trinity, glory to Thee. *(Byzantine Horologion, Troparion at Nocturns. ca. 6th to 8th cent.)*

The divine nature is really and entirely identical with each of the three persons, all of whom can therefore be called one: I and the Father are one. *(St. Thomas Aquinas)*

It is not easy to find a term which appropriately defines such great excellence, unless it is better to say that this Trinity is one God from Whom, through Whom, and in Whom all things exist. *(Cf. Rom. 11,36) (St. Augustine of Hippo)*

In the Father resides unity, in the Son equality, and in the Holy Ghost the perfect union of unity and equality. These three qualities are all one because of the Father, all equal because of the Son, and all united because of the Holy Ghost. *(St. Augustine of Hippo)*

God dwells in our heart by faith, and Christ by his Spirit, and the holy Spirit by his purities; so that we are also cabinets of the mysterious Trinity; and what is this short of heaven itself, but as infancy is short of manhood, and letters of words? *(Jeremy Taylor)*

We are enclosed in the Father, and we are enclosed in the Son, and we are enclosed in the Holy Ghost. And the Father is enclosed in us, and the Son is enclosed in us, and the Holy Ghost is enclosed in us:

Almightiness, All Wisdom, All Goodness: one God, one Lord. *(Julian of Norwich)*

Statement

Now the Catholic faith is this; that we worship one God in Trinity, and Trinity in Unity, neither confounding the Persons, nor dividing the substance, for there is one Person of the Father, another of the Son, and another of the Holy Ghost; but the godhead of the Father, of the Son, and of the Holy Ghost is one, the glory equal, the majesty co-eternal . . . *(Athanasian Creed)*

Word-Pictures

Think of the Father as a spring of life begetting the Son like a river and the Holy Ghost like a sea, for the spring and the river and the sea are all one nature. Think of the Father as a root, of the Son as a branch, and of the Spirit as a fruit, for the substance in these three is one. The Father is a sun with the Son as rays and the Holy Ghost as heat. The holy Trinity transcends by far every similitude and figure. So when you hear of an offspring of the Father, do not think of a corporeal offspring. And when you hear that there is a Word, do not suppose him to be a corporeal word. And when you hear of the Spirit of God, do not think of wind and breath. Rather, hold your persuasion with a simple faith alone. For the concept of the Creator is arrived at by analogy from his creatures. *(John of Damascus)*

Christopher Columbus had a tremendous devotion to the Blessed Trinity. He invoked the Trinity at the beginning of every enterprise, and everything he wrote began with the words: 'In the Name of the Most Holy Trinity.'

When he presented to the Council of Salamanca (that assembly of all the learned of science and theology) his theory of the New World to be discovered, he began: 'I come before you in the Name of the Most Holy Trinity, because our sovereigns have commanded me to submit to your wisdom a project which has certainly come to me inspired by the same Holy Spirit.'

On his third voyage in 1598, he vowed to consecrate to the Trinity the first land that he would discover, and hence the island he reached was called Trinidad. *(Anon)*

See also: A37 Christ the King
A47 The Spirit of Truth
B28 The Father who draws us to himself
B40 One God
C47 The Indwelling Spirit

LIBERATION FROM FEAR

'When these things begin to take place, stand erect, hold your heads high, because your liberation is near at hand.' *Luke 21:28*

Quotations

Nothing in life is to be feared. It is only to be understood. *(Marie Curie)*

Fear is the foundation of safety. *(Tertullian)*

It will be quite enough to receive the evils which come upon us from time to time, without anticipating them by the imagination. *(St. Francis de Sales)*

The weight of fear is the anchor of the heart. *(Pope St. Gregory I)*

The free man is he who does not fear to go to the end of his thought. *(Leon Blum)*

Dodgers often dodge into the danger they would avert. Don't dodge anything except sin, sir, and you will be all right. *(Stonewall Jackson)*

A good scare is worth more to a man than good advice. *(E. W. Howe)*

Those who love to be feared, fear to be loved; they themselves are of all people the most abject; some fear them, but they fear everyone. *(Jean Pierre Camus)*

Let me assert my firm belief that the only thing we have to fear is fear itself—nameless, unreasoning terror which paralyses needed efforts to convert retreat into advance. *(Franklin D. Roosevelt)*

If you have a fearful thought, share it not with a weakling, whisper it to your saddle-bow, and ride forth singing. *(King Alfred)*

Proverbs

Keep your fears to yourself but share your courage. *(English proverb)*

Fear makes men ready to believe the worst. *(Latin proverb)*

Statement

In the use of all freedoms, the moral principle of personal and social responsibility is to be observed. In the exercise of their rights, individual men and social groups are bound by the moral law to have respect both for the rights of others and for their own duties toward others and for the common welfare of all. Men are to deal with their fellows in justice and civility. *(Second Vatican Council—'Religious Freedom')*

Word-Pictures

Dunkirk is set in a coastline riddled by shoals, sandbanks and narrow passages, hazards that were increased as most of the rescue work had to be done at night. Moreover, owing to the shallow water, ships larger than destroyers were prevented from reaching the pier.

The scene was unforgettable. Against an inferno of bursting high explosive, troops waded out to small boats and rafts that carried them to the waiting rescue vessels. It was a nightmare for the wounded. Rescue parties of stout-hearted and strong-backed sailors carried them on board. The devil's chorus of guns, bullets and bombs grew greater with every passing hour. The reverberations could be heard from the English coast, where watchers strained their eyes to catch each ominous flash on the horizon.

Then the news broke to the world: 335,000 men rescued; British casualties throughout the campaign, 'exceeding 30,000 killed, missing and wounded.'

At south-eastern ports, the whole population turned out to welcome back the men from Dunkirk. The Churches, the Salvation Army, the WVS and many other organisations had piles of food and hot tea ready. There were gifts of cigarettes and of chocolate. Crowds cheered them off from railway stations. Union Jacks fluttered, together with hastily improvised banners bearing words like 'Bravo BEF' and 'Welcome Home'. Weary as they were, many of the men contrived a cheery smile and an exchange of badinage as they saw their welcome.

The free world hailed the evacuation as a victory for freedom. And victory it was, compared with the disaster which had been so narrowly averted. *(From the Second World War Victory Book)*

Fear is one of the passions of human nature of which it is impossible to divest it. You remember the Emperor Charles V, when he read upon the tombstone of a Spanish nobleman, 'Here lies one who never knew fear,' wittily said, 'Then he never snuffed a candle with his fingers.' *(Samuel Johnson)*

The tragic loss of life that resulted from the sinking of the liner Titanic more than fifty years ago brought about at least one good effect.

After the British ship struck an iceberg in the North Atlantic and sank with a loss of 1,500 lives, the International Ice Patrol was formed to prevent similar tragedies.

Almost 50 nations are now members of this safety agency. Its planes and ships are constantly on patrol during the ice season to warn other vessels of danger from icebergs.

Four reasons were given for the incredibly high toll of life in this accident: 1. there were too few lifeboats; 2. the crew was unfamiliar with the ship; 3. the ship was travelling too fast; 4. the liner's officers were overconfident. *(Anon)*

'The Grey Dawn'

He knows not Advent's meaning who has never sat
By twilight in a dreary cell, its window dim;
Even by day comes little light into the narrow space.
Evening falls, slowly steals away the sun.

Night throws her gloomy mantle round the room,
Terrifying, impenetrable.

Will it always be night?
Will ne'er a ray of sunshine pierce the gloom?

And a new day lead on to joy?
A faint light glimmers through the narrow rift, a witness

That the sun sets never and soon will rise again,
Yes, that the light on which men turned their backs.

The Lord will bring again, with power and glory,
And found his everlasting kingdom!

I believe in Advent! *(Max Josef Metzger. Catholic Priest martyred in prison, 1944)*

See also: B3 Joy in Christ
B14 Freedom to serve
C2 Joy of salvation

THE JOY OF SALVATION

'God will guide Israel in joy by the light of his glory with his mercy and integrity for escort.' *Baruch 5:9*

Quotations

Joy is the echo of God's life within us. *(Joseph Marmion)*

Divine care supplies everybody with the means necessary for salvation, so long as he on his part does not put up obstacles. *(St. Thomas Aquinas)*

God wills all men to be saved that are saved, not because there is no man whom He does not wish saved, but because there is no man saved whose salvation He does not will. *(St. Augustine of Hippo)*

Salvation is seeing that the universe is good, and becoming a part of that goodness. *(Clutton Brock)*

The terms for 'salvation' in many languages are derived from roots like salvus, saos, whole, heil, which all designate health, the opposite of disintegration and disruption. Salvation is healing in the ultimate sense; it is final cosmic and individual healing. *(Paul Tillich)*

Salvation is free for you because someone else paid. *(Anon)*

The way to be saved is not to delay, but to come and take. *(Dwight L. Moody)*

No man has the right to abandon the care of his salvation to another. *(Thomas Jefferson)*

If you have no joy in your religion, there's a leak in your Christianity somewhere. *(W. A. Sunday)*

Proverbs

Salvation is from God only. *(Latin proverb)*

The knowledge of sin is the beginning of salvation. *(Latin proverb)*

Word-Pictures

There is no expeditious road
To pack and label men for God,
And save them by the barrel-load. *(Francis Thompson)*

Joy is distinctly a Christian word and a Christian thing. It is the reverse of happiness. Happiness is the result of what happens of an agreeable sort. Joy has its springs deep down inside, and that spring never runs dry, no matter what happens. Only Jesus gives that joy. He had joy, singing its music within, even under the shadow of the cross. It is an unknown word and thing except as He has sway within. *(Samuel Gordon)*

See also: B3 Joy in Christ

SHARING POSSESSIONS

'If anyone has two tunics he must share with the man who has none.'
Luke 3:10

Quotations

Be not anxious about what you have, but about what you are. *(Pope St. Gregory)*

Goods which are not shared are not goods. *(Fernando de Rojas)*

In a shared fish, there are no bones. *(Democritus of Abdera)*

Man should not consider his material possessions as his own, but as common to all, so as to share them without hesitation when others are in need. Whence the apostle says: 'Command the rich of this world . . . to offer with no stint, to apportion largely.' *(St. Thomas Aquinas)*

There is no savour like that of bread shared among men. *(Antoine de Saint-Exupery)*

For well you know that not life nor health nor riches nor honour nor dignity nor lordship is your own. Were they yours, you could possess them in your own way. But in such an hour a man wishes to be well, he is ill; or living, and he is dead; or rich, and he is poor; or a lord, and he is made a servant and vassal. All this is because these things are not his own, and he can only hold them in so far as may please him who has lent them to him. *(St. Catherine of Siena)*

Proverbs

All possessions of mortals are mortal. *(Latin proverb)*

Everything goes to him who wants nothing. *(French proverb)*

He who shares honey with the bear has the least part. *(English proverb)*

Humour

'Grandma,' asked a youngster, 'were you once a little girl like me?'
'Yes, dear.'
'Then," continued the child, 'I suppose you know how it feels to get an ice-cream cone when you don't expect it!'

One child said to another, 'If one of us would get off this tricycle, I could ride it much better.'

Teacher asked Peter how he would divide 10 potatoes equally among 20 people. Peter promptly replied, 'I'd mash them.'

Two children at a Sunday School picnic found a third who had no lunch. Remembering the lesson on the loaves and fishes in the Bible, Ronny said to his friend Timmy, 'We are going to share our lunch with our new friend, aren't you, Timmy?'

The postman stared doubtfully at the formidable looking animal lying on the doorstep. 'What kind of dog is that?' he asked the little old lady.

'I don't rightly know,' she said. 'My brother sent it from Africa.' 'Well,' the postman hesitated, 'it's the oddest looking dog I've ever seen.'

The prim lady nodded her head. 'You should have seen it before I cut its mane off.'

Statement

The distribution of goods should be directed toward providing employment and sufficient income for the people of today and of the future. Whether individuals, groups or public authorities make the decisions concerning this distribution and the planning of the economy, they are bound to keep these objectives in mind. They must realise their serious obligation of seeing to it that provision is made for the necessities of a decent life on the part of individuals and of the whole community. *(Second Vatican Council—'The Church Today')*

Word-Pictures

I heard recently of a Christian speaker in Hyde Park who declared rhetorically, expecting the answer 'Yes': 'If you had two houses, you would give one to the poor, wouldn't you?' 'Yes,' said the man to whom the question was directed, 'indeed I would.' 'And if you had two motor cars,' went on the orator, 'you would keep one and give the other away?' 'Yes, of course,' said the man. 'And if you had two shirts, you would give one away?' 'Hey, wait a minute,' said the man, 'I've got two shirts.' *(Douglas Woodruff)*

The Holy Supper is kept, indeed,
In whatso we share with another's need;

Not what we give, but what we share.
For the gift without the giver is bare. *(James Russell Lowell)*

See also: A7 Poor in Spirit
A21 Feeding the hungry
A33 Love your neighbour
B41 Generosity

PERSONAL PEACE

'They will live secure, for from then on he will extend his power to the ends of the land. He himself will be peace.' *Micah 5:4*

Quotations

We should have much peace if we would not busy ourselves with the sayings and doing of others. *(Thomas à Kempis)*

Thy peace shall be in much patience. *(Thomas à Kempis)*

The springs of human conflict cannot be eradicated through institutions, but only through the reform of the individual human being. *(General Douglas MacArthur)*

Peace is liberty in tranquility. *(Cicero)*

Where there is peace, God is. *(George Herbert)*

If we will have peace without a worm in it, lay we the foundations of justice and good will. *(Oliver Cromwell)*

Thinking about interior peace destroys interior peace. The patient who constantly feels his pulse is not getting any better. *(Hubert Van Zeller)*

Peace is not made at the council tables, or by treaties, but in the hearts of men. *(Herbert Hoover)*

Peace is not an absence of war, it is a virtue, a state of mind, a disposition for benevolence, confidence, justice. *(Baruch Spinoza)*

My religion is based on truth and non-violence. Truth is my God and non-violence is the means to reach Him. *(Mohandas Gandhi)*

We have to make peace without limitations. *(Harold Lindsell)*

Peace demands a mentality and a spirit which, before turning to others, must first permeate him who wishes to bring peace. Peace is first and foremost personal, before it is social. And it is precisely this spirit of peace which it is the duty of every true follower of Christ to cultivate. *(Pope Paul VI)*

Scrawled on the back of a van: 'Make love not war; ask driver for details.' *(Anon)*

Proverbs

Peace within makes beauty without. *(English proverb)*

Peace without truth is poison. *(German proverb)*

Statement

Peace cannot be obtained on earth unless personal values are safeguarded and men freely and trustingly share with one another the riches of their inner spirits and their talents. A firm determination to respect other men and peoples and their dignity, as well as the studied practice of brotherhood, are absolutely necessary for the establishment of peace. Hence peace is likewise the fruit of love, which goes beyond what justice can provide.

For this reason, all Christians are urgently summoned 'to practice the truth in love' *(Eph. 4:15)* and to join with all true peacemakers in pleading for peace and bringing it about. *(Second Vatican Council—'The Church Today')*

Word-Pictures

Peace is not won
By man's eternal strife,
Peace is the power of God
In human life.
It dwells with joy and love,
Is manifest in grace;
The star above His crib,
The light that is His face. *(Anon)*

Give us, O God, the vision which can see thy love in the world in spite of human failure. Give us the faith, the trust, the goodness in spite of our ignorance and weakness. Give us the knowledge that we may continue to pray with understanding hearts, and show us what each one of us can do to set forth the coming of the day of universal peace. *(Frank Bormann, Apollo 8, Christmas Eve 1968).*

See also: A2 Integrity
B19 Conscience
C17 International peace

THE INSTITUTION OF MARRIAGE

'There was a wedding at Cana in Galilee. The mother of Jesus was there and Jesus and his disciples had also been invited.' *John 2:1*

Quotations

And when will there be an end of marrying? I suppose, when there is an end of living! *(Tertullian)*

Marriage is an order in which the profession must be made before the noviciate. *(Jean Pierre Camus)*

Marriage is our last, best chance to grow up. *(Joseph Barth)*

Marriage is not like the hill of Olympus, wholly clear, without clouds. *(Thomas Fuller)*

Marriage is like twirling a baton, turning handsprings, or eating with chopsticks; it looks so easy till you try it. *(Helen Rowland)*

The form of matrimony consists in an inseparable union of minds; a couple pledged to one another in faithful friendship. The end is the begetting and upbringing of children, through marriage intercourse and shared duties in which each helps the other to rear children. *(St. Thomas Aquinas)*

When men and women marry, the union should be made with the consent of the bishop, so that the marriage may be according to the Lord and not merely out of lust. Let all be done to the glory of God. *(St. Ignatius of Antioch)*

It is clear that marriage, even in the state of nature and certainly long before it was raised to the dignity of a sacrament, was divinely instituted in such a way that it should be a perpetual and indissoluble bond, which cannot therefore be dissolved by any civil law. *(Pope Pius VI)*

How shall we ever be able adequately to describe the happiness of that marriage which the Church arranges, the Sacrifice strengthens, upon which the blessing sets a seal, at which the angels are present as witnesses, and to which the Father gives His consent? *(Tertullian)*

Proverbs

Marriage is a covered dish. *(Swiss proverb)*

Marriage is Heaven and Hell. *(German proverb)*

Don't praise marriage on the third day, but after the third year. *(Russian proverb)*

Humour

All marriages are happy. It's the living together afterwards that causes all the trouble. *(Farmer's Almanac)*

Falsely your Church seven sacraments does frame: Penance and Matrimony are the same! *(Richard Duke)*

Nowadays two can live as cheaply as one large family used to! *(J. Adams)*

Student 'To whom was Minerva married?'
Professor 'My boy, when will you learn that Minerva was the Goddess of Wisdom? She wasn't married.'

A neighbour's four-year-old daughter confided to me one day, 'When I grow up, I'm going to marry Danny.'

I asked her why she was going to marry the boy next door and she replied seriously, 'I have to, I'm not allowed to cross the street where the other boys live.'

An old Negro accused of deserting his wife was brought before the judge. After the judge had lectured him severely on the sin and serious character of desertion, he asked the old Negro: 'What have you to say?'

'Judge,' solemnly answered the old Negro: 'you done git me wrong. I ain't no deserter. I is a refugee.'

'Tis easy enough to be twenty-one:
'Tis easy enough to marry;
But when you try both games at once
'Tis a bloody big load to carry. *(The Midlands: Traditional)*

Statements

Since the Creator of all things has established the conjugal partnership as the beginning and basis of human society, and by His grace, has made it a great mystery in Christ and the Church *(cf. Eph. 5:32)* the apostolate of married persons and of families is of unique importance for the Church and civil society. *(Second Vatican Council—'Laity')*

Thus a man and a woman, who by the marriage covenant of conjugal love 'are no longer two, but one flesh' *(Mt. 19:6)* render mutual help and service to each other through an intimate union of their persons and of their actions. Through this union they experience the meaning of their oneness and attain to it with growing perfection day by day. As a mutual gift of two persons, this intimate union, as well as the good of the children, imposes total fidelity on the spouses and argues for an unbreakable oneness between them.

Authentic married love is caught up into divine love and is governed and enriched by Christ's redeeming power and the saving activity of the Church. Thus this love can lead the spouses to God with powerful effect and can aid and strengthen them in the sublime office of being a father or a mother. *(Second Vatican Council—'The Church Today')*

Word-Pictures

'Adam and Eve must have scolded each other roundly during their 900 years together. Eve would have said, "You ate the apple!" And Adam would have replied, "But why did you give it to me?" There is no doubt that during their long life, they encountered numberless evils as they sighed over their Fall. It must have been an extraordinary regime! And so Genesis is a remarkable book of wisdom and reason.'

This was the kind of table talk you might have heard if Martin Luther had asked you to a meal in 1536. Having plumped for the marriage of the clergy, his mind constantly ran on the inconveniences of the married state. He had his strict side, too, and put up a notice to warn the University students of Halle against prostitutes, and said that if he had his way, such women should be broken on the wheel and flayed for ruining young men. The students should pray God to provide them with pious wives, he said, adding grimly: 'You will have trouble enough as it is.' *(Douglas Woodruff)*

A group of cinema engineers classified the following as the 10 most dramatic sounds in the movies: a baby's first cry; the blast of a siren; the thunder of breakers on rocks; the roar of a forest fire; a fog-horn; the slow drip of water; the galloping of horses; the sound of a distant train whistle; the howl of a dog; the wedding march.

And one of these sounds causes more emotional response and upheaval than any other, has the power to bring forth almost every human emotion: sadness, envy, regret, sorrow, tears, as well as supreme joy. It is the sound of the wedding march. *(James Florn)*

We speak traditionally of the marriage knot or the bond of marriage. The Latin phrase is *nodus Herculeus*, and part of the marriage service was for the bridegroom to loosen *(solvere)* the bride's girdle, not to tie it. In the Hindu marriage ceremony, the bridegroom knots a ribbon round the bride's neck. Before the knot is tied, the bride's father may refuse consent, but immediately it is tied, the marriage is indissoluble. The Parsees bind the hands of the bridegroom with a sevenfold cord, seven being a sacred number. The ancient Carthaginians tied the thumbs of the betrothed with a leather lace. *(Anon)*

Over 50 years ago, a newlywed lost her wedding ring near the farm house in Kansas where she and her husband lived.

Now 57 years later, at the age of 81, the elderly women rejoices that her long missing wedding band has at last been returned to her. It was found by her granddaughter close to the spot where it had disappeared. She noticed a glint on the ground and picked up the dirt-encrusted ring. *(Anon)*

The Texas oil man was getting married and was nervous about it. He told the minister that the fee would be in proportion to the brevity of the service, and that if he used a long service, he wouldn't receive a cent. When the wedding day came, the couple stood before the minister, in the bride's home, and the minister said to the man, 'Take her?'—to the woman, 'Take him?' and then closed the ceremony by pronouncing, 'Took . . .'—a whole ceremony in five words. *(Anon)*

See also: B6 The Family
B30 Married Love

THE OLD TESTAMENT LAW

'The precepts of the Lord are right, they gladden the heart. The command of the Lord is clear, it gives light to the eyes.' *Psalm 19:8*

Quotations

Men of most renowned virtue have sometimes by transgressing most truly kept the law. *(John Milton)*

Probably all laws are useless; for good men do not need laws at all, and bad men are made no better by them. *(Demonax the Cynic)*

What is hateful to you, do not to your fellow: that is the whole Law: all the rest is interpretation. *(Rabbi Hillel)*

There are 70 ways of studying Torah; one is in silence. *(Rabbi Tcharkover)*

The Torah is truth, and the purpose of knowing it is to live by it. *(Maimonides)*

The Torah lives—even in a hovel, up to its neck in dirt. *(Anon)*

Proverbs

The beginning and the end of the law is kindness. *(Jewish proverb)*

Without Law, civilization dies. *(Jewish proverb)*

Word-Pictures

Alice While you talk, he's gone.
More And go he should, if he were the Devil himself, until he broke the law!
Roper So now you'd give the Devil benefit of law?
More Yes. What would you do? Cut a great road through the law to get after the Devil?
Roper I'd cut down every law in England to do that.
More Oh? And when the last law was down, and the Devil turned round on you—where would you hide, Roper, the laws all being flat? This country's planted thick with laws from coast to coast—Man's laws, not God's—and if you cut them down—and you are just the man to do it—d'you really think you could stand upright in the winds that would blow then? Yes, I'd give the Devil benefit of law, for my own safety's sake. *(Robert Bolt, 'A Man for all Seasons')*

When Rabbis of Judaism used the word 'Torah' or Law, a complicated concept was involved.

(1) Technically the Torah refers to the Pentateuch or 'the Five Books of Moses

(2) In another sense 'the Torah' designates the actual scroll containing the Five Books of Moses

(3) In a general sense, Torah is all of Jewish Law

(4) In the widest use of the word, 'Torah' refers to Judaism as a religion or philosophy

See also: A29 True Obedience
B4 Christ the Covenant of God
B31 The Commandments of Life

THE HUMANITY OF CHRIST

They said, 'This is Joseph's son, surely?' *Luke 4:22*

Quotations

Christ as God is the fatherland where we are going. Christ as man is the way by which we go. *(St. Augustine of Hippo)*

By a Carpenter, mankind was created and made, and by a Carpenter, meet it was that man should be repaired. *(Erasmus)*

To know Jesus and Him crucified is my philosophy, and there is none higher. *(St. Bernard)*

I see His blood upon the rose
And in the stars the glory of His eyes,
His body gleams amid eternal snows,
His tears fall from the skies. *(Joseph M. Plunkett)*

'Gentle Jesus, meek and mild' is a snivelling modern invention, with no warrant in the Gospels. *(George Bernard Shaw)*

Tell me the picture of Jesus you have reached and I will tell you some important traits about your nature. *(Oscar Pfister)*

Poor creature though I be, I am the hand and foot of Christ. I move my hand and my hand is wholly Christ's hand, for deity is become inseparably one with me. I move my foot, and it is aglow with God. *(Symeon the New Theologian)*

He became what we are that he might make us what he is. *(St. Athanasius of Alexandria)*

Proverbs

It is a man who counts; I call upon gold, it answers not; I call upon cloth, it answers not; it is man who counts. *(Ghanaian proverb)*

He is a man who acts like a man. *(Danish proverb)*

Statement

The truth is that only in the mystery of the incarnate Word does the mystery of man take on light. For Adam, the first man, was a figure of Him who was to come, namely, Christ the Lord. Christ, the final Adam, by the revelation of the mystery of the Father and His love, fully reveals man to man himself and makes his supreme calling clear. *(Second Vatican Council—'The Church Today')*

Word-Pictures

It was at that time that a man appeared—if 'man' is the right word—who had all the attributes of a man but seemed to be something greater. His actions were superhuman, for he worked such wonderful and amazing miracles that I for one cannot regard him as a man; yet in view of his likeness to ourselves I cannot regard him as an angel either. *(Josephus)*

Turn a deaf ear therefore when any one speaks to you apart from Jesus Christ, who was of the family of David, the child of Mary, who was truly born, who ate and drank, who was truly persecuted under Pontius Pilate, was truly crucified and truly died . . . But if, as some godless men, that is unbelievers, say, he suffered in mere appearance (being themselves mere appearances), why am I in bonds? *(St.Ignatius)*

A little known religious poet of early New England, Edward Taylor, put into words the main point of Incarnation-theology in this way: 'God's only Son doth hug Humanity Into his very Person.' *(Anon)*

St. John Fisher, on the way out of the Tower of London to the scaffold where he was to be beheaded, opened his New Testament at random with the prayer: 'Lord, show me some comforting thought this day.' When he looked at the page, his eye fell on the words in St. John: 'This is eternal life, that they may know thee the only true God and Jesus Christ whom thou hast sent.' He closed the book gently. 'Here is wisdom enough for me unto my life's end,' he said. *(Anon)*

See also: A37 Christ the King
B3 Joy in Christ
B16 Christ forgives our sins
C45 The divinity of Christ

GOD'S MESSENGERS

'Then I heard the voice of the Lord saying: "Whom shall I send? Who will be our messenger?" I answered, "Here I am, send me."' *Isaiah 6:8*

Quotations

But not everyone who speaks in the spirit is a prophet, but only if he follows the conduct of the Lord. *(Teaching of the Twelve Apostles)*

The prophet is to be no mere announcer, he is rather God's agent who by the 'word' accomplishes what he foretells, whether good or bad. *(Fleming James)*

The prophet is primarily the man, not to whom God has communicated certain divine thoughts, but whose mind is illuminated by the divine spirit to intercept aright the divine acts; and the act is primary. *(William Temple)*

Prophets were twice stoned—first in anger, then, after their death, with a handsome slab in the graveyard. *(Christopher Morley)*

We have made this memorial to commemorate those who have fought already, and to train those who shall fight hereafter. *(Inscription in the Chapel of Modern Martyrs, St. Paul's Cathedral)*

Leave it to the people, if they are not prophets, they are the sons of prophets. *(Talmud)*

The wisest prophets make sure of the event first. *(Horace Walpole)*

Humour

St. Jerome in his study kept a great big cat,
It's always in his pictures, with its feet upon the mat.
Did he give it milk to drink, in a little dish?
When it comes to Fridays, did he give it fish?
If I lost my little cat, I'd be sad without it;
I should ask St. Jerome what to do about it;
I should ask St. Jerome, just because of that,
For he's the only saint I know who kept a pussy cat. *(Anon)*

Word-Pictures

St. Albert (called 'the Great'), was a young German who went to the University of Padua and in 1223 joined the Dominicans, drawn by the preaching of their Master-General, Jordan of Saxony. Albert became one of the greatest minds of his time, a scientist as well as a theologian, bringing Aristotle into harmony with the Faith. He started a new university in Cologne. One of his students was a silent young Dominican named Thomas of Aquino, of whom he hoped great things. They worked together at Paris and elsewhere. Albert was elected Provincial for Germany in 1254, but resigned three years later; he felt his job was research and teaching.

In 1260, he was made Bishop of Ratisbon, where there were many difficulties and troubles; once again he realised he was no administrator; he resigned in 1262 and went back to teach at Cologne. St. Thomas was now in Paris, but Albert kept in close touch with him; and it was a sad blow to Albert when St. Thomas died, still under 50, in 1274. 'The Light of the Church is extinguished,' said Albert and often shed tears when people spoke about his great pupil. Sometimes he had to defend St. Thomas's writing against those who criticised them as untraditional. But meanwhile old age had come upon him, and he died at Cologne in 1280. He was beatified in 1622 and declared a Doctor of the Church in 1931. *(Anon)*

See also: B2 The Good News
B9 Revelation
B24 Go tell Everyone

THE BEATITUDES

'A blessing on the man who puts his trust in the Lord, with the Lord for his hope.' *Jeremiah 17:7*

Quotations

Innocence and knowledge make a man blessed. *(St. Ambrose)*

A blessed life may be defined as consisting simply and solely in the possession of goodness and truth. *(St. Ambrose)*

Never undertake anything for which you wouldn't have the courage to ask the blessings of heaven. *(Georg Christian Lichtenberg)*

Blessed is the man who is too busy to worry in the daytime and too sleepy to worry at night. *(Anon)*

It is not written, blessed is he that feedeth the poor, but he that considereth the poor. A little thought and a little kindness are often worth more than a great deal of money. *(John Ruskin)*

Blessed is he who expects nothing, for he shall never be disappointed. *(Alexander Pope)*

Blessed are the simple, for they shall have much peace. *(Thomas à Kempis)*

Blessed is the man who has a skin of the right thickness. He can work happily in spite of enemies and friends. *(Henry T. Bailey)*

Reflect upon your present blessings, of which every man has many; not on your past misfortunes, of which all men have some. *(Charles Dickens)*

Proverb

Blessings ever wait on virtuous deeds. *(English proverb)*

Statement

Christians who take an active part in modern socioeconomic development and defend justice and charity should be convinced that they can make a great contribution to the prosperity of mankind and the peace of the world. Whether they do so as individuals or in association, let their example be a shining one. After acquiring whatever skills and experience are absolutely necessary, they should in faithfulness to Christ and His gospel observe the right order of values in their earthly activities. Thus their whole lives, both individual and social, will be permeated with the spirit of the beatitudes, notably with the spirit of poverty. *(Second Vatican Council—'The Church Today')*

Word-Pictures

Blessed are they who have the gift of making friends, for it is one of God's best gifts. It involves many things, but above all, the power of going out of one's self, and appreciating whatever is noble and loving in another. *(Thomas Hughes)*

It is manifest that men are made blessed by the obtaining of divinity. And as men are made just by the obtaining of justice, and wise by the obtaining of wisdom, so they who obtain divinity must needs in like manner become gods. Wherefore everyone that is blessed is a god, but by nature there is only one God; but there may be many by participation. *(Boethius)*

The pursuit of God is the desire of beatitude, the attainment of God is beatitude. We pursue after Him by loving Him, we attain to Him, not indeed by becoming what He is, but by coming close to Him, as it were, in some marvellous intellectual fashion, wholly illumined and wholly embraced by His holiness. For He is Light itself and by that Light are we permitted to be illumined. *(St. Augustine of Hippo)*

Blessings we enjoy daily, and for the most of them, because they be so common, men forget to pay their praises. But let not us, because it is a sacrifice so pleasing to him who still protects us, and gives us flowers, and showers, and meat and content. *(Izaak Walton)*

See also: B2 The Good News
B3 Joy in Christ
C2 Joy of Salvation

LOVE YOUR ENEMIES

'Love your enemies, do good to those who hate you, bless those who curse you.' *Luke 6:27*

Quotations

The first duty of love is to listen. *(Paul Tillich)*

Where there is no love, pour love in, and you will draw out love. *(St John of the Cross)*

Love will conquer hate. *(Mohandas Gandhi)*

Love with no condition. *(Paul Tournier)*

Love your enemies, for they tell you your faults. *(Benjamin Franklin)*

Never cease loving a person, and never give up hope for him, for even the Prodigal Son who had fallen most low, could still be saved. The bitterest enemy and also he who was your friend could again be your friend; Love that has grown cold can kindle again. *(Soren Kierkegaard)*

If we are bound to forgive an enemy, we are not bound to trust him. *(Thomas Fuller)*

Proverbs

There is no little enemy. *(French proverb)*

Charity gives itself rich; covetousness hoards itself poor. *(German proverb)*

He who plants trees loves others besides himself. *(English proverb)*

Humour

Love your enemy–it will drive him nuts. *(Eleanor Doan)*

I choose my friends for their good looks, my acquaintances for their good characters, and my enemies for their intellects. A man cannot be too careful in the choice of his enemies. *(Oscar Wilde)*

One day, little Jane was seated alone at a small table while her parents sat with their guests at the large table. This greatly displeased Jane. Before eating, Jane's parents thought it would be nice for

Jane to be included in the group although she was seated separately, so father asked her to say the blessing. This was her prayer: 'Lord, I thank Thee for this table in the presence of mine enemies. Amen.'

A magician was sailing the Pacific, right after World War II, entertaining the passengers. With each amazing feat of magic, a parrot, who perched on his shoulder would squawk, 'Faker, faker.' No matter what the magician did, rabbits out of hats, vanishing bird cage and all, he would repeatedly cry, 'Faker, faker.' The magician and parrot became bitter enemies. Finally the magician promised that he would do a trick that would out-Houdini Houdini. The night came, the wand was waved, the 'woofle dust' was sprinkled. At that minute the ship hit a floating mine, which blew the ship to pieces. The next morning on a make-shift life raft, the parrot was perched at one end, the magician at the other. Finally the parrot hopped over and said, 'O.K. Buddy, you win, but what did you do with the ship?'

Statement

Respect and love ought to be extended also to those who think or act differently than we do in social, political, and religious matters, too. In fact, the more deeply we come to understand their ways of thinking through such courtesy and love, the more easily will we be able to enter into dialogue with them. *(Second Vatican Council—'The Church Today')*

Word-Pictures

Irene Laure was born in Marseilles, the daughter of a businessman. She used to steal her father's socks to give them to poor workers.

She became a nurse and married Victor, a seaman and pupil of the French Communist leader, Marcel Cachin.

In World War II, she was in the Resistance in Marseilles. After her son had been tortured by the Gestapo, her hatred reached the point where she wanted every German dead and their country 'wiped off the map of Europe.'

At war's end, she was elected Member of Parliament and Secretary General of the Socialist Women of France. As such, she attended a conference in Switzerland aimed at restoring the unity of Europe.

She was horrified to find Germans there, and at once packed her bag. But before she could leave, someone asked her, 'How do you hope to rebuild Europe without the Germans?'

She stayed on for three nights of sleepless turmoil.

A voice inside her told her to let go of her blinding hate. 'I needed a miracle,' she says. 'I hardly believed in God, but He performed that miracle. I apologised to the Germans, not for my Resistance fight, but for having desired their total destruction.'

She went to Germany, addressed ten of its eleven provincial

parliaments, and spoke to hundreds of thousands in meetings and on the radio.

Because of her, prominent Germans went to France and apologised to the French people, on the radio and in the press, for what had happened during the war. *(Anon)*

In 1941, Mama took me back to Moscow. There I saw our enemy for the first time. If my memory is right, nearly 20,000 German war prisoners were to be marched in a single column through the streets of Moscow.

The pavements swarmed with onlookers, cordoned off by soldiers and police. The crowd were mostly women. Russian women with hands roughened by hard work, lips untouched by lipstick and thin hunched shoulders which had borne half the burden of the war. Every one of them must have had a father or a husband or brother or a son killed by the Germans.

They gazed with hatred in the direction from which the column was to appear. At last we saw it.

The generals marched at the head, massive chins stuck out, lips folded disdainfully, their whole demeanour meant to show superiority over their plebeian victors . . .

The women were clenching their fists. The soldiers and policemen had all they could do to hold them back.

All at once something happened to them.

They saw German soldiers, thin, unshaven, wearing dirty, bloodstained bandages, hobbling on crutches or leaning on the shoulders of their comrades; the soldiers walked with their heads down.

The street became dead silent—the only sound was the shuffling of boots and the thumping of crutches.

Then I saw an elderly women in broken-down boots push herself forward and touch a policeman's shoulder, saying: 'Let me through.' There must have been something about her that made him step aside.

She went up to the column, took from inside her coat something wrapped in a coloured handkerchief and unfolded it. It was a crust of black bread. She pushed it awkwardly into the pocket of a soldier, so exhausted that he was tottering on his feet. And now suddenly from every side women were running towards the soldiers, pushing into their hands bread, cigarettes, whatever they had.

The soldiers were no longer enemies. They were people. *(Yevtushenko)*

See also: A9 Relationships
A33 Love your neighbour
B15 Jesus friend of outcasts
B52 God is Love

TALK

'For a man's words flow out of what fills his heart.' *Luke 6:45*

Quotations

Many a man's tongue broke his nose. *(Seumas MacManus)*

A sharp tongue is the only edge tool that grows sharper with constant use. *(Washington Irving)*

Gossip, unlike river water, flows both ways. *(Michael Korda)*

Some people talk like the watch which ticks away the minutes but never strikes the hour. *(Samuel Johnson)*

Don't say all you'd like to say lest you hear something you wouldn't like to hear. *(Seumas MacManus)*

Much talkativeness is the sign of a feeble mind, and an undisciplined will. *(Archbishop Ullathorne)*

Conversation is the image of the mind. As the man is, so is his talk. *(Publius Syrus)*

Speaking without thinking is shooting without aiming. *(W. G. Benham)*

There are few wild beasts more to be dreaded than a talking man having nothing to say. *(Jonathan Swift)*

The wise hand does not all that the foolish mouth speaks. *(George Herbert)*

Think twice before you speak and then say it to yourself. *(Elbert Hubbard)*

I suspect that the real reason that an Englishman does not talk is that he cannot leave off talking. I suspect that my solitary countrymen, hiding in separate railway compartments, are not so much retiring as a race of Trappists as escaping from a race of talkers. *(G. K. Chesterton)*

Proverbs

Man is caught by his tongue, and an ox by his horns. *(Russian proverb)*

From saying to doing is a long stretch. *(French proverb)*

Don't let your tongue cut off your head. *(Persian proverb)*

He who talks much is sometimes right. *(Spanish proverb)*

Humour

Why is the word 'tongue' feminine in Greek, Latin, Italian, Spanish, French and German? *(Austin O'Malley)*

A small boy on his way to church for the first time, was being briefed by his elder sister. 'They won't allow you to talk,' she warned him.
'Who won't?' asked the boy.
'The Hushers.' *(Sign)*

A little boy was saying his go-to-bed prayers in a very low voice. 'I can't hear you, dear,' his mother whispered.
'Wasn't talking to you,' said the small one firmly.

Charles Lamb was giving a talk at a mixed gathering and someone in the crowd hissed. Finally Lamb calmly said, 'There are only three things that hiss, a goose, a snake and a fool. Come forth and be identified.'

Word-Pictures

Aesop, the philosopher of the Fables, was asked one day what was the most useful thing in the world. 'The tongue,' he replied. And what (they asked), is the most harmful thing in the world? 'The tongue,' he replied once more. *(Anon)*

Aesop has a fable of three bulls that fed in a field together in the greatest peace and safety. A lion had long watched them in the hope of making prey of them, but found little chance so long as they kept together. He therefore began secretly to spread evil and slanderous reports of one against another till he fermented jealousy and distrust among them. Soon they began to avoid each other and each took to feeding alone. This gave the lion the opportunity it had been wanting. He fell on them singly and made an easy prey of them all.

Anyone who would cultivate the art of conversation should learn that listening to others is often more important than talking to them. These words of wisdom deserve reflection:
1. Nature has given to man one tongue, but two ears, that we may hear from others as much as we speak. *(Epictetus)*
2. It takes a great man to make a good listener. *(Helps)*

3. A good listener is not only popular everywhere, but after a while he knows something. *(Mizner)*
4. To be a judicious and sympathetic listener will go far toward making you an agreeable companion, self-forgetful, self-possessed, but not selfish enough to monopolize the conversation. *(Jack)*

On one occasion when Mohamet and his friend Ali were together, they met a man who, imagining some ill-treatment, began abusing Ali.

Ali bore the insults for a long while, but at last lost patience and returned railing for railing. When Mohamet heard this, he walked away, and left the two disputants to settle their differences as best they could. When, later on, Ali met Mohamet, he asked reproachfully, 'Why did you go away like that and leave me to bear such insults alone?' Mohamet replied, 'My friend, while that rude man was insulting you so cruelly and you kept silent there were ten angels guarding you and answering him; but as soon as you began returning his insults they left you, and I also came away.' *(Anonymous)*

In ancient Sparta, the citizens were stoical, military-minded and noted for their economy of speech. Legend has it that when Philip of Macedon was storming the gates of Sparta, he sent a message to the besieged king saying, 'If we capture your city we will burn it to the ground.' A one-word answer came back: 'If'. *(Norman Lewis)*

See also: A2 Integrity
A9 Relationships
A47 The Spirit of Truth
B53 Consecrated in Truth

THE CHURCH FOR ALL MEN

'Grant all the foreigner asks so that all the peoples of the earth may come to know your name.' *1 Kings 8:43*

Quotations

The religion of Jesus begins with the verb 'follow' and ends with the word 'go'. *(Anon)*

But the brightness of the Catholic and only true Church proceeded to increase in greatness, for it ever held to the same points in the same way, and radiated forth to all the race of Greeks and barbarians the reverent, sincere, and free nature, and the sobriety and purity of the divine teaching as to conduct and thought. *(Eusebius of Caesarea)*

It seems to me, as I have been saying, that catholicity is not only one of the notes of the Church, but, according to the divine purposes, one of its securities. *(Cardinal Newman)*

The Church of Jesus Christ is neither Latin nor Greek nor Slav, but Catholic. Accordingly, she makes no difference between her children, and Greek, Latins, Slavs and members of all other nations are equal in the eyes of the Apostolic See. *(Pope Benedict XV)*

The Church is catholic, that is, universal:
(a) first with regard to place . . . The Church has three parts, one on earth, a second in heaven, a third in purgatory:
(b) the Church is universal with regard to all conditions of human beings; nobody is rejected whether they be masters or slaves, men or women . . .
(c) it is universal in time, and those are wrong who allow it a limited span of time, for it began with Abel and will last even to the end of the world. *(St Thomas Aquinas)*

There is no geography for the Catholic as a Catholic. *(Archbishop Hughes)*

The Church of Christ is the world's only social hope and the sole promise of world peace. *(Sir Douglas Haig)*

Proverbs

He who is near the Church is often far from God. *(French proverb)*

In the visible Church the true christians are invisible. *(German proverb)*

Statement

So it is that this messianic people, although it does not actually include all men, and may more than once look like a small flock, is nonetheless a lasting and sure seed of unity, hope and salvation for the whole human race. Established by Christ as a fellowship of life, charity, and truth, it is also used by Him as an instrument for the redemption of all, and is sent forth into the whole world as the light of the world and the salt of the earth. (cf. Mt. 5:13-16). *(Second Vatican Council—'The Church')*

Word-Pictures

The universality of the Church is very well illustrated by the way the European countries (the French always excepted) are quite content that their national patron saints should be foreigners. The English are content with St George of Cappadocia, and do not mind sharing him with Russians and Genoese and Catalans: the Spaniards long ago settled for St James, the Germans for St Boniface from Devon, the Dutch for St Willobrod, also from South England, and the Irish for glorious St Patrick, a Romano-British character from somewhere this side of St George's Channel. As for the Scots, they have accepted an Anglo-Saxon princess, side by side with the Galilean St Andrew. *(Douglas Woodruff)*

A Moravian missionary named George Smith went to Africa. He had been there only a short time and had only one convert, a poor woman, when he was driven from the country. He died shortly after, on his knees, praying for Africa. He was considered a failure.

But a company of men stumbled on the place where he had prayed and found a copy of the Scriptures he had left. Presently they met the one poor woman who was his convert.

A hundred years later his mission counted more than 13,000 living converts who had sprung from the ministry of George Smith. *(A. J. Gordon)*

'I regret to say,' reported an Indian minister to me at an annual meeting of his congregation, 'that during the last year, there has been no improvement in Church members.' This way of putting it was a slight misuse of English in an endeavour to say that no new members had been received during the year; but I think he was speaking better than he knew and unconsciously explaining the lack of numerical progress. 'The trouble with this Church,' declaimed another Indian minister in my hearing 'is that there are no surprises in it.' He might have been speaking at the end of a long ministry in western suburbia. *(Norman Goodall: One Man's Testimony)*

See also: A6 Light of the World
A13 The Church is for sinners
A43 Believing Community
B17 The Church—Bride of Christ

COPING WITH GRIEF

'When the Lord saw her, he felt sorry for her. "Do not cry," he said.'
Luke 7:13

Quotations

There is no grief which time does not lessen and soften. *(Cicero)*

Grief and death were born of sin, and devour sin. *(St. John Chrysostom)*

There is no greater grief than, in misery, to recall happier times. *(Dante)*

To weep is to make less the depth of grief. *(William Shakespeare)*

Sorrow makes us all children again, destroys all differences in intellect. The wisest knows nothing. *(Ralph Waldo Emerson)*

Happiness is beneficial for the body but it is grief that develops the powers of the mind. *(Marcel Proust)*

Grief knits two hearts in closer bonds than happiness ever can, and common suffering is a far stronger link than common joy. *(Alphonse De Lamartine)*

The true way to mourn the dead is to take care of the living who belong to them. *(Edmund Burke)*

The young man who has not wept is a savage, and the old man who will not laugh is a fool. *(Santayana)*

Genuine grief is like penitence, not clamorous, but subdued. *(Josh Billings)*

Proverbs

He that conceals his grief finds no remedy for it. *(Turkish proverb)*

You cannot prevent the birds of sorrow from flying over your head, but you can prevent them from building nests in your hair. *(Chinese proverb)*

He who would have no trouble in this world must not be born in it. *(Italian proverb)*

Word-Pictures

A little girl came home from a neighbour's house where her little friend had died. 'Why did you go?' questioned her father.

'To comfort her mother,' replied the child.

'What could you do to comfort her?' the father continued.

'I climbed into her lap and cried with her,' answered the child. *(Anon)*

A missionary translator, labouring amongst a tribe in the mountains of Mexico, found it hard to get the right word for 'comfort'. One day his helper asked for a week's leave, and explained that his uncle had died and he wanted some days off to visit his bereaved aunt 'to help her heart around the corner.' That was just the expression the missionary needed. *(Anon)*

I would maintain the sanctity of human joy and human grief. I bow in reverence before the emotions of every melted heart. We have a human right to our sorrow. To blame the deep grief which bereavement awakens, is to censure all strong human attachments. The more intense the delight in their presence, the more poignant the impression of their absence; and you cannot destroy the anguish unless you forbid the joy. A morality which rebukes sorrow rebukes love. When the tears of bereavement have had their natural flow, they lead us again to life and love's generous joy. *(James Martineau)*

Power is the reward of sadness. It was after the Christ had wept over Jerusalem that he uttered some of his most august words; it was when his soul had been sorrowful even unto death that his enemies fell prostrate before his voice. Who suffers, conquers. The bruised is the breaker. *(Francis Thompson)*

See also: A25 Courage
B38 The suffering servant
B49 Coping with doubt
C18 Compassion

FORGIVENESS

'I tell you that her sins, her many sins, must have been forgiven her, or she would not have shown such great love.' *Luke 7:47*

Quotations:

To err is human, to forgive divine. *(Alexander Pope)*

And you will say to life; Forgive. *(Yevtushenko)*

Humanity is never so beautiful as when praying for forgiveness or else forgiving another. *(Jean Paul Richter)*

No one true penitent forgets or forgives himself; an unforgiving spirit towards himself is the very price of God's forgiving him. *(Cardinal Newman)*

There are many kinds of alms, the giving of which helps us to obtain pardon for our sins; but none is greater than that by which we forgive from our heart a sin that some one has committed against us. *(St. Augustine of Hippo)*

He who cannot forgive others breaks the bridge over which he must pass himself. *(George Herbert)*

Forgiveness is man's deepest need and highest achievement. *(Horace Bushnell)*

It is easier for the generous to forgive, than for the offender to ask forgiveness. *(J. Thomson)*

Proverbs

Know all and you will pardon all. *(Greek proverb)*

They who forgive most shall be most forgiven. *(English proverb)*

Word-Pictures

A Russian prince through the prerogative of Napoleon, was permitted to bring pardon to one convict in a French prison. Every person he interviewed professed innocence and said he was unjustly punished. At last he found one who with sorrow confessed his guilt and acknowledged himself deserving of the punishment. To him he said,

'I have brought you pardon. In the name of the Emperor, I pronounce you a free man.' *(Anon)*

Someone asked Luther, 'Do you feel sure that you have been forgiven?' He answered, 'No, but I'm sure as there's a God in heaven.'

The Duke of Wellington was about to pronounce the death sentence on a confirmed deserter. Deeply moved, the great General said, 'I am extremely sorry to pass this severe sentence, but we have tried everything, and all the discipline and penalties have failed to improve this man who is otherwise a brave and good soldier.'

Then he gave the man's comrades an opportunity to speak for him. 'Please, your Excellency,' said one of the men, 'there is one thing you have never tried. You have not tried forgiving him.' The General forgave him and it worked; the soldier never again deserted and ever after showed his gratitude to the Iron Duke. *(Anon)*

Rabbi Leo Beck, a German scholar who took on the leadership of German Jews in Hitler's time, is a fine example of forgiveness. He was five times arrested, and finally sent to a concentration camp, where he served on the convicts' committee of management. On the very day he was to have been shot, the Russian troops arrived. Beck could have escaped at once, but stayed behind to argue with the Russians, to persuade them to spare the lives of the German camp-guards. The Russians decided that the camp-guards should be handed over to the inmates. Beck then argued with the inmates and managed to persuade them not to take the vengeance that they were thirsting for. Later on he went to the USA and worked hard for the Council of Christians and Jews. He died in 1957, aged 80. *(Anon)*

See also: A26 The Sacrament of Penance
A27 As we forgive those
B16 Christ forgives our sins
C27 The Father who receives us back
C40 Reconciliation

PREJUDICE

'There are no more distinctions between Jew and Greek, slave and free, male and female, but all of you are one in Christ Jesus.' *Galatians 3:28*

Quotations

Dogs bark at every one they do not know. *(Heraclitus)*

Prejudices are what rule the vulgar crowd. *(Voltaire)*

Ignorance is less remote from the truth than prejudice. *(Denis Diderot)*

Prejudice is the child of ignorance. *(William Hazlitt)*

It is never too late to give up your prejudices. *(Henry David Thoreau)*

The man who never alters his opinion is like standing water, and breeds reptiles of the mind. *(William Blake)*

A prejudice is a vagrant opinion without visible means of support. *(Ambrose Bierce)*

To be prejudiced is always to be weak. *(Samuel Johnson)*

Never try to reason the prejudice out of a man. It was not reasoned into him and cannot be reasoned out. *(Sydney Smith)*

Prejudice is never easy unless it can pass itself off for reason. *(William Hazlitt)*

Proverbs

Drive out prejudices by the door, they will come back by the window. *(French proverb)*

No physician can cure the blind in mind. *(Jewish proverb)*

Humour

. . . Being a star has made it possible for me to get insulted in places where the average Negro could never hope to go and get insulted. *(Sammy Davis Jr.)*

I read a joke in one of the columns that said you were playing golf on Long Island and the pro asked you for your handicap and you told him, 'I'm a coloured, one-eyed Jew, do I need anything else,' *(Sammy Davis Jr.)*

The folly of snap judgements of others is well illustrated by the story of the late Bishop Potter of New York. He was sailing for Europe on one of the great transatlantic liners. When he went on board, he found another passenger was to share the cabin with him. After going to see his accommodation, he came up to the pursers desk and inquired if he could leave his gold watch and other valuables in the ship's safe. He explained that ordinarily he never availed himself of that privilege, but he had been to his cabin and had met the man who was to occupy the other berth and judging from his appearance, he was afraid that he might not be a very trustworthy person. The purser accepted the responsibility of caring for the valuables and remarked: 'It's all right, Bishop, I'll be very glad to take care of them for you. The other man has been up here and left his for the same reason.' *(Sunday School Times)*

Statement

As a consequence, the Church rejects, as foreign to the mind of Christ, any discrimination against men or harassment of them because of their race, colour, condition of life, or religion. *(Second Vatican Council—'Non-Christians')*

Word-Pictures

If you do not like me because I am ignorant, I can be sent to school and educated. If you do not like me because I am dirty, I can be taught to wash and be clean. If you do not like me because of my unsocial habits, I can be taught how to live in society. But if you do not like me because of the colour of my skin, I can only refer you to the God who made me. *(A negro priest in 1958)*

Robert was born at Aldershot; his mother was Japanese and father English. When Robert started school, he was tormented by the other children. One Christmas, his parents bought him a watch, but this was taken from him by some other older children and thrown against the school wall. The school crossing warden asked Robert one day why he was walking over a mile to school and crossing a busy road instead of using the school bus. His parents had wanted him to use the bus but Robert had refused. He told the traffic warden he was frightened of the other children because they called him a 'wog', a 'chink' and a 'bloody jap'! He walked to school for three weeks until one day, when crossing the road he was knocked down by a car and killed. *(A. P. Castle)*

Air Commodore MacDonald Somerville saw a young punk rock group tramp out into the hazardous Scottish blizzard and succeed in resuing a couple who almost certainly would otherwise have died. 'I always thought of pop groups as hairy kids pumping away on their ukeleles,' he says, 'but these are very fine young fellows with a terrific social conscience.'

We've all got trenchant views, blinkered prejudices, and the tendency to slap labels on people. This might teach some of us to accept that punk rockers can be brave . . . teenagers can be responible . . . missionaries can be bounders. *(Daily Mail)*

See also: A40 Equality of Women
A41 Spiritual blindness
B15 Jesus friend of outcasts
C16 Liberation from fear

COME FOLLOW ME

'Another to whom he said 'Follow me', replied, 'Let me go and bury my father first.' But he answered, 'Leave the dead to bury their dead.'
Luke 9:59–60

Quotations

On account of him there have come to be many Christs in the world, even all who, like him, loved righteousness and hated iniquity. *(Origin of Alexandria)*

Happy are they who know that discipleship simply means the life which springs from grace, and that grace simply means discipleship. *(Dietrich Bonhoeffer)*

He who stops being better stops being good. *(Oliver Cromwell)*

There's but the twinkling of a star between a man of peace and war. *(Nicholas Butler)*

You can't be the salt of the earth without smarting someone. *(Anon)*

The attempts of Christians to be Christians now are almost as ridiculous as the attempts of the first men to be human. *(G. A. Studdert-Kennedy)*

There are two words used a great deal by Jesus in the Gospels. One is 'Come' and the other is 'Go'. It's no use coming unless you go, and it's no use going unless you come. *(Anon)*

When we have travelled all ways, we shall come to the End of all ways, who says, 'I am the way'. *(St. Ambrose)*

To love God is to will what He wills. *(Charles de Foucauld)*

Notice outside a North London Church: 'Wanted—Workers for God. Plenty of Overtime.' *('Peterborough' in the Daily Telegraph)*

Word-Pictures

Near the southern shore of Lake Tanganyika stands a church and on its pulpit is a brass plate commemorating the life of James Lawson. Born in the midlands in the early part of this century, he offered himself as a missionary and after training was appointed to Africa. Despite his training, he would still have been very much of a novice during his first months overseas. There were local customs to be learnt and language to be mastered so he had very little time to fulfil his calling, for, going to an unhealthy spot, within a year he was dead. Such waste! Such futility! Yet that isn't altogether how the Christian sees it. On the memorial plate with his name are the words 'Not what I did, but what I strove to do.' Perhaps in the long run that is the measure by which all of us are judged. *(Anon)*

He comes to us as One unknown, without a name, as of old, by the lake-side, he came to those men who knew him not. He speaks to us the same word 'Follow thou me!' and sets us to the tasks which he has to fulfil for our time. He commands. And to those who obey him, whether they be wise or simple, he will reveal himself in the toils, the conflicts, the sufferings which they shall pass through in his fellowship, and as an ineffable mystery, they shall learn in their own experience Who he is. *(Albert Schweitzer: The Quest of the Historical Jesus)*

A tired, starving hunter emerged from the forest where he had been wandering, dropped his rifle and ran to embrace a stranger who just entered the clearing from the opposite direction.

'Thank heaven, mister!' he exclaimed. 'I've been lost for two days. Am I glad to see you!'

'What are you so glad about,' murmured the other man. 'I've been lost for a week!'

We often look for leadership from those poorly qualified to give it. While it may not be too serious in small matters, there is danger of real tragedy in more important affairs. *(Anon)*

See also: A22 Seeking God
B11 Vocation
B24 Go tell everyone
C41 Starting afresh

INTERNATIONAL PEACE

'Now towards her I send flowing peace, like a river, and like a stream in spate the glory of the nations.' *Isaiah 66:12*

Quotations

The Christian order, since its purpose is peace, is essentially an order of liberty. It is the cooperative effort of men and peoples toward the progressive realisation in all spheres of life of the ends God has assigned to humanity. *(Pope Pius XII)*

The purpose of all war is peace. *(St. Augustine of Hippo)*

The most disadvantageous peace is better than most just war. *(Erasmus)*

Peace cannot be kept by force. It can only be achieved by understanding. *(Albert Einstein)*

War is much too serious a matter to be entrusted to the military. *(Georges Clemenceau)*

Peace is better than war, because in peace the sons bury their fathers, but in war fathers bury their sons. *(Croesus)*

In War: Resolution. In Defeat: Defiance. In Victory: Magnanimity. In Peace: Good Will. *(Winston Churchill)*

I hate war as only a soldier who has lived it can, only as one who has seen its brutality, its futility, its stupidity. *(Dwight D. Eisenhower)*

If man does find the solution for world peace, it will be the most revolutionary reversal of his record we have ever known. *(George C. Marshall)*

There are two world powers, the sword and the spirit, but the spirit has always vanquished the sword. *(Napoleon)*

In modern warfare there are no victors; there are only survivors. *(Lyndon B. Johnson)*

If we wish to have true peace, we must give it a soul. The soul of peace is love. It is love that gives life to peace, more than victory or defeat, more than self-interest or fear or weariness or need. The soul of peace is love, which for us believers comes from the love of God and expresses itself in love for men. *(Pope Paul VI)*

Proverbs

Better a bad peace than a good war. *(Jewish proverb)*

No one can have peace longer than his neighbour pleases. *(Dutch proverb)*

Statement

It is our clear duty, then to strain every muscle as we work for the time when all war can be completely outlawed by international consent. This goal undoubtedly requires the establishment of some universal public authority acknowledged as such by all, and endowed with effective power to safeguard, on the behalf of all, security, regard for justice, and respect for rights.

Peace must be born of mutual trust between nations rather than imposed on them through fear of one another's weapons. Hence everyone must labour to put an end at last to the arm's race, and to make a true beginning of disarmament, not indeed a unilateral disarmament, but one proceeding at an equal pace according to agreement and backed up by authentic and workable safeguards. *(Second Vatican Council—'The Church Today')*

Word-Pictures

The peace concluded on 24th June 1502 between England and Scotland was called 'Perpetual Peace'. In the agreement Margaret, daughter of Henry VIII, was betrothed to James IV of Scotland. However, the Scots invaded England in 1513! The name has been given to other treaties, as that between Austria and Switzerland in 1471 and between France and Switzerland in 1516. *(Anon)*

We utterly deny all outward wars and strife and fightings with outward weapons for any end, or under any pretence whatever; this is our testimony to the whole world. The Spirit of Christ by which we are guided is not changeable, so as once to command us from a thing as evil, and again to move unto it; and we certainly know, and testify to the world, that the Spirit of Christ, which leads us into all truth, will never move us to fight and war against any man with outward weapons, neither for the kingdom of Christ, nor for the kingdoms of this world. *(An extract from A Declaration from the Harmless and Innocent People of God, Called Quakers, presented to Charles II in 1660.)*

Waste of Muscle, waste of Brain,
Waste of Patience, waste of Pain,
Waste of Manhood, waste of Health,
Waste of Beauty, waste of Wealth,
Waste of Blood, and waste of Tears,
Waste of Youth's most precious years,
Waste of ways the Saints have trod,
Waste of Glory, waste of God—War!
(G. A. Studdert-Kennedy)

There is a huge statute of Christ holding a cross standing on the Andes, between the countries of the Argentine and Chile. The story of that statute is worth knowing. Once the Argentine and Chile were about to go to war with one another. They were quarrelling over some land which each said belonged to them. So both countries started to prepare for war. Then on Easter Sunday, bishops in Argentine and Chile began to urge peace. They went round their countries crying out for peace in the name of Christ. The people did not want war and in the end they made their governments talk peace with one another, instead of war. The big guns, instead of being used for fighting, were melted down and made into the great big bronze statue of Christ. It now stands on the mountains between the two countries. Written on it are the words 'These mountains shall fall and crumble to dust before the people of Chile and the Argentine shall forget their solemn convenant sworn at the feet of Christ'. *(M. Nassan)*

See also: A33 Love your neighbour
B34 Human rights
C10 Love your enemies
C4 Personal Peace

COMPASSION

'A Samaritan traveller who came upon him was moved with compassion when he saw him.' *Luke 10:33*

Quotations

Pity melts the mind to love. *(John Dryden)*

Man is never nearer the Divine than in his compassionate moments. *(Joseph H. Hertz)*

The compassion that you see in the kindhearted is God's compassion: he has given it to them to protect the helpless. *(Sri Ramakrishna)*

A tear dries quickly, especially when it is shed for the troubles of others. *(Cicero)*

We must learn to regard people less in the light of what they do or omit to do, and more in the light of what they suffer. *(Dietrich Bonhoeffer)*

Compassion is the basis of all morality. *(Arthur Schopenhauer)*

If we do not help a man in trouble, it is as if we caused the trouble. *(Nachman of Bratslav)*

When a man has compassion for others, God has compassion for him. *(Talmud)*

Proverbs

One heart is mirror to another. *(Jewish proverb)*

The comforter's head never aches. *(Italian proverb)*

Word-Pictures

The Buddha said: 'If villainous bandits were to carve you limb from limb with a two-handled saw, even then the man that should give way to anger would not be obeying my teaching. Even then be it your task to preserve your hearts unmoved, never allow an ill word to pass your lips, but always to abide in compassion and goodwill, with no hate in your hearts, enfolding in radiant thoughts of love the bandit (who tortures you), and proceeding thence to enfold the whole world in your radiant thoughts of love, thoughts great, vast and beyond measure, in which no hatred is nor thought of harm.' *(Translated by T. W. Rhys Davids)*

See also: A17 Gentleness
A23 Mercy
A33 Love your neighbour
C46 Loving kindness

FRIENDSHIP

'Jesus came to a village, and a woman named Martha welcomed him into her house.' *Luke 10:38*

Quotations

True friendship ought never to conceal what it thinks. *(St. Jerome)*

It is mutual respect which makes friendship lasting. *(Cardinal Newman)*

Friendships begun in this world will be taken up again, never to be broken off. *(St. Francis de Sales)*

Friendship is a disinterested commerce between equals. *(Oliver Goldsmith)*

A friend is someone who can see through you and still enjoys the show. *(Anon)*

A friend is the one who comes in when the whole world has gone out. *(Anon)*

Friendship is like money, easier made than kept. *(Samuel Butler)*

To know someone here or there with whom you feel there is understanding in spite of distances or thoughts unexpressed—that can make of this earth a garden. *(Johann Wolfgang Von Goethe)*

Every man should keep a fair-sized cemetry, in which to bury the faults of his friends. *(Henry Ward Beecher)*

True friendship is a plant of slow growth, and must undergo and withstand the shocks of adversity before it is entitled to the appellation. *(George Washington)*

The best way to keep your friends is not to give them away. *(Anon)*

A friendship that makes the least noise is very often the most useful; for which reason I prefer a prudent friend to a zealous one. *(Joseph Addison)*

Proverbs

A friend is one who warns you. *(Jewish proverb)*

Friendship is the marriage of the soul. *(French proverb)*

Hold a true friend with both your hands. *(Nigerian proverb)*

Humour

You, sir, are a foul-weather friend. *(Harpo Marx)*

A friend married is a friend lost. *(Henrik Ibsen)*

Friendship is far more tragic than love. It lasts longer. *(Oscar Wilde)*

Word-Pictures

Lord Brooke was so delighted with the friendship of Sir Philip Sydney that he ordered to be engraved upon his tomb nothing but this—'Here lies the friend of Sir Philip Sydney'.

The following story is from Ernest Gordon's account of life and death in a Japanese P.O.W. camp on the River Kwai.

It was the custom among prisoners from the Argyll regiment for every man to have a 'mucker'—that is, a pal or friend with whom he shared or 'mucked in' everything he had.

'It seemed pretty certain to everyone,' Dusty continued 'that the mucker was going to die. Certain, that is, to everyone but Angus. He had made up his mind that his mucker would live. Someone had stolen his mucker's blanket. Angus gave him his own. Every meal-time, Angus would show up to draw his ration. But he didn't eat it. He would bring it round to give to his friend. Stood over him, he did, and made him eat it. Going hungry was hard on Angus, mind you, because he was a "big man".' As Dusty talked on, I could see it all happening—Angus drawing on his own strength, through his will, and depleting his own body to make his friend live.

'His mates noticed that Angus had taken to slipping out of the camp at night,' Dusty went on. 'These excursions could only have one purpose. He was visiting the Thai villages; it was taken for granted that he had joined the black marketeers! Angus, of all people! This shocked the others for he was known as a man of high principles!

'As the men died in the camp, it became possible for others to come into possession of objects of some value—watches, shorts, knives and so on. These were highly prized by the Thais, who would gladly pay for them in the paper money known as "Bahts", worth about one-and-sixpence each. Or they would barter for the goods, offering medicine or duck eggs.

'Although Angus' mates thought that he was trying to make a bit of money for himself, they didn't begrudge it to him,' said Dusty. 'Perhaps you can guess the end of the story. The mucker got better.

Then Angus collapsed. Just pitched on his face and died.' 'And what did the docs say caused it? I asked.' 'Starvation', answered Dusty, 'complicated by exhaustion, and all for his friend.' *(Ernest Gordon, 'Miracle on the River 'Kwai')*

See also: A9 Relationships
A33 Love your neighbour
B15 Jesus friend of outcasts

OUR FATHER IN HEAVEN

'Father, may your name be held holy, your kingdom come.' *Luke 11:2*

Quotations

God's love for us is not greater in heaven than it is now. *(St. Thomas Aquinas)*

Our Heavenly Father never takes anything from His children unless He means to give them something better. *(George Mueller)*

He is not to be gotten or holden by thought, but only by love. *(Julian of Norwich)*

Whoever falls from God's right hand, is caught into his left. *(Edward Markham)*

Beware of the man whose god is in the skies. *(Bernard Shaw)*

I am always humbled by the infinite ingenuity of the Lord, who can make a red barn cast a blue shadow. *(E. B. White)*

It is the heart which experiences God and not the reason. *(B. Pascal)*

Short arm needs man to reach to Heaven, so ready is Heaven to stoop to him. *(Francis Thompson)*

Our love for God is tested by the question of whether we seek Him or His gifts. *(Ralph W. Sockman)*

Proverbs

God puts a good root in the little pig's way. *(French proverb)*

God is a good worker, but He loves to be helped. *(Spanish proverb)*

God punishes with one hand and blesses with the other. *(Yiddish proverb)*

Word-Pictures

God and the soldier we alike adore,
When on the brink of danger, not before;
The danger past, both are alike requited,
God is forgotten and the soldier slighted. *(Euricius Cordus)*

Thou madest man, he knows not why,
He thinks he was not made to die,
And Thou hast made him: Thou art just. *(Alfred Lord Tennyson)*

St. John Chrysostom, summoned before the Roman Emperor Arcadius, and threatened with banishment, is said to have replied; 'Thou canst not banish me, for the world is my Father's house.'

'Then I will slay thee,' exclaimed the Emperor wrathfully.

'Nay, but thou canst, for my life is hid with Christ in God.'

'Your treasures shall be confiscated,' was the grim reply.

'Sire, that cannot be. My treasures are in heaven, as my heart is there.'

'But I will drive thee from men and thou shalt have no friends left.'

'That you cannot do either, sire, for I have a Friend in heaven Who has said, "I will never leave thee nor forsake thee".'

The following lines were found scratched on the wall of a bomb-blasted air-raid shelter in Germany after the Second World War.

I believe in the light,
even when the sun doesn't shine.
I believe in love,
even when it isn't given.
I believe in God,
even when his voice is silent. *(Anon)*

See also: A22 Seeking God
B28 The Father who draws us to Himself
C27 The Father who receives us back

RISE ABOVE MATERIALISM

'A man's life is not made secure by what he owns, even when he has more than he needs.' *Luke 12:15*

Quotations

Riches are not forbidden, but the pride of them is. *(St. John Chrysostom)*

The most grievous kind of destitution is to want money in the midst of wealth. *(Seneca)*

He who seeks only the glory of God finds it in poverty and in abundance. *(St. Francis de Sales)*

He is rich enough who is poor with Christ. *(St. Jerome)*

He is rich in spirit who has his riches in his spirit or his spirit in his riches; he is poor in spirit who has no riches in his spirit, nor his spirit in his riches. *(St. Francis de Sales)*

Unless our civilisation is redeemed spiritually, it cannot endure materially. *(Woodrow Wilson)*

The poor man, rich in faith, who toils for the love of God and is generous of the little fruit of his labours, is much nearer to heaven than the rich man who spends a fortune in good works from no higher motive than his natural inclination to benevolence. *(Archbishop Ullathorne)*

Be sure, as long as worldly fancies you pursue, you are a hollow man—a pauper lives in you. *(Angelus Silesius)*

What horror has the world come to when it uses profit as the prime incentive in human progress, and competition as the supreme law of economics! *(Dom Helder Camara)*

It is not that things are illusory, but their separateness in the fabric of Reality is illusory. *(Anon)*

If you cannot have everything, make the best of everything you have. *(Anon)*

Proverbs

Spend less than you earn and you'll never be in debt. *(Yiddish proverb)*

When money speaks, the truth is silent. *(Russian proverb)*

Humour

One reason why it's hard to save money is that our neighbours are always buying something we can't afford. *(Anon)*

Money is made round to slip through your fingers. *(Edwin L. Brooks)*

The Scotsman sent an indignant letter to the editor of the newspaper. He said that if any more stories about stingy Scotsmen appeared in the columns, he was going to stop borrowing the paper.

A burglar had entered a poor minister's house at midnight, but was disturbed by the awakening of the occupant of the room he was in.

Drawing his weapon, he said, 'If you stir you are a dead man. I'm hunting for your money.'

'Let me get up and turn on the light,' said the minister, 'and I'll hunt with you.'

A six-year-old went into a bank and asked to see the Manager. A courteous clerk showed her into his private office. She explained that her girl's club was raising money for a new clubroom and would he please contribute?

The banker laid a pound note and a penny on the desk and said, 'Take your choice, Miss.'

She picked up the penny and said, 'My mother always taught me to take the smallest piece.' Picking up the pound note also, she added, 'But so I won't lose this penny, I'll wrap it in this piece of paper.' *(Anon)*

Statements

Wealth which is constantly being augmented by social and economic progress, must be so distributed amongst the various individuals and classes of society that the common good of all . . . be thereby promoted. *(Pope Pius XI—'Quadragesimo Anno')*

What we have already said and the experience of our people lead to the rejection of capitalism, both in its economic aspects as well as in its ideological foundation which favours individualism, profit, and the exploitation of man by man himself. Thus we must strive to create a qualitatively different society. *(Catholic Bishops of Peru)*

Since in our times, variations of materialism are rampant everywhere, even among Catholics, the laity should not only learn doctrine more carefully, especially those main points which are the subjects of controversy, but should also provide the witness of an evangelical life in contrast to all forms of materialism. *(Second Vatican Council—'Laity')*

Word-Pictures

Jesus, *on whom peace*, has said:
The world is a bridge,
Pass over it,
But build not your dwelling there. *(Inscription on the great Mosque in Fateh-pur-Sikri, Delhi)*

A London newspaper offered a prize for the best definition of money. This was the winning answer:
Money is an instrument that can buy you everything but happiness and pay your fare to every place but heaven.

One has risen from the dead, and the rich confess this at their table, and yet poor Lazarus, in millions, continues to hunger at their door. The point of this parable is not as is often suspected, the consoling pipedream of heaven for poor Lazarus. It is addressed exclusively to the rich man. It is not meant to console the poor with hope of recompense beyond the grave, but to warn the rich of damnation and to incite them to hear and act in the world. *(Helmut Gollwitzer)*

To any man worth his salt, the desire for personal gain is not his chief reason for working. It is the desire to achieve, to be a success, to make his job something worthy of his mettle and self-respect. Money plays an important part in this—it is stupid to deny it—but it is not the most important part . . . It is no regret to me that I was not the son of a rich man. My father indeed had riches, but of the mind, not of the pocket. The least valuable thing a parent can endow a strong, healthy son with is money. Counsel, correction and example should count far more in equipping him for the battle of life. *(Lord Nuffield)*

Nobody is more parochial than the materialist, for it is the essence of parochialism to assume that nothing exists outside one's own parish. The materialist, like John Wesley, takes the world for his parish. Unlike Wesley, he does not realise that there are other parishes. *(Arnold Lunn)*

See also: A7 Poor in spirit
A21 Feeding the hungry
C29 Not through luxury

THE LIGHT OF FAITH

'It was for faith that our ancestors were commended.' *Hebrews 11:2*

Quotations

The infused light of the habit of faith discovers the meaning of the articles of the Creed just as the mind's natural power of abstraction discovers the first evidences of reason. *(St. Thomas Aquinas)*

Faith, after all, is a divine operation wrought in the dark, even though it may seem to be embodied in intellectual arguments and historical facts. *(R. H. Benson)*

Faith declares what the senses do not see, but not the contrary of what they see. It is above them, not contrary to them. *(Pascal)*

Faith is illuminative, not operative; it does not force obedience, though it increases responsibility; it heightens guilt, it does not prevent sin; the will is the source of action. *(Cardinal Newman)*

Ultimately, faith is the only key to the universe. The final meaning of human existence, and the answers to the questions on which all our happiness depends cannot be found in any other way. *(Thomas Merton)*

Faith, like light, should always be simple, and unbending; while love, like warmth, should beam forth on every side, and bend to every necessity of our brethren. *(Martin Luther)*

Faith depends not on intellectual, but on moral conditions. *(R. H. Benson)*

There is no love without hope, no hope without love, and neither hope nor love without faith. *(St. Augustine of Hippo)*

Belief is a truth held in the mind. Faith is a fire in the heart. *(Joseph Newton)*

Faith opens the door to understanding, unbelief closes it. *(St. Augustine of Hippo)*

The deep secret of the mystery of faith lies in the fact that it is a 'baptism' in the death and sacrifice of Christ. We can only give ourselves to God when Christ, by His grace, dies and rises again spiritually within us. *(Thomas Merton)*

Statements

The People of God believes that it is led by the Spirit of the Lord, who fills the earth. Motivated by this faith, it labours to decipher authentic signs of God's presence and purpose in the happenings, needs and desires in which this People has a part along with other men of our age. For faith throws a new light on everything, manifests God's design for man's total vocation, and thus directs the mind to solutions which are fully human. *(Second Vatican Council—'The Church Today')*

Word-Pictures

The most celebrated lighthouse of antiquity was the one erected by Ptolemy Soter in the island of Pharos, opposite Alexandria. Josephus says it could be seen at a distance of 42 miles. It was one of the seven wonders of the ancient world.

Of modern lighthouses, the most famous are the Eddystone, 14 miles southwest of Plymouth, the Cordouan lighthouse, at the entrance of the Gironde in France, and the Bell Rock, which is opposite the Firth of Tay. The Bartholdi Statue of Liberty, in New York harbour, is 305 feet high. Eddystone light is 133 feet high and lights a radius of approximately 13 miles. *(Anon)*

The story is told of the Poet Coleridge who had listened to quite a vehement argument by a visitor against religious instructions of the young. His caller had concluded with the statement of his determination not to prejudice his children in any form of religion, but to allow them at maturity to choose for themselves. Coleridge made no immediate comment, but shortly afterwards asked this same visitor if he would like to see his garden. Receiving a reply in the affirmative, he led his guest to a strip of lawn overgrown with weeds.

'Why, this is no garden. It is nothing but a weed-patch,' said the guest.

'Oh,' replied Coleridge, 'that is because it has not come to its age of discretion. The weeds you see have taken the opportunity to grow and I thought it unfair of me to prejudice the soil toward roses and strawberries.' *(Anon)*

I imagine most people think that, as soon as Henry VIII secured the title 'Defender of the Faith' from Leo X, he put it on the coins of the realm, where it has remained ever since. He was extremely eager for some special title from the Holy See to match what the Kings of France and Spain had—'Most Christian' or 'Catholic'. In fact, while he used it in the Great Seal, it did not appear on the coins of himself or any of his successors until, as the Vicar of Bray sings 'George in pudding-time came o'er'. Putting Fid Def on the coinage was a clever idea of the Whigs who imported him, for the sake of the Protestant succession, and the faith he was brought in to defend against the Catholic Stuarts was the Protestantism for writing against which the title had been conferred nearly 200 years before. *(Douglas Woodfuff)*

See also: B33 Faith and Good works
C30 Increase our faith

ZEAL FOR WHAT IS RIGHT

'Jesus said to his disciples, "I have come to bring fire to the earth, and how I wish it were blazing already."' *Luke 12:49*

Quotations

No sacrifice is more acceptable to God than zeal for souls. *(Pope St. Gregory)*

We are often moved with passion, and we think it to be zeal. *(Thomas à Kempis)*

There are few catastrophes so great and irremediable as those that follow an excess of zeal. *(R. H. Benson)*

Zeal without knowledge is always less useful and effective than regulated zeal, and very often it is highly dangerous. *(St. Bernard)*

Dear Crito, your zeal is invaluable, if a right one; but if wrong, the greater zeal, the greater the danger. *(Socrates)*

I prefer to do right and get no thanks rather than to do wrong and get no punishment. *(Marcus Cato)*

There is only one way of seeing things rightly, and that is seeing the whole of them. *(John Ruskin)*

Zeal dropped in charity is good; without it, good for nothing; for it devours all it comes near. *(William Penn)*

Always do right. This will gratify some people and astonish the rest. *(Mark Twain)*

Never explain your actions. Your friends don't need it and your enemies won't believe you anyway. *(Anon)*

Zeal is fit only for wise men but is found mostly in fools. *(Anon)*

Do not act as if you had 10,000 years to throw away. Be good for something while you live, and it is in your power. *(Marcus Aurelius)*

Proverbs

To perfect diligence nothing is difficult. *(Chinese proverb)*

Zeal without knowledge is fire without light,
Zeal without prudence is frenzy. *(English proverb)*

Humour

'Ethics,' the man told his son, 'is vital to everyday living. For example, today an old friend paid me back a loan with a new £20 note. As he was leaving, I discovered he'd given me two notes stuck together. Immediately a question of ethics arose: Should I tell your mother?'

Here lies the body of Joshua Gray
Who died defending his right of way.
His right was clear,
His will was strong,
But he's just as dead as if he'd been wrong. *(Anon)*

Word-Pictures

In 1956, the Vicar-general of the Singapore diocese discovered that it included a small island 750 miles away, far off in the ocean south of Java. (It is called Christmas Island; not the only one.) It is about 16 miles by 12 miles, no harbour, cliffs rising straight up 1,000 feet out of the sea; visitors are hauled up in a small boat by a buoy.

The island was uninhabited until phosphate deposits were found some years ago; now there are over 2,000 people, of whom a number are Catholics—Chinese, Malayan and a few Australians.

The Vicar-general went by the phosphate company's ship and said Mass on the island for the first time: later he sent another priest to prepare the children for their first communion.

Before this time some of the Catholic families had a custom of going to Singapore once a year to get to the sacraments: this meant a round trip of 1,500 miles. *(Catholic Herald)*

One of the stories told of a persecution in China in the old days is about a Chinese Christian lad named Paul Moy. He was dragged before the local mandarin, who tried to induce him to renounce the Christian faith. Other persuasions having failed, the mandarin tried bribery, and promised the boy a purse of silver.

'I thank your Excellency, but a purse of silver is not enough.'

'Very well: I will give you a purse of gold.'

'Excellency, that is still not enough.'

The magistrate had not expected such obstinate bargaining on the part of one so young and was rather annoyed.

'Well, what do you want, then?'

'Most noble, Excellency, if you ask me to renounce the Faith you will have to give me enough to buy a new soul.'

He completed his glorious witness when he was beheaded a few days later. *(Anon)*

The word for sincerity in the Greek original of the New Testament means 'judged in the sunlight'; and the English word is derived from the Latin 'sine cera', which means 'without wax'. In the days when art flourished in ancient Greece, it was the common practice to repair with 'invisible' wax any vase or statue that had, as a result of carelessness or misadventure, been damaged.

A rich man or a person of high rank might employ a sculptor to chisel his bust in marble. Sometimes, if the chisel slipped, the end of the nose would be chipped off. Rather than go to all the trouble of making a new bust, the sculptor would so mend the features with wax that the flaw could not be detected unless by very close scrutiny. He would then palm off on the customer his defective workmanship. If the client happened to be a knowing person, he would carry the finished statuette out of the studio into the open before paying for it, and examine it carefully in the sunlight: otherwise, in course of time, he would have the chagrin of seeing the nose drop off his statuette in the heated room of his house. The statue was not 'sincere', not 'without wax', and could not bear careful scrutiny in the sunlight.

See also: A2 Integrity
C8 God's messengers
C39 Doing God's will

LORD OF ALL NATIONS

'I am coming to gather the nations of every language. They shall come to witness my glory.' *Isaiah 66:18*

Quotations

For the whole Church which is throughout the whole world possesses one and the same faith. *(St Irenaeus)*

Catholicism is a deep matter, you cannot take it up in a tea-cup. *(Cardinal Newman)*

Catholicism is the sum of all religions and the queen of them. *(R. H. Benson)*

The Catholic Church alone teaches as matters of faith those things which the thoroughly sincere person of every sect discovers, more or less obscurely for himself, but dares not believe for want of external sanction. *(Coventry Patmore)*

True Catholicity is commensurate with the wants of the human mind; but persons are often to be found who are surprised that they cannot persuade all men to follow them, and cannot destroy dissent, by preaching a portion of the divine system, instead of the whole of it. *(Cardinal Newman)*

Science can make a neighbourhood of the nations, but only Christ can make the nations into a Brotherhood. *(John Holland)*

Statements

It is our will that all the peoples who are ruled by the administration of our clemency shall practice that religion which the divine Peter the apostle transmitted to the Romans, for the religion which he introduced is clear even to this day. It is evident that this is the religion that is followed by the pontiff Damasus and by Peter, bishop of Alexandria, a man of apostolic sanctity. We command that those persons who follow this rule shall embrace the name of Catholic Christians. The rest, however, who we adjudge demented and insane, shall sustain the infamy of heretical dogmas, their meeting places shall not receive the name of churches, and they shall be smitten first by divine vengeance and secondly by the retribution of our own initiative, which we shall assume in accordance with the divine judgement. *(Edict of the Emperors Gratian, Valentinian, and Theodosius to the People of Constantinople. Feb. 28, 380)*

While she transcends all limits of time and of race, the Church is destined to extend to all regions of the earth and so to enter into the history of mankind. Moving forward through trial and tribulation, the Church is strengthened by the power of God's grace promised to her by the Lord, so that in the weakness of the flesh she may not waver from perfect fidelity, but remain a bride worthy of her Lord; that moved by the Holy Spirit she may never cease to renew herself, until through the cross she arrives at the light which knows no setting. *(Second Vatican Council—'The Church')*

Word-Pictures

This our European structure, built upon the noble foundations of classical antiquity, was formed through, exists by, is consonant to, and will stand only in the mould of, the Catholic Church. Europe will return to the faith, or she will perish. The faith is Europe. And Europe is the faith. *(H. Belloc: Europe and the Faith)*

If Mr Hilaire Belloc means that Europe would be nothing without the faith and that its raison d'être has been and remains to dispense the faith to the world, Mr Belloc is right in saying that Europe is the faith. But speaking absolutely, no! Europe is not the faith and the faith is not Europe: Europe is not the Church and the Church is not Europe. Rome is not the capital of the Latin world. Rome is the capital of the world. Urbs caput orbis. The Church is universal because she is born of God, all nations are at home in her, the arms of her crucified Master are stretched above all races, above all civilizations. She does not bring nations the 'benefits of civilization', but the blood of Christ and supernatural beatitude. *(J. Maritain: The Things That Are Not Caesar's)*

The Church is of her nature apostolic, mindful of the commission to go out into all the world with the Gospel, and it shows a reasonable largeness of mind to treat the moon as part of the world, since it originally was part of it. So we must commend the parish priest of Buxton, in Derbyshire, who has bought a plot of land on the moon, to erect the first Catholic Church there. He has paid for it with a dollar bill which he found in the plate, from a sound feeling that the moon is in the dollar area. We can be quite sure that those who travel in rockets and space ships will be in urgent need of spiritual consolation at the end of their journey. It is of course a little uncertain who has the power to sell space on the moon, and the lawyers have not yet got busy verifying titles. But that is no reason for delaying public manifestations of sympathetic interest in a satellite, or for not trying to influence the moon, seeing for how long and how profoundly lunar influences have played upon the human intelligence. *(Douglas Woodruff)*

See also: A6 Light of the World
B8 The Cosmic Christ
B28 The Father who draws us to Himself
C12 The Church for all men

HUMILITY

'For everyone who exalts himself will be humbled and the man who humbles himself will be exalted.' *Luke 14:16*

Quotations

Humility is the mother of salvation. *(St. Bernard)*

The science of humility rests upon the knowledge of God and of oneself. *(Archbishop Ullathorne)*

For he is less in need who is without a garment, than he who is without humility. *(Pope St Gregory I)*

There is something in humility which strangely exalts the heart. *(St. Augustine of Hippo)*

Humility in oneself is not attractive, though it is attractive in others. *(Dom Chapman)*

True humility makes no pretence of being humble, and scarcely ever utters words of humility. *(St. Francis de Sales)*

To feel extraordinarily small and unimportant is always a wholesome feeling. *(R. H. Benson)*

Golden deeds kept out of sight are most laudable. *(B. Pascal)*

Humility like darkness reveals the heavenly lights. *(Henry D. Thoreau)*

You grow up the day you have your first real laugh at yourself. *(Ethel Barrymore)*

An able yet humble man is a jewel worth a kingdom. *(William Penn)*

I believe the first test of a truly great man is his humility. *(John Ruskin)*

A mountain shames a molehill until both are humbled by the stars. *(Author unknown)*

Proverbs

Too humble is half proud. *(Yiddish proverb)*

Don't make yourself so big. You are not so small. *(Jewish proverb)*

Statement

Following Jesus who was poor, the laity are neither depressed by the lack of temporal goods nor puffed up by their abundance. Imitating Christ who was humble, they have no obsession for empty honours (cf. Gal. 5:26) but seek to please God rather than men, ever ready to leave all things for Christ's sake (cf. Lk. 14:26) and to suffer persecution for justice' sake. *(Second Vatican Council—'Laity')*

Word-Pictures

A man who celebrated his fiftieth wedding anniversary recently says, 'A man is always as young as he feels, but seldom as important.'

If I could give you information of my life, it would be to show how a woman of very ordinary ability has been led by God in strange and unaccustomed paths to do in His service what He has done in her. And if I could tell you all, you would see how God has done all, and I nothing. I have worked hard, very hard—that is all, and I have never refused God anything. *(Florence Nightingale)*

I do not know what I may appear to the world; but to myself I seem to have been only a boy playing on the seashore, and diverting myself in now and then finding a smoother pebble or a prettier shell than ordinary whilst the great ocean of truth lay all undiscovered before me. *(Isaac Newton)*

Some American tourists one day visited the home of Beethoven. A young woman among them sat down at the great composer's piano and began to play his Moonlight Sonata. After she had finished, she turned to the old caretaker and said: 'I presume a great many musicians visit this place every year.' 'Yes,' he replied. 'Paderewski was here last year.' 'And did he play on Beethoven's piano?' 'No,' he said, 'he wasn't worthy.' *(Anon)*

There is a story of a rabbi and a cantor and a humble synagogue cleaner who were preparing for the Day of Atonement. The rabbi beat his breast, and said 'I am nothing, I am nothing.' The cantor beat his breast, and said 'I am nothing, I am nothing.' The cleaner beat his breast, and said 'I am nothing, I am nothing.' And the rabbi said to the cantor 'Look who thinks he's nothing.' *(Alan Paton)*

A certain French Marquis was raised to his grand and exalted state from very humble surroundings. He had been a shepherd in his earlier days, and so, in his palace, he had one room known as 'the shepherd's room'. In that room were reproductions of hills and valleys and running streams and rocks and sheepfolds. Here were the staff he had carried and the clothes he had worn as a lad when herding his sheep. When asked one day the meaning of this, he replied, 'If ever my heart is tempted to haughtiness and pride, I go into that room and remind myself of what I once was.' *(Anon)*

See also: A2 Integrity
A7 Poor in Spirit
A10 Be Perfect
B20 Growth to Maturity

THE HUMAN CONDITION

'A perishable body presses down the soul, and this tent of clay weighs down the teeming mind.' *Wisdom 9:15*

Quotations

Left to itself, human nature tends to death, and utter apostasy from God, however plausible it may look externally. *(Cardinal Newman)*

The heart sometimes finds out things that reason cannot. (R. H. Benson)

Relying on God has to begin all over again, everyday, as if nothing had yet been done. *(C. S. Lewis)*

Man is being filled with error. This error is natural, and, without grace, ineffaceable. Nothing shows him the truth; everything deceives him. *(Pascal)*

The world owes all its onward impulse to men ill at ease. The happy man inevitably confines himself within ancient limits. *(Nathaniel Hawthorne)*

We are all as God made us, and oftentimes a great deal worse. *(Miguel de Cervantes)*

The goodness of God knows how to use our disordered wishes and actions, often lovingly turning them to our advantage while always preserving the beauty of His order. *(St. Bernard)*

To what shall I compare this life of ours? Even before I can say, 'it is like a lightning flash or a dewdrop,' it is no more. *(Sengai)*

So blind is our mortality, and so unaware what will fall, so unsure also what manner of mind we will have tomorrow, that God could not lightly do man a more vengeance than in this world to grant him his own foolish wishes. *(St. Thomas More)*

Humour

A witty French bishop was once asked why he kept up a country home which he seldom visited. 'Do you not know,' he replied, 'that I must have some place where, though I never go to it, I can always imagine that I might be happier than where I am?' *(Anon)*

Word-Pictures

Our inner unrest manifests itself when we feel we are alive and yet vulnerable; that we cannot stand alone; that we are full of positive energies and yet full of weakness. We are tormented by our overpowering egoism; it asserts our own right to life, and yet we also have a great need of others. Where and how can we achieve peace, integration, equilibrium for our personalities? *(Pope Paul VI)*

I was on the point of putting an end to my life—the only thing that held me back was my art. For indeed it seemed to me impossible to leave this world before I had produced all the works that I felt the urge to compose; and thus I have dragged on this miserable existence. *(Ludwig van Beethoven)*

THE NOTHING PEOPLE

None-Volunteers

They do not lie;
They just neglect to tell the truth.
They do not take;
They simply cannot bring themselves to give.
They do not steal;
They scavenge.
They will not rock the boat;
But did you ever see them pull an oar?
They will not pull you down;
They'll simply let you pull them up,
And let that pull you down.
They do not hurt you;
They merely will not help you.
They do not hate you;
They merely cannot love you.
They will not burn you;
They'll only fiddle while you burn.
They are the nothing people;
The sins-of-omission folk;
The neither-good-nor-bad-
And-therefore-worse.
Because the good, at least keep busy
trying, and the bad try just as hard.
Both have that character
that comes from caring, action, and
conviction, so give me every time an

honest sinner, or even a Saint.
But, God and Satan,
Get together, and protect me from the
nothing people. *(Anon)*

See also: A15 Sin
A38 Original Sin
B22 Death
B49 Coping with doubt
C37 Temptation

THE FATHER WHO RECEIVES US BACK

'His father saw him and was moved with pity. He ran to the boy, clasped him in his arms and kissed him tenderly.' *Luke 15:20*

Quotations

The Lord is loving unto man, and swift to pardon, but slow to punish. Let no man therefore despair of his own salvation. *(St. Cyril of Jerusalem)*

For no one is redeemed except through unmerited mercy, and no one is condemned except through merited judgement. *(St. Augustine of Hippo)*

How inconsistent it is to expect pardon of sins to be granted to a repentance which they have not fulfilled. This is to hold out your hand for merchandise, but not produce the price. For repentance is the price at which the Lord has determined to award pardon. *(Tertullian)*

Repeated sickness must have repeated medicine. You will show your gratitude to the Lord by not refusing what the Lord offers you. You have offended but still can be reconciled. You have One Whom you may satisfy, and Him willing. *(Tertullian)*

Pardon, not wrath, is God's best attribute. *(Bayard Taylor)*

When thou attackest the roots of sin, fix thy thought upon the God whom thou desirest rather than upon the sin which thou abhorest. *(Walter Hilton)*

Proverbs

He who forgives ends the quarrel. *(African proverb)*

Late repentance is seldom true. *(Latin proverb)*

Humour

A small boy, repeating the Lord's Prayer one evening, prayed: 'And forgive us our debts as we forgive those who are dead against us.' *(Anon)*

Word-Pictures

A London man claims the distinction of landing a job with the same company he was caught stealing from.

'I only stole because I had been out of work for 11 months and had no money,' the 55-year old man explained. He was arrested for taking tea, sugar, biscuits, and sweets from a factory in the East End. When he was put on probation for two years and hired as a labourer for £56 a week by the same company, he made this comment: 'I really intend to show the management that their goodness isn't going to be abused.' *(Anon)*

Someone once asked Charles Dickens what was the best short story in the English language, and his reply was—'The Prodigal Son'.

Oh, the comfort, the inexpressible comfort of feeling safe with a person; having neither to weigh thoughts nor measure words, but to pour them all out, just as they are, chaff and grain together, knowing that a faithful hand will take and sift them, keep what is worth keeping, and then, with the breath of kindness, blow the rest away. *(George Eliot)*

See also: A26 Sacrament of Penance
B28 The Father who draws us to Himself
C20 Our Father in Heaven
C41 Starting afresh

LORD OF THE OPPRESSED

'From the dust he lifts up the lowly, from the dungheap he raises the poor to set him in the company of princes.' *Psalm 112*

Quotations

Poverty comes from God, but not dirt. *(The Talmud)*

Satan now is wiser than of yore,
And tempts by making rich,
not making poor. *(Alexander Pope)*

The rich will do everything for the poor but get off their backs. *(Karl Marx)*

The accumulation of vast wealth while so many are languishing in misery is a grave transgression of God's law, with the consequence that the greedy, avaricious man is never at ease in his mind: he is in fact a most unhappy creature. *(Pope John XXIII)*

A poor man with nothing in his belly needs hope and illusion, more than bread. *(Georges Bernanos)*

Proverbs

It is no disgrace to be poor—which is the only good thing you can say about it. *(Jewish proverb)*

Poverty is a blessing hated by all men. *(Italian proverb)*

God help the poor, for the rich can help themselves. *(Scottish proverb)*

Statement

Those who are oppressed by poverty, infirmity, sickness, or various other hardships, as well as those who suffer persecution for justice sake—may they all know that in a special way they are united with the suffering Christ for the salvation of the world. *(Second Vatican Council—'The Church')*

Word-Pictures

No, it is not God's will that a few rich people enjoy the goods of this world and exploit the poor. No, it is not God's will that some people remain poor and abject forever. No, religion is not the opiate of the people; it is a force that exalts the lowly and casts down the proud, that feeds the hungry and sends the sated away empty. *(Third World Bishops)*

King Oswin was troubled to think of Bishop Aidan's long journeys on foot on the rough roads and among the stony crags of Yorkshire, and he knew that the Bishop must often find it difficult to cross the rivers, for there were few bridges. So he gave him a fine horse with royal trappings, to help him on his journeys. One day as Aidan was riding the horse over the moorlands, he met a beggar who asked for alms. At once he dismounted and gave the horse to the poor man, and went on his way on foot. This was told to the king, who felt rather hurt that Aidan should have given away the horse he had particularly chosen for him as a gift. As they were going into dinner, he said to him, 'Have I not many less valuable horses which might have been given to the beggar?' And Aidan, who was ever a friend of the poor, replied with his ready wit, 'What sayest thou, King? Is that son of a mare more precious in thy sight than the son of God?'

They went into the hall, and Aidan took his place at the table, but the king, who had been out hunting, stood warming himself at the fire with his attendants. Suddenly he ungirded his sword and threw himself at Aidan's feet, asking his forgiveness.

'I will never speak any more of this,' he said, 'nor will I ever judge what, or how much, you shall give to the sons of God.' *(Phyllis Garlick)*

Yes, the first woman I saw, I myself picked up from the street. She had been half eaten by the rats and ants. I took her to the hospital but they could not do anything for her. They only took her in because I refused to move until they accepted her. From there, I went to the municipality and I asked them to give me a place where I could bring these people, because on the same day I had found other people dying in the streets. The health officer of the municipality took me to the temple, the Kali Temple, and showed me the 'dormashalah' where the people used to rest after they had done their worship of the Kali goddess. It was an empty building; he asked me if I would accept it. I was very happy to have that place for many reasons, but especially knowing that it was a centre of worship and devotion of the Hindus. Within 24 hours, we had our patients there and we started the work of the home for the sick and dying who are destitute. Since then, we have picked up over 23,000 people from the streets of Calcutta of which about 50 per cent have died. *(Mother Teresa)*

Elsbeth Rosenfield, who died in Birmingham on 2nd March 1970, at the age of 79, was one of the most remarkable people to emerge from the fires of Nazi persecution. The eldest child of a Jewish father and a Christian mother, she grew up as a Christian in Berlin before the First World War. Under the Weimar Republic, she became a social worker, and in 1920 married a member of the Social Democratic Party in the Prussian Parliament. He happened also to be a Jew. When Hitler came to power, her husband immediately retired, while Elsbeth herself, under the Nuremburg race laws, was classified as a 'non-aryan'. Compelled to move from place to place, they managed eventually to send their children to England in 1939, in hope of being able to follow soon after. At the last moment, only one permit arrived, and at Elsbeth's insistence, her husband—the one in immediate danger—left to join the children.

At this point, though she had no intention of abandoning her Christian faith, she succeeded in persuading a Rabbi in Berlin to register her as a member of the Jewish community so that she could share in their lot and help in any way possible. She then worked in Munich until she was compelled to go into hiding. Subject for two years to constant danger of discovery and deportation, she came to realise how many Germans were prepared, at the risk of their own lives, to help their persecuted Jewish fellow-citizens. Eventually, she escaped to Switzerland, where, after some months in hospital, she resumed her social work among refugees.

In 1946, she rejoined her family in London, where she was invited by the Foreign Office to work among German prisoners of war, lecturing to them about the Nazi treatment of Jews and others, and helping in their rehabilitation. Her husband died in 1947, and in 1952 she returned to Germany. Thereafter she spent half the year as a social worker in German prisons, and half with her family in England. In 1963, she told the story of her life in a remarkable series of broadcasts in the BBC Midland Regional programme. The story was subsequently published under the title 'The Four Lives of Elsbeth Rosenfield'. Four lives indeed, yet bound together by that love of God and one's fellow man which leaves no room for hatred of an enemy.

(W. W. Simpson)

See also: A21 Feeding the Hungry
B15 Jesus, friend of outcasts
B38 The Suffering Servant
B50 The Good Shepherd

NOT THROUGH LUXURY

'Woe to those ensconced so smugly in Zion and to those who feel so safe on the mountain of Samaria.' *Amos 6:1*

Quotations

Avarice and luxury, those pests which have ever been the ruin of every great state. *(Livy)*

Luxury—something you don't really need and can't do without. *(Anon)*

Luxury makes a man so soft, that it is hard to please him, and easy to trouble him; so that his pleasures at last become his burden. Luxury is a nice master, hard to be pleased. *(Mackenzie)*

There has never yet been a man in our history who led a life of ease whose name is worth remembering. *(Theodore Roosevelt)*

We act as though comfort and luxury were the chief requirements of life, when all that we need to make us really happy is something to be enthusiastic about. *(Charles Kingsley)*

Comfort comes as a guest, lingers to become a host and stays to enslave. *(Lee Bickmore)*

Luxuries are what other people buy. *(David White)*

It is easier to renounce worldly possessions than it is to renounce the love of them. *(Walter Hilton)*

You must either conquer the world or the world will conquer you. You must be either master or slave. *(Cardinal Newman)*

But not all solicitude about temporal affairs is forbidden, only such as is superfluous and out of due order. *(St. Thomas Aquinas)*

Let temporal things serve thy use, but the eternal be the object of thy desire. *(Thomas à Kempis)*

We should enjoy spiritual things but only use corporal things. *(St. Francis de Sales)*

Proverbs

We would all live in luxury, if we didn't have to eat. *(Yiddish proverb)*

A full cup must be carried steadily. *(English proverb)*

Word-Pictures

Croesus, King of Lydia, born in 590 BC, had immense wealth and lived luxuriously. He filled his house with all manner of costly treasures. He thought he was the happiest of mortals. Solon, one of the seven wise men of Greece, paid him a visit and was received into a magnificent chamber. Solon showed no surprise or admiration. The king, angry at his indifference, asked Solon, 'Why do you not think me the most truly happy?' Solon replied, 'No man can be esteemed truly happy but he whose happiness God continues to the end of his life.' *(Anon)*

One symptom of our physical and mental obesity which I'd never noticed so sharply before is the astonishing success of two growth industries—slimming and consumer protection. In other words we are desperate to be told how to cope with having too much of everything. Does an African farmer need to be told how to spend his money? Does an Indian mother of 10 need to be told how to slim?

Can't we stop and see what a fantastic way of life we have in this country? Can't we realise that losing a little fat is no catastrophe? Listening to all the grumbles about hardship—and then looking with new eyes at the reality of the way most people live—it seems to me that the more we have the less mature we have become. Which is a pity, because I am afraid that if we can't adjust to a more realistic standard of living, we're in for a tough time. The growing unrest of poorer countries, the finite quantity of natural resources, and historical necessity mean that there's a lot to come off yet. Then we will have something to grumble about. *(from 'Good Housekeeping')*

A big spider, which lived in the roof of an old house, decided to come and live a little lower down. So he spun a thread and came sliding down it and made a new web. He then began to catch flies and make himself fat and because he became fat he also became very stupid. He was very pleased with himself one day as he was walking round his web and he looked up and saw the thread going up in the air. 'What's the use of that?' he said and he broke it. Immediately, he went crashing down with his web to the floor beneath and killed himself. *(M. Nassan)*

A miser in France used to keep all his gold and precious things in a cellar under the floor of his house. One day he went down through a secret trap-door at the top of the cellar to gloat over his treasure. Then the trap-door banged down so that he could not get out. No one in the house knew about the cellar and the miser could not be found. People searched all over the place without finding him. After a long time, they gave up and the house was sold. The new people who bought the house wanted some new building done and the cellar was found. When it was opened, the miser was found sitting at a table with all his gold glittering around him. The dead man had even eaten a candle before dying of hunger. *(M. Nassan)*

See also: A7 Poor in Spirit
A21 Feeding the Hungry
C21 Rise above materialism

INCREASE OUR FAITH

'The apostles said to the Lord, 'Increase our faith.' *Luke 17:5*

Quotations

For they conquer who believe they can. *(Virgil)*

A faint faith is better than a strong heresy. *(St. Thomas More)*

Believe that you have it, and you have it. *(Erasmus)*

Faith means battles; if there are no contests, it is because there are none who desire to contend. *(St. Ambrose)*

It is love makes faith, not faith love. *(Cardinal Newman)*

Human reason is weak, and may be deceived, but true faith cannot be deceived. *(Thomas à Kempis)*

The man who says, Unless I feel, I will not believe, is as narrow and foolish as the man who says, Unless I understand, I will not believe. *(R. H. Benson)*

For faith is the beginning and the end is love, and God is the two of them brought into unity. After these comes whatever else makes up a Christian gentleman. *(St. Ignatius of Antioch)*

People only think a thing's worth believing in if it's hard to believe. *(Armiger Barclay)*

It is cynicism and fear that freeze life; it is faith that thaws it out, releases it, sets it free. *(Harry Emerson Fosdick)*

All the scholastic scaffolding falls, as a ruined edifice, before one single word—faith. *(Napoleon I)*

A Christian is not a man who is trying to do something, he is a man who has received something; a man to whom something has happened and who simply cannot keep it to himself. *(Peter Marshall)*

Those who have the faith of children have also the troubles of children. *(R. H. Benson)*

Word-Pictures

As I look back over my career in the Fire Service, I am vividly reminded of the Psalmist's words: 'The Lord is close to the broken-hearted'. I began fire-fighting 34 years ago in Belfast and after the last war moved to London.

Naturally, in the course of my work I have witnessed many harrowing incidents. I am a member of the Catholic Evidence Guild and my Faith has firmly implanted within me the conviction that Our Lord is present in a very special way in times of great danger.

My most gruesome and frightening experiences are so firmly fixed in my memory that I will never be able to forget either their horrifying details or the feeling of reassurance which accompanied them. I can still see a burning wall collapse and bury three fellow firemen—it happened in 1952. I can hear the rumble of collapsing floorboards which trapped three other friends—it happened a year later. Some experiences will never fade into the past. I can forget what someone said to me a few hours ago but I always hear the voices of the 50 people who were trapped on the upper floors of the Leinster Towers Hotel. The cries are three years old, but they are just as loud to me now as they were then.

The sights, sounds and smell of the rail crashes at Harrow Weald and Lewisham will always be with me. The horror of Moorgate will live on for me, as it surely will for many others.

We were three days working in the tunnel where the temperature rose to 110 degrees Fahrenheit and the stench of decomposing bodies forced us to resort to breathing apparatus and made it impossible for us to work for more than 10 minutes at a time. One of the things that sticks most doggedly in my mind was the expression on the face of the driver when his corpse was uncovered—it was almost a smile. I had seen the same expression on the face of the Perth–Euston driver all those years before in Harrow Weald. In times of death or disaster, man is not alone. My work has brought me into contact with suffering and carnage. I know at those times He has always been with me. *(Patrick Knight)*

We ourselves must be convinced of the need for a living, true and active faith. Even more today when the difficulties are so much greater. It is not enough to have a vague, weak and uncertain faith which is purely one of sentiment and habit, made up of theories, doubts and reservations. Nor is it enough to hold a faith which just accepts what it pleases, or which seeks to avoid difficulties by denying assent to truths which themselves are both difficult and mysterious. *(Pope Paul VI)*

Bruce Larson tells a story in his book *Edge of Adventure.* It's about a letter found in a baking-powder tin wired to the handle of an old pump, which offered the only hope of drinking water on a very long and seldom-used trail across the Amargosa Desert in USA; the letter read as follows:

'This pump is alright as of June 1932. I put the new leather sucker washer into it, and it ought to last several years. But this leather washer dries out and the pump has got to be primed. Under the white rock, I buried a bottle of water. There's enough water in it to prime the pump, but not if you drink some first. Pour in about one-quarter, and let her soak to wet the leather. Then pour in the rest, medium fast and pump like crazy. You'll get water. The well has never run dry. Have faith. When you get watered up, fill the bottle and put it back like you found it for the next feller.
(Signed) Desert Pete.

P.S.—Don't go drinking up the water first. Prime the pump with it first, and you'll get all you can hold.'

See also: B33 Faith & Good Works
C22 The Light of Faith

THANKSGIVING

'Finding himself cured, one of them turned back praising God at the top of his voice and threw himself at the feet of Jesus and thanked him.'
Luke 17:15–16

Quotations

Give thanks frequently to God for all the benefits he has conferred on you, that you may be worthy to receive more. *(St. Louis IX of France)*

Gratitude is a duty which ought to be paid, but which none has a right to expect. *(Rousseau)*

What is gladness without gratitude? And where is gratitude without God?. *(Coventry Patmore)*

One act of thanksgiving when things go wrong with us is worth a thousand thanks when things are agreeable to our inclination. *(Bl. John of Avila)*

When I find a great deal of gratitude in a poor man, I take it for granted there would be as much generosity if he were rich. *(Alexander Pope)*

Gratitude is born in hearts that take time to count up past mercies. *(Charles E. Jefferson)*

Awake with a winged heart, and give thanks for another day of loving!. *(Kahlil Gibran)*

The finest test of character is seen in the amount and the power of gratitude we have. *(Milo H. Gates)*

Gratitude is the most exquisite form of courtesy. *(Jacques Maritain)*

Proverbs

Gratitude is the heart's memory. *(French proverb)*

We never know all we should be grateful to God for. *(Jewish proverb)*

Word-Pictures

I own that I am disposed to say grace upon twenty other occasions in the course of the day besides my dinner. I want a form for setting out upon a pleasant walk, for a moonlight ramble, for a friendly meeting, or a solved problem. Why have we none for books, those spiritual repasts—a grace before Milton, a grace before Shakespeare—a devotional exercise proper to be said before reading the Faere Queen? *(Charles Lamb)*

God is He who created the heavens and the earth and sent down water from the clouds, then brought forth with it the fruits as a sustenance for you, and He has made the ships subservient to you, that they might run their course in the sea by His command, and He has made the rivers subservient to you.

And He has made subservient to you the sun and the moon pursuing their courses, and He has made subservient to you the night and the day. And He gives you of all that you ask Him, and if you count God's favours, you will not be able to number them; surely man is very unjust, very ungrateful. *(The Qu'ran)*

The church nursery-school teacher had placed a lovely bouquet of daffodils on a table in the nursery room. When little Sandra came into the room, she was fascinated by the flowers and said to her teacher, 'Aren't these pretty telephones God made? I think I'll call God up and say, "Thank you for the pretty flowers".' *(Anon)*

In 1939, Sgt. Maj. Robert MacCormack saved the life of his commanding officer, Major Harry Parkin, on a battlefield in France. He has just received his thirty-fifth annual letter of thanks from Parkin, now an estate agent in Richmond, Yorkshire, 'Dear Bob,' Parkin wrote, 'I want to thank you for the thirty-five years of life which ordinarily I would not have had were it not for you. I am grateful to you.'

Today upon a bus, I saw a lovely maid
with golden hair;
I envied her—she seemed so gay—and
wished I were as fair.
When suddenly she rose to leave, I saw
her hobble down the aisle;
She had one foot and wore a crutch, but
as she passed, a smile.
Oh, God, forgive me when I whine;
I have two feet—the world is mine!

And then I stopped to buy some sweets.
The lad who sold them had
Such charm, I talked with him—he said
to me;

'It's nice to talk with folks like you.
You see,' he said, 'I'm blind.'
Oh, God, forgive me when I whine;
I have two eyes—the world is mine!

Then, walking down the street, I saw a
 child with eyes of blue.
He stood and watched the others play;
It seemed he knew not what to do.
I stopped for a moment, then I said:
'Why don't you join the others, dear?'
He looked ahead without a word, and then
I knew he could not hear.
Oh, God, forgive me when I whine;
I have two ears—the world is mine!

With feet to take me where I'd go,
With eyes to see the sunset's glow,
With ears to hear what I would know,
Oh, God, forgive me when I whine;
I'm blessed, indeed! The world is mine. *(Anon)*

See also: A17 Gentleness
A39 The Glory of God
A48 Prayer & worship
B41 Generosity

PRAYER

'Now will not God see justice done to his chosen who cry to him day and night even when he delays to help them?' *Luke 18:7*

Quotations

Prayer is conversation with God. *(Clement of Alexandria)*

The daily prayers of the faithful make satisfaction for those daily, tiny, light faults from which this life cannot be free. *(St. Augustine of Hippo)*

In a single day I have prayed as many as a hundred times, and in the night almost as often. *(St Patrick)*

Men by petitioning may merit to receive what almighty God arranged before the ages to give them. *(Pope St Gregory I)*

Prayer is the noblest and most exalted action of which man is capable through the Grace of God. *(Archbishop Ullathorne)*

Prayer is the most important thing in my life. If I should neglect prayer for a single day, I should lose a great deal of the fire of faith. *(Martin Luther)*

He prays best who does not know that he is praying. *(St. Anthony)*

But before all things it is good to begin with prayer, as thereby giving ourselves up to and uniting ourselves with God. *(Pseudo-Dionysius)*

Prayer in itself properly is nought else but a devout intent directed unto God, for the getting of good and the removing of evil. *(Anon)*

Pray as you can and do not try to pray as you can't. *(Dom Chapman)*

All that should be sought for in the exercise of prayer is conformity of our will and the divine will, in which consists the highest perfection. *(St. Teresa of Jesus)*

I have so much to do that I must spend several hours in prayer before I am able to do it. *(John Wesley)*

Our prayers should be for blessings in general, for God knows best what is good for us. *(Socrates)*

Certain thoughts are prayers. There are moments when, whatever be the attitude of the body, the soul is on its knees. *(Victor Hugo)*

A prayer in its simplest definition is merely a wish turned Godward. *(Phillips Brooks)*

Proverbs

Pray as though no work would help, and work as though no prayer would help. *(German proverb)*

Prayer is the pillow of religion. *(Arab proverb)*

If you pray for another, you will be helped yourself. *(Yiddish proverb)*

Humour

Priest 'Do you say your prayers at night, little boy?'
Jimmy 'Yes, Father.'
Priest 'And do you always say them in the morning, too?'
Jimmy 'No, Father, I ain't scared in the daytime.'

Hodge's Grace
Heavenly Father bless us,
And keep us all alive;
There's 10 of us for dinner
And not enough for five. *(Anon)*

One evening six-year old Bobby asked his father for a pet. 'Sorry, son,' his father said, 'not now. But if you pray real hard for two months, perhaps God will send you a baby brother.'

Bobby prayed faithfully for a month, but it seemed futile to pray longer so he gave up.

How surprised he was, when a month later, a little baby boy arrived at their home, or so Bobby thought when he saw a squirming bundle beside his mother. His proud father drew back the cover and Bobby saw another baby. Twins!

'Aren't you glad you prayed for a baby brother?' asked his father.

'I sure am,' said the boy. 'But aren't you glad I stopped praying when I did?' *(Together)*

A man once went out lion hunting. Suddenly he saw a big lion coming towards him. He waited with his gun until the lion got nearer, to make sure that he would not miss it. Then he pulled the trigger and nothing happened! He had no bullets in his gun. Terrified he went down on his knees, shaking all over. The lion came bounding up and seeing him on his knees it too went down on its knees. 'What are you doing?' asked the man, trembling with fright. 'I'm saying my grace before meals,' said the lion! *(Anon)*

Statement

The spiritual life, however, is not confined to participation in the liturgy. The Christian is assuredly called to pray with his brethren, but he must also enter into his chamber to pray to the Father in secret (cf Mt. 6:6); indeed, according to the teaching of the Apostle Paul, he should pray without ceasing. *(Second Vatican Council—'Liturgy')*

Word-Pictures

One day, a mother noticed that her little girl was in her room a long time and she had said she was going in to pray to Jesus. Finally, when the little girl came out, her mother asked her what she was doing in her room for such a long time when she had just gone in to pray. 'I was just telling Jesus that I love Him and He was telling me that He loves me. And we were just loving each other.' *(Anon)*

While journeying on horseback one day, St. Benedict met a peasant walking along the road.

'You've got an easy job,' said the peasant, 'Why don't I become a man of prayer? Then I too would be travelling on horseback.'

'You think praying is easy,' replied the Saint. 'If you can say one "Our Father" without any distraction, you can have this horse.'

'It's a bargain,' said the surprised peasant.

Closing his eyes and folding his hands he began to say the Our Father aloud: 'Our Father, who art in heaven, hallowed be Thy name, Thy kingdom come . . .'

Suddenly he stopped and looked up.

'Shall I get the saddle and bridle too?'

Visitors to the famous Gallery in St. Paul's Cathedral, London, can hear the guide's whisper travel around the whole dome, the sound bouncing back many times from the smooth wall. If you put your ear close to the wall, you can hear what is said on the opposite side of the dome, even though it may be said in the lowest of tones.

A number of years ago, a poor shoemaker whispered to his young lady that he could not afford to marry her as he hadn't money enough to buy any leather, and his business was ruined. The poor girl wept quietly as she listened to this sad news.

A gentleman on the other side of the gallery, which is 198 feet across, heard this story and the shoemaker's whispered prayer, and he decided to do something about it. When the young shoemaker left St. Paul's, the gentleman followed him, and after finding out where he lived, had some leather sent along to the shop. Imagine how delighted the poor man was! He made good use of this gift, and his business prospered so that he was able to marry the girl of his choice. It was not till a few years later that he learned the name of his unknown friend. It was the Prime Minister of Great Britain, William Gladstone. *(Anon)*

The intrinsic characteristic of prayer is trust. Let me explain. If the relationship between man and God is that which Christ inaugurated and established, then prayer is no longer a monologue. It is no longer a voice crying in the darkness, but is a real dialogue, and a response not only to a divine precept but also to a promise. 'Pray, and your prayers will be heard.' *(Pope Paul VI)*

See also: A22 Seeking God
A48 Prayer & Worship
B25 Quiet—time for prayer
B29 The Eucharist

EQUALITY

'The Lord is a judge who is no respecter of personages.'
Ecclesiasticus 35:12

Quotations

Equality consists in the same treatment of similar persons. *(Aristotle)*

As men, we are all equal in the presence of death. *(Publius Syrus)*

All animals are equal, but some animals are more equal than others. *(George Orwell)*

All men are born equal but the tough job is to outgrow it. *(Don Leary)*

All men are equal on the turf and under it. *(Lord George Bentinck)*

The equality existing among the various social members consists only in this: that all men have their origin in God the Creator, have been redeemed by Jesus Christ, and are to be judged and rewarded or punished by God exactly according to their merits or demerits. *(Pope St Pius X)*

The Lord so constituted everybody that no matter what colour you are, you require the same amount of nourishment. *(Will Rogers)*

Equality is a mortuary word. *(Christopher Fry)*

Proverbs

Equality begins in the grave. *(French proverb)*

In the public baths, all men are equal. *(Yiddish proverb)*

Statement

Since all men possess a rational soul and are created in God's likeness, since they have the same nature and origin, have been redeemed by Christ, and enjoy the same divine calling and destiny, the basic equality of all must receive increasingly greater recognition. *(Second Vatican Council—'The Church Today')*

Word-Pictures

From the time of the first fairy-tales, men had always believed ideally in equality; they had always thought that something ought to be

done, if anything could be done, to redress the balance between Cinderella and the ugly sisters. The irritating thing about the French was not that they said this ought to be done: everybody said that. The irritating thing about the French was that they did it.
(G. K. Chesterton)

I have a dream that one day this nation will rise up and live out the true meaning of its creed: 'We hold these truths to be self-evident; that all men were created equal'.

I have a dream that one day on the red hills of Georgia, the sons of former slaves and the sons of former slave owners will be able to sit down together at the table of brotherhood.

I have a dream that one day even the state of Mississippi, a state sweltering with the heat of injustice, sweltering with the heat of oppression, will be transformed into an oasis of freedom and justice. I have a dream that my four little children will one day live in a nation where they will not be judged according to the colour of their skin but by the content of their character.

I have a dream today.

I have a dream that one day every valley shall be exalted, every hill and mountain shall be made low, the rough places will be made plain, and the crooked places will be made straight, and the glory of the Lord shall be revealed and all flesh shall see it together. This is our hope. This is the faith that I go back to the South with. With this faith, we will be able to hew out of the mountain of despair a stone of hope. With this faith, we will be able to transform the jangling discords of our nation into a beautiful symphony of brotherhood. With this faith, we will be able to work together, to pray together, to struggle together, to go to jail together, knowing that we will be free one day. *(Martin Luther King)*

See also: A9 Relationships
A40 Equality of Women
B34 Human Rights
B44 The dignity of the individual

THE VALUE OF LITTLE THINGS

'In your sight, Lord, the whole world is like a grain of dust that tips the scales, like a drop of morning dew falling on the ground.' *Wisdom 11:22*

Quotations

Great acts take time. *(Cardinal Newman)*

It is marvellous how our Lord sets His seal upon all that we do, if we will but attend to His working, and not think too highly upon what we do ourselves. *(R. H. Benson)*

From a little spark may burst a mighty flame. *(Dante)*

God does not want us to do extraordinary things; He wants us to do the ordinary things extraordinarily well. *(Bishop Gore)*

The great doing of little things makes the great life. *(Eugenia Price)*

Do little things as if they were great, because of the majesty of the Lord Jesus Christ who dwells in thee. *(Blaise Pascal)*

The greatest thing for us is the perfection of our own soul; and the saints teach us that this perfection consists in doing our ordinary actions well. *(Archbishop Ullathorne)*

Never do anything that thou canst not do in the presence of all. *(St. Teresa of Avila)*

Between the great things we cannot do and the little things we will not do, the danger is that we will do nothing. *(H. G. Weaver)*

He does most in God's great world who does his best in his own little world. *(Thomas Jefferson)*

If I cannot do great things, I can do small things in a great way. *(J. F. Clarke)*

Love's secret is always to be doing things for God, and not to mind because they are such very little ones. *(Frederick W. Faber)*

Humour

Be grateful for little things. It's true that the world is getting crowded, but can you imagine if Noah had taken four of everything? *(Orben)*

Word-Pictures

To illustrate to his students the power of little things, Professor Tait had a heavy iron joist suspended from the roof of his laboratory by a strong cord, and then began to throw small paper pellets at it, striking it square each time. At first there was no perceptible movement of the joist, but after a continuous barrage of paper pellets, the iron joist commenced to sway from side to side and swing like a pendulum. *(Anon)*

In a fabulous
necklace
I had to admire
the anonymous string
by which the whole thing
was strung together. *(Helder Camara)*

A holy Christian life is made up of a
number of small things:
  Little words, not eloquent sermons;
  Little deeds, not miracles of battle
  Or one great, heroic deed of martyrdom;
The little constant sunbeam,
not the lightning.

The avoidance of little evils,
  Little inconsistencies, little weaknesses,
  Little follies and indiscretions,
  And little indulgences of the flesh make up
The beauty of a holy life. *(Andrew Bonar)*

I long to accomplish a great and noble task, but it is my chief duty to accomplish small tasks as if they were great and noble. Green, the historian, tells us that the world is moved along, not only by the mighty shoves of its heroes, but also by the aggregate of the tiny pushes of each honest worker. *(Helen Keller)*

To live well in the quiet routine of life; to fill a little space because God wills it; to go on cheerfully with a petty round of little duties, little avocations; to smile for the joy of others when the heart is aching—who does this, his works will follow him. He may not be a hero to the world, but he is one of God's heroes. *(Anon)*

Over 10,000 people in Provence, France, owe their homes and environment to a little known peasant shepherd. Elezard Bouffier lived alone, in 1910, in a barren region where there were very few trees. While tending his flock in the Autumn, the shepherd would pick up each acorn that he saw. In the early Spring, while watching the sheep, he would prod the earth with his staff and drop in a nut. He did this each year between 1910 and 1947. At his death, the barren countryside was covered by trees and teeming with wild life. It is now the pleasant site of a new housing development. *(A. P. Castle)*

See also: A5 Unselfishness
A18 Balance in Nature
B20 Growth to Maturity
B33 Faith and Good Works

HOPE

'Ours is the better choice, to meet death at men's hands, yet relying on God's promise that we shall be raised up by him.' *2 Maccabees 7:14*

Quotations

If you do not hope, you will not find what is beyond your hopes. *(Clement of Alexandria)*

What can be hoped for which is not believed? *(St. Augustine of Hippo)*

No man is able of himself to grasp the supreme good of eternal life; he needs divine help. Hence there is here a two-fold object, the eternal life we hope for, and the divine help we hope by. *(St. Thomas Aquinas)*

As long as matters are really hopeful, hope is a mere flattery or platitude; it is only when everything is hopeless that hope begins to be a strength at all. Like all the Christian virtues, it is as unreasonable as it is indispensable. *(G. K. Chesterton)*

We promise according to our hopes, and perform according to our fears. *(La Rochefoucauld)*

He who wants to enjoy the glory of the sunrise must live through the night. *(Anon)*

Hope is the struggle of the soul, breaking loose from what is perishable, and attesting her eternity. *(Herman Melville)*

Hope is the only good that is common to all men; those who have nothing else possess hope still. *(Thales)*

The word which God has written on the brow of every man is Hope. *(Victor Hugo)*

Proverbs

The man who lives only by hope will die with despair. *(Italian proverb)*

Hope is the poor man's income. *(Danish proverb)*

While there is life there is hope. *(Latin proverb)*

Humour

Bill 'Have you ever realized any of your childhood hopes?'
Pete 'Yes; when mother used to comb my hair, I often wished I didn't have any.'

Word-Pictures

When Sir Walter Scott was a boy, he was considered a great dullard. His accustomed place in the schoolroom was the ignominious dunce corner, with the high-pointed paper cap of shame on his head. When about twelve years old, he happened to be in a house where some famous literary guests were being entertained. Robert Burns, the Scottish poet, was standing admiring a picture under which was written the couplet of a stanza. He inquired concerning the author. None seemed to know. Timidly a boy crept up to his side, named the author, and quoted the rest of the poem. Burns was surprised and delighted. Laying his hand on the boy's head, he exclaimed, 'Ah, bairnie, ye will be a great man in Scotland some day.' From that day Walter Scott was a changed lad. One word of encouragement set him on the road to greatness. *(Indian Christian)*

Sir Walter Raleigh is believed to have written this poem in the Tower of London on the night before his execution.

Even such time, that takes in trust
Our youth, our joys, our all we have,
And pays us but with earth and dust;
Who, in the dark and silent grave,
When we have wandered all our ways,
Shuts up the story of our days,
But from this earth, this grave, this dust,
My God shall raise me up, I trust.

In 79 AD, the city of Pompeii in southern Italy was destroyed in the eruption of nearby Mount Vesuvius. Less well known is another town, Herculaneum, which suffered in the same catastrophe. This town was a popular first century resort until that day Mount Vesuvius exploded and buried it under sixty-five feet of solidified mud and lava.

Herculaneum is interesting in that it was not a wealthy town like Pompeii. Excavations at the site have uncovered blocks of tenements in which the poor lived. The ruins of Herculaneum speak about the lives of ordinary people.

In one old house uncovered in 1938, in a small room on the second floor of a tenement, there was found imbedded into a stucco wall panel a small cross. It is an important find because it is among the earliest evidence of the Christian religion in the Roman Empire.

The archeologist sees this cross and knows that a Christian lived here, a Christian who was very poor, a Christian who was almost isolated from a larger pagan community. Thus this cross is of some interest. The believer sees this cross and begins to understand a great deal about this room and its occupant(s). There was hope in this tiny room, hope in the midst of what must have been a very meagre existence. There was freedom from the Fates that ruled the lives of so many people in ancient days. There was light that comes from the knowledge that one is loved. For in this room lived a Christian, one who believed in Jesus, one who believed that the ultimate meaning of the universe is life-nourishing love. Could anything destroy this hope?

See also: A6 Light of the World
A19 Patience
B21 Trust in God
C1 Liberation from fear

THE DAY OF THE LORD

'The day is coming now, burning like a furnace; and all the arrogant and evildoers will be like stubble.' *Malachi 3:19*

Quotations

Judgement cannot be pronounced on a man until he has run his course. *(St. Thomas Aquinas)*

God postpones the collapse and dissolution of the universe (through which the bad angels, the demons, and men would cease to exist), because of the Christian seed, which He knows to be the cause in nature of the world's preservation. *(St. Justin Martyr)*

All who set not their minds on this world are accounted fools; but who will be the merrier in the world that is to come? *(R. H. Benson)*

For when the judgement is finished, this heaven and earth shall cease to be, and there will be a new heaven and a new earth. For this world shall pass away by transmutation, not by absolute destruction. *(St. Augustine)*

If we judge ourselves, we will not be judged by God. *(Jean Pierre Camus)*

God himself, sir, does not propose to judge man until the end of his days. *(Samuel Johnson)*

If we have to answer for our lives after death, those people who have made other people unhappy will be the ones really in trouble with the Boss. *(Jimmy Savile OBE)*

Proverb

Don't try to fill a sack that's full of holes. *(Jewish proverb)*

Statement

For God has called man and still calls him so that with his entire being he might be joined to Him in an endless sharing of a divine life beyond all corruption. Christ won this victory when He rose to life, since by His death He freed man from death. Hence to every thoughtful man a solidly established faith provides the answer to his anxiety about what the future holds for him. *(Second Vatican Council—'The Church Today')*

Word-Pictures

The last judgement is not fable or allegory, but vision. Vision or imagination is a representation of what eternally exists, really and unchangeably. Fable or allegory is formed by the daughters of memory. Imagination is surrounded by the daughters of inspiration.

The Hebrew Bible and the Gospel of Jesus are not allegory, but eternal vision or imagination of all that exists. *(William Blake)*

A 200-seater amphitheatre, costing £20,000, was built overlooking Sydney Harbour, Australia, in 1925, for the Second Coming of Christ. Members of 'The order of the Star of the East,' led by Hindu mystic Krishnamurti, believed that Christ would soon return to earth in human form and walk across the Pacific Ocean to the amphitheatre. When he did not arrive by 1929, the group dissolved, and a block of flats now occupies the site. *(Anon)*

One day in 1883, recorded history's most violent cataclysm came to pass. It occurred when the volcanic island of Krakatoa in the East Indies blew up. All that was left was a cavity 1,000 feet deep in the ocean floor. Nearly thirty-six thousand persons were killed—and the resultant tidal wave encircled the Earth four times. *(Anon)*

Then one of the soldiers, without waiting for orders and without a qualm for the terrible consequences of his action but urged on by some unseen force, snatched up a blazing piece of wood, and climbing on another soldier's back, hurled the brand through a golden aperture giving access on the north side to the chambers built round the Sanctuary . . . A runner brought the news to Titus as he was resting in his tent after the battle. He leapt up as he was and ran to the Sanctuary to extinguish the blaze . . . Thus the Sanctuary, in defiance of Caesar's wishes, was set on fire. *(Josephus—'The Jewish War')*

See also: A31 Heaven
A42 Life after Death
B22 Death

TEMPTATION

'Jesus was led by the Spirit through the wilderness, being tempted there by the devil for forty days.' *Luke 4:1*

Quotations

The devil cannot lord it over those who are servants of God with their whole heart and who place their hope in Him. The devil can wrestle with, but not overcome them. *(Shepherd of Hermas)*

The devil tempts that he may ruin; God tempts that He may crown. *(St. Ambrose)*

No man is so perfect and holy as not to have sometimes temptations; and we cannot be wholly without them. *(Thomas à Kempis)*

God does not punish people for what they would have done, but for what they do. *(St. Thomas Aquinas)*

Inconstancy of mind, and small confidence in God, is the beginning of all evil temptations. *(Thomas à Kempis)*

It is one thing to be tempted, another thing to fall. *(Shakespeare)*

To realize God's presence is the one sovereign remedy against temptation. *(Fenelon)*

It is good to be without vices, but it is not good to be without temptations. *(Walter Bagehot)*

As the Sandwich-Islander believes that the strength and valour of the enemy he kills passes into himself, so we gain the strength of the temptations we resist. *(Ralph Waldo Emerson)*

To pray against temptations, and yet to rush into occasions, is to thrust your fingers into the fire, and then pray they might not be burnt. *(Secker)*

Following the path of least resistance makes both rivers and men crooked. *(Anon)*

No man is matriculated to the art of life till he has been well tempted. *(George Eliot)*

Proverbs

God promises a safe landing but not a calm passage. *(Bulgarian proverb)*

The heron's a saint when there are no fish in sight. *(Bengalese proverb)*

Humour

The Devil, having nothing else to do.
Went off, to tempt My Lady Poltagrue.
My Lady, tempted by a private whim,
To his extreme annoyance, tempted him. *(Hilaire Belloc)*

Don't worry about avoiding temptation—as you grow older, it starts avoiding you. *(Farmer's Almanac)*

'I can resist everything,' said the young lady, 'except temptation.' *(Anon)*

A shop-keeper, seeing a boy hanging about outside where there was a tempting display of various fruits, went out to him and said, 'What are you trying to do, young man; steal my apples?'

'No, sir,' said the boy, 'I'm trying not to!' *(Anon)*

Statement

To be sure, the disturbances which so frequently occur in the social order result in part from the natural tensions of economic, political, and social forms. But at a deeper level they flow from man's pride and selfishness, which contaminate even the social sphere. When the structure of affairs is flawed by the consequences of sin, man, already born with a bent toward evil, finds there new inducements to sin, which cannot be overcome without strenuous efforts and the assistance of grace. *(Second Vatican Council—'The Church Today')*

Word-Pictures

God is better served in resisting a temptation to evil than in many formal prayers. This is but twice or thrice a day; but that every hour and moment of the day. So much more is our continual watch than our evening and morning devotion. *(William Penn)*

One 82-year old Father Christmas put too much enthusiasm into his job last Christmas and found himself out of work. The pensioner was paid to sit in his red coat and white beard in a Nottingham store and speak kindly to the shy children.

When they would whisper their wishes in his ear, however, he began to melt. 'I couldn't bear to see them go away disappointed,' he said later, 'There were a lot of toys on the shelves nearby that no one seemed to be buying. So I started handing them to some of the children as an extra present.' While store officials sympathized with the sentiment, they insisted on the hard facts of commercial life. The old man was politely sacked.' *(Anon)*

The guides to Westminster Abbey miss a great chance. They should make much more of that great event in the Abbey's history which happened in the closing years of the reign of Edward I. That otherwise sagacious monarch placed excessive reliance on the monks at Westminster as a community specially bound to the royal house, his father, Henry III, having been virtually the re-founder of the Abbey. So when he was collecting treasure for his great campaign against the Scots, he deposited it in the Abbey crypt, thinking there could be no safer place. But while he was away in the north, as he was from 1298 onwards, temptation crept in. Some monks sowed hemp in their cloisters and graveyard, for its quick-growing foliage to conceal what went on, while others, in alliance with what would now be called outside interest, began filching the miscellaneous treasures leaving the crown alone, but taking vases and pots and other things of gold and silver by river to the City.

One monk drew suspicion upon the community because he could not refrain from boasting how very rich he had suddenly become. When the theft was discovered, and its magnitude, equivalent to perhaps two million pounds, the Abbot and all the community were arrested and lodged in the Tower. All except eight of them were cleared, and one of the lay accomplices was prevailed upon before his execution to take the full blame on himself, telling a highly improbable tale of how he had effected an entrance from the outside.

Henry VIII did not bring this up, as he might have done, perhaps because Edward I managed to track down the receivers and get most of the treasure back. This last item should come as a relief to the monks of Ampleforth, who claim to be the descendants of the monks of Westminster. It was this unhappy experience that caused the Kings of England to keep their treasure in the Tower. *(Douglas Woodruff)*

See also: A15 Sin
A38 Original Sin
B19 Conscience
C26 The human condition

DISCERNING GOD'S WILL

'My lord, the Lord,' Abram replied, 'how am I to know that I shall inherit it?' *Genesis 15:8*

Quotations

The principal effect of love is to unite the wills of those who love, so as to make of them but one and the same will. *(Pseudo-Dionysius)*

No one may prefer his own will to the will of God, but in everything we must seek and do the will of God. *(St. Basil)*

Nothing, therefore, happens unless the Omnipotent wills it to happen: He either permits it to happen, or He brings it about Himself. *(St. Augustine of Hippo)*

It is not a question of who or what you are, but whether God controls you. *(J. Wilbur Chapman)*

God's will is as energetic in the bewildering rush of the current as in the quiet sheltered backwater. *(R. H. Benson)*

It is the duty of those who are zealous for God's good pleasure to make inquiry as to what it is right for them to do. *(St. Basil)*

The will of God is the measure of things. *(St. Ambrose)*

It needs a very pure intention, as well as great spiritual discernment, always to recognise the divine voice. *(R. H. Benson)*

God's will is as much in sickness as in health. *(St. Francis de Sales)*

We should fulfill the commands of God with insatiable desire, ever pressing onward towards greater achievements. *(St. Basil)*

We always find it more acceptable to have God speaking to us directly rather than through our wives! But we may learn a great deal by listening to what He says to us through them. *(Paul Tournier)*

Statement

The intellectual nature of the human person is perfected by wisdom and needs to be. For wisdom gently attracts the mind of man to a quest and a love for what is true and good. Steeped in wisdom, man passes through visible realities to those which are unseen.

It is finally, through the gift of the Holy Spirit, that man comes by faith to the contemplation and appreciation of the divine plan. *(Second Vatican Council—'The Church Today')*

Word-Pictures

This I know is God's own truth, that pain and troubles and trials and sorrows and disappointments are either one thing or another. To all who love God, they are love tokens from him. To all who do not love God and do not want to love him they are merely a nuisance. Every single pain that we feel is known to God because it is the most loving touch of his hand. *(Edward Wilson (who died with Scott in the Antarctic))*

I fled Him down the nights and down the days;
  I fled Him, down the arches of the years;
I fled Him, down the labyrinthine ways
  Of my own mind; and in the midst of tears
I hid from Him, and under running laughter. *(Francis Thompson 'The Hound of Heaven')*

See also: A41 Spiritual Blindness
B11 Vocation
B47 Dying to self
C39 Doing God's Will

DOING GOD'S WILL

'This,' God added, 'is what you must say to the sons of Israel: 'I Am has sent me to you.' *Exodus 3:14*

Quotations

As regards the will of God, even if some take scandal, we must not let this hamper our freedom of action. *(St. Basil)*

A broken heart and God's will done would be better than that God's will should be avoided. *(R. H. Benson)*

In his will is our peace. *(Dante Alighieri)*

The greatness of a man's power is the measure of his surrender. *(William Booth)*

Life is nothing but a play and a pretence, and His will must be done, however much we rebel at it. *(R. H. Benson)*

The Lord doesn't want the first place in my life, He wants all of my life. *(Howard Amerding)*

A man's heart is light when he wills what God wills. *(St. Thomas Aquinas)*

Blessed are they who do not their own will on earth, for God will do it in heaven above. *(St. Francis de Sales)*

Proverbs

The favourite place of God is in the heart of man. *(Yiddish proverb)*

If God willed it, brooms would shoot. *(Jewish proverb)*

Word-Pictures

Our prayers do not change God's mind, elicit his pity or reverse a sentence . . . they allow God to put into operation (in me and through me) something He has willed all along. *(Hubert van Zeller)*

'Nothing in the hands of God is evil; not failure, not thwarting, not the frustration of every hope or ambition, not death itself. All in his hands is success, and will bear the more fruit the more we leave it to him, having no ambitions, no preoccupations, no excessive preferences or desires of our own.' *(Archbishop Goodier)*

There was a man here last night—you needn't be afraid that I shall mention his name—who said that his will was given up to God, and who got mad because the omnibus was full and he had to walk to his lodgings. *(Dwight L. Moody)*

Dr Mason of Burma once wanted a teacher to visit and labour among a warlike tribe and asked his converted boatman if he would go. He told him that as a teacher he would receive only four rupees per month whereas as boatman he was then receiving fifteen rupees.

After praying over the matter, the boatman returned to the doctor and the following conversation occurred:

'Well, Shapon,' said the doctor, 'what have you decided? Will you go for four rupees a month?'

'No, teacher,' replied Shapon, 'I will not go for four rupees a month but I will go for Christ.' *(Anon)*

Many people would be willing to renounce worldly pleasures if they received convincing proof that the ultimate rewards would make the deal worthwhile. But if such a deal could be made, it would not be due to love, but to business discernment. The object of the training can only be achieved by a loving donation of ourselves, uncertain of reward. Christ himself put the matter exactly. 'My doctrine,' he said, 'is not mine but his that sent me. If any man will do his will, he shall know of the doctrine whether it be of God.' The abandonment of our own interests and our surrender to his guidance must be the first step. After that, our trust will grow.

Evelyn Underhill has a good illustration of the situation. She supposes someone looking at a great cathedral, a mass of grey stone with the windows showing a dark, dusty colour. It does not look very cheerful. But if we push open the doors and go in, we suddenly see that all the windows are really brightly coloured glass . . . You cannot see the glory if you stand outside, asking sneeringly what proof there is that the inside is beautiful. You have to go in yourself. *(John Bagot Glubb 'The Way of Love')*

'Will you please tell me in a word,' said a Christian woman to a minister, 'what your idea of consecration is?' Holding out a blank sheet of paper, the pastor replied, 'It is to sign your name at the bottom of this blank sheet, and let God fill it in as He wills.' *(Anon)*

See also: A41 Spiritual Blindness
B11 Vocation
B47 Dying to self
C38 Discerning God's Will

RECONCILIATION

'It was God who reconciled us to himself through Christ and gave us the work of handing on this reconciliation.' *2 Corinthians, 5:18*

Quotations

It takes two sides to make a lasting peace, but it only takes one to make the first step. *(Edward M Kennedy)*

Clean your fingers before you point at my spots. *(Benjamin Franklin)*

He that accuses all mankind of corruption ought to remember that he is sure to convict only one. *(Edmund Burke)*

We must not be unjust and require from ourselves what is not in ourselves. *(St. Francis de Sales)*

Our task is to work for the expression of God's reconciliation here and now. We are not required to wait for a distant 'heaven' when all problems will have been solved. What Christ has done, he has done already. We can accept his work or reject it; we can hide from it or seek to live by it. But we cannot destroy it, for it is the work of the eternal God. *(Council of African Churches)*

Reconciliation sounds a large theological term, but it simply means coming to ourselves and arising and going to our Father. *(John Oman)*

A reconciliation that does not explain that error lay on both sides is not a true reconciliation. *(Midrash: Genesis Rabbah)*

Word-Pictures

A love of reconciliation is not weakness or cowardice. It demands courage, nobility, generosity, sometimes heroism, an overcoming of oneself rather than of one's adversary. At times it may even seem like dishonour, but it never offends against true justice or denies the rights of the poor. In reality, it is the patient, wise art of peace, of loving, of living with one's fellows, after the example of Christ, with a strength of heart and mind modelled on his. *(Pope Paul VI)*

A soldier asked a holy monk if God accepted repentance. He said, 'Tell me, if your cloak is torn, do you throw it away?' The soldier replied, 'No, I mend it and use it again.' The old man said to him, 'If you are so careful about your cloak, will not God be equally careful about his creature?' *(Anon)*

In 1914, Clayton was one of the four curates whom Portsea contributed to the forces as chaplains. After serving with the 16th Division, he was transferred in 1915 to the 6th Division in the Ypres Salient. There, men were dying at the rate of 250 a day, and the lucky ones were those who got a bullet through the brain instead of coughing out their poisoned lungs or lingering mangled in the mud. It was a unique problem that this unique man tackled at Talbot House (Toc H in the language of the army signaller), a soldier's club in a back street in Poperinghe. Men, even on a few days' leave, needed human brotherhood; Clayton gave it. Religion was not pressed on men, but more and more came to value the long garret, stretching the whole length and breadth of the house, which formed the chapel.

When peace came, Clayton recognised the need for special training for ex-servicemen seeking ordination. For some years, nothing better than a disused prison at Knutsford was available; but that did not trouble him. When Knutsford was well established, he turned to what was to become his life's work, the establishment, first in London, then in the cities of Britain and in many other lands, of branch houses of Toc H to preserve the spirit of the trenches, and, as he put it, to 'teach the younger generation class reconciliation and unselfish service'. *(The Guardian)*

See also: A26 Sacrament of Penance
A27 As we forgive those
B16 Christ forgives our sins
C14 Forgiveness

STARTING AFRESH

'All I can say is that I forget the past and I strain ahead for what is still to come.' *Philippians 3:14*

Quotations

It is not of much use to be entreated to turn over a new leaf, when you see no kind of reason for doing so. *(R. H. Benson)*

The meaning of life is to see. *(Hui-Neng)*

Every exit is an entry somewhere else. *(Tom Stoppard)*

Nothing is more expensive than a start. *(Nietzsche)*

Proverbs

It is better to begin in the evening than not at all. *(English proverb)*

For a web begun, God sends thread. *(Italian proverb)*

There is nothing new except what hath been forgotten. *(English proverb)*

He who begins many things finishes but few. *(Italian proverb)*

A good beginning makes a good ending. *(English proverb)*

Word-Pictures

There was an old sailor my grandfather knew,
Who had so many things that he wanted to do,
That just when he thought it was time to begin,
He couldn't—because of the state he was in! *(Anon)*

Not forever can one enjoy the stillness and peace. But misfortune and destruction are not final. When the grass has been burnt by the fire on the Steppe, it will grow anew in summer. *(Mongolian Steppe)*

We must aim above all at an inner renewal, a liberation from the mere following of conventions, a new departure in our way of thinking. More than anything else, we must lament our shortcomings before God, and the community of our brethren. We must renew the self-understanding each must have of himself or herself as a child of God, as a Christian, as a member of the Church. *(Pope Paul VI)*

An escaped convict from Devil's Island, the penal colony off the French Guiana coast, died some time ago, after devoting 35 years to helping the sick.

The man, sentenced to life imprisonment in connection with a murder in Marseilles, was granted asylum on the pearl fishing island of Margarita.

Since he was a doctor, he devoted his remaining years to curing the ills of the islanders. Although he was never able to obtain official authorisation as a doctor, he was allowed by local authorities to practice.

When he died at 72, several hundred neighbours gathered to pay their last respects to the man who had done so much to relieve their physical ills.

A young burglar fleeing across a rooftop heard the crash of glass behind him. Looking back, he saw a policeman falling through a skylight. The 26-year old thief went back and supported the officer until help came. Then he was arrested and sentenced to twenty months in prison. Four months later, a judge reviewed the case, saluted the man's 'outstanding gallantry' and set him free. Headlines heralded the former burglar as a hero.

He soon found that public esteem was short-lived. Every attempt to get a permanent job met with failure. Three employers discharged him when they learned of his past. Nine others refused to hire him because he told the full truth at job interviews.

The embittered man complained: 'If I hadn't stayed to save that policeman's life, I would probably not be in this fix now. But I'll never go back to crime.' *(Anon)*

See also: A25 Courage
B14 Freedom to serve
C1 Liberation from fear

THE RISEN LORD

'Three days afterwards, God raised him to life and allowed him to be seen, not by the whole people but only by certain witnesses.' *Acts 10:40*

Quotations

The root of all good works is the hope of the resurrection; for the expectation of the reward nerves the soul to good works. *(St. Cyril of Jerusalem)*

Let us consider, beloved, how the Lord is continually revealing to us the resurrection that is to be. Of this He has constituted the Lord Jesus Christ the first-fruits, by raising Him from the dead. *(Pope St. Clement I)*

Our Lord has written the promise of the resurrection, not in books alone, but in every leaf in springtime. *(Martin Luther)*

Many meetings and conferences with bishops were held on this point, and all unanimously formulated in their letters the doctrine of the Church for those in every country, that the mystery of the Lord's Resurrection from the dead could be celebrated on no day save Sunday, and that on that day alone we should celebrate the end of the paschal feast. *(Eusebius of Caesarea)*

The night of Easter is spent in keeping the vigil (pervigilia) because of the coming of our King and Lord, that the time of His resurrection may not find us sleeping, but awake. The reason for this night is twofold: either because He then received back His life when He suffered, or because He is later to come for judgement at the same hour at which He arose. *(St. Isidore)*

Easter, like all deep things, begins in mystery and it ends like all high things, in great courage. *(Bliss Perry)*

The Gospels do not explain the resurrection; the resurrection explains the Gospels. Belief in the resurrection is not an appendage to the Christian faith; it *is* the Christian faith. *(J. S. Whale)*

The resurrection did not result in a committee with a chairman, but in a fellowship with an experience. *(Anon)*

Humour

Just before Easter one year, this item appeared in a police log: '8.26

pm, church—lights will be on throughout the village church for the rest of the weekend; vicar trying to speed up the Easter lilies.' *(H.C.R.)*

I was showing my husband an egg which was speckled rather than all white like the rest. 'The Easter Bunny must have laid this one,' I said. 'Perhaps she did,' he answered absently, and returned to his paper. 'I always thought the Easter Bunny was a he,' I reflected. 'Look,' said my husband, putting down his paper, 'it's hard enough for a rabbit to lay eggs without being a male too.' *(Mrs George Maskell)*

Statement

When Jesus rose up again after suffering death on the cross for mankind, he manifested that he had been appointed Lord, Messiah, and Priest forever (cf. Acts 2:36; Heb. 5:6; 7:17–21), and he poured out on his disciples the Spirit promised by the Father (cf. Acts 2:33). The Church, consequently, equipped with the gifts of charity, humility and self-sacrifice, receives the mission to proclaim and to establish among all peoples the kingdom of Christ and of God. *(Second Vatican Council—'The Church')*

Word-Pictures

It is also stated that after his execution and entombment he disappeared entirely. Some people actually assert that he had risen; others retort that his friends stole him away. I for one cannot decide where the truth lies. *(Josephus)*

Over the magnificent mausoleum that holds the mortal remains of Queen Victoria and those of her royal husband are inscribed the words: 'Here at last I will rest with thee, and with thee in Christ I shall also rise again.'

Easter's meaning for those who formerly were without hope and without a true direction in life is a source of ever-recurring wonder. Some of the effects of Christ's Resurrection were eloquently described nearly 1,600 years ago by St. John Chrysostom in his Easter message:

'Those who were formerly living in the shame of sin are now living in confidence and in justice.

'They are not only free, but saints;
'Not only saints but just men;
'Not only just men but sons;
'Not only sons but heirs;

'Not only heirs, but brothers of Christ;
'Not only brothers of Christ but his co-heirs;
'Not only His co-heirs, but His members;
'Not only His members, but temples;
'Not only temples, but instruments of the Holy Spirit.'

The word Easter derives from Eostre, the pagan goddess of Spring, and to the Saxons, April was 'ostermonud'—the month of the ost-end wind (wind, that is, from the east) so that Easter became by association the April feast, which lasted eight days.

But Easter Sunday nowadays is the first Sunday after the first full moon following 21 March, and can therefore fall as early as 22 March, or as late as 25 April. For many years in earlier times, it was quite a popular belief that the Sun danced on Easter day. Sir John Suckling (1609–1642) wrote:

'But oh, she dances such a way,
No sun upon an Easter day
Is half so fine a sight.'

We do not believe that any longer, but we still have an affection for the 'Easter Egg'. The presentation of eggs at Eastertime is a practice that goes back to Persian times, when it was held that there were two contending forces in the world, those of Germuzd and Ahriman (Good and Evil). The egg was, so to speak, the 'bone of contention' between these opposite forces. The Jews, Egyptians and Hindus also clung to the idea and made symbolic presentations of eggs to each other. In due course, Christians adopted the custom, signifying by the new life within the egg the resurrection of Christ. They also coloured the eggs they gave red, so as to represent to their friends the Blood of the Redemption. *(W. A. Dickins)*

One ancient symbol of Christian belief in the resurrection is the phoenix. This bird symbolised hope and the continuity of life after death. According to legend, only one phoenix could live at a time. The Greek poet Hesiod, writing in the 8th century BC, said it lived nine times the lifespan of the long-living raven.

When the bird felt death approaching, it built itself a pyre of wild cinnamon and died in the flames. But from the ashes there then arose a new phoenix, which tenderly encased its parent's remains in an egg of myrrh and flew with them to the Egyptian city of Heliopolis, where it laid them on the Altar of the Sun. These ashes were said to have the power of bringing a dead man back to life. Scholars now think that the germ of the legend came from the orient, and was adopted by the sun-worshiping priests of Heliopolis as an allegory of the sun's daily setting and rebirth.

In Christian art, the resurrected phoenix became a popular symbol of Christ risen from the grave.

See also: A44 Meeting Christ in the Sacraments
C43 The Living One
C45 The Divinity of Christ
C47 The Indwelling Spirit

THE LIVING ONE

'You believe because you can see me. Happy are they who have not seen and yet believe.' *John 20:29*

Quotations

Taking all the evidence together, it is not too much to say that there is no single historic incident better or more variously supported than the resurrection of Christ. *(B. F. Westcott)*

Christ has conquered death, not only by suppressing its evil effects, but by reversing its sting. By virtue of the Resurrection, nothing any longer kills inevitably but everything is capable of becoming the blessed touch of the divine hands, the blessed influence of the will of God upon our lives. However compromised by our faults, or however cast down by circumstances our position may be, we can at any moment, by a total redressment, wholly readjust the world around us and take up our lives again in a favourable sense. To those who love God, all things are turned to good. *(Pierre Teilhard de Chardin)*

Word-Pictures

In the time of Cuspius and Tiberius Alexander, many of the miracle-worker's followers came forward and declared to the adherents of their master that although he had died, he was now alive and would free them from slavery. *(Josephus)*

They took away what should have been my eyes,
(But I remembered Milton's Paradise).
They took away what should have been my ears,
(Beethoven came and wiped away my tears).

They took away what should have been my tongue,
(But I had talked with God when I was young).
He would not let them take away my soul—
Possessing that, I still possess the whole. *Helen Keller*

The basic meaning of the Resurrection is the liberation of Jesus Christ. John Masefield in his play tells in imagination how Procla, the wife of Pilate, sent for Longinus, the centurion in charge of the crucifixion, and asked him what happened. 'He was a fine young man,' said Longinus, 'but when we were finished with him, he was a poor broken thing on a cross.' 'So you think,' said Procla, 'that he is finished and ended?' 'No, madam, I do not,' said Longinus, 'He is set free throughout the world where neither Jew nor Greek can stop his truth.' *(William Barclay)*

Years ago, on Princes Street, Edinburgh, with its beautiful setting, one of the many shop windows displaying art treasures in beautiful paintings attracted the eye of a passing gentleman. He was gazing intently at a painting of the 'Crucifixion'. It had been a long time since this man had allowed any thoughts like those suggested by the canvas to enter his mind, but the artist's portrayal brought back the memory of long forgotten truths, and he was impressed and troubled.

Suddenly he became aware of the presence at his side of a little ragged lad who was also looking intently at the painting.

'That's Jesus, sir, on the cross. They nailed him there with that crown of thorns on his head, and killed him, sir. He was a good man. He died for us, and that's his mother standing there, sir, looking at what they did to him.' The gentleman felt a lump rise in his throat as the boy continued—'And he died, sir, for our sins and they buried him yonder, sir.' It was too real, and the man turned away to continue his walk in Princes Street. He felt a tugging at his coat tails. Turning round he saw the boy who had been telling the story standing looking into his face. The boy blurted out breathlessly, 'I forgot to tell you, sir. I forgot to tell you, he rose again.' *(Anon)*

An old cathedral stood on the site of the present St Paul's in London. It perished in the great fire of 1666. After the fire, the brilliant young architect, Christopher Wren, designed a new cathedral which took 35 years to erect. The first stone that Wren picked up from the ruins of the old building bore a Latin inscription whose meaning is 'I shall rise again'.

See also: A44 Meeting Christ in the Sacraments
C42 The Risen Lord
C45 The Divinity of Christ
C47 The Indwelling Spirit

FEED MY SHEEP

'Lord, you know I love you,' Jesus said to him, 'Feed my sheep.'
John 21:17

Quotations

Advice is seldom welcome; and those who want it the most always like it the least. *(Lord Chesterfield)*

To profit from good advice requires more wisdom than to give it. *(Churton Collins)*

I divide the world in three classes—
the few who make things happen,
the many who watch things happen,
the overwhelming majority who have no notion of what happens.
(Nicholas Murray Butler)

All that is necessary for the victory of evil is that good men do nothing. *(Edmund Burke)*

O God, thou knowest how busy I must be this day. If I forget thee, do not thou forget me. *(Sir Jacob Asterley, before the battle of Edgehill)*

I saw the shepherd fold the sheep,
With all the little lambs that leap.

O Shepherd Lord, so I would be
Folded with all my family. *(Wilfrid Meynell)*

The Good Shepherd laid down His life for His sheep, that he might convert His Body and Blood in our sacrament, and satisfy the sheep Whom he had redeemed with the nourishment of His own Flesh. *(Pope St. Gregory I)*

Proverbs

It never troubles a wolf how many the sheep be. *(English proverb)*

The wolf eats oft of the sheep that have been warned. *(English proverb)*

Word-Pictures

Cardinal Heenan was ordered by his doctors to rest, and was staying at a country house in Hertfordshire. He had hardly arrived, when a letter reached him from a Catholic layman so upset by the reforms of the Second Vatican Council that he had decided to leave the Church—although, he added dourly, the Cardinal would hardly be interested in the worries of such an unimportant person.

Back went the swift reply: 'I am a shepherd, and you are one of my flock. I shall return to London immediately to meet you and discuss your difficulties.' *(Anon)*

When the archaeologists were digging in the ruins of Nineveh they came upon a library of plaques containing the laws of the realm. One of the laws reads, in effect, that anyone guilty of neglect would be held responsible for the result of his neglect . . . If you fail to teach your child to obey, if you fail to teach him to respect the property rights of others, you and not he are responsible of your neglect. *(William Tait)*

Some years ago a great actor was asked at a drawing-room function to recite for the pleasure of his fellow-guests. He consented and asked if there was anything they specially wanted to hear. After a minute's pause, an old minister asked for Psalm 23. A strange look came over the actor's face. He paused for a moment, then said, 'I will,' on one condition—that after I have recited it, you, my friend, will do the same.'

'I!' said the preacher, in surprise, 'I am not an elocutionist, but, if you wish it, I shall do so.'

Impressively, the actor began the Psalm. His voice and intonation were perfect. He held his audience spellbound, and, as he finished, a great burst of applause broke from his guests. As it died away, the old man rose and began to declaim the same psalm. His voice was not remarkable, his tone was not faultless, but, when he finished, there was not a dry eye in the room.

The actor rose and his voice quivered as he said, 'Ladies and gentlemen, I reached your eyes and ears: he has reached your hearts. The difference is just this: I know the Psalm but he knows the Shepherd.' *(Anon)*

Is there any greater pathos in our world than the number of youth, miles outside our churches, who are longing for a Saviour, looking pathetically toward revolutionaries like Che Guevara, or to the student who burned himself alive in Prague? Do you know the hush that comes down when either of them are mentioned? Why no hush for Jesus! Because we have got him lost in our violent Establishment in which the Church is seen as just 'part of the show'; preaching the love of God, silent about the bestialities and obscenities. *(Lord George MacLeod)*

See also: A21 Feeding the Hungry
B52 The Good Shepherd

THE DIVINITY OF CHRIST

'The Father who gave them to me is greater than anyone and no one can steal from the Father. The Father and I are one.' *John 10:29–30*

Quotations

Just as every human being is one person, that is, a rational soul and body, so, too, is Christ one Person, the Word and Man. *(St. Augustine of Hippo)*

The Son is the Image of the invisible God. All things that belong to the Father He expresses as the Image; all things that are the Father's he illumines as the splendour of His glory and manifests to us. *(St. Ambrose)*

There is one Doctor active in both body and soul, begotten and yet unbegotten, God in man, true Life in death, Son of Mary, and Son of God, first able to suffer and then unable to suffer, Jesus Christ our Lord. *(St. Ignatius of Antioch)*

We profess two wisdoms in Christ, the uncreated wisdom of God and the created wisdom of man. *(St. Thomas Aquinas)*

One difference between Christ and other men is this: they do not choose when to be born, but He, the Lord and Maker of history, chose His time, His birthplace, and His mother. *(St. Thomas Aquinas)*

A God on the cross! That is all my theology. *(Jean Lacordaire)*

If Socrates would enter the room, we should rise and do him honour. But if Jesus Christ came into the room, we should fall down on our knees and worship Him. *(Napoleon)*

If Jesus Christ is not true God, how could he help us? If he is not true man, how could he help us? *(Dietrich Bonhoeffer)*

I consider the Gospels to be thoroughly genuine; for in them there is the effective reflection of a sublimity which emanated from the Person of Christ; and this is as Divine as ever the divine appeared on earth. *(Goethe)*

If the life and death of Socrates were those of a man, the life and death of Jesus were those of God. *(Jean Jacques Rousseau)*

He that cried in the manger, that sucked the paps of a woman, that hath exposed himself to poverty, and a world of inconveniences, is the Son of the Living God, of the same substance with his Father, begotten before all ages, before the morning-stars; he is God eternal. *(Jeremy Taylor)*

Word-Picture

The cell was a concrete box too narrow to sit down. One could only bend one's knees a little, so that they were thrust up against the door, and the position becomes so agonizing that it is hard not to cry out. To pray in such circumstances is not easy, but it is a great and sweet solace if one can do so, and one must try with all one's strength to love more, not less. I had to struggle not to sink below the level of love and fall back into the realm of hatred, anger and revenge; to love Romulus Luca (the prison guard) not for a moment but continuously. I had to drive my soul to do this as one may push a vehicle with locked brakes. It was now that I came to understand Luca, his blindness and narrow hatred, his reactions which were like those of a dog rendered savage by being chained too long, or of a slave put in charge of slaves, with no freedom except to torment them. And then my thoughts went to those, whom it was natural and easy to love. I found that now I loved them differently, now that I had learnt to love Romulus Luca . . . And it was in that cell, my legs sticky with filth, that I at last came to understand the divinity of Jesus Christ, the most divine of all men, the one who had most deeply and intensely loved, and who had conceived the parable of the lost sheep. *(Petru Dumitriu—Incognito)*

See also: A37 Christ the King
A44 Meeting Christ in the Sacraments
B4 Christ, the Covenant of God
B8 The Cosmic Christ
B46 Christ the Sacrament of God

LOVING KINDNESS

'By this love you have for one another, everyone will know that you are my disciples.' *John 13:35*

Quotations

Kindness gives birth to kindness. *(Sophocles)*

Kindness is the golden chain by which society is bound together. *(Goethe)*

Kindness has converted more sinners than zeal, eloquence and learning, *(Frederick W. Faber)*

People are lonely because they build walls instead of bridges. *(J. F. Newton)*

The art of saying appropriate words in a kindly way is one that never goes out of fashion, never ceases to please and is within the reach of the humblest. *(Frederick W. Faber)*

Charity gives peace to the soul. For whoever loves God above all things rests his heart in the eternal peace. *(Archbishop Ullathorne)*

To give pleasure to a single heart by a single kind act is better than a thousand head-bowings in prayer. *(Saadi)*

It has been said that charity is the pardoning of the unpardonable and the loving of the unlovable. *(R. H. Benson)*

To love is to admire with the heart; to admire is to love with the mind. *(Theophile Gautier)*

Love is the noblest frailty of the mind. *(John Dryden)*

That best portion of a good man's life—His little, nameless unremembered acts of kindness and of love. *(William Wordsworth)*

Don't look for flaws as you go through life;
It is easy enough to find them.
It is wise to be kind, and sometimes blind,
And to look for the virtues behind them. *(Anon)*

Proverbs

One can pay back the loan of gold, but one dies forever in debt to those who are kind. *(Malayan proverb)*

Help thy brother's boat across, and lo! thine own has reached the shore. *(Old Hindu proverb)*

Word-Pictures

His room was in a poor, but densely populated part of Liverpool. Children played outside his door. He was found in August. The doctor estimated he had died in mid-February, during the bitterest cold! Nobody had missed him: and he may never have been found, had not some housebreakers tried to rob his gas meter!

In the scullery of her Portsmouth home, the body of a 70-year-old woman was discovered. It was almost decomposed. She had been dead for about four years. For four years, no one could have called on her!

And Annie Driver of Stepney, London said:
'No one comes here, and I don't know any one to go and visit. I haven't any relatives, and I haven't any friends left now. They're all dead and gone. Once I got ill at night and I was afraid. I thought I was going to die all alone. I crawled to the window. I was choking and I couldn't breathe. I shouted for help and I hammered on the window. It was hours and hours before anyone heard me.' *(John Dickson Pope)*

(Two detectives are discussing a young murderer who is being shielded by an elderly aunt.) 'I know it,' he said. 'She'll forgive him without question, whatever he's done to her and however high we hang him. *And he knows it.* It's no use you blaming her. She can't help herself. She's only a vehicle. That's Disinterested Love, chum, a force, like nuclear energy. It's absolute.' *(Margery Allingham—'Hide My Eyes')*

There are 10 strong things. Iron is strong, but fire melts it. Fire is strong, but water quenches it. Water is strong, but the clouds evaporate it. Clouds are strong, but wind drives them away. Man is strong, but fears cast him down. Fear is strong, but sleep overcomes it. Sleep is strong, yet death is stronger. But loving kindness survives death. *(The Talmud)*

John Wesley, on one of his countless travels, discovered he was sharing a carriage with an Army Officer. Their conversation was lively and interesting but the officer's contribution was punctuated by swear words and blasphemies. The gentle Wesley was most disturbed by this language but made an effort not to show his displeasure.

When they stopped to change the coach horses, Wesley seized the opportunity to have a word with the officer. "I wonder if I might ask you a favour", Wesley asked. The officer, pleasantly surprised, agreed. "We will be travelling some distance together", Wesley said, "And if I should forget myself and use a swear word in front of the ladies, perhaps you would kindly correct me?" The officer immediately took the point, and Wesley's method of reproof worked perfectly. *(Anon)*

See also: A17 Gentleness
A33 Love your neighbour
B41 Generosity
C18 Compassion

THE INDWELLING SPIRIT

'If anyone loves me he will keep my word, and my Father will love him, and we shall come to him and make our home with him.' *John 14:23*

Quotations

I pray thee, O God, that I may be beautiful within. *(Socrates)*

Your treasure house is within. It contains all you will ever need. Use it fully instead of seeking vainly outside yourself. *(Hui Hai)*

However well of Christ
you talk and preach,
unless He lives within,
He is beyond your reach. *(Angelus Silesius)*

'Too few people have experienced the divine image as the innermost possession of their own souls. Christ only meets them from without, never from within the soul.' *(C. G. Jung)*

'The centre of the soul is God, and when the soul has attained to him according to the whole capacity of its being, and according to the force of its operation, it will have reached the last and deep centre of the soul, which will be when with all its powers it loves and understands and enjoys God.' *(St. John of the Cross)*

The gift of the Holy Ghost closes the last gap between the life of God and ours . . . When we allow the love of God to move in us, we can no longer distinguish ours and his; he becomes us, he lives us. It is the first fruits of the spirit, the beginning of our being made divine. *(Austin Farrer)*

Statement

Christ is now at work in the hearts of men through the energy of His Spirit. He arouses not only a desire for the age to come, but, by that very fact, He animates, purifies, and strengthens those noble longings too by which the human family strives to make its life more human and to render the whole earth submissive to this goal. *(Second Vatican Council—'The Church Today')*

Word-Pictures

'I came here to find the Truth, Master.'
'Why wander around and neglect your precious treasure at home?' the master replied.

'What do you call my precious treasure?'
Master replied 'That which asks the question is the treasure.' *(Cheng-tao Ke)*

And after this I saw God in a point; by which sight I saw that He is in all things . . . I saw truly that God doth everything, be it never so little . . . As all that hath being in nature is of God's making, so is every thing that is done in property of God's doing . . . There is no Doer but He . . . And therefore the Blessed Trinity is ever full pleased in all His works. All this He showed fully blissfully, as if to say thus:

'See, I am God. See, I am in all things. See, I never leave my hands off my works, and never shall without end. See, I lead everything to the end I ordain it to, from without beginning, by the same mighty power, wisdom and love that I made it with. How should anything be amiss?' *(Dame Julian of Norwich—'Revelations of Divine Love')*

Your daily life is your temple and your religion.
Whenever you enter into it take with you your all.
Take the plough and the forge and the mallet and the lute,
The things you have fashioned in necessity or for delight.
For in reverie you cannot rise above your achievements, nor fall lower than your failures.
And take with you all men:
For in adoration you cannot fly higher than their hopes, nor humble yourself lower than their despair. *(Kahlil Gibran)*

Rossini was an Italian who composed some beautiful music. He was once given a beautiful watch by the King of France. He was very proud of this watch because it was a royal gift. A few years after he had been given it, he showed it to a friend. His friend told him that although he had had the watch for years he did not know its real value.

'Impossible,' said Rossini. 'Lend it to me for a moment,' said his friend. Taking the watch, he touched a secret spring and an inner case flew open revealing a beautiful little painting of Rossini himself. The composer had never known that the painting was there. *(M. Nassan)*

I was dusting the bedroom when I discovered God,
I've often looked for him, or it, before,
Upstairs, downstairs, in my lady's chamber,
But never there where I found it—
  Last place you'd think to look!
Don't think I'm going to tell you right away
Where I found it!

After all, it took me forty years,
So why should I make it easy for you?
You can damn well wait for a couple more lines at least.
Well now, where was I?
Oh, yes, in the bedroom
Discovering God.
Well, where do you think it was then?
I'll bet you'll never guess.
It was here in me all the time!
(Like Maeterlinck's Blue Bird
Poignantly sitting at home—
That was a heartbreaker film for me to see
When I was an evacuee)

Funny really
Doesn't seem to equate with housework
  Me walking round with the Godhead inside me.
I went in Woolworth's later,
  Met several friends,
But it didn't seem to show.

Just as well, really;
After all, they never show theirs to me. *(Brenda Rogers)*

See also: B44 The dignity of the individual
B51 One with Christ
C48 One in us
C49 Receive the Holy Spirit

ONE IN US

'Father, may they be one in us, as you are in me and I am in you.'
John 17:21

Quotations

I pray that in them there may be a union based on the flesh and spirit of Jesus Christ, Who is our everlasting life, a union of faith and love, to which nothing is to be preferred, but especially a union with Jesus and the Father. *(St. Ignatius of Antioch)*

Man's perfection is to be like God . . . in unity of spirit, whereby man not only becomes one with God in the sense that he wills the same things as God, but in the sense that he is unable to will what God does not will. *(William of St. Thierry)*

You all are fellow-travellers, God-bearers (theophoroi) and temple bearers (naophoroi), Christ-bearers (Christophoroi). *(St. Ignatius of Antioch)*

Every rational soul ought with all its strength to desire to approach God and to be united to Him through the perception of His invisible presence. *(Walter Hilton)*

The soul that is united with God is feared by the devil as though it were God himself. *(St. John of the Cross)*

The deepest prayer which I could ever say is that which makes me One with that to which I pray. *(Angelus Silesius)*

The end of love is no other thing than the union of the lover and the thing loved. *(St. Francis de Sales)*

It is Christ that prays in every soul in whom He lives. *(R. H. Benson)*

It is not only by the imitation of Christ, but by actual union with Him, that love becomes and remains the driving force of the soul. *(R. H. Benson)*

None understand better the nature of real distinction than those who have entered into unity. *(John Tauler)*

Word-pictures

Jesus said '. . . the Kingdom is within you and without you. If you know yourselves, then you will be known, and you will know that you are sons of the living Father. But if you do not know yourselves, then you are in poverty and you are poverty.'

Jesus said: 'Whoever knows the All but fails to know himself, lacks everything.' *(The Gospel according to Thomas)*

'There is a spirit in the soul, untouched by time and flesh, flowing from the spirit, remaining in the spirit, itself wholly spiritual. In this principle is God, ever verdant, ever flowing in all the joy and glory of his actual self. Sometimes I have called that principle the Tabernacle of the soul, sometimes a spiritual light, anon I say it is a Spark. But now I say it is more exalted over this and that than the heavens are exalted above the earth. So now I name it in a nobler fashion . . . It is free of all names, and void of all forms. It is one and simple as God is one and simple, and no man can in any wise behold it.' *(Meister Eckhart)*

I was in an underground train, a crowded train in which all sorts of people jostled together, sitting and strap-hanging—workers of every description going home at the end of the day. Quite suddenly I saw in my mind, but as vividly as a wonderful picture, Christ in them all. But I saw more than that: not only was Christ in everyone of them, living in them, dying in them, rejoicing in them, sorrowing in them—but because He was in them and because they were here, the whole world was here too, here in this underground train: not only the world as it was at this moment, not only all the people in all the countries of the world, but all the people who had lived in the past, and all those yet to come.

I came out into the street and walked for a long time in the crowds. It was the same here, on every side, in every passer-by—Christ. *(Caryll Houselander, A Rocking-horse Catholic)*

See also: B44 The dignity of the individual
B51 One with Christ
C47 The Indwelling Spirit
C49 Receive the Holy Spirit

RECEIVE THE HOLY SPIRIT

'As the Father sent me, so am I sending you.' After saying this he breathed on them and said, 'Receive the Holy Spirit.' *John 20:21–22*

Quotations

Those who have the gale of the Holy Spirit go forward even in sleep. *(Brother Lawrence)*

The Holy Spirit is the living interiority of God. *(Romano Guardini)*

The whole future of the human race depends on bringing the individual soul more completely and perfectly under the sway of the Holy Spirit. *(Isaac T. Hecker)*

Whatever we are, that we are by the divine goodness; and this goodness is specially attributed to the Holy Ghost. *(Pope Leo XIII)*

The Spirit of God first imparts love; he next inspires hope, and then gives liberty; and that is about the last thing we have in many of our churches. *(Dwight L. Moody)*

Every time we say 'I believe in the Holy Spirit', we mean that we believe there is a living God able and willing to enter human personality and change it. *(J. B. Phillips)*

Love can be used either as an essential name of the divine nature or as a personal name of a divine person—then it is the proper name of the Holy Ghost, as Word is the proper name of the Son. *(St. Thomas Aquinas)*

The Holy Spirit Himself, which also operates in the prophets, we assert to be an effluence of God, flowing from Him and returning back again like a beam of the sun. *(Athenagoras)*

I should as soon attempt to raise flowers if there were no atmosphere, or produce fruits if there were neither light nor heat, as to regenerate men if I did not believe there was a Holy Ghost. *(Henry Ward Beecher)*

A gift is freely given, and expects no return. Its reason is love. What is first given is love; that is the first gift. The Holy Ghost comes forth as the substance of love, and Gift is His proper name. *(St. Thomas Aquinas)*

Humour

The Bishop was gradually getting through a large Confirmation, and one small boy came up whom the Bishop seemed to remember he had seen already. Still, he thought he must be mistaken, and confirmed the boy. When later on the same boy appeared for the third time, however, the Bishop bent down and whispered: 'I've confirmed you already, haven't I?' The boy pointed to one of the assistant clergy. 'Yes,' he said 'but that priest over there keeps wiping it off.'

Statement

For, wherever they live, all Christians are bound to show forth, by the example of their lives and by the witness of their speech, that new man which they put on at baptism, and that power of the Holy Spirit by whom they were strengthened at Confirmation. Thus other men, observing their good works, can glorify the Father (cf. Mt. 5:16) and can better perceive the real meaning of human life and the bond which ties the whole community of mankind together. *(Second Vatican Council—'The Missions')*

Word-Pictures

Mei was a little Chinese girl, three-years-old, dark-eyed with black hair. Her mother had been put in prison for refusing to surrender her Christian Faith (this was in the 1950's) and Mei had to go with her because there was nowhere else for her to go. The Christian prisoners were closely guarded, but the guards let Mei run about everywhere.

Amongst the prisoners was a bishop, and some priests and nuns. They could not say Mass, but there were still priests outside. They used to send in loaves to the prisoners, with consecrated hosts secretly hidden in them by arrangement, so the prisoners were able to receive communion.

Once, one Chinese woman was in solitary confinement. Nobody was allowed to visit her, but the guards did not count Mei. So the little girl took the Blessed Sacrament to her, hidden in her closed fist held demurely in her sleeves.

Later on, Mei's mother was released, and returned with Mei to her village. There was still a missionary priest there, and Mei kept asking him to give her Holy Communion. She was still only four, but she knew all about it, and the priest let her make her first Communion, and a month afterwards she was confirmed.

When the priest was expelled from China, he said goodbye sadly to Mei and her mother, and hoped they would be left alone. He never heard how they got on, but he remembers how Mei said, 'I'm not afraid: I've been confirmed.' *(Anon)*

Pure and genuine love always desires above all to dwell wholly in the truth, whatever it may be, unconditionally. Every other sort of love desires, before anything else, means of satisfaction, and for this reason, is a source of error and falsehood. Pure and genuine love is in itself spirit of truth. It is the Holy Spirit. The Greek word, which is translated spirit, means literally fiery breath, breath mingled with fire, and it represented, in antiquity, the notion which science represents today by the word energy. What we translate by 'spirit of truth' signifies the energy of truth, truth as an active force. Pure love is this active force, the love that will not at any price, under any condition, have anything to do with either falsehood or error. *(Simone Weil)*

See also: A47 The Spirit of Truth
A46 Priesthood of the Laity
C47 The Indwelling Spirit

APPENDICES

APPENDIX ONE

For use with the Roman Catholic
three year cycle of
Readings

The material is arranged in three parts, A, B and C to correspond with the three year cycle. The themes are those which are suggested by one or more of the Sunday readings.

Part A *Advent*	*Theme*	*Text*	*Section*	*Related Sections*
1st Sunday	The value of time	*Rm.13;11*	A1	A19/B25/C34
2nd Sunday	Integrity	*Is.11;5*	A2	B19/B20/B26/C23
3rd Sunday	Perseverance	*Mt.11;6*	A3	A19/B49/C30/C35
4th Sunday	Emmanuel—Mary's Child	*Is.7;14*	A4	A37/B4/B8/B46/C45
Of the Year	*(for Christmas see Year B)*			
2nd Sunday	Man for others—unselfishness	*Is.49;3*	A5	A33/B41/B47/C34
3rd Sunday	Light of the World	*Ps.27;1*	A6	A37/B4/B8/B46
4th Sunday	Poor in Spirit	*Mt.5;3*	A7	A11/C21/C25/C29
5th Sunday	The light of example	*Mt.5;16*	A8	A9/A33/B24
6th Sunday	Relationships	*Mt.5;37*	A9	A33/B6/B30/B52/C10/C19
7th Sunday	Seeking perfection	*Mt.5;48*	A10	A20/A22/B26/C47
8th Sunday	Divine Providence	*Mt.6;26*	A11	A7/A19/B21/C39
9th Sunday	Holy Scripture	*Mt.7;24*	A12	B2/B9/B24/C6
10th Sunday	The Church is for sinners	*Mt.9;13*	A13	B17/C12/C27
11th Sunday	The successors of the Apostles	*Mt.10;1*	A14	A24/A45/B13
12th Sunday	Sin	*Rm.5;12*	A15	A13/A38/C37
13th Sunday	The Saints	*Mt.10;41*	A16	A10/B26/B51/C8
14th Sunday	Gentleness	*Mt.11;30*	A17	A19/B41/C18/C46
15th Sunday	Balance in Nature	*Rm.8;20*	A18	B32/B39/B42/C34
16th Sunday	Patience	*Mt.13;28*	A19	A11/B21/C39
17th Sunday	The Kingdom of God	*Mt.13;52*	A20	A31/B17/B51/C39
18th Sunday	Feeding the hungry	*Mt.14;16*	A21	A33/B15/C21/C29
19th Sunday	Seeking God	*1 Kings 19;12*	A22	A10/B28/C16/C38
20th Sunday	Mercy	*Is.56;1*	A23	A17/C14/C18/C46
21st Sunday	Papacy	*Mt.16;18*	A24	A14/B13/B17/C44
22nd Sunday	Courage	*Mt.16;21*	A25	B35/C13/C41
23rd Sunday	Sacrament of Penance	*Mt.18;18*	A26	A27/B16/C14/C40
24th Sunday	As we forgive those	*Mt.18;22*	A27	A26/B16/C14/C40
25th Sunday	Work	*Mt.20;8*	A28	A1/A18/A36/A39
26th Sunday	True Obedience	*Phil.2;7*	A29	A14/A32/B13/B31/C25
27th Sunday	The Jewish People	*Is.5;7*	A30	A12/B36/C8
28th Sunday	Heaven	*Is.25;7*	A31	A20/B3/B51/C48
29th Sunday	Civic Duty	*Mt.22;21*	A32	A29/B14/B33/B34
30th Sunday	Love your neighbour	*Mt.22;39*	A33	A9/B52/C10/C19
31st Sunday	Hypocrisy & Ambition	*Mt.23;3*	A34	A2/A15/B26/B44
32nd Sunday	Preparing for death	*Mt.25;13*	A35	A42/B21/B22/B23/B41
33rd Sunday	Using talents	*Mt.25;15*	A36	A1/A28/A39
34th Sunday	Christ the King	*1 Cr.15;25*	A37	A4/A44/B4/B8

Lent

1st Sunday	Original Sin	*Rm.5;12*	A38	A15/B10/C26/C37
2nd Sunday	The glory of God	*Mt.17;2*	A39	A20/B40/C31/C39
3rd Sunday	The equality of women	*Jn.4;27*	A40	B34/B44/C33
4th Sunday	Spiritual blindness	*Jn.9;26*	A41	A22/B49/C26
5th Sunday	Life after death	*Jn.11;25*	A42	A31/B22/C35

Eastertide *(for Easter Day see Year C)*

2nd Sunday	Believing community	*Acts 2;42*	A43	B17/B36/C12
3rd Sunday	Meeting Christ in the sacraments	*Lk.24;30–31*	A44	A37/B4/B46/B51/C45
4th Sunday	The Priesthood	*Ps.23;1*	A45	A14/A46/B13
5th Sunday	Priesthood of the laity	*1 Pet.2;9*	A46	B10/B44/C49
6th Sunday	The Spirit of Truth	*Jn.14;16–17*	A47	B53/C47/C48
7th Sunday	Worship	*Acts 1;14*	A48	B25/B29/C32

Part B

Advent	*Theme*	*Text*	*Section*	*Related Sections*
1st Sunday	Waiting on the Lord	*Mk.13;35*	B1	A1/A22/A35/B21/C36
2nd Sunday	The Good News	*Is.40;9*	B2	B9/B12/B24/C2
3rd Sunday	Joy in Christ	*I Th.5;16*	B3	B51/C2/C47
4th Sunday	Christ, Covenant of God	*Rm.16;25*	B4	A37/A44/B10/B46

Christmas

Christmas Day	A Saviour is born for us	*Lk.2;11*	B5	A4/B3/C2/C7
Sunday in Octave	The family	*Eccl.3;2*	B6	A9/B30/C5
1st January	Mary, Mother of God	*Lk.2;16*	B7	A4/A40/C7/C45
2nd Sunday	The Cosmic Christ	*Jn.1;1*	B8	A4/A37/B4/C45
Epiphany	Revelation	*Eph.3;3*	B9	A12/B2/B24/C8/C38
Sunday after Epiphany	Baptism	*Mk.1;8*	B10	A38/B36/C26/C47/C49

Of the Year

2nd Sunday	Vocation	*1 Sm.3;10*	B11	A10/A22/C16/C38
3rd Sunday	On a mission	*Mk.1;15*	B12	B2/B24/C12/C16
4th Sunday	Authority	*Mk.1;27*	B13	A14/A24/A29/A32/B14
5th Sunday	Freedom to serve	*1 Cr.9;22*	B14	B34/B45/C1
6th Sunday	Jesus, friend of outcasts	*Mk.1;40*	B15	A21/A33/B38/C3
7th Sunday	Christ forgives our sins	*Mk.2;5*	B16	A15/A26/A27/C22 /C27/C40
8th Sunday	The Church—Bride of Christ	*Ho.2;21*	B17	A13/B36/C12
9th Sunday	Sunday	*Mk.2;27*	B18	A48/B29
10th Sunday	Conscience	*Mk.3;29*	B19	A2/A10/A34/B45/C47
11th Sunday	Growth to maturity	*Mk.4;28*	B20	A2/A7/A10/B28
12th Sunday	Trust in God	*Mk.4;40*	B21	A11/A19/B52/C39
13th Sunday	Death	*Wm.1;13*	B22	A35/A42/B47/C36
14th Sunday	Pastoral care of the sick	*2 Cr.12;9*	B23	A35/A52/B38

15th Sunday	Go tell everyone	*Mk.6;7.13*	B24	B2/B12/C8
16th Sunday	Quiet—time for prayer	*Mk.6;31*	B25	A1/A10/C32/C47
17th Sunday	The whole man	*Eph.4;2*	B26	A2/A10/B20
18th Sunday	Bread from heaven	*John 6;32–33*	B27	A21/A52/B29
19th Sunday	The Father who draws us to Himself	*John 6;44*	B28	B40/C20/C27
20th Sunday	The Eucharist	*John 6;55–56*	B29	A44/B27/B18
21st Sunday	Married love	*Gn.2;24*	B30	B8/C13
22nd Sunday	The Commandments of life	*Js.1;21*	B31	A29/C6/C39
23rd Sunday	The wonders of God	*Mk.7;37*	B32	A18/B39
24th Sunday	Faith and good works	*Js.2;17*	B33	C22/C30
25th Sunday	Human Rights	*Js.3;16*	B34	A21/A40/B44/C1/C33
26th Sunday	The Grace of God	*N.11;25*	B35	B51/B52/C55
27th Sunday	The Family of God	*Hebrews 2;11*	B36	B10/B34/C12/C17/C24
28th Sunday	True Wisdom	*Wm.7;7*	B37	A2/B20/B26
29th Sunday	The Suffering Servant	*Is.53;11*	B38	B15/B49/C13
30th Sunday	The Lord who works marvels	*Ps.126;3*	B39	A18/B32
31st Sunday	One God	*Deut. 6;4*	B40	B30/B54/C27
32nd Sunday	Generosity	*Mk.12;43*	B41	A5/C18/C46
33rd Sunday	Signs of the time	*Mk.13;28*	B42	A18/B34/C17
34th Sunday	Christ the King	*(see A37)*		

Lent

1st Sunday	Forty Days of Lent	*Mk.1;12*	B43	B47/C37/C40/C41
2nd Sunday	The Dignity of the individual	*Rm.8;34*	B44	B26/B34/B45/C47
3rd Sunday	Free Will	*Jn.2;25*	B45	A2/B26/B44
4th Sunday	Christ the Sacrament of God	*Jn.3;14*	B46	A44/B16/B51
5th Sunday	Dying to self	*Jn.12;24*	B47	A5/A7/A10/B26

Eastertide *(for Easter Day see Year C)*

2nd Sunday	Christian unity	*Acts 4;32*	B48	A20/B17/B36/B51
3rd Sunday	Coping with doubt	*Lk.24;38*	B49	C13/C22/C30/C41
4th Sunday	The Good Shepherd	*Jn.10;11*	B50	B15/B38/C44
5th Sunday	One with Christ	*Jn.15;4*	B51	B25/C47/C48
6th Sunday	God is Love	*1 Jn.4;8*	B52	A9/A33/B30/C10
7th Sunday	Consecrated in truth	*Jn.17;19*	B53	A47/C11/C23
Trinity Sunday	Trinity	*Mt.28;19–20*	B54	A37/A47/B28/B40/C47

Part C

Advent	*Theme*	*Text*	*Section*	*Related Sections*
1st Sunday	Liberation from fear	*Lk.21;28*	C1	B3/B14/C2
2nd Sunday	Joy of Salvation	*Bar.5;9*	C2	B3/B14/C1
3rd Sunday	Sharing possessions	*Lk.3;10*	C3	A7/A21/A33/B41
4th Sunday	Personal peace	*Micah 5;4*	C4	A2/B19/C17

Of the Year *(for Christmas see Year B)*

2nd Sunday	The institution of marriage	*Jn.2;1*	C5	B6/B30
3rd Sunday	The Old Testament Law	*Ps.19;8*	C6	A29/B4/B31
4th Sunday	The humanity of Christ	*Lk.4;22*	C7	A37/B3/B16/C45
5th Sunday	God's messengers	*Is.6;8*	C8	B2/B9/B24
6th Sunday	The Beatitudes	*Jemh.17;7*	C9	B2/B3/C2
7th Sunday	Love your enemies	*Lk.6;27*	C10	A9/A33/B15/B52
8th Sunday	Talk	*Lk.6;45*	C11	A2/A9/A47/B53
9th Sunday	The Church for all men	*1 Kgs.8;43*	C12	A6/A13/A43/B17
10th Sunday	Coping with grief	*Lk.7;13*	C13	A25/B38/B49/C18
11th Sunday	Forgiveness	*Lk.7;47*	C14	A26/A27/B16/C27/C40
12th Sunday	Prejudice	*Gal.3;28*	C15	A40/A41/B15/C1
13th Sunday	Come follow me	*Lk.9;59–60*	C16	A22/B11/B24/C41
14th Sunday	International peace	*Is.66;12*	C17	A33/B34/C4/C10
15th Sunday	Compassion	*Lk.10;33*	C18	A17/A23/A33/C46
16th Sunday	Friendship	*Lk.10;38*	C19	A9/A33/B15
17th Sunday	Our Father in heaven	*Lk.11;12*	C20	A22/B28/C27
18th Sunday	Rise above materialism	*Lk.12;15*	C21	A7/A21/C29
19th Sunday	The light of Faith	*Hb.11;2*	C22	B33/C30
20th Sunday	Zeal for what is right	*Lk.12;49*	C23	A2/C8/C39
21st Sunday	Lord of all nations	*Is.66;18*	C24	A6/B8/B28/C12
22nd Sunday	Humility	*Lk.14;11*	C25	A2/A7/A10/B20
23rd Sunday	The human condition	*Wis.9;15*	C26	A15/A38/B22/B49/C37
24th Sunday	The Father who receives us back	*Lk.15;20*	C27	A26/B28/C20/C41
25th Sunday	Lord of the oppressed	*Ps.112*	C28	A21/B15/B38/B50
26th Sunday	Not through luxury	*Amos 6;1*	C29	A7/A21/C21
27th Sunday	Increase our Faith	*Lk.17;5*	C30	B33/C22
28th Sunday	Thanksgiving	*Lk.17;15–16*	C31	A17/A39/A48/B41
29th Sunday	Prayer	*Lk.18;7*	C32	A22/A48/B25/B29
30th Sunday	Equality	*Ecclus 35;12*	C33	A9/A40/B34/B44
31st Sunday	The value of little things	*Wis.11;22*	C34	A5/A18/B20/B33
32nd Sunday	Hope	*2 Mac 7;14*	C35	A6/A19/B21/C1
33rd Sunday	The Day of the Lord	*Mal.3;19*	C36	A31/A42/B22

Lent

1st Sunday	Temptation	*Lk.4;1*	C37	A15/A38/B19/C26
2nd Sunday	Discerning God's will	*Gen.15;8*	C38	A41/B11/B47/C39
3rd Sunday	Doing God's will	*Ex.3;14*	C39	A41/B11/B47/C38
4th Sunday	Reconciliation	*2 Cr.5;18*	C40	A26/A27/B16/C14
5th Sunday	Starting afresh	*Phil.3;14*	C41	A25/B14/C1

Eastertide

Easter Sunday	*Risen Lord*	*Acts 10;40*	C42	A44/C43/C45/C47
2nd Sunday	The Living One	*Jn.20;29*	C43	A44/C42/C45/C47
3rd Sunday	Feed my sheep	*Jn.21;17*	C44	A21/B52
4th Sunday	The divinity of Christ	*Jn.10;29–30*	C45	A37/A44/B4/B8/B46
5th Sunday	Loving kindness	*Jn.13;35*	C46	A17/A33/B41/C18
6th Sunday	The indwelling Spirit	*Jn.14;23*	C47	B44/B51/C48/C49
7th Sunday	One in us	*Jn.17;21*	C48	B44/B51/C47/C49
Pentecost	Receive the Holy Spirit	*Jn.20;21–22*	C49	A46/A47/C47

APPENDIX TWO

For use with the Anglican Alternative Calendar

Before Christmas

	Theme	*Suitable sections*
9th Sunday	The Creation	A18/A39/B28/B32/B39/C20
8th Sunday	The Fall	A13/A15/A28/A38/B45/C26/C37
7th Sunday	The Election of God's people: Abraham	A30/A43/B4/B36/B40
6th Sunday	The Promise of Redemption: Moses	A29/B4/B9/B40/C6/C20/C35
5th Sunday	The Remnant of Israel	A3/A7/A22/A30/B1/B38/C1

Advent

1st Sunday	The Advent Hope	A1/A2/A4/B1/C1/C2/C35
2nd Sunday	The Word of God in the Old Testament	A12/A30/B4/C6/C8
3rd Sunday	The Forerunner	A2/A5/A7/A22/C25/C29
4th Sunday	The Annunciation	A4/A40/B7/B41/B44/C7

After Christmas

1st Sunday	The Incarnation	A4/B4/B7/B46/C7
2nd Sunday	The Holy Family	A4/B6/B7/B30/C5/C7

After Epiphany

1st Sunday	Revelation: The Baptism of Jesus	B9/B10/B11/C7
2nd Sunday	Revelation: The First Disciples	A14/B2/B9/C16
3rd Sunday	Revelation: Signs of Glory	A39/B9/B32
4th Sunday	Revelation: The New Temple	A20/B4/B9/C45
5th Sunday	Revelation: The Wisdom of God	A12/B2/B9/B37/C9
6th Sunday	Revelation: Parables	A12/B9/B24

Before Easter

9th Sunday	Christ the Teacher	A6/B2/B24/B50/C9
8th Sunday	Christ the Healer	B3/B23/B32/B46/C13
7th Sunday	Christ the Friend of Sinners	A13/A44/B15/B16/B50

Lent

1st Sunday	The King and the Kingdom: Temptation	A15/A38/C26/C37
2nd Sunday	The King and the Kingdom: Conflict	A15/A38/C15/C28/C37
3rd Sunday	The King and the Kingdom: Suffering	A35/B15/B38/C13/C38
4th Sunday	The King and the Kingdom: Transfiguration	A39/B8/C23/C45
5th Sunday	The King and the Kingdom: The Victory of the Cross	A29/A37/B38/C10
Palm Sunday	The Way of the Cross	A29/B15/B38/B39
Easter Sunday		A42/C42/C43/C45

After Easter

1st Sunday	The Upper Room/The Bread of Life	A44/B27/B29
2nd Sunday	The Emmaus Road/The Good Shepherd	B50/C44
3rd Sunday	The Lakeside/The Resurrection and the Life	C42/C43
4th Sunday	The Charge to Peter/The Way, the Truth and the Life	A47/C44
5th Sunday	Going to the Father	B28/C20/C27
Sunday after Ascension	The Ascension of Christ	A39/B51/C48
Pentecost		A47/B53/C47/C48
Trinity Sunday		B40/B54/C20/C45/C48

After Trinity

1st Sunday	The People of God/The Church's Unity and Fellowship	A43/B48/C48
2nd Sunday	The Life of the Baptized/The Church's confidence in Christ	B17/B21/C12
3rd Sunday	The Freedom of the Sons of God/The Church's mission to the individual	B14/B44/C1/C12
4th Sunday	The New Law/The Church's mission to all men	A13/A33/B12/B52/C10
5th Sunday	The New Man	A5/A10/B26/B47/C47
6th Sunday	The More Excellent Way	A10/B11/C38/C39/C47
7th Sunday	The Fruit of the Spirit	A2/A5/A17/A19/B3/B41/C46
8th Sunday	The Whole Armour of God	A3/B21/B35/C32/C35
9th Sunday	The Mind of Christ	A6/A23/A27/A33/C18/C39
10th Sunday	The Serving Community	A1/A7/A21/B14/C3/C17
11th Sunday	The Witnessing Community	A8/A32/A43/B24/B33/C21
12th Sunday	The Suffering Community	A7/A21/B15/B38/C13/C18
13th Sunday	The Family	A46/B6/B32/C5
14th Sunday	Those in Authority	A14/A32/B13
15th Sunday	The Neighbour	A9/A33/C10/C46
16th Sunday	The Proof of Faith	A29/B21/B33/C1/C22
17th Sunday	The Offering of Life	A2/A5/A39/A46/A48/B47
18th Sunday	The Life of Faith	A1/A10/C22/C30
19th Sunday	Endurance	A3/A19/A25/B21/B49/C13
20th Sunday	The Christian Hope	A20/A31/B51/C35
21st Sunday	The Two Ways	A19/A23/C18/C46
22nd Sunday	Citizens of Heaven	A16/A20/A31/B51

APPENDIX THREE

For School Use

The Human Condition

Ambition	A34	Pain	B38
Balance in Nature	A18	Prejudice	C15
Death	B22 & A35	Seeking God	A22
Conscience	B19	Signs of the Times	B42
Doubt	B49	Sin	A15
Grief	C13	Spiritual blindness	A41
Human Condition	C26	Temptation	C37
Hypocrisy	A34	Work	A28
Original Sin	A38		

Relationships

Family	B6	Love your neighbour	A33
Feeding the hungry	A21	Married Love	B30
Friendship	C19	Reconciliation	C40
Human Rights	B34	Relationships	A9
Love your enemies	C10	Sharing	C3

God

Father who draws us to Himself	B28	Lord who works marvels	B39
Glory of God	A39	One God	B40
God is Love	B52	Spirit of Truth	A47
Indwelling Spirit	C47	Trinity	B54

Communication with God

Covenant of God	B4	Prayer	C32
God's will	C38 & C39	Providence	A11
Good News	B2	Revelation	B9
Holy Scripture	A12	Vocation	B11
Mission	B12	Worship	A48

Christ

Christ the Covenant of God	B4	Jesus friend of outcasts	B15
Christ the King	A37	Light of the World	A6
Cosmic Christ	B8	Lord of all nations	C24
Divinity of Christ	C45	Risen Lord	C42
Emmanuel	A4	Living One	C43
Humanity of Christ	C7	Suffering Servant	B38

The Church

Authority	B13	Feed my sheep	C44
Believing Community	A43	Jewish People	A30
Church for all men	C12	Mary, Mother of God	B7
Church triumphant	A16	The Pope	A24
Church—Bride of Christ	B17	Priesthood	A45
Church for sinners	A13	Priesthood of Laity	A46
The Family of God	B36	Successors of the Apostles	A14

The Sacraments of God

Baptism	B10	Marriage	C5
Bread of Heaven	B27	Meeting Christ in the sacraments	B46
Christ the Sacrament	B46	Ministry of Priesthood	A45
Confirmation	C49	Pastoral care of the sick	B23
The Eucharist	B29	Sacrament of Reconciliation	A26
The Grace of God	B35		

Virtues, Gifts and Qualities

Civic Duty	A32	Mercy	A23
Compassion	C26	Obedience	A29
Courage	A25	Patience	A19
Equality	C33	Personal peace	C4
Faith and good works	B33	Perseverance	A3
Generosity	B41	Poor in spirit	A7
Gentleness	A17	Seeking perfection	A10
Growth to maturity	B20	Talents	A36
Hope	C35	Talk	C11
Humility	C25	Trust in God	B21
Integrity	A2	Unselfishness	A5
Joy	B3	Value of little things	C34
Light of example	A8	Value of time	A1
Loving kindness	C46	International peace	C17

Liturgical days and Seasons

Advent	A1-A4/B1-B4/C1-C4	Lent	A38-A42/B43-B47/C37-C41
Christmas	A4, B5, C7	Easter	C42-C43
Epiphany	B9	Pentecost	A47/C47/C48

The Last Things

Death	B22	Heaven	A31
Day of the Lord	C36	Life after death	A42

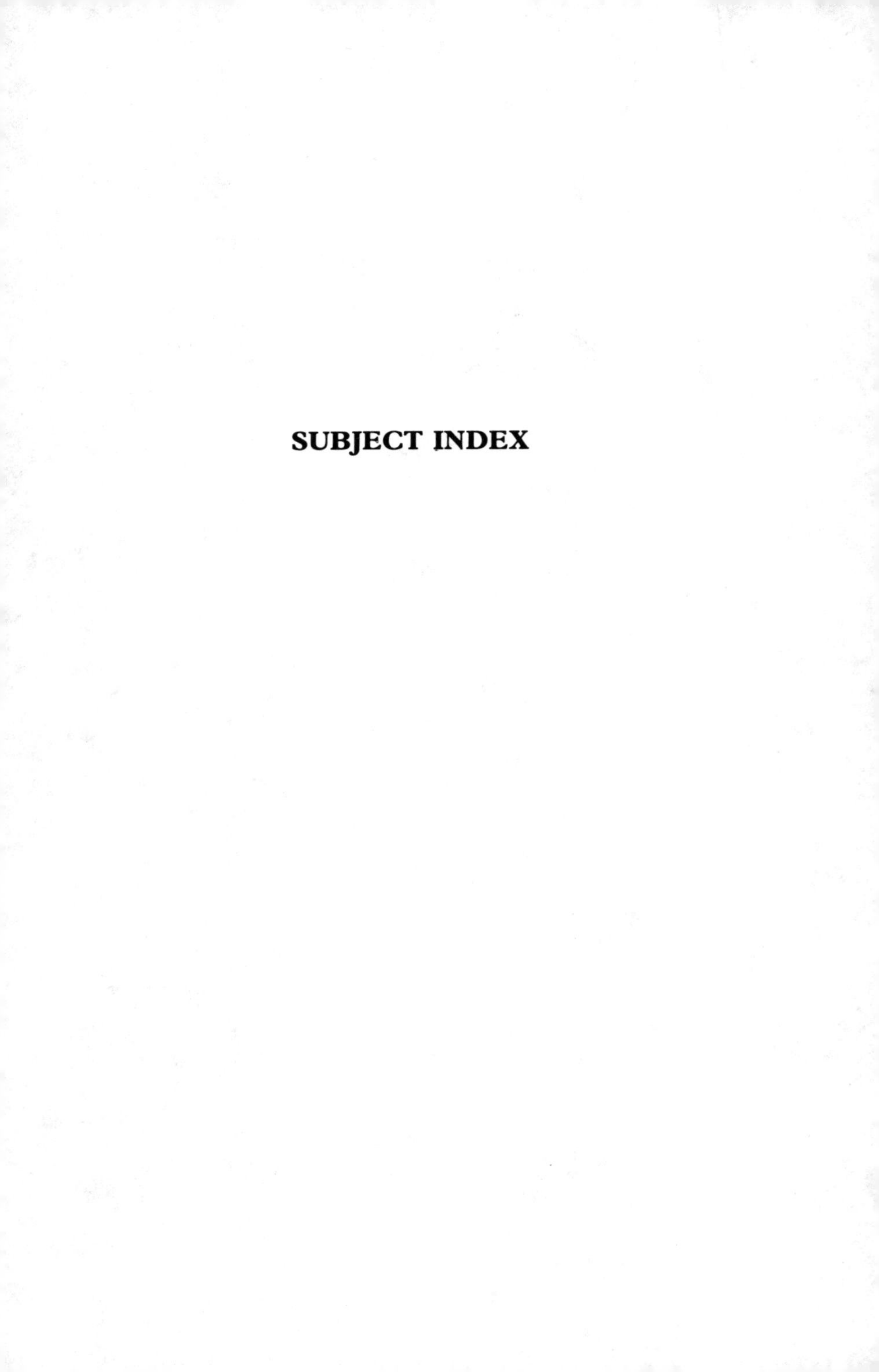

SUBJECT INDEX

SUBJECT INDEX

INDEX OF SOURCES

INDEX OF SOURCES

A

B

ACKNOWLEDGEMENTS

The author and publishers would like to thank the following publishers for permission to reproduce passages from the publications listed:
EVANS BROTHERS LTD; *The Small Woman* by Alan Burgess.

W. COLLINS PUBLISHERS; *Miracle on the River Kwai* by Ernest Gordon; *Autobiography* by Yevtushenko; *History and Human Relations* by Herbert Butterfield; *Naught for your Comfort* by Trevor Huddleston; *Mere Christianity* by C. S. Lewis; *Something Beautiful for God* By Malcolm Muggeridge; *Dying we Live* by Kathe Kunn; *The Plain Man looks at the Apostles' Creed* by William Barclay; *Incognito* by Petru Dumitrui; *Journey for a Soul* by George Appleton.

S.C.M. PRESS; *Odds Against* by Ernest Marvin; *Christianity in Africa* by Cecil Northcott; *Letters and Papers from Prison* by Dietrich Bonhoeffer (Enlarged Edition 1971); *The Cost of Discipleship* by Dietrich Bonhoeffer; *Interpreting the Cross* by Max Warren.

BAPTIST TIMES; *The Fellowship of God* by Dr Philip Potter.

EYRE & SPOTTISWOODE LTD; *The Secret Archives of the Vatican* by Luisa Ambrosini.

GEORGE ALLEN & UNWIN LTD; *Lord of the Rings* by J. R. R. Tolkien.

HODDER & STOUGHTON LTD.; *Through the Year with Cardinal Heenan* by Cardinal Heenan; *In Spite of Dungeons* by S. J. Davies; *The Trumpet of Conscience* by Martin Luther King.

AMNESTY INTERNATIONAL; Quotation by Salvador de Madariaga.

VICTOR GOLLANCZ LTD; *The Nine Taylors* by Dorothy L. Sayers; *A Year of Grace* by Victor Gollancz.

WILLIAM HEINEMANN LTD.; *The Velveteen Rabbit* by Margery Williams.

ADAM & CHARLES BLACK; *The Quest for the Historical Jesus* by Albert Schweitzer.

A. D. PETERS & CO. LTD; *An Only Child* by Frank O'Connor.

DAILY EXPRESS; *Girl Writing to a make-believe Father.*

HULTON EDUCATIONAL PUBLICATIONS LTD; *The Way of the Hindu* by Swami Yogeshananda.

THE GUARDIAN; Obituary of Tubby Clayton.

SHEED & WARD LTD; *Considerations* by Hubert Van Zeller; *A Rocking Horse Catholic* by Caryll Houselander.

DAILY MIRROR; *Stinkers of the Season* by Marje Proops.

ASSOCIATED CATHOLIC PUBLICATIONS LTD (THE UNIVERSE); *52 Talks for Young People* by Maurice Nassan S. J.; *Woodruff at Random* edited by Mary Craig.

CATHOLIC TRUTH SOCIETY; Translation of *Divino Afflante Spiritu.*

CATHOLIC INSTITUTE FOR INTERNATIONAL RELATIONS; *This is Progress* a translation of *Populorum Progressio.*

THE DAILY TELEGRAPH: *Hymn and Prayer for Civil Servants.*

RELIGIOUS EDUCATION PRESS; *Orders from Christ* by John Foster.

HEINEMANN EDUCATIONAL BOOKS; *A Man for All Seasons* by Robert Bolt.

ALFRED KNOPF INC; *The Prophet* by Kahlil Gibran.

LAWRENCE POLLINGER LTD; *Phoenix* from *Complete Poems* by D. H. Lawrence .

FRANKLIN WATTS LTD; *St Francis of Assisi* by Douglas Liversidge.

YORKSHIRE COMMITTEE FOR COMMUNITY RELATIONS; *Religion in a multi-faith school.*

CASSELL LTD; *Lord Nuffield* by E. Gillbank.

GEOFFREY CHAPMAN LTD; *The Documents of Vatican II* edited by Walter M. Abbott, S. J.

HEINEMANN EDUCATIONAL BOOKS LTD; *A Man for all Seasons* by Robert Bolt.